ROUTLEDGE LIBRARY EDITIONS:
POLITICAL GEOGRAPHY

Volume 16

GEOGRAPHY OF ELECTIONS

GEOGRAPHY OF ELECTIONS

P.J. TAYLOR AND R.J. JOHNSTON

Routledge
Taylor & Francis Group
LONDON AND NEW YORK

First published in 1979

This edition first published in 2015
by Routledge
2 Park Square, Milton Park, Abingdon, Oxon, OX14 4RN

and by Routledge
711 Third Avenue, New York, NY 10017

Routledge is an imprint of the Taylor & Francis Group, an informa business

British Library Cataloguing in Publication Data
A catalogue record for this book is available from the British Library

ISBN: 978-1-138-80830-0 (Set)
eISBN: 978-1-315-74725-5 (Set)
ISBN: 978-1-138-81426-4 (Volume 16)
eISBN: 978-1-315-74761-3 (Volume 16)
Pb ISBN: 978-1-138-81427-1 (Volume 16)

Publisher's Note
The publisher has gone to great lengths to ensure the quality of this reprint but points out that some imperfections in the original copies may be apparent.

Disclaimer
The publisher has made every effort to trace copyright holders and would welcome correspondence from those they have been unable to trace.

Geography of Elections

P.J. TAYLOR and R.J. JOHNSTON

CROOM HELM LONDON

Croom Helm Ltd, 2-10 St John's Road, London SW11
ISBN 0-7099-0056-2
First published by Penguin Books Ltd, 1979

British Library Cataloguing in Publication Data

Taylor, P. J.
Geography of elections.
1. Elections 2. Geography, Political
I. Title II. Johnston, Ronald John
324'.2 JF1041

ISBN 0-7099-0056-2

Printed in Great Britain by
Biddles Ltd, Guildford, Surrey

For Margaret and Pete,
Joyce and John.

Contents

Contents

List of Figures

List of Figures

List of Tables

List of Tables

Preface

Most readers of this book will cast their vote for political parties and their candidates on numerous occasions during their lifetime. Competitive party voting has become an accepted part of the 'western' way of doing things. People normally cast their votes in their home area where their vote is subsequently counted to help produce a representative for them. *Geography of Elections* is about some of the implications of this geographical basis to the organization of elections.

We hope that this book will be of interest to three groups of potential readers. First, students of politics will find a small part of their subject area brought together and viewed in what may prove to be a slightly different light. Our treatment of elections is obviously not complete from a political scientist's point of view but we trust that our particular perspective, with its emphasis on spatial aspects of elections, will prove to be of some use within their wider spectrum. To a large degree we have selected parts of the politics literature and reorganized it into a geographical framework. We trust that the original authors, to whom we are greatly indebted, forgive us.

Secondly, we hope that our specific treatment of elections appeals to the layman interested in such matters. To some degree the geographical approach is a straightforward, simple view of elections on the ground. We have intended that our discussions of all the various topics with which we deal are self-contained within the book and require no previous reading, but merely an average interest in the party politics going on around the reader. Our discussions are supported by numerous maps and diagrams which are intended to clarify arguments and to help readers see elections in their basic geographical context.

Finally, students of geography should find topics of interest in the following pages. In geography in general, the political dimension has normally been under-valued and relatively neglected. Hence, recent introductory human geography text books on the spatial organization of society deal almost solely with economic and social topics to the exclusion of political aspects of society. We hope that this book contributes a little towards rectifying this anomaly in human geography. There are numerous applications of ideas and concepts from human geography set within a new political context. Quite simply, electoral patterns reflect and help produce the overall human geography of a region or state. This book attempts to illustrate this assertion.

Although it has not been our purpose to cover all political aspects of elections, we have attempted a more comprehensive approach relating to geographical coverage. There are numerous books which deal with the elections of single states; in this book we are explicitly cross-national in our arguments. Discussion ranges from Austria to Australia as we try to provide the reader with a wide spectrum of electoral examples. We hope that all readers will profit from this aspect of this book.

Geography of Elections emanates from conversations between the authors at a conference in January 1976. The speed at which these original ideas have been translated into reality owes much to the secretarial and cartographic staffs in the Geography Departments at Newcastle and Sheffield Universities. Special mention should be made of Mrs Olive Teasdale, who drew the majority of the maps and diagrams, and Mrs Joan Dunn who typed most of the manuscript.

Finally we dedicate this book to our parents who were originally responsible for 'socializing' us politically to provide the roots out of which this book has grown.

Peter J. Taylor
R. J. Johnston

Part One

Preliminaries

1 Geography and Electoral Studies

The study of elections has been a continuing source of inter-disciplinary conflict, largely between political scientists and sociologists: the latter are accused of taking the politics out of voting studies (Key and Munger, 1959), whereas the former are accused of insufficient attention to sociology (Sheingold, 1973). Geographers have not been involved in this conflict, and it is no intention of ours that this book should launch a triangular contest. We make no claims for any distinctive discipline of electoral geography and have no imperial ambitions; our aim is to illustrate the richness of inter-disciplinary study of voting, from a geographical bias.

Although the roots of electoral geography can be traced to the early years of this century (Siegfried, 1913; Kareil, 1916; Sauer, 1918), research by geographers into various aspects of voting has never been more than slight in its volume. With the possible exception of French work, the heritage for current workers in electoral geography consists only of a disconnected set of isolated studies, few in number and limited in purpose. More recently, geographers have developed a greater interest in the topic of elections. An initial programmatic statement suggested a limited scope for electoral geography, based on a traditional concern with maps (Prescott, 1959), but growing awareness of the value of quantitative approaches and of the richness of work in other disciplines has widened the geographer's horizons quite considerably (McPhail, 1971). A small annual volume of research is now published on electoral themes, which has led one author to claim – much more than we would – that 'Geography is particularly important in that it can add an entirely new dimension to the study of elections' (Busteed, 1975, p. 3).

As in most disciplines, new developments in geography produce excesses, and there are some studies which, on hindsight, have produced rather obvious results. Others have explored interesting corners of the field, however, and have unearthed some fascinating findings. It is their impact which justifies our writing a *geography of elections*, despite an obvious reliance on a wide range of material from other disciplines, notably political science and sociology.

There is no set of topics which can be designated as exclusively the domain of electoral geographers, as indicated by our catholic sources in this book. The result is thus a survey of relevant material which is clearly inter-disciplinary in what we hope is the best sense of that term. Research results and hypotheses from within and beyond the usually defined boundaries of geography are integrated here in a survey of three major topics. The only criterion for inclusion has been relevance to the theme, so that although much of the research is not geographical in origin it is clearly geographical in interest; conversely, all of the works cited, whether by geographers or not, are of interest to those who would understand the full complexity of elections.

Modern human geography is often defined as having a focus on the spatial distributions of phenomena and the processes by which these are generated. In such studies, the adjective 'geographical' is used as synonymous with spatial or locational effects. To summarize, human geographers are concerned with the spatial organization of society (Morrill, 1970; Abler, Adams and Gould, 1971). This organization comprises two elements: (1) the *de facto* organization, which is the 'natural' reflection of society in spatial patterns – the continuous geographical distributions; and (2) the *de jure* organization, which is the set of spatial patterns explicitly defined for administrative purposes (Cox, 1973). The pattern of social areas or neighbourhoods in a city is an example of *de facto* organization, whereas that of parliamentary constituencies or congressional districts exemplifies that of *de jure* organization.

Given this general definition of the geographer's sphere of

influence, we can identify the many geographical elements in a typical election. Within a city, for example, voters are registered by their home addresses. Where these are depends on which parts (sectors) of the housing market they have access to; the most affluent have most choice and select the more 'desirable' areas, whereas the poorest have least choice and are usually allocated to certain prescribed areas. In some societies, other variables – such as race or religion – may combine with class to influence residential choice. The result in all cases is spatial segregation by socio-economic criteria, and perhaps by others as well. It is very often the case that these same criteria are important in shaping people's political attitudes, and hence how they vote. We might anticipate, therefore, that the spatial patterns of voting – usually for various political parties – will also indicate segregation of people with different views and will reflect the underlying socio-economic segregation. The extent of the associations between these patterns – at all spatial scales and not just within cities – is a basic feature of geographical research into elections.

Within the patterns just outlined, where a person lives may have a still subtler connection with his or her voting behaviour. The location of a home prescribes who are the occupiers' neighbours, and in many cases whom they have as friends and acquaintances. This pattern of social contacts may be a major element of the social environment within which voters make up their minds on how to vote, for different social milieux may involve different biases in terms of political discussion and advice. Further, different areas may receive different levels of attention from parties and their candidates in the attempts to win votes, thereby extending the range of the locational or geographical influences on voting decisions.

Finally, where a voter lives determines by whom he is represented, which may or may not be the candidate(s) for whom he voted. The determining factor is the set of *de jure* spatial districts – often termed constituencies – which form the organizational framework for elections and send the representatives to the parliament or similar assembly. The location of constituency boundaries can influence the political complexion of the district, and hence the nature of its representation, and so geographers are interested in the boundary-drawing process. Further, the location of these boundaries can have major influences on the overall election result, through the translation of votes into patterns of representation, which can produce a peculiarly geographical influence on representation.

We have identified three main foci of geographical interest in electoral studies. First, there is the *geography of voting* itself; secondly, there is the set of *geographical influences on voting*; and finally, there is the *geographical influence on representation*. These three form the framework for the remainder of the book; to provide initial illustration of each so as to set the scene for the greater detail to come, we conclude the present chapter with an example of a classical study from each substantive area.

The geography of voting in Ardèche, France

Many studies of the geography of voting involve the comparison of two or more maps, thereby associating the distribution of votes – usually for a particular political party – with various other distributions. From such associations causal connections are often inferred. This cartographic approach – now somewhat superseded by statistical methods of comparing distributions – has deep roots in French geography and is often associated with the work of André Siegfried, the 'father' of electoral geography.

André Siegfried and his *géographie électorale* have not always been without their critics in political science. He is sometimes viewed as an 'environmental determinist', that is, a researcher who explains social phenomena by relating them causally to the physical environment. Geography has had its fair share of such simplistic thinkers but Siegfried is not one of them. Although he is sometimes credited with the statement that in northern France 'the granite votes for the right and the chalky soil for the left' (Dogan, 1967, p. 183), Siegfried does not imply any such direct causal relationships in his researches. There is however, 'a correspondence between nature of the soil, agrarian landscape, type of dwelling, distribution of land ownership, degree of stratification in society, the stronger persistence of tradition, and political orientation' (Dogan, 1967, p. 183).

Dogan presents another example in which physical geography is superficially related to voting. In Italy the higher the land the greater the conservatism. This is not because land nearer to Heaven preserves more Christian ideals, but rather it is related to land ownership and the resulting stratification – 'Thus geography leads back to economy, and this to history' (Dogan, 1967, p. 183). Such explanations are based upon social factors which are themselves based in part upon the physical environment.

These relationships between the physical environment, the social environment and voting are excellently illustrated by Siegfried's study of voting in the département of Ardèche, on the west bank of the Rhône, during the period of the Third Republic (1871–1940). In this (Siegfried, 1949), he interpreted the pattern of party votes as reflecting the spatial organization of society there, which in its turn reflects variations in the physical environment. The associations which he deduced were extremely constant in election after election. Those cantons favouring parties of the left in 1871 still did so in 1936, for example. In all, Siegfried classified the 31 cantons into 17 of the left and 11 of the right, with only three which varied greatly in their support during the long period.

What factors led to the spatial polarization of cantons within Ardèche? Siegfried's conclusions on this are summarized in Figure 1.1. The main element in the physical base of the department is its geology, which is reflected by altitudinal variations in the landscape. In turn, these variations have influenced the types of productive activity – both agricultural and the incipient manufacturing industries – and in terms of human patterns are shown as variations in farm sizes and population agglomerations. Political attitudes are coloured by these different social and economic environments, and are reflected in the voting map.

Figure 1.1 and the short paragraph above are gross simplifications of a 136-page research monograph, which includes over fifty maps of voting patterns and another twenty used to help provide

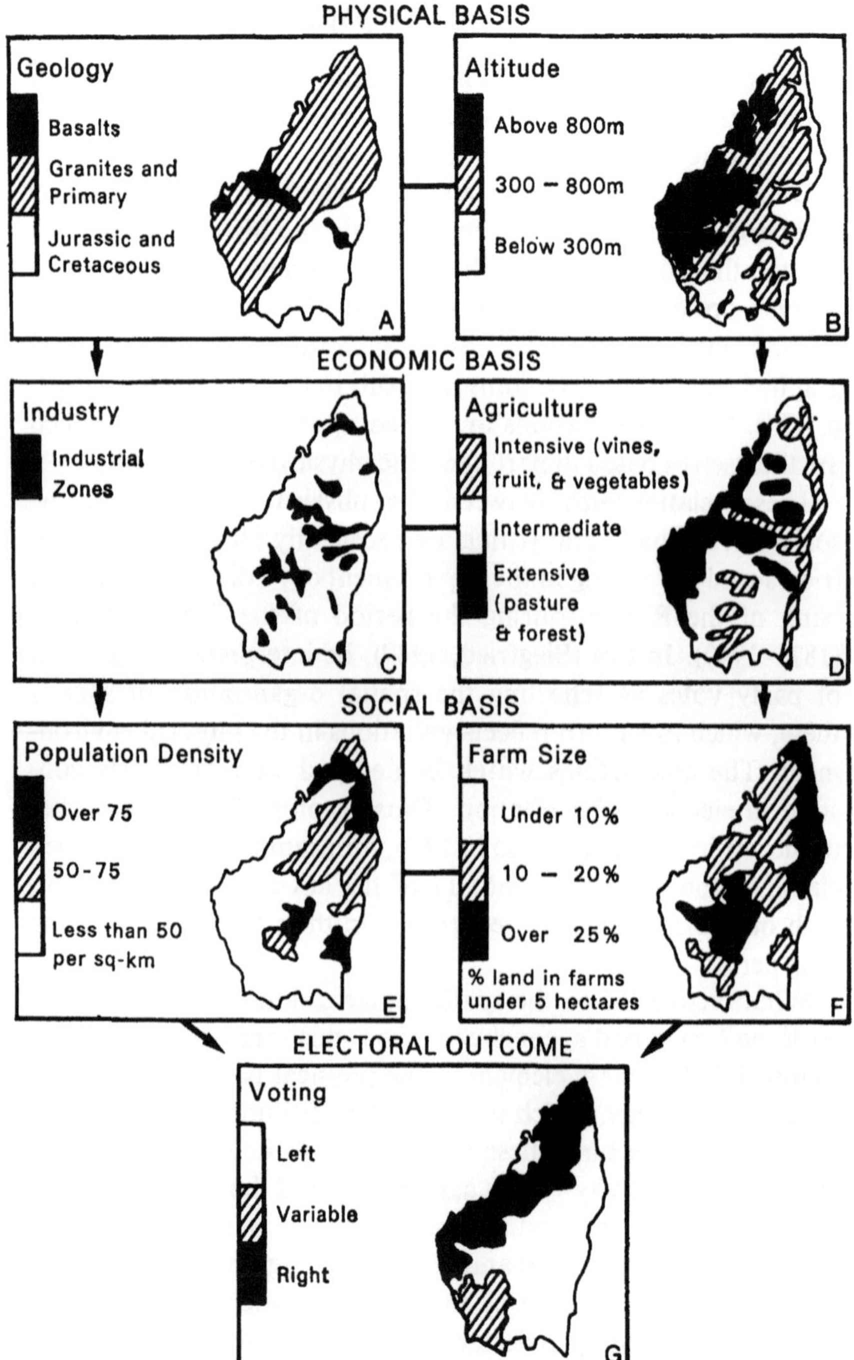

Figure 1.1 The geography of voting in Ardèche, France

an account for those patterns. The essence of Siegfried's approach is clear, however. Through careful consideration of the appeals of the parties of the left and the right, he could identify those aspects of the social and economic milieux most likely to underlie the voting decisions, and was then able to trace those aspects back to the physical environment. The argument is supported through map comparisons. Modern studies are more likely to use statistical procedures, and to stop short of tracing the associations back to the physical environment, but neither the method nor the conclusion was irrelevant to this early example from rural France, which provides a classic prototype of the geography of voting.

Geographical influences in voting in the American south

The notion of geographical influences is commonly taken to mean effects due to the physical environment, and in this way the Ardèche study may be seen as illustrating geographical influences. Most modern interpretations of the adjective 'geographical' relate to locational factors underlying behaviour, however, and this is how we will interpret the term here. We have already indicated that Siegfried, in effect, produced socio-economic explanations of voting in Ardèche in any case. Here we concentrate on geographical or locational influences on voting patterns.

No study better illustrates the geographical or locational influences on voting than the seminal work on politics in the American south by V. O. Key Jr (1949). Being the work of a political scientist, his analysis is steeped in the states' political history, and he interprets twentieth-century, southern politics as reflecting conservative and reactionary victories in the separatist and populist movements of the nineteenth century. The result is a one-party façade for national politics (i.e. supporting Democrat Party candidates) but a virtual lack of political parties within the states, where the Democrat Party primary elections, to select party candidates, are much more important in the contests for most offices than the subsequent run-off in the 'real' election, whose result is usually a formality. Key (1949, p. 16), thus describes the Democrat Party as 'purely a holding company for a congress of transient squabbling factions, most of which fail to meet the standards of permanence, cohesiveness, and responsibility that characterize the [concept of a] . . . political party'.

The lack of any coherent political groups in succeeding elections makes the criteria by which electors decide how to vote somewhat different from those used when they can match their own attitudes against those of the competing parties. Thus in Alabama, Key (1949, p. 37) found 'a tenuous and impermanent factional organization [which] confuses the voters and makes for electoral decisions based on irrelevancies'. The separate southern states have produced different reactions to this confusing situation; in Alabama, the lack of clearly recognizable differences between candidates has led to an excessive localism in voting patterns.

Key terms this localism a 'friends-and-neighbours' effect, by which voting decisions are greatly influenced by the location of the elector's residence relative to those of the candidates. Each contestant in a Democrat primary might expect to perform particularly well in his home county and its neighbours, therefore. This is illustrated by the contest in the 1946 gubernatorial primary. One of the candidates – Boozer – won only 16 per cent of the votes across the whole state, but built up a considerably greater volume of support in and around his home county (Figure 1.2); nevertheless one of his rivals – Folsom – also received a strong friends-and-neighbours vote not only around his existing home in the north of the state but also around his boyhood home in the south-east. Having two nodes of major support was crucial to his success in defeating Boozer (Folsom won 29 per cent of the votes in all), and clearly illustrates the effect of a simple geographical influence on voting behaviour.

Geographical influences on representation: the New York menagerie

In almost all elections it is very rare for a party to get an equal percentage of both the votes cast and the seats contested, and so

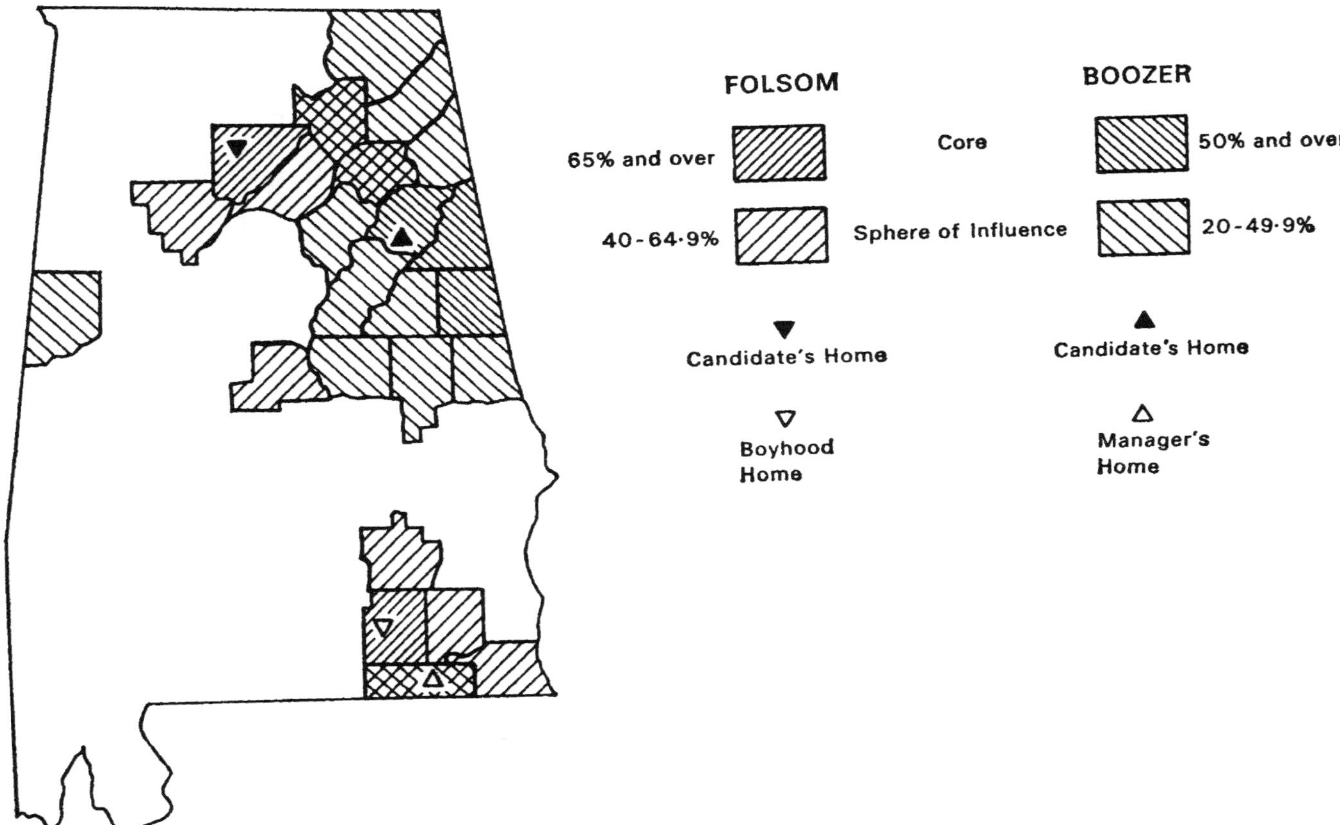

Figure 1.2 'Friends-and-neighbours' voting in the 1946 Alabama primary election

a lot of research effort has focused on the relationship between votes received and seats won. The degree of disparity between the two proportions varies considerably. At elections in Great Britain, the United States and other 'Anglo-Saxon democracies', the discrepancy is often quite large; in the systems operated in most European countries, it is generally much less pronounced.

The discrepancy between seats and votes has frequently been purposively produced in the United States by the careful location of constituency (district) boundaries relative to the distributions of voters of different political persuasions. Such geographical influences on representation were first noted in 1812 when Governor Elbridge Gerry redistricted Massachusetts for the purpose of electing the state senate. In the subsequent election, members of his party won 29 of the 49 seats although they won less votes than did their opponents. The governor's name has been immortalized as the first 'gerrymanderer' and the practice is now an accepted feature of the American political scene. As might be expected, it is the cause of much controversy, so that its investigation involves propaganda as much as academic research. To illustrate such work we use an example which is both academic and polemic – Tyler and Wells's (1961, 1962) writings on the drawing of congressional district boundaries in New York.

Tyler and Wells have dubbed New York as a 'two-party state with a one-party legislature', which refers to the fact that although the Democrats traditionally win as many votes as the Republicans, they rarely offer any serious challenge to the Republican hegemony when it comes to winning seats. The 1958 state election was a typical example; the Democrats won 50·3 per cent of all the votes cast for state senator, but in terms of seats the margin of victory was 34–24 in favour of the Republican Party. At the same time, the Democrats won 50·2 per cent of the votes for candidates to the State Assembly, but 92 of the 150 seats were won by their opponents.

The boundaries for congressional districts, used in the elections to the Federal House of Representatives, are drawn by the state legislature and those produced for New York in 1961 were conceived by the victors of 1958. The map of New York City pro-

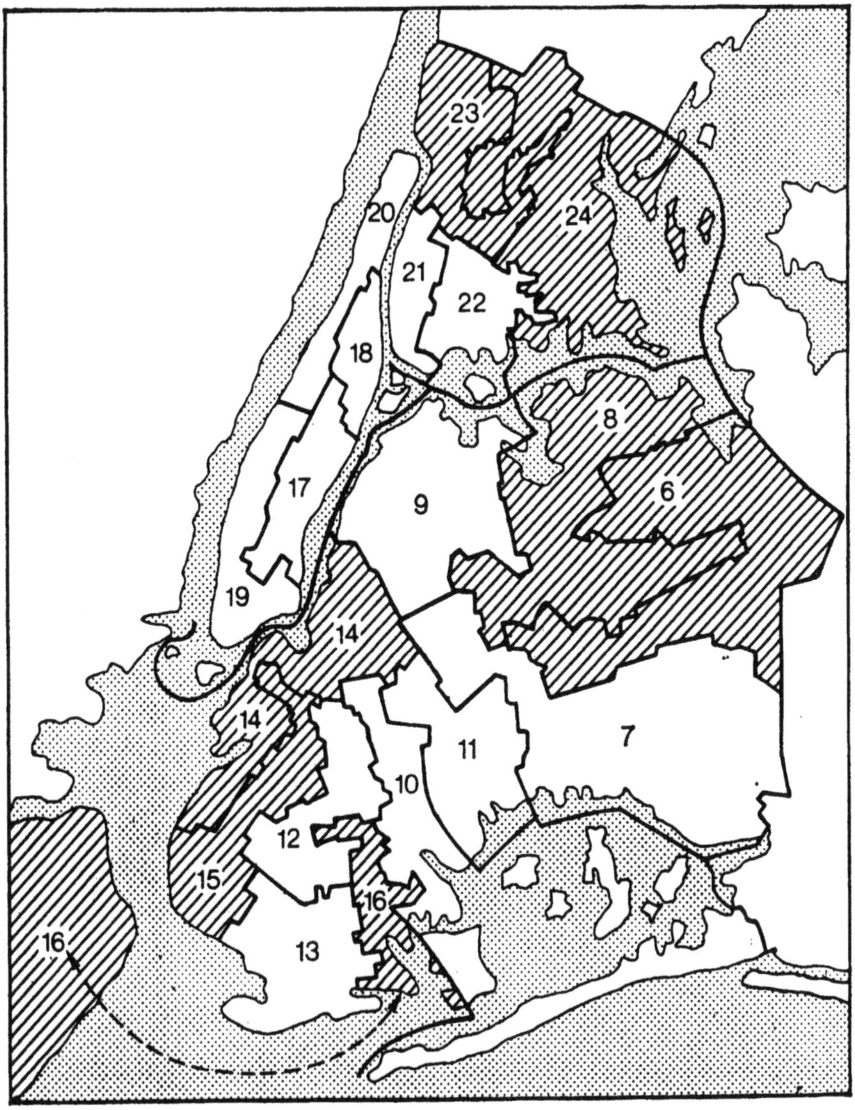

Figure 1.3 New York City Congressional Districts, 1961

duced by the Republican-controlled legislature is shown in Figure 1.3. Their problem within the city was to produce Republican districts in a traditional Democrat stronghold, and their solutions are geographically very ingenious. In Brooklyn, for example, many widely separated Republican areas were linked to produce the very irregularly shaped 15th and 16th districts, with the latter including Staten Island. Perhaps the most irregular boundary of all is that in the Bronx which divided the 24th district from the 22nd and 23rd, the design being an attempt to keep the 24th as a Republican seat, despite an influx of Democrat supporters.

In their propaganda against this gross manipulation of boundaries to distort representation, Tyler and Wells (1961) refer to it as the 'New York menagerie'. Governor Gerry's manipulation produced a district whose shape resembled a salamander – hence the term gerrymander. In New York, Tyler and Wells 'identified': a camel biting the tail of a barking dachshund; a mechanical dinosaur with key attached; a vulture flying towards its rather large egg; a fiery dragon; a snake suffering from indigestion after swallowing a giraffe; a chicken with its head being cut off; and, finally, an upside-down pregnant crocodile! (For the less-well-versed political biologists, the above fauna are the 14th, 15th, 16th, 24th, 23rd, 6th and 8th districts respectively.)

There can be no doubt that the *de jure* spatial organization depicted in Figure 1.3 has a major influence on election results and hence on the geography of representation. Such a situation is true of several countries which have no legal prescriptions preventing such a manipulation of boundaries, but the same result can apply when such laws exist (Taylor, 1973). During the present century, each of the three main parties has won 44 per cent of the votes at a British election. With such a poll: in 1906 the Conservative Party suffered a landslide defeat; in 1910 the Liberal Party were able to form a minority government; and in 1964 the Labour Party could form a majority government. Such variations on the same figure illustrate the point that different distributions of party supporters across a set of constituencies can produce very different electoral outcomes in terms of seats won from the same overall poll.

Conclusions

The three topics which we have identified here are all of current interest, particularly since electoral reform is an important issue in a number of countries. Before treating them in detail, however, we must consider the ways in which votes are cast, are translated into parliamentary seats, and are analysed by academics and others. This involves a discussion of electoral laws and procedures, which are the foundations of any geography of elections since they determine the types of data available for testing ideas on the geography of voting, geographical influences in voting, and geographical influences on representation. This discussion forms the bulk of the next chapter, as a backdrop to the substantive analyses of the following seven.

Following our introduction to electoral methods and electoral data in Chapter 2, the next six chapters form three groups, each dealing with one of the substantive topics identified above. Thus, Chapters 3 and 4 focus on the geography of voting, outlining, first, the spatial development of party cleavages and, secondly, the social bases to the geography of voting which reflect those cleavages. In the next group, Chapters 5 and 6 investigate the geographical influences in voting; in the first, the focus is on the influence of the candidate's home location on his pattern of support, whereas in the second it is the effect of local issues and campaigns which receives attention. Then in Chapters 7 and 8 we look at the geography of representation, at the translation of votes into seats and the biases in this process which can be produced by electoral cartography. In Chapter 7, the focus is on electoral abuses, on the manipulation of constituencies for particular ends; in Chapter 8 the topic of electoral reform is treated, highlighting the problems of avoiding bias and the myth of nonpartisan cartography.

Most of the material in this book is concerned with the interactions between political actors (parties and candidates) and voters, pointing out the geographical context within which elections take place. Such an orientation avoids one of the major topics of political science, the distribution of power. Clearly a strong geography of voting, and significant geographical influences in voting, should lead to consequential geographies of power for the elected candidates and parties. Our final chapter investigates this topic, highlighting the influence of electoral systems on the nature of representation and the allocation of electoral power.

2 Electoral Systems and Electoral Data

The concept of democracy creates a variety of images, but in defining it, most people would probably come close to the Oxford English Dictionary's description, which is 'government by the people, direct or representative'. Direct government involving every member of the society is possible only in very small communities, or in particular instances and on specific issues in larger ones, as with the use of referenda in some societies. Most government is by representatives, and in a majority of countries by elected representatives (in 1976 only one European country – Spain – had no elected body involved in the detail of its government). The initial purpose of agreed government (which is different from superimposed government, in which a powerful group imposes its rule on a weaker one), was to provide goods and services that individuals could not provide for themselves, such as defence from hostile countries. Governments were appointed, constituted, or elected for the purpose of raising taxes to provide these services, of which defence was usually the most important – it is still a major stimulus to the growth of governmental power, for instance in many countries during World War II. Increasingly, as greater proportions of national populations have been given a say in government through the electoral process, the provision of services has been handed over to governments, because of 'market failure' in the private sector of an economy (Tullock, 1976). To provide an acceptable level of living for all, governments in many countries now provide a wide range of welfare and other services. Government began as a protective institution, but its main functions are now productive, in the generation of employment and the repair of failures in the capitalist market system (Buchanan, 1974).

Elections

Governing, then, is a major task in most societies. In the absence of imposed governments, which are usually supported by a strong military presence, government is provided by representatives elected for the task by the adult population. Elections perform several functions. They provide for popular control, ensuring that those who govern are, within the constraints of the choices offered to the voters, the most popular with the electorate, which guarantees that citizen support will be given to the government. If held regularly they also ensure that government is responsible, since the representatives are then answerable to the electorate every so often (usually between two and five years); in this role, they also provide a channel of communication between governors and governed.

Who are the members of a government? How do they achieve office? Some, like cabinet ministers in the United States, are appointees of elected representatives; most are themselves directly elected. Who then elects them, and how are they represented by them? The nature of representation has long been a vital discussion topic among political philosophers (see Birch, 1971), much of their debate stemming from the works of people such as Thomas Hobbes (1588–1679), and from a speech by Edmund Burke in 1774 to the citizens of Bristol. Thus the representative might be considered a *delegate*, acting on instructions from those who elected him; he might be a *stereotype*, a sample representing a certain group within society, with the government as a whole comprising a set of stereotypes who in total are a mirror image in miniature of the society they represent; he might be a *symbol*, indicative of a certain decision – such as that every British Labour government should include one Welshman; or he might be a *trustee*, someone selected by a group because it is believed he will act in their, and perhaps also the whole society's, best interests. In a sense, too much may be asked of many representatives, demanding that they combine several roles which in certain circumstances could be contradictory. Citizens expect governments to act in the national interest; trade unionists expect their executive to pursue the interests of the whole membership. But a government member or a trade union leader is also expected to favour the interests of the particular group who elected him, which may well go against the greater interest. Which then should he do? The answer depends in part on whom he represents. As the suffrage has been extended, so that in many countries all adults are now electors, and as the functions of government have become manifold, so the loyalties of the representative have become divided. In some countries (e.g. Ireland), he is still expected to act mainly as a stereotype, as the member for a certain group of people for whom he is expected to work (Chubb, 1963); in others (e.g. the United Kingdom), he is much more a delegate, elected to perform certain tasks and to pursue certain policy ends which he has undertaken, as a member of a group of representatives – a political party. The other roles must be performed in each case, but they are generally subservient to the major one.

Whatever the theory of representation which dominates the political ethos of a country, in most cases representatives are elected by a procedure which developed out of the concept of the representative as a stereotype. The constituency was and is a particular section of the population, characterized by the single criterion of where they live. The first parliaments were called together by monarchs to legitimize their rule and to validate certain actions they wished to take, such as the raising of taxes, which required the support of others. The monarchs were landowners, as were the representatives they called together; the latter were usually in some way subservient to the monarch, depending on him to legitimize their ownership of land and also of labour, which was often either to be taxed by, or enlisted into the armies of, the monarch. Parliaments obtained their power in the concessions yielded by the monarch in return for their cooperation.

With the increasing complexity of societies, parliamentary representation and power was widened as monarchs, and the permanent ruling groups (governments) supporting them, sought assistance from a greater range of people. And so the commercial leaders of the various communities were co-opted and as these people became more numerous they were invited to send elected representatives. In each place – county or borough usually – the landowners, merchants and tradesmen met to elect their representatives, whose tasks were to protect the interests of their local peers, as well as of their own class generally. Over time, class interests came to dominate, as we shall show in the next chapters, and the range of class interests to be represented has increased as the suffrage has been extended by governments forced into obtaining wider public legitimation of their rule. And yet the place has remained the basic unit for conducting elections; government members may now largely act as class delegates (or as delegates of some other section of the population such as a religious group), but the electorate to whom they are responsible is not that class as a whole, nor even some part of it, but all the residents of a particular place. Societies continue to be organized in territorial units, local governments provide certain services for defined areas, and spatially-defined constituencies provide the representatives for national governments.

The conflict between various theories of representation sets up various contradictions. In a number of countries, some of these conflicts revolve around the concept of proportional representation and lead to calls for electoral reform. (Not all of which may point in the same direction: whilst in Britain in the mid-1970s there has been a growing demand for electoral reform based on the West German system, in West Germany there have been requests for adoption of the British system!) Our aim in this book is not to pay much more than passing attention to these conflicts (Chapter 9 is the major reference to them), but rather to focus on the electoral base to political power. Our overview of 'Western democratic' societies is that the organization and conduct of elections, and the results of these, are key elements in the distribution of political power. In the present book, we analyse – as geographers – the nature of elections.

The quantitative importance of elections

The importance of such analysis can be illustrated by a few simple figures. In the general elections closest to 1970 (those covering the period 1968–72), about 152 million votes were cast in the countries of western Europe (the nine of the present E.E.C., plus Austria, Finland, Iceland, Malta, Norway, Sweden and Switzerland), and another 139 million in seven other countries whose elections are discussed in this book (Australia, Canada, Israel, Japan, New Zealand, South Africa and the United States). And this 291 million votes is undoubtedly an underestimate; in many of the elections referred to, voters cast more than one ballot for different offices, and in most countries local government elections are held on an annual or biennial rota.National elections are held in many other countries outside Europe; in some the voter may be presented with no choice of candidates – and although this aspect of democracy is frequently removed temporarily after non-electoral changes of government, the use of elections in general is spreading (into Spain and Portugal within Europe in recent years). Clearly, the vote is an important expression of political attitudes. Prescott (1969) estimated that there were seventy-one countries in which the voting returns at national elections were suitable to geographical analysis, and another fifty-seven in wh.ch they were not; undoubtedly, this is an understatement.

Such figures are but the tip of the iceberg, referring only to national elections and to those held in the so-called 'Western democracies'. Elections are held at many levels within individual countries, as well as in countries which we do not normally associate with such democratic acts. (Russia, for example, holds elections. They may be very carefully stage-managed and the results wholly contrived, but nevertheless they do involve many millions of people giving some form of legitimation to those who rule them.) Although they may not be everyday events, therefore, elections are major events, both because they involve large numbers of people, and because of their role in the allocation of power within society.

The analysis of elections depends on how they are conducted –

the electoral laws and procedures – and on the detail with which they are reported – the electoral data. Both of these topics are clearly crucial in any analysis of the geography of elections, and so the purpose of the present chapter is to outline the sorts of system and the data on which geographical analyses are based.

Electoral laws

A very great variety of methods is used to conduct elections, ranging from the relatively informal counting of hands at the annual general meeting of a small society to the complex voting machines used in many American states. No attempt is made to list them all here, for no authoritative catalogue is available (for a useful start, see Lakeman, 1974), and in any case the purpose of the book is to analyse rather than to describe. Consequently, our review focuses on the main methods only, with particular reference to elections held at national levels and for major *de jure* spatial units within nations – states, provinces, counties, cities etc.

Two main types of election are discussed in this book, according to their function. The first are ***elections of persons***, at which votes are cast for candidates, or groups of candidates, standing for some particular office; the second are ***issue elections***, at which votes are cast to indicate attitudes on a particular issue, such as British membership of the E.E.C. or whether California should have stricter regulations for the operation of nuclear power plants. The former are usually elections for assemblies or parliaments of some kind (these terms are sometimes used here as synonyms for similar bodies, such as city councils), although they may be concerned with the election of individuals to a particular office – United States presidents, for example, or county dog-catchers; the issue elections are typically referenda or plebiscites at which, either because it is a constitutional requirement or because a government wishes to know public opinion on an issue, voters are invited to present a formal and unambiguous statement of their views on major issues. We shall deal with these two types of election in turn in the present section.

A wide range of different electoral systems is used for the elections of persons. Three distinct characteristics can be used to categorize them: the number of votes that the elector has; the way in which votes are allocated; and the number of representatives to be elected for each constituency. Employing these characteristics, we have identified three major electoral systems – the system based on *pluralities,* that based on the expression of *several preferences*, and that based on a choice between *party lists.* In each of the first two, a further subdivision is made according to the *number of representatives per constituency.* The main features of each system, plus mixed systems which combine characteristics of two or more, are outlined in the following subsections, together with recent examples of their operation.

1. The Plurality System

Although not peculiar to Great Britain, nor even to those parts of the world once ruled from London, the plurality system is predominantly operated in English-speaking countries; elections have a long history in Britain, and have evolved in the way outlined above, whereas in many other countries they are relatively novel, replacing many centuries of imposed hegemony. A plurality is often equated with 'a majority', but the plurality system is not necessarily based on overall majorities, although it may produce them; better descriptions of the system are provided by the alternative terms frequently used in the United States – 'first past the post' and 'winner takes all'. The major feature of a plurality-based election is that the person with most votes wins. In two adjacent Welsh constituencies in the February 1974 general election the results were:

Carmarthen

Candidate	*Party*	*Votes*	*Percentage*
Jones	Labour	17,165	34·29
Evans	Plaid Cymru	17,162	34·28
Owen-Jones	Liberal	9,698	19·37
Dunn	Conservative	6,037	12·06

Llanelli

Candidate	*Party*	*Votes*	*Percentage*
Davies	Labour	28,941	57·76
Richards	Conservative	7,496	14·96
Evans	Liberal	7,140	14·25
Williams	Plaid Cymru	6,620	12·02
Hitchen	Communist	507	1·01

Both seats were won by the Labour Party candidate. In Llanelli, Davies was a clear victor, with more than half of all the votes cast and four times as many as his nearest opponent, but in Carmarthen, Jones was the favoured candidate of only just over one-third of the voters, and almost as many preferred the Plaid Cymru candidate, Evans (who got his revenge by winning at the next election, eight months later!). With only two candidates and one member to be elected, the winner is bound to have a majority of support from the electors, but the greater the number of candidates the greater the probability that the victorious candidate has the endorsement of less than half of the electorate. As we shall see in Chapter 7, this has important implications for the geography of representation, with some variations depending on the type of plurality electoral system employed.

(i) *The plurality system in single-member constituencies*

This is the system just described for the two Welsh constituencies; it is now universally applied in the United Kingdom for elections to the Westminster parliament (a history can be obtained from Butler, 1963 or Steed, 1975), although not for the various assemblies elected in the Ulster province since 1973. It is also used widely in British local government elections, although occasionally it is replaced by the multi-member system described below.

The system is a very simple one, both for the voter and for the vote counter, although some would claim that its simplicity in fact creates difficulties for the voter, who must make a single decision out of what may be a lot of conflicting influences. A list of the candidates is provided, with many countries now also giving an indication of their party affiliations, and the voter selects one, usually by marking a cross against that person's name. (Voting machines are used in many American states, with the button or lever replacing the pencil, and with automatic tallying of the votes.) Counting is then straightforward, and the candidate with most votes is declared elected.

Canada, New Zealand and South Africa are among the countries which use this system for electing the lower houses of their national parliaments (New Zealand has no upper house), using more or less the same procedures that apply in Britain. Elections for most of the congressmen in the United States House of Representatives are organized in a similar way, with each congressional district in each state returning a single member; in a few states, however, extra seats in the House, allocated to them because of population growth, have in the past been voted for by the whole state - again by a plurality system - because of reapportionment difficulties (Jewell, 1962), but this is now illegal. Some states have one representative only, of course. U.S. senators are also elected by pluralities. Each of the fifty states has two senators, each elected for a different six-year term so that the gap between senatorial elections is alternately two years and four years.

In all of these elections, as we shall illustrate later (Chapters 7 and 8), a crucial determinant of the representation that ensues is the location of the constituency boundaries. Many voters have no personal representation because they preferred a losing candidate; in our Welsh example, over half of the Llanelli voters obtained the representative that they wanted, but in Carmarthen nearly two-thirds did not. A number of Carmarthens, in each of which the Plaid Cymru candidate lost narrowly, could severely bias representation relative to voter preferences, which is why the single-member plurality system has long been under attack; it survives because of the vested interests of those who win under it.

(ii) *Multi-member plurality systems*

In some plurality systems more than one representative is to be returned from a single contest: if for example 5 are to be elected then the winners are the top 5 in a ranking of candidates by the number of votes cast for each.

There are two major variants of this system. In the first, each elector has as many votes as there are representatives to be elected. Thus in May 1973 elections were held for the councils to govern the new English Metropolitan Districts. Most wards were to return three members, and so each elector had three votes. In this case, the election was a 'one-off'; not only were the top three to be declared elected, but it was laid down that the top candidate was to serve for three years, the second for two years and the third for one. A single-member plurality contest was thereafter to be held each year to return one representative who would serve a three-year term. Most New Zealand city and borough councils are elected in multi-member plurality contests of this kind. Wards are rare, and even where they exist, they return up to five representatives at one time. Until 1974, for example, Christchurch City Council had nineteen members, all of them elected by the city as a whole in the triennial at-large election, at which each voter had up to nineteen votes. Many did not use all nineteen; many others apparently used some odd criteria to aid their decisions, such as length of the candidate's name (Blydenburgh, 1974; Bush, 1975; Johnston, 1974a).

The other major variant of this system is where the elector has fewer votes than the number of representatives required from his constituency. The Japanese Diet comprises 511 members in its lower house, representing 124 constituencies. Up to 1976, there were 491 members from the constituencies, of which 43 returned three members each, 39 returned four, 41 sent five and only one, the Amami Islands, was a single-member constituency (Stockwin, 1975, p. 82). Whatever the number of representatives to be returned by a constituency, however, the elector has only one vote, so he must decide not only which party to support but also, if more than one candidate is fielded by it, which of that party's candidates. (Details of the campaigning that this system produces are given in Chapter 6, p. 284.) The nature of the system creates problems for the parties, regarding how many candidates to field. In a three-member constituency, a party expecting to get thirty per cent of the votes might be better advised to field only one candidate and be virtually certain of his election, than to nominate two who might split the vote between them and both be defeated. (In the 1976 general election, the Liberal Democratic Party fielded 319 candidates for the 511 seats; the next largest party – the Socialist – fielded only 162 (*The Times*, 4 December 1976)). Each was clearly as good as the other as a predictor of success: 78 per cent of the L.D.P. candidates were elected and 75 per cent of the Socialists.)

This system, termed by Lakeman (1974, p. 86) the single non-transferable vote, was used in Great Britain from 1867 to 1884. It is very unlikely to result in proportional representation, although it is probably somewhat fairer to smaller parties than the single-member plurality system; a proposal to introduce the single-member system in Japan was dropped by the Liberal Democratic Party in 1973 in the face of opposition protest that it would have produced an even greater bias towards that party, perhaps sufficient to give them the two-thirds majority in the lower house of the Diet that would allow them to over-ride the views of the upper house. (The L.D.P. won 46·9 per cent of the votes in the 1972 general election, and 55·2 per cent of the seats (Stockwin, 1974, pp. 83–91). In 1976, the L.D.P. won 41·9 per cent of the votes and 48·7 per cent of the seats (*The Times*, 7 December 1976).)

A number of hybrids based on this system have been used in the United States, with voters getting more than one vote but fewer votes than the total number of representatives to be elected. Thus, in 1968, a new Junior College Board of Trustees was established in Los Angeles and 133 candidates were nominated for the seven positions on it. A primary was held, at which each elector was given seven votes, and the top fourteen candidates went forward to a run-off. The contest was non-partisan, and important determinants of the number of votes received by each candidate were: their position on the ballot paper; which newspaper, if any, endorsed them; whether they had a Spanish or Jewish surname; and whether they were Edmund G. Brown Jr, son of the governor who defeated Nixon in 1962 (Mueller, 1970).

Perhaps even more horrendous for the voter was the 1964 election to the Illinois House of Representatives. Because of an inter-party impasse over re-districting the state, the House had to be elected at-large. There were 236 candidates for the 177 seats (each party was restricted to 118 nominees, two-thirds of the seats, to ensure some minority representation). Each elector had 177 votes. As machines were used only in Chicago and two other cities, many electors faced a ballot paper one foot wide and three feet long! They were allowed: (1) to make one mark signifying a vote for all 118 of one party's candidates (as in the list systems – see below), and not cast their other 59; (2) to vote a single-party ticket, plus 59 other individual selections; or (3) to make up to 177 individual selections. Large numbers were expected not to vote – the poll was on the same day as the 1964 presidential election – but 97 per cent of those voting for president also voted for the State House. 85 per cent voted for one party only, 10 per cent for one party plus some others, and only 5 per cent voted for individuals from different parties (Andrews, 1966).

(iii) *A weighted plurality system: electing the American president*

A special case of the plurality system, in which the constituencies are weighted by their populations, is used for elections of the American president, which proceeds by stages. First, a variety of procedures is used to produce a number of state delegates to each major party's national nominating convention, with the number of state delegates usually determined by the party's performance in that state at the previous presidential election. Next the nominating conventions elect the party candidates for the presidency and vice-presidency. Thirdly, the population of each state votes to send a number of electors to the electoral college. Finally, the college elects the president. (If no candidate receives a majority of electoral college votes, however, the election shifts to the House of Representatives for a fifth stage.)

The first two stages are not obligatory under the law – it is not only the two major parties who can nominate candidates – but the others are enshrined in the Constitution of 1787. Three possible methods of electing a president had been considered: by the Congress; by the people; and by the state governments (Dahl, 1956). The last alternative was that chosen. The president was to be the choice of a majority of the population, as represented in the electoral college by the number of members of Congress – two senators plus the number of members of the House of Representatives who are allocated decennially on a population basis by the Bureau of the Census. How the members of the electoral college were to be determined was left to the state governments to decide, and only in the present century have all states adopted the plurality system, whereby the electors sent are those on the slate of the candidate who wins a plurality of the votes in the election held on the first Tuesday in November.

Primary elections are not an obligatory method for producing the state's delegation to the national nominating conventions. The first was held in Florida in 1904. In recent years, to provide for greater public participation in the process, the use of primaries has spread widely, and they were held in thirty states in 1976. Elsewhere, a variety of procedures is employed. In Colorado, for example, each party held a caucus in each of the state's 2300 precincts (polling districts), with each meeting having a number of delegates to be elected, by proportional representation, to their county or city convention. The number of delegates is a function of the number of registered party members in the precinct. The city and county conventions in turn elect delegates to the state convention, which elects the state delegation to the national convention (*The Times*, 22 May 1976).

Where primaries are held, a variety of rules may be applied (Polsby and Wildavsky, 1964). Among the more important are:

(1) They may be open or closed. In a closed primary only registered members of a party may vote. In an open primary – as in Wisconsin – electors can vote in either primary, *but in only one*. This latter system can lead to 'cross-voting'. In the 1976 primaries, for example, a Democrat Party member might have believed (a) that Carter was certain to be his party's nominee, and (b) that in the presidential election Carter had a better chance of beating Reagan than Ford. He may therefore have voted in the Republican primary for Reagan, seeing this as in Carter's best interests.

(2) The delegates may be elected because they are associated

with a certain candidate, or they may be elected in their own right, to act as trustees for the state's interests. In some states, delegates are pledged to vote for a certain candidate in the nominating convention *at the first ballot only*. This is why Reagan hoped that Ford wouldn't get more than half the delegate vote at Kansas City in August 1976, after which some of Ford's committed voters might have transferred their allegiance to him, through personal commitment to Reagan's cause.

(3) Presidential candidates may have to enter a primary formally, or they may be voted for without their consent (a 'write-in'). Some candidates prefer not to enter in some primaries – in an opponent's home state, for example – for fear that a bad showing is worse than no contest.

(4) The primary may be only to decide which presidential candidate is preferred. Often called a 'beauty contest', this may run parallel to the selection of delegates or merely to advise the state convention which elects the delegates to the national gathering.

Election of delegates can also be by a variety of procedures. In 1972, for example, in some states the Democratic primaries were organized on a winner-takes-all basis; the candidate who received most votes won the pledges of the whole delegation. In others, the delegation was allocated to each candidate in proportion to his share of the total state poll (proportional representation). In a third group, delegates were allocated to each county according to the party's strength there, and a winner-take-all plurality was operated in each (Lengle and Shafer, 1976; see Chapter 9, p. 449).

After the nominating conventions comes the presidential contest which, although it is usually presented as between two major candidates (Ford and Carter in 1976) plus a number of minor-party tickets, is in fact a series of weighted single-member plurality elections, with votes being cast for slates of delegates committed to one or other of the candidates. The winning candidate receives the support of the whole state delegation even if he obtains only a one-vote margin of success over his nearest challenger. In 1948, Truman beat Dewey by only 33,612 out of 3,984,046 votes cast in Illinois, and so won all 28 of the state's electoral college votes. He won California's 25 votes by an even

Table 2.1 Voting at two American presidential elections

State	1960			1976		
	Republican	*Democrat*	*Electoral College*	*Republican*	*Democrat*	*Electoral College*
Alabama	237,981	324,050	D–11*	495,744	644,375	D–9
Alaska	30,953	29,809	R–3	39,008	22,994	R–3
Arizona	221,241	176,781	R–4	417,413	294,668	R–6
Arkansas	184,508	215,049	D–8	266,713	495,909	D–6
California	3,259,722	3,224,099	R–32	3,837,202	3,709,815	R–45
Colorado	402,242	330,629	R–6	566,364	447,006	R–7
Connecticut	565,513	657,055	D–8	712,414	641,010	R–8
Delaware	96,373	99,590	D–3	109,926	122,610	D–3
District of Columbia†				25,184	127,562	D–3
Florida	795,476	748,700	D–10	1,375,296	1,561,383	D–17
Georgia	274,472	458,638	R–12	469,129	951,636	D–12
Hawaii	92,295	92,410	D–3	140,003	147,375	D–4
Idaho	161,597	138,853	R–4	203,874	126,175	R–4
Illinois	2,368,988	2,377,846	D–27	2,319,173	2,218,056	R–26
Indiana	1,175,120	952,358	R–13	1,166,670	1,002,936	R–13
Iowa	722,381	550,565	R–10	631,667	618,898	R–8
Kansas	561,474	363,213	R–8	501,759	429,003	R–7
Kentucky	602,607	521,855	R–10	524,171	609,410	D–9
Louisiana	230,980	407,339	D–10	606,204	683,512	D–10
Maine	240,608	181,159	R–5	234,434	231,283	R–4
Maryland	489,538	565,808	D–9	648,980	735,618	D–10
Massachusetts	976,750	1,487,174	D–16	1,004,598	1,391,201	D–14
Michigan	1,620,428	1,687,269	D–20	1,855,924	1,667,000	R–21
Minnesota	757,915	779,933	D–11	817,349	1,067,536	D–10
Mississippi	73,561	108,362	Other–8*	360,911	372,448	D–7
Missouri	962,221	972,201	D–13	916,903	984,413	D–12
Montana	141,841	134,891	R–4	169,308	146,291	R–4

Nebraska	380,553	232,542	R–6	349,736	230,152	R–5
Nevada	52,387	54,880	D–3	100,786	92,023	R–3
New Hampshire	157,989	137,772	R–4	185,472	147,168	R–4
New Jersey	1,363,324	1,385,415	D–16	1,477,858	1,420,668	R–17
New Mexico	153,733	156,027	D–4	207,718	199,225	R–4
New York	3,446,419	3,830,085	D–45	3,060,695	3,336,665	D–41
North Carolina	655,420	713,136	D–14	736,602	921,119	D–13
North Dakota	154,310	123,963	R–4	146,559	130,325	R–3
Ohio	2,217,611	1,944,248	R–25	1,992,415	2,000,001	D–25
Oklahoma	533,039	370,111	R–8*	539,948	528,761	R–8
Oregon	408,060	367,402	R–6	482,093	481,881	R–6
Pennsylvania	2,439,956	2,556,282	D–32	2,187,038	2,315,494	D–27
Rhode Island	147,502	258,032	D–4	172,138	216,991	D–4
South Carolina	188,558	198,129	D–8	342,409	443,901	D–8
South Dakota	178,417	128,070	R–4	151,619	146,153	R–4
Tennessee	556,577	481,453	R–11	632,731	821,594	D–10
Texas	1,121,310	1,167,567	D–24	1,876,316	2,031,562	D–26
Utah	205,361	169,248	R–4	335,144	180,974	R–4
Vermont	98,131	69,186	R–3	98,982	77,746	R–3
Virginia	404,521	362,327	R–12	834,542	810,636	R–12
Washington	629,273	599,298	R–9	679,631	643,333	R–9
West Virginia	395,995	441,786	D–8	311,012	430,404	D–6
Wisconsin	895,175	830,805	R–12	1,003,039	1,037,056	D–11
Wyoming	77,451	63,331	R–3	92,831	62,267	R–3
Total	34,108,157	34,226,731	R–220* D–309* Other–8*	38,413,635	40,156,213	R–241 D–297

Sources: 1960 R. M. Scammon *America Votes 9* Congressional Quarterly, Washington, 1972, p. 7.
1976 *New York Times* 4, November 1976, p. 32.

* 6 of the 11 Democrat electors in Alabama and the 8 unpledged Democrats in Mississippi voted for Senator H. F. Byrd, as did one of the Oklahoma Republican electors.

† The residents of the District of Columbia were enfranchised only in 1964.

smaller margin with a plurality of only 17,865 over Dewey out of the 4,021,538 ballots cast. The closest election overall, in recent years, however, was in 1960, when the Kennedy–Johnson ticket won by a margin of only 118,574 votes (0·17 per cent of the national total) over Nixon–Cabot Lodge, but because its successes included five of the seven states returning more than twenty members of the electoral college (Illinois' 27 were won by a margin of only 8,858: see Table 2.1) its margin in the college was 84 (276 were needed for absolute victory). In 1976, there were few very tight contests – the closest being Oregon which the Republican candidate (Ford) won by 212 votes out of 963,974. Carter's lead of about 2 percentage points in the popular vote produced a comfortable electoral college victory.

As indicated in Table 2.1, the weighted plurality system of winner-takes-the-whole-state-delegation does not ensure that electoral college membership reflects the popular vote. Consequently, it is possible, although not very likely, for a president to be elected on a minority of the votes (in 1960, if the right states had been won, this minority could have represented a plurality in only twelve states) which leads, as we shall see in Chapter 9, to persistent claims for reform of the system.

2. Preferential Systems

In plurality contests, as we have just seen, electors simply indicate the candidate they most prefer (or the candidates, if the contest is multi-membered with plural voting). But no information is given in either case of their feelings about the others, about, for example, who their second choice would be if for some reason they could not have their first, who their third choice would be, and so on. One consequence of this is that, as we saw for the Carmarthen election (p. 40), a candidate may be elected whom many more people have voted against than for. To counter this, systems have been devised to produce consensus candidates – those who are least disliked, or whom a majority of voters would prefer to certain others. There are two major variants of this procedure, differing in the number of representatives returned per constituency.

(i) *Single-member preferential systems: (a) the alternative vote*

The 'pure' form of preferential voting for a single-member constituency is the alternative vote (A.V.), in which the elector orders all the candidates in a rank, from the one most preferred to the least, although in some systems an elector does not have to express a preference for every one of them. These preferences are then used to produce a consensus representative; the one, that is, who is eventually supported by at least half (plus one) of the electors.

Operation of the system begins by counting the first preference votes; if any candidate receives more than half of these, he is declared elected, since he already meets the criterion of having the support of at least half of the electorate. If no candidate receives an absolute majority of first preference votes, the one with the smallest total is eliminated and his second preferences are distributed among the others, being added to their first preference totals. This procedure continues until one candidate reaches the 50 per cent level or, in the case of a system where electors do not have to express all their preferences, until there are no further preferences to allocate, in which case the candidate with most votes wins. As illustrations of this procedure, we have data for three divisions of the State of Victoria at the 1974 Australian general election for the House of Representatives:

Gippsland	*First preference*	Henty	*First preference*	McMillan	*First preference*
Nixon	32,484	Child	28,111	Hewson	13,650
Bowron	2,123	Farrell	2,408	Broadhurst	1,666
Condern	2,533	Fox	24,953	Dent	13,345
Oakes	17,456	Hughes	1,191	Hilton	2,273
				Murphy	24,201

In Gippsland, Nixon won nearly 60 per cent of the votes, and was declared elected without any allocation of preferences. No candidate received a majority of the votes in Henty, however (Child got 49·61 per cent), and so Hughes was eliminated and his second preferences distributed as

	To Child	to Farrell	to Fox
	774	115	302
making total	28,885	2,523	25,225

which gave victory to Child with 50·78 per cent of the votes. Finally, in McMillan several distributions were necessary:

	Broad-hurst	Dent	Hewson	Hilton	Murphy
First preferences	1,666	13,345	13,650	2,273	24,201
Broadhurst's second preferences	—	1,025	156	51	434
making total	—	14,370	13,806	2,324	24,635
Hilton's second preferences	—	175	2,041	—	108
making total	—	14,545	15,847	—	24,743
Dent's second preferences	—	—	14,263	—	282
making total	—	—	30,110	—	25,025

Despite his large lead on the first preferences, therefore, Murphy was eventually defeated, largely by a combination of Dent's and Hewson's votes. These two were members of the two parties, Liberal and Country, which have formed the only non-Labor governments in Australia since 1940, ruling as a federal coalition. In many seats they do not compete against each other, the exceptions to this being divisions which contain rural and urban portions and which both feel they have a chance of winning, thereby gaining another M.P. and greater power within the coalition. There is little fèar that they will lose to the Labor (A.L.P.) candidate unless he gets over fifty per cent of the first preferences, since most second preferences from Liberal candidates go to Country and vice versa. This is what happened in McMillan, and indeed it was to cater for such competition between members of à coalition without ensuring the defeat of both that the system was introduced in Australia in 1918, since when it has been used for all Federal House of Representatives elections (Graham, 1962).

If only two parties are contesting a seat, however, the system is of little value, and indeed for all federal elections in Australia between 1937 and 1961 second preferences had to be allocated in only 19 per cent of the constituencies, and the ordering of candidates from that on the first preferences was changed in only 5 per cent of the contests (Rydon, 1968). In part this is because of the nature of the bipartisan contests, with absolute majorities occasionally impeded on the first preferences by minor parties whose supporters can thus voice their opinions without necessarily 'wasting' their vote (see Chapter 9, p. 457); in part it reflects the gerrymanders (intentional and otherwise) in the definition of Australian constituencies (Jaensch, 1970).

One undesirable consequence of the use of the A.V. system in Australia is the 'donkey vote', whose prevalence is undoubtedly also associated with the compulsory voting rule there. Electors who vote in this way simply rank-order the candidates from 1 onwards, straight down the ballot paper, so that the greater the number of donkey votes cast, the greater the number of first preferences given to the candidate at the top of the ballot, on which the ordering is alphabetical. As a consequence, there has been a preponderance of members elected with surnames beginning with the letters A–K, and parties clearly seek candidates whose surnames begin with early letters in the alphabet (Masterman, 1964). It has been estimated that as many as eight constituencies have been won and lost on the donkey vote in a single election, although at no time influencing the final decision about which party formed the government (Mackerras, 1970).

Single-member preferential systems: (b) the double-ballot

A variant of the Australian procedure is practised in the elections for the French National Assembly, and also for the leadership contests in the British Conservative and Labour Parties (Rose, 1976). In France, people do not rank order the candidates, but merely express their first preference, as in a single-member plurality contest. If no candidate wins more than half of the votes, then a second ballot is held a week later, and some of the candidates from the first contest may withdraw; in any case, the person with most votes in the second ballot, irrespective of whether they form a majority, is elected. In broad outline, the system has been in use – on and off – since 1852; at some stages candidates could stand in the second ballot without contesting the first, but at present only candidates who won votes from 10 per cent or more of the total electorate on the first ballot can stand again (Campbell, 1958). During the intervening week, the candidates and their parties often make pacts, with one withdrawing, perhaps, and asking his supporters to vote for the other, which is very similar to the suggestions on allocation of preferences given by Australian candidates.

Three examples, none of them involving a first-ballot victory, from the 1958 French general election illustrate the procedure (Williams, 1970, pp. 290–91).

	Seine-St Denis 3		Herault 3		Aisne 1	
Party	*First*	*Second*	*First*	*Second*	*First*	*Second*
Communist	23,233	25,409	12,239	13,676	7,914	
Socialist	5,146		12,284	15,244	8,945	15,076
M.R.P.	6,511		6,325			
Gaullist	11,456	22,903	7,643	16,905	9,980	
Extreme right	981		2,744			
Other right	1,183				13,202	24,694
Total votes	48,510	48,312	41,235	45,825	40,041	39,720
Total electorate	61,558	61,558	59,165	59,165	52,704	52,704

In Seine-St Denis 3, three candidates were forced to withdraw because they received fewer than 6156 votes, and the M.R.P. (Mouvement Républicain Populaire) candidate did too, producing a straight fight between the Communist and the Gaullist, which the former won. Two such pacts apparently were made in Aisne 1, creating a straight right/left contest, won in this case by the candidate of the right, but in Herault 3 the left-wing parties seem not to have agreed and, despite each obtaining many more votes (presumably because of the larger turnout). they were defeated by the single candidate of the right. Clearly, there are complicated bargains to be struck during this week, which can be crucial to the final composition of the assembly and the power of the parties within it.

Run-off elections of this type are also common in the United States, particularly in the states of the south and adjacent areas where the Democrat party predominates. In eleven states the Democrat party holds run-off primaries between the leading contenders in the first primary, on the argument that since the Democrat candidate is virtually certain to win the general election, he should get the endorsement of a majority of the party members, which is not likely to occur if there are many candidates (Chapter 6, p. 276: Ranney, 1965). In Los Angeles, the mayoralty election is similarly held in two stages. At the first in 1969 there were 26 candidates, with 731,423 votes being cast, and at the second there were only 2 (including the incumbent mayor, Yorty), with an extra 124,751 being persuaded to vote by the issues raised in the two-month campaign between the two ballots (McPhail, 1971). (See also p. 205.)

Preferences and election results: a paradox

The A.V. system, and the second ballot to a lesser extent, seems to be a fairer system than the plurality, although in effect it is only a modification of the plurality and is very unlikely to produce proportional representation. But if we take a hypothetical situation of three candidates, A, B and C we might get:

Candidate	*First preference votes*	*Second preferences*	
A	10,000	C 9,000	B 1,000
B	9,500	C 9,000	A 500
C	5,000	A 2,500	B 2,500

which would be won, according to the A.V. system, by A. Yet a moment's perusal of the data suggests that if all second preferences were added to all first preferences the results would be A 13,000, B 13,000 and C 23,000!

A lot of work has been reported on this general problem of the meaning of preferences, much of it being based on what is called Arrow's theorem, after the distinguished economist Kenneth J. Arrow, who showed (Arrow, 1951) that if three voters A, B and C were each asked to rank-order three candidates and produced the following rankings:

Rank	1	2	3
Voter A	Labour	Conservative	Liberal
Voter B	Liberal	Labour	Conservative
Voter C	Conservative	Liberal	Labour

the following inconclusive results would occur:

(1) two voters (A and B) put Labour before Conservative, so Labour is preferred to Conservative overall;

(2) two voters (A and C) put Conservative before Liberal, so Conservative is preferred to Liberal overall;

(3) two voters (B and C) put Liberal before Labour, so Liberal is preferred to Labour overall.

In other words, Labour is preferred to Conservative, Conservative is preferred to Liberal, but Liberal is preferred to Labour: there is no consensus candidate! This can easily happen in real elections. If one assumes, reasonably from survey data (Butler and Stokes, 1969), that at Britain's 1966 election: (1) 76 per cent of Conservative voters would have given their second preferences to Liberal: (2) 74 per cent of Labour voters would have given their second preferences to Liberal; and (3) 56 per cent of Liberal voters would have given their second preferences to Labour: then, at the Norfolk South election (Colman and Pountney, 1975a, 1975b) whereas the first preference voting of: Conservative 16,968; Labour 16,849; Liberal 4,079; made the Conservative candidate the most preferred, the third preferences, showing the candidate whom the voters liked least, would have read: Conservative 14,836; Labour 14,661; Liberal 8,399; which would have made the Conservative the least preferred. Who should have won?

(ii) *Multi-member preferential systems: the single transferable vote*

In this system, the elector again rank-orders the candidates from 1 to a given number, knowing that more than one of them will be elected. It was first used in 1918, in Ireland, for electing the Sligo Town Council and was then adopted for elections to the lower house of the Irish parliament (The Dail) in that country's 1922 Constitution (O'Leary, 1961). Advancement of the method's value was largely the work of the Proportional Representation Society, which continues to campaign in Great Britain (as the Electoral Reform Society) for use of the single transferable vote (S.T.V.) in multi-member constituencies. They consider it the most suitable method for giving voters a wide freedom of choice, away from the impress of the party machine, and at the same time approaching, if not producing, proportional representation. In Ireland, the case was made strongly that S.T.V. ensured representation of minorities, which the English plurality system did not, and this was a crucial issue for the Protestant population of the incipient state. After the Sligo election, Lloyd George's government realized that its use would temper the strength of the Sinn Fein movement, hence the adoption of S.T.V. there but not in England (Chapter 8, p. 422). The Maltese parliament, the lower house of the Tasmanian parliament, the Australian Senate, the 1973 Northern Ireland Assembly and the 1975 Northern Ireland Constitutional Convention all use S.T.V.

Details of the system's use vary from place to place. In Ireland, for example, electors may make their ballots non-transferable by not ranking all candidates, but in Australia such a ballot-paper would be considered as spoiled and not be counted. Nevertheless, the general procedures are the same. Once voting is completed, the first preferences are counted and the number necessary for election is determined, usually by what is known as the Droop quota, which is:

$$\left(\frac{\text{Total number of first preferences cast}}{\text{Number of seats in the constituency}+1}\right)+1$$

so that in a constituency with 20,000 votes cast and four members to be elected the quota would be $\frac{20,000}{5}+1$ or 4001. The denominator is the number of seats *plus one* and not the number of seats, since 1/n of the votes (where n = the number of seats) are not needed for victory. In the above example $\left(\frac{1}{n+1}+1\right)\times$ votes = 4001 and no other candidate could beat the four who exceeded that – they would be elected.

If any candidates have first preference vote totals exceeding the quota the one with most votes is declared elected. He may have more votes than the quota, in which case the excess votes would be 'wasted', in that they are irrelevant to the victory (see Chapters 7 and 8). To avoid waste the excess votes – or surplus – are distributed as second preferences, so that if the quota was 4001 and A got 5000 votes, 999 second preferences would be distributed to the other candidates. But which 999? Clearly there can be no answer to this, and so all 5000 second preferences are distributed, but 'weighted' (diminished in value) by 999/5000 so that nevertheless only 999 extra votes are allocated to the other candidates. To illustrate this, assume a constituency with nine candidates competing for three seats. Voting went:

Candidate	A	B	C	D	E	F	G	H	I	Total
First preference votes	400	200	200	1000	200	300	100	100	100	2600

Quota = (2600/3+1)+1 = (2600/4)+1 = 651

Candidate D exceeded the quota and was elected. His second preferences were allocated by his supporters as follows:

Candidate	A	B	C	D	E	F	G	H	I	Total
D's second preferences	100	50	50	—	400	300	60	20	20	1000

He has a surplus of 349 to be distributed, and so the second preferences, weighted by 349/1000, are added to the first preferences for the other eight, as follows:

Candidate	A	B	C	D	E	F	G	H	I	Total
First preference votes	400	200	200	1000	200	300	100	100	100	2600
D's second preferences	100	50	50	—	400	300	60	20	20	1000
Weighted (reduced by a factor of $\frac{349}{1000}$)	35	17	17	—	140	105	21	7	7	349
Total	435	217	217	—	340	405	121	107	107	1949

After allocation of preferences, the candidate with the highest number of votes is declared elected, if his total now exceeds the quota, and his surplus is distributed in the same way as before except that if any of his second preferences are for a candidate already elected, these are replaced by the third preferences on those ballots; similarly some of his votes may be second (or lower) preferences from others already elected, and again the next lowest preferences on the relevant ballots are substituted.

If, as with our hypothetical example, no candidate exceeds the quota of 651 and there are still seats to be filled, the procedure used in the alternative vote system is operated. The candidate with the lowest number of votes is eliminated, and his second preferences (or lower ones where relevant) are allocated. A candidate may then exceed the quota, in which case the procedure already outlined is applied again; if all candidates still fail to exceed the quota, the one with the lowest total is eliminated, and so on.

The two procedures of distributing the surpluses for elected candidates and eliminating the bottom candidates continue until all of the seats are filled. With large constituencies, returning say ten candidates, as occurs in Australian full Senate elections, this may be a long and complex process, especially when filling the last seats where many of the higher preferences are given to already-elected or eliminated candidates.

If votes can be made non-transferable, then the last candidate to be elected may be below the quota. Table 2.2 illustrates the results of the total count in a small Irish constituency. The leading Fianna Fail candidate – Power – was declared elected on the first preferences, and his surplus of 1313 distributed. McEvoy of

Table 2.2 The Irish general election in Kildare, 1973

Seats to be filled	3				Total first preference votes		27,701
Electoral quota	7581						
Party		Fianna Fail			Fine Gael	Labour	
Candidate	Power	Boyland	Dooley	Malone	McEvoy	Bermingham	Non-Transferable
First preference votes	8894	4898	1441	6581	1716	6791	
Power's surplus (1313)	—	704	449	56	23	81	
New total	—	5602	1890	6637	1739	6872	32
McEvoy's votes (1739)	—	31	43	1268	—	365	
New Total	—	5633	1933	7905	—	7237	
Malone's surplus (324)	—	7	9	—	—	309	
New Total	—	5640	1941	—	—	7546	
Dooley's votes (1941)	—	1549	—	—	—	204	188
New total	—	7189	—	—	—	7750	

Source: Knight and Baxter-Moore (1973, p. 132)

Fine Gael was then eliminated, and the 73 per cent of his second preferences going to Malone were just sufficient to get the latter elected. After Malone's surplus of only 324 was distributed, most of it to the Labour candidate (Fine Gael and Labour were in coalition), Dooley, the third Fianna Fail candidate, was eliminated, and although most of his second preferences went to Boyland, the 11 per cent going to Bermingham were sufficient to give the Labour candidate the third seat.

The S.T.V. system's main advantage is the choice it gives to the electors. With large constituencies, it usually produces results which are close to proportional representation but, as is now the case in Ireland, with small constituencies the match of votes and seats may be poor (Paddison, 1976); in Kildare, the three Fianna Fail candidates won nearly 60 per cent of the votes but only one of the three seats (Table 2.2).

In elections based on the S.T.V. system, parties are faced with the same decisions as under the single non-transferable system used in Japan (p. 42); how many candidates should they field? The main influence on their answer is the number of seats they expect to win, but the details of how the system is operated are also relevant. For example, if Fianna Fail had fielded only two candidates in the Kildare contest, they might easily have won two seats. If they had been able (successfully) to direct all their supporters to give their first preferences to Power and their second preferences to Boyland, then Power would have received 15,233 votes; his surplus of 7652 would all have gone to Boyland, who would have been elected. This assumes that people vote for party, and party only, which in Irish politics is not usually so. As we discuss in more detail in Chapters 5 and 9 (p. 290), a major feature in Irish voting is support for local candidates, to represent parts of constituencies, and so if Fianna Fail had not nominated Dooley, some of his first preferences might have gone to another party's candidate. Also in some constituencies parties must aim at particular sections of the electorate, particularly the Protestant minority, as illustrated in a study of the Donegal North-East constituency (Sacks, 1970). Having nominated Dooley, the problem for Fianna Fail was that sufficient of his second preferences (or of Power's third preferences: Table 2.2) were either allocated to the Labour candidate or were non-transferable, so that Boyland's chances of election were wrecked.

Party solidarity in the allocation of preferences is the important feature of S.T.V. elections from the point of view of the parties, a feature which the Northern Irish quickly learned in the mid-1970s (Laver, 1976). This is very apparent in the Australian Senate elections, in which local issues are of very minor importance (Chapter 6, p. 287) and most electors use the 'how-to-vote' cards distributed by the parties (which also avoids the donkey vote, although as a further step to minimize its influence the Electoral Act of 1940 introduced a lottery for the location of candidates on the ballot, rather than putting them in alphabetical order. To ensure that all candidates in one party are together, however, each party can nominate one member to enter the lottery and the others are placed after him on the ballot: Hughes and Graham, 1968, p. 284). Thus at the 1974 Senate election for Victoria the Australian Labor Party nominated six candidates for the ten seats. The distribution of the first preference votes was:

Brown 850,879 Primmer 1,261 Button 1,059 Poyser 1,578
Melzer 2,493 Cox 1,808

with Brown getting 99 per cent of the total. His 683,568 surplus votes were allocated as follows:

Primmer 681,400 Button 386 Poyser 178 Melzer 207 Cox 155

with over 99 per cent following the party directive; only 1202 were allocated to candidates of other parties. The A.L.P. candidates received 41 per cent of the first preference total and won five seats, Cox being the unlucky one.

3. List Systems

This is both the most frequent type of electoral system and the one with most variants (Lakeman, 1974, gives the countries using the major systems). The basic features are: (1) voting is entirely party-oriented; (2) elections are for multi-member, sometimes very large, constituencies (national in the cases of Israel and the Netherlands); and (3) electors may be allowed to discriminate among a party's candidates, but only within one party. Such features are typical of the electoral systems of nearly all countries in western and northern Europe, and were also common in eastern Europe before the Communist takeovers in the late 1940s.

In most list system elections, the voters are presented with a ballot containing lists of candidates submitted by each of the parties contesting the constituency. They must decide to support one of these parties, *and one only*, irrespective of the number of members to be elected. This is often all that they need do, leaving to the party leaders the decision as to which candidates are actually elected; thus the electors may give 40 per cent of the votes to party A, entitling it to four seats, and these go to the top four candidates the party have placed on their list.

Handing over the actual choice of members to the parties is typical of voting in Italy, for example, where some of the constituencies return over 30 members. But the chance of making one's own choices within the party selection is usually offered. In Italy, for example, voters can indicate a personal preference for up to three candidates of their chosen party (four if more than fifteen members are to be returned); in Belgium they can indicate one preference only; in Luxembourg they can express two preferences, both of which can be for the same candidate.

We will not go into the full details of personal voting in each country, but use the Danish example as a more detailed illustration of its procedures (Pedersen, 1966). Parties there can choose among three different ways of organizing their lists – and they can use different methods in different constituencies. In describing these systems we identify two different types of votes: impersonal votes, in which the electors accept the order of candidates on the party list; and personal votes, in which the electors indicate their preference for one or more of those on their chosen party list.

(1) *The simultaneous list* allocates the impersonal votes equally to each member of a party list. In the example here, a party has

three nominees; of the 900 votes given to the party, 600 are 'impersonal' votes, and the other 300 are personal votes. The voting may then read:

Candidate	A	B	C
Personal votes	200	10	90
Impersonal votes	200	200	200
Total	400	210	290

so that, if the party won two seats with its total of 900 votes, A and C would be elected. In a district, a party may list all of its candidates simultaneously, or only some.

(2) *The local list* method allows the local branch of a party to nominate, for its part of the constituency, which of the party's candidates is to top the list in their district, and this person is indicated in bold type. Electors who vote for the party list are expressing a preference for that candidate; others may vote for other candidates. Thus we might have a two-district constituency, in which the first branch nominates B and the second nominates A; the voting for that party alone might then be as follows:

Candidate	A	B	C
District I – nominated candidate B			
Party list votes (impersonal votes)	0	200	0
Personal votes	10	0	50
District II – nominated candidate A			
Party list votes (impersonal votes)	300	0	0
Personal votes	0	40	70
Total	310	240	120

so that if two members are to be returned they will be A and B, who benefit from their selection by the local party machines.

(3) *The party list* method is one in which the central party organization determines a single rank ordering to be used in all districts in the constituency, against which the individual elector can express his own preference for one candidate. All party votes go to the top candidate on the list and election is determined by

allocating surpluses down the list. Thus, in a constituency with the six candidates in a party receiving the following votes:

Candidate	A	B	C	D	E	F
Party votes	400	0	0	0	0	0
Personal votes	20	20	40	130	20	10
Total	420	20	40	130	20	10

three candidates are to be elected, and the electoral quota (see below) is 180. Candidate A is declared elected; his surplus of 240 goes to B, who has 260 and is elected; his 80 surplus go to C giving him 120, but D gets the final seat because of his 130 personal votes.

Personal voting is quite common in Denmark, and the parties are free to use whichever of the three list systems they prefer, in each constituency and district, allowing them to decide which is to their greatest benefit. At the general election of 9 January 1975 in the Aarhus constituency, for example, 339,832 votes were cast for the various party lists, of which nearly 41 per cent were personal votes. One of the parties contesting the fourteen seats for the constituency was the Konservative Folkeparti, which fielded six candidates, winning 16,784 votes and one seat. The distribution of its votes among the six is shown in Table 2.3. In every district some candidates, it will be seen, received only a personal vote; this absence of an impersonal vote distributed among all candidates means that no district listed all simultaneously. In five districts (5, 6, 7, 9, 10) all candidates but one received only a personal vote, which means a party list was used, with the nominee at the top of the list getting personal votes as well. In the other five districts (1, 2, 3, 4, 8) several candidates received impersonal votes, implying a local list or simultaneous listing of some candidates only. Lowzow was elected (he received the largest percentage of personal votes), thanks largely to his position at the top of the list in districts 7, 9 and 10.

This example of how the list system operates in Denmark illustrates both the voting procedures and the way in which the successful candidates within a party are identified. The other important procedure is that which determines how many seats

Table 2.3 Voting for the Konservative Folkeparti: Aarhus constituency, 1975 general election

	Candidate (personal votes are in parentheses)					
District	*Bendix*	*Gammelgaard*	*Lowzow*	*Nielsen*	*E. S. Petersen*	*A. Petersen*
1	633 (271)	311 (133)	104 (104)	306 (131)	686 (294)	7 (7)
2	369 (157)	459 (195)	33 (33)	160 (68)	256 (109)	2 (2)
3	504 (206)	364 (149)	105 (105)	724 (296)	677 (277)	5 (5)
4	1074 (467)	518 (225)	97 (97)	320 (139)	384 (167)	3 (3)
5	59 (59)	29 (29)	78 (78)	1 (1)	30 (30)	705 (164)
6	104 (104)	58 (58)	165 (165)	5 (5)	47 (47)	1883 (666)
7	88 (88)	55 (55)	1140 (443)	16 (16)	31 (31)	3 (3)
8	1157 (471)	106 (43)	123 (123)	22 (9)	100 (41)	19 (19)
9	50 (50)	58 (58)	1068 (420)	7 (7)	47 (47)	3 (3)
10	52 (52)	36 (36)	1294 (533)	2 (2)	41 (41)	1 (1)
Total	4090 (1925)	1994 (981)	4207 (2101)	1563 (674)	2299 (1084)	2631 (873)

Source: *Statistiske Arbog fur Arahus*, 1976.

each party has won in each constituency. This is done by calculating an electoral quota, of which there are several types (see Lakeman, 1974). One of the commonest is the *d'Hondt rule* (sometimes known as the largest average). The total number of votes cast for all candidates of each party is added up, and successively divided by whole numbers from 1 to n, where n is the number of members to be returned from the constituency. Seats are then allocated to the parties with the n largest quotients. For example, in a constituency returning five members, in which therefore n is 5, voting might be like this:

Party	A	B	C	D	E
Total votes	10,000	2,000	1,500	6,500	4,500
Divided by: 1	10,000	2,000	1,500	6,500	4,500
2	5,000	1,000	750	3,250	2,250
3	3,333	667	500	2,167	1,500
4	2,500	500	375	1,625	1,125
5	2,000	400	300	1,300	900

The five largest quotients (which are underlined) allocate three seats to party A and one each to parties D and E; allocation of the seats within each party then follows the rules outlined above. A modification of this rule, used in Denmark, Norway and Sweden (Elder, 1975), is the *Sainte-Lague formula* in which the denominators are 1·4, 3, 5, 7, 9, . . . rather than 1, 2, 3, . . . n; this formula is both less generous to large parties than the d'Hondt and also relatively more severe on small parties. In our example it would allocate one more seat to D and one less to A than would the d'Hondt, as follows:

Party	A	B	C	D	E
Total votes	10,000	2,000	1,500	6,500	4,500
Divided by: 1·4	7,143	1,429	1,071	4,643	3,214
3	3,333	667	500	3,169	1,500
5	2,000	400	300	1,300	900
7	1,429	286	214	929	643
9	1,111	222	167	722	500

At the 1975 Danish general election, application of the formula in the Aarhus constituency produced the distribution of seats shown in Table 2.4.

In Luxembourg, the *largest remainder* rule is used. The intent is to obtain proportional representation within the constituency, but it is rare that the party percentages of the total vote are exact multiples of the quota percentage. Thus the vote might be distributed as follows:

Party	A	B	C	D	E
Percentage of the vote	41	8	6	27	18

and if there were five seats, the quota would be 20 per cent. Three seats can immediately be allocated, to A (two) and D, and the remainders are then calculated:

Party	A	B	C	D	E
Percentage of the vote	41	8	6	27	18
Less quota of 20%	40	0	0	20	0
Remainders	+1	+8	+6	+7	+18

The remaining two seats go to the parties with the largest remainders, B and E. Finally, in this list of examples, in Italy seats are allocated in each constituency using a quota formula of:

$$\frac{\text{Total number of votes cast in the constituency}}{\text{Number of members to be returned}+2}$$

and seats are allocated to all parties who receive votes exceeding the quota. Thus an example might be a constituency with 24,500 votes and 5 members to be returned, giving a quota of 3500 (24,500/7). If the votes were distributed in the same way as above, allocation of seats would be (subtracting 3500 or multiples of it):

Party	A	B	C	D	E
Votes	10,000	2000	1500	6500	4500
Seats	2	0	0	1	1
Surplus Votes	3000	2000	1500	3000	1000

Table 2.4 Application of the Sainte-Lague formula, Aarhus Constituency, 1975 General Election

	Denominator (the largest 14 quotients are underlined)						
Party	*Votes*	1·4	3	5	7	9	11
Socialdemokratiet	111,107	79,362	37,036	22,221	15,872	12,345	10,101
Radikale Venstre	23,842	17,030	7947				
Konservative Folkeparti	16,784	11,989	5595				
Retsforbundet	7477	5341					
Socialistik Folkeparti	17,676	12,626	5892				
Kommunistike Parti	13,567	9691					
Centrum-Demokraterne	6762	4830					
Kristeligt Folkeparti	18,516	13,226	6172				
Venstre	73,891	52,779	24,630	14,778	10,556		
Venstre-Socialisterne	9368	6691					
Fremskridtspartiet	40,842	29,173	13,614	8168			
Uden for partierne	63	45					

Source: *Statistiske Efterretninger*, January 1975

in which case only four seats are allocated. The fifth goes into a national pool in which all the surplus votes from the constituencies are amalgamated, and they are allocated according to a new quota for this 'national constituency'.

4. Mixed Systems

We have suggested that a major aim of many electoral systems is to ensure proportional representation, with each party's percentage of the national vote equalled by its percentage of the parliamentary seats. None of the various constituency-based systems that we have discussed here is bound to produce proportional representation (we indicate why in Chapters 7 and 8) although some, notably the single-member plurality system, are more likely to produce results further from the ideal than are others. For this reason, some countries have adopted methods of combining a constituency-based voting pattern with a national 'topping-up' which aims to correct any deviations from the norm of proportional representation.

In Denmark the major element in the electoral system is, as we have indicated, a list system by which seventeen constituencies return between 2 and 17 members to the Folketing. In addition to these 135 seats, however, there are a further 40, which are allocated so as to ensure proportional representation among the major parties. Parties qualify for this second-round allocation by meeting one of the following criteria: (1) one parliamentary seat in the constituency allocation; (2) at least two per cent of the national poll; and (3) at least as many votes in each of two of the country's three zones (Greater Copenhagen, Jutland and the Islands) as the average votes per seat there. The seats are then allocated among the parties so that their national percentages of the votes and the Folketing seats are as nearly equal as possible; after the 1975 election the maximum difference was only 0·7 percentage points. Table 2.5 illustrates how this 'topping-up' was necessary after the 1975 election, because of the over-representation of the three largest parties from the constituency contests. Sweden has a similar system, except that the number of second-

Table 2.5 The 'topping-up' process to produce proportional representation: the Danish general election of January 1975

Party	*Votes (%)*	*Constituency Seats (%)*	*'Topping-up' Seats*	*Total Seats (%)*
Socialdemokratiet	913,155 (30·5)	51 (37·8)	2	53 (30·3)
Radikale Venstre	216,553 (7·2)	8 (5·9)	5	13 (7·4)
Konservative Folkeparti	168,164 (5·6)	3 (2·2)	7	10 (5·7)
Socialistik Folkeparti	150,963 (5·0)	5 (3·7)	4	9 (5·1)
Kommunistike Parti	127,837 (4·3)	3 (2·2)	4	7 (4·0)
Centrum-Demokraterne	66,316 (2·2)	0 (0·0)	4	4 (2·3)
Kristeligt Folkparti	162,734 (5·4)	5 (3·7)	4	9 (5·1)
Venstre	711,298 (23·8)	39 (28·9)	3	42 (24·0)
Venstre-Socialisterne	63,579 (2·1)	0 (0·0)	4	4 (2·3)
Fremskridtspartiet	414,219 (13·8)	21 (15·6)	3	24 (13·7)
Total	2,994,818	135	40	175

Source: *Statistike Efterretninger*, January 1975

round seats had to be reduced from 40 to 39 to avoid a repetition of the embarrassing tie between government and opposition which occurred in 1972.

The other form of 'topping-up' is practised in West Germany, and also in Iceland, and has been proposed in a modified form for the United Kingdom (Hansard Society, 1976). Each person votes twice at a national election in West Germany. His first vote is for a local representative, and is cast in one of the 248 constituencies which operate a single-member plurality system. His second vote is for a party list, which is compiled for the Land (the province encompassing his home constituency); the party which gets his list vote need not be the same as that which gets his constituency vote – a variant which the Hansard Committee proposal would not allow in the United Kingdom. The list votes for each party are then totalled separately for the ten Länder, and the proportional entitlement of each party is determined by the d'Hondt rule, although only parties with at least five per cent of the Land vote are entitled to allocations in the second round. Thus in Hesse at the 1949 election the result was (Pollock, 1952, p. 1060):

Party	C.D.U. (C.S.V.)	S.P.D.	F.D.P./ D.V.P./ B.D.Y.	K.P.D.	Independent
Constituency seats	3	12	7	0	0
Percentage of Land (list) votes	21·3	32·1	28·0	6·7	11·9
List seats	6	1	5	2	0
Total seats (with percentage)	9 (25)	13 (36)	12 (33·3)	2 (5·5)	0

The S.P.D. won 12 out of 22, a majority, of the constituency contests (we explain why this sort of result occurs in Chapters 7 and 8) despite getting less than a third (32·1 per cent) of the party list votes. Four parties qualified for allocations in the second round, when a further 14 seats were distributed (no independent got 5 per cent of the Land total); only one of these went to the S.P.D. Exact proportional representation was not achieved, however, because 11·9 per cent of the votes (Land votes won by the Independent) did not qualify for second-round seats, but comparison of percentage of final seats with percentage of valid Land votes shows:

Party	C.D.U. (C.S.V.)	S.P.D.	F.D.P./ D.V.P./ B.D.Y.	K.P.D.
Percentage of total seats	25	36	33·3	5·5
Percentage of valid Land votes	24·1	36·4	31·7	7·6

and no substantial distortions.

One of the quirks of this system, as it is applied, is that the size of the Bundestag varies. There should be 496 seats distributed, 248 for constituencies and 248 for the Land lists. It may be the case, however, that in any one Land a party wins more constituency seats than it is apparently entitled to according to the d'Hondt rule. The extra seats are not taken away; instead the Bundestag is expanded, as it had to be in both 1957 and 1961, to cater for such an event. A more interesting and significant characteristic, however, may be the type of representation achieved by the various parties. In 1949 the K.P.D. won 15 seats, all of them on the Land lists. Since the 1951 election, only three parties – the C.D.U. (C.S.V.), the S.P.D. and the F.D.P. – have won such seats, and the F.D.P., despite getting as much as 12·1 per cent of the national list vote, has won no constituency seats in that period (Roberts, 1975, p. 214). Thus constituency representation and government formation may be very different; if the system were applied in the United Kingdom, virtually all of the Liberals elected might be individuals picked by the party machine to go on the party lists rather than trustees chosen in the constituencies.

In the plurality system, votes cast for losing candidates are 'wasted votes', in that they have no influence on the result of the election in terms of the proportion of seats won by the relevant party. This leads to what is often known as 'tactical voting', by which supporters of a party who feel it is bound to lose in their constituency vote for another, usually third, party to defeat their major opponent. In list system elections, wasted votes do not exist; every one counts towards the allocation of seats, and so tactical voting is irrelevant. Under the German 'mixed' system, support for small parties produces large numbers of wasted votes in the constituency contests, but not in the Land lists. Voters and parties are aware of this, and ballots are cast accordingly; at the 1969 election, 38 per cent of those who voted for the F.D.P. in the Land lists did not support its candidates in the constituency contests (Fisher, 1973).

A recently introduced electoral system presents a novel hybrid of the list system with aspects of preferential voting. It is to be used to elect the Legislative Council (upper house) in South Australia, and its final form represents the result of much conflict and bargaining between the Labor Party there and the strongly entrenched rural interests in the pre-existing Council, whose support was needed for a constitutional amendment to reform the electoral system (Blewett, 1976). The Council was reconstituted with 22 members, 11 of whom were to be returned at an election held every three years. There are no electoral districts; votes are cast for party lists in a state-wide constituency, but when a voter has chosen a list, he can indicate his preferences by ranking candidates. A major controversy in the development of the system concerned the threshold proportion of the votes below which minor parties would be excluded from the allocation of seats. The final decision was for a threshold of half the electoral quota; any party whose list received less than $\frac{1}{2}(N/n+1)$ votes (N is the number of votes, n the number of seats) would have its preferences allocated to other parties.

5. Referenda and Plebiscites

In most referenda and similar expressions of preference the decision on the issue goes with the largest number of votes over the whole territory, making them equivalent to single-member plurality elections. In the vast majority of cases, voters are faced with a simple alternative, as in the referendum on Britain's continued membership of the E.E.C. in June 1975 (Kirby and Taylor, 1976) when the choice was between withdrawal or staying in.

Hence the final decision is that of a majority of those voting, though not necessarily of all electors if there is either a large number of abstentions or a small margin in the preferences (or both). Other referenda with similar characteristics include those held (if demanded) every seven years in the Welsh counties on Sunday opening of public houses (Carter and Thomas, 1969), and the 'initiatives' which in eleven American states can be held on any issues if sufficient voters, often a large number, demand one. Proposition 15, voted on by California electors during their presidential primary elections in June 1976, was an example of the importance these initiatives can have. In California, five per cent of the number of people voting in the last gubernatorial election must request a poll if one is to be held (more than twenty were voted on in 1976). Proposition 15 urged much greater safety standards for nuclear power stations, and the power industry claimed that these would force the closure of stations because of the expense; the measure was defeated, 66 per cent of the votes cast being against it.

Similar rules for local governments operate in some states. Philadelphians spent much of the spring of 1976 trying to collect 145,448 valid signatures on a petition requesting a poll which would be a vote of confidence in the city's mayor, re-elected only in the previous November (they were successful but a vote was not held in November 1976 because of a Supreme Court ruling). Most local governments must hold referenda before they can raise taxes for certain projects, amalgamate with other areas, or borrow money on the loan market in excess of a certain sum; Los Angelenos in June 1976 defeated a proposition for a 0·5 per cent increase in local sales tax to finance a new commuter railway system. Sometimes the choices are not as clear-cut, as in the triennial liquor poll in New Zealand at which voters opt for one of: (1) continuance (i.e. private market provision with 10 o'clock closing of pubs and no Sunday opening); (2) prohibition; and (3) state control (i.e. nationalization).

In federal systems, referenda may have to be carried not only by a majority of the population but also by a certain proportion of the member states, thereby ensuring that the populous states do not dominate the smaller ones. Australian referenda must be carried in four of the states, as well as by a national majority, and a similar rule applies for the Swiss cantons, six of which count as only one-half. The regulations for constitutional amendments in the United States are akin to this, requiring a two-thirds vote in Congress, and confirmation by three-quarters of all state legislatures.

Referenda are much more popular in some countries than others, being used either as means of ensuring popular support for certain actions (as in Switzerland, and also in Ireland where if constitutional amendments are not carried by both the Dail and the Senate they must go to a referendum or be lost) or, some would argue, by governments who wish to avoid making unpopular decisions. They were a favourite device of de Gaulle, who had several during his period of rule in the French Fifth Republic, to gain public support and circumvent parliament (Williams, 1970), and have been quite frequent in Australia; that held in 1975 was Britain's first national poll on a specific issue, however.

Electoral Data

The methods of analysis which can be applied to any election result depend on the level of detail at which the result is published. In part, this is a function of the electoral law, whose nature determines the minimum data set which must be made available to indicate to the electors the consequences of their actions. The plurality law typical of Britain and the United States requires the smallest volume of published data – the number of votes cast per candidate in each constituency, although in the United States, and also in Australia and New Zealand, data on the distribution of votes are made available at a sub-constituency scale. For preferential electoral systems, on the other hand, the electoral law requires that information be given on the distribution of intra-party preferences, and of inter-party rankings too in the case of S.T.V. Again, such data need only be made available by constituency (as in Ireland) but they may also be reported for smaller units.

Whatever the detail of the electoral law, the constituency is the basic reporting unit for election results, and data must be published for each to provide the necessary level of public information. (In some countries – such as South Africa – it should be noted, identifying the location of the constituency boundaries with any accuracy is extremely difficult.) In the United Kingdom and in Ireland, the ballot papers for all polling divisions in a constituency are amalgamated prior to the count, so that no sub-constituency data are made available. Elsewhere – in Australia, Canada, and the United States, for example – votes are tallied according to the division of the constituency in which the voter lives. In New Zealand they are counted and published for the booths at which they were cast (there is no compulsion there for the voter to use a particular booth). For no country, however, is it possible to gain access to the individual ballot papers, and so determine exactly who voted for whom, or what. As a consequence, to fill out their analyses of the election results social scientists have developed methods of conducting sample surveys from which they can estimate the answers to various questions concerning the correlates and determinants of voting behaviour.

We can, therefore, identify two types of data which are used for geographical analyses of elections; the actual voting records, made available by *de jure* spatial units, and the results of surveys of party preferences and voting acts. The former refer to population aggregates, whereas the latter refer to individuals: although in all surveys the investigators undertake not to identify individual respondents, they are able to aggregate their respondents into whatever groups they wish. With such data, analysts want not only to tally the number of votes going to each party, for example, but to investigate such questions as, 'which population groups supported which party?', 'in which places did groups deviate from general trends?'. This involves matching the electoral data with other sets of information. Each type of data has its own requirements with regard to statistical analysis, and each has its peculiar disadvantages; in the present section we look at these aspects of electoral data as a final introductory framework to the analyses reported in the rest of this book.

Voting Records and Ecological Analyses

One of the basic questions of electoral geography is undoubtedly some variant of 'what is the spatial pattern of voting for a particular party/candidate/issue?'. This can be answered by simple cartographic methods, as in the atlases of election results produced by several authors (e.g. Kinnear, 1968). A simple example of such a treatment is Figure 2.1, which shows the percentage of the votes gained by the Republican candidate (Nixon) at the 1960 American presidential election in each of the ten counties of the state of New Hampshire.

Maps such as that in Figure 2.1 with a very small number of observations provide a pictorial rather than a tabular presenta-

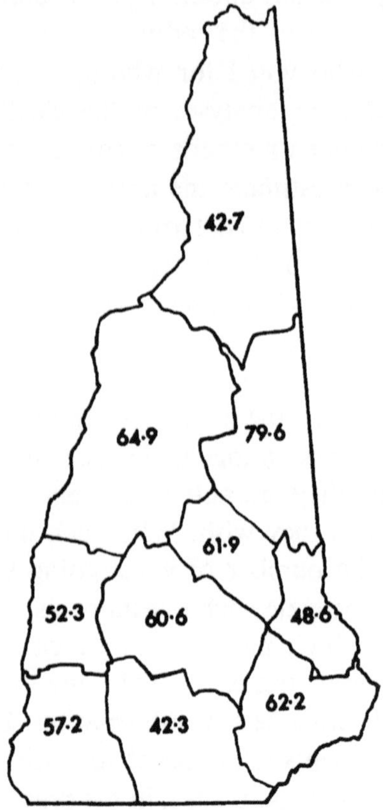

Figure 2.1 The votes for Nixon in the counties of New Hampshire, 1960 presidential election, as percentages of all votes cast in each county

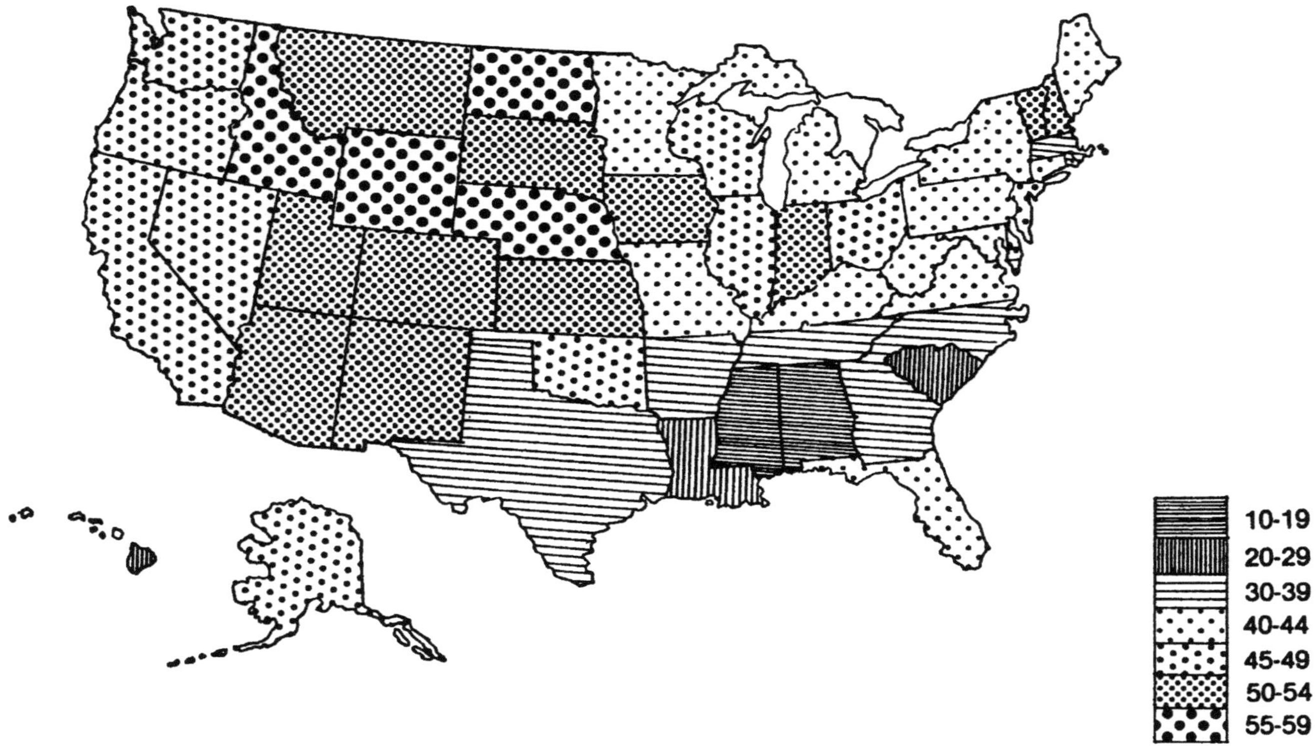

Figure 2.2 The votes for Nixon in the states of the U.S.A., 1968 presidential election. as percentages of all votes cast in each state

tion of a set of numbers, from which it is possible to read off directly the Republican performance in each county and see that, for example, the range of values was from 42.4 to 79.6 per cent but that there was a clear clustering in the low sixties. For data sets with larger numbers of observations, the values usually have to be grouped into categories, as in Figure 2.2 which shows the percentage of the votes gained by the Republican candidate (Nixon again) in each of the fifty states in the 1968 presidential election. With this many observations, a summary of the information on the map is needed in order to 'see the wood for the trees'. Figure 2.3 provides such a summary in the form of a fre-

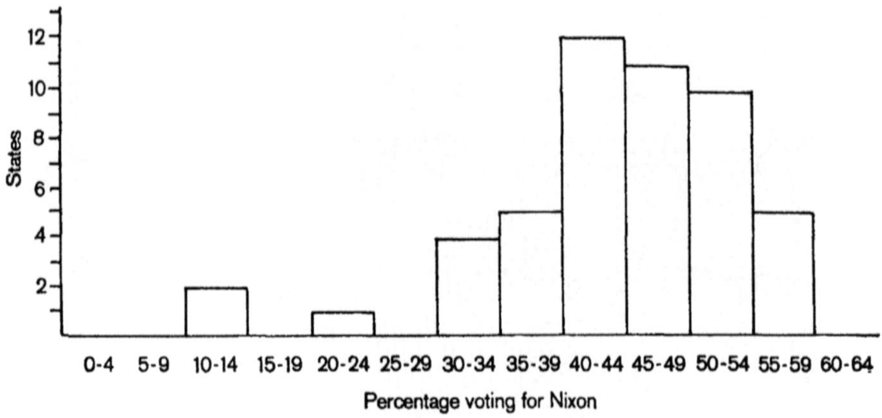

Figure 2.3 Frequency distribution of the percentages mapped in Figure 2.2

quency distribution in which each column indicates the number of states in each percentage category. Frequency distributions, and associated summary statistics indicating the average value and the extent of the scatter of observations around that value, are important tools in our analysis of the geography of representation in Chapters 7 and 8.

Map comparisons

Maps and frequency distributions, therefore, provide useful answers to the question about the spatial pattern of voting;

those maps in Figures 2.1 and 2.2 indicate where Nixon did well and badly at the relevant elections, whereas the frequency distribution in Figure 2.3 illustrates the extent of the spatial variation in the voting for Nixon in 1968, at the state level. Having described a pattern, the next stage in an inquiry is usually to ask the question, 'why does the spatial pattern of votes have that form?'. In the positivist scientific methodology, to which most of the work reported in this book would be ascribed, answering this question involves the testing of hypotheses which suggest either causal links or non-causal associations between patterns; the hypotheses are usually derived from the results of earlier or similar studies or, very rarely, from intuitive flashes which suggest new insights.

In geographical work, such hypothesis-testing involves the comparison of two maps (Taylor, 1977). Returning to our New Hampshire example, we might reason that Republican candidates generally get stronger support from farmers than do Democrat candidates, and from this hypothesize that Nixon should have done better in the more rural counties of the state. Figure 2.4 shows the percentage of each county's residents categorized by the American Bureau of the Census as 'rural farm', and comparison of this with Figure 2.1 suggests the validity of the hypothesis (Republican support is generally weakest in the southern counties, where rural farm residents are few in number).

Correlation and regression

Map comparison by 'eyeballing' is a very subjective way of testing a hypothesis, and so analysts have adopted the precise language of inferential statistics which allows an unambiguous statement – one which should be the same whoever is analysing the data – concerning the degree of similarity between two maps (Taylor, 1977; Johnston, 1978a). The commonest statistical technique used for such purposes is that of *linear correlation and regression*. The data are made to fit a linear equation of the form

$$Y = a + bX$$

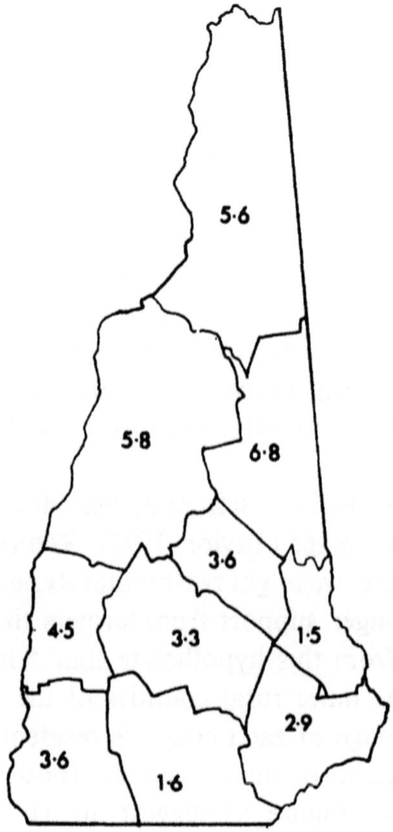

Figure 2.4 Percentage of the residents of each New Hampshire county categorized as 'rural farm' in the 1960 Census

where *X* is the independent variable (the cause), *Y* is the dependent variable (the effect) and *a* and *b* are the parameters of the equation (constant for a particular set), to be estimated by what is known as the least-squares method.

The equation just given describes a straight line plotted through a scatter of points on a two-dimensional graph in such a way that it is as close as possible to all of those points. ('As close as possible' is defined as minimizing the sum of the squared distances between the points and the line, these distances being measured on the *Y* axis, that of the dependent variable.) Figure 2.5 shows this 'regression line' (as it is called) for the two variables depicted in Figures 2.1 and 2.4, where, for the New

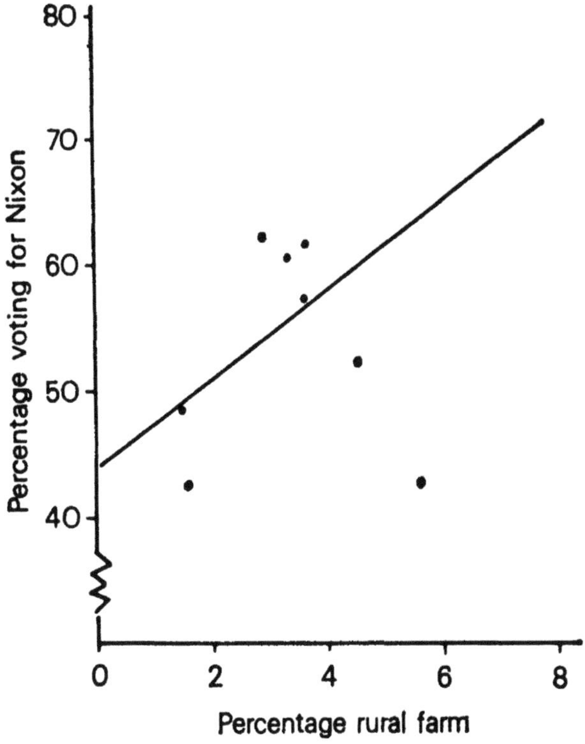

Figure 2.5 Regression of the data shown in Figure 2.1 against those portrayed in Figure 2.4

Hampshire data, the full equation turns out to be $Y = 43{\cdot}40 + 3{\cdot}53X$ (pictorially *a* is shown as the distance up the *Y* axis where the line hits it, and *b* is the gradient). The equation (or graph) indicates: (1) that the baseline of Republican support – when $X = 0$ – is 43·40 per cent of the votes; and (2) that for every increase of one percentage point in the rura farm component compared to the total population, the Republican percentage of the vote increases by just over 3·5 points.

A regression line indicates the trend in a relationship between two variables; an associated statistic – the linear correlation coefficient, r_{YX} – indicates how accurately the regression line fits the scatter of points. Thus on Figure 2.5 we see that although the general trend of the relationship is upwards – that Republican voting increases with increases in rural farm residents – some of the observations (i.e. for certain counties) are a considerable distance from the straight line. The correlation coefficient indicates the goodness-of-fit of the regression line. The value of r_{YX} varies between $+1{\cdot}0$ and $-1{\cdot}0$: if it is $+1{\cdot}0$ then all of the observations actually lie on the line; if it is $-1{\cdot}0$ then again there is perfect fit; all of the observations lie on the line (but the line slopes downwards to the right, indicating that as the value of X increases that of Y decreases – such an inverse relationship is known as a negative correlation; the b parameter associated with such a relationship would also be negative). If r_{YX} is 0·0, then there is no pattern or trend in the observations at all; and if it is between 0·0 and either $+1{\cdot}0$ or $-1{\cdot}0$ there is some relationship but not a perfect one. The true extent of the goodness-of-fit is usually assessed by squaring the value of the correlation coefficient and interpreting this as the proportion of the spatial variation in Y which can be accounted for by the spatial variation in X. For our New Hampshire data in Figure 2.5 the value of r_{YX} is 0·55 which when squared ($r^2{}_{YX} = 0{\cdot}30$) indicates that a little under one-third of the spatial pattern of Republican voting in New Hampshire can be accounted for by the spatial pattern of the 'rural vote'.

Inspection of the regression line and the scatter of observations around it in Figure 2.5 indicates that some of the counties deviate much more from the general trend than do others. The extent of each individual deviation can be measured as the 'residual from the regression', which is the distance from the individual observation to the regression line, that is between its actual value of Y and that estimated for it from the general trend (the line). The residual values clearly indicate the observations for which the pattern given by the regression line fails – at least relatively; they suggest places where other influences are at work to produce the voting behaviour and indicate where future research needs to be done.

Ecological correlations and fallacies

The implication of the regression and correlation results just discussed is that, to a certain extent (about a third of the total pattern), rural residents were more likely to vote for Nixon in New Hampshire in 1960 than were non-rural residents. This, however, is only an inference; the data do not show that rural residents voted for Nixon, only that Nixon obtained more votes in the more rural areas. Such an inference is often known as an *ecological correlation*, since it is based on the study of population aggregates rather than of individuals. Use of such methods introduces the possibility of a variety of fallacious inferences.

Ecological correlations are extremely useful as indicators of the associations between spatial patterns and are widely used to test for hypothesized associations between voting patterns and other spatial distributions (Dogan and Rokkan, 1969). The extent to which they can be used depends, however, on the degree to which the *de jure* spatial units for which vote totals are reported coincide with those units for which other data – such as the results of census tabulations – are collected and made available. In the United States, the Bureau of the Census provides a great wealth of data, for example, not only for the states, the counties, and the congressional districts, but also for much smaller areas whose boundaries often coincide with those of voting precincts. In the United Kingdom, parliamentary constituencies are amalgamations of local government units and data can be assembled from censuses to describe the characteristics of constituencies (Miller, Raab and Britto, 1974). Since 1966, census data have been published by constituency. Several European countries similarly provide data which can be analysed at the constituency level (Rokkan and Meyriat, 1969), but this is not the case in some other countries – New Zealand, for example.

A major problem of using aggregate data in this manner concerns what is now known as the *ecological fallacy*, which involves inferring incorrectly from the aggregate level to that of the individual. The classic statement on this problem was made by Robinson (1950), using data on Negro percentages and illiteracy rates within the American population. Using data for census divisions (of which there are nine) and states (48 at that time) he found very high correlations (Figure 2.6) from which it would seem reasonable to infer high illiteracy rates among Negroes.

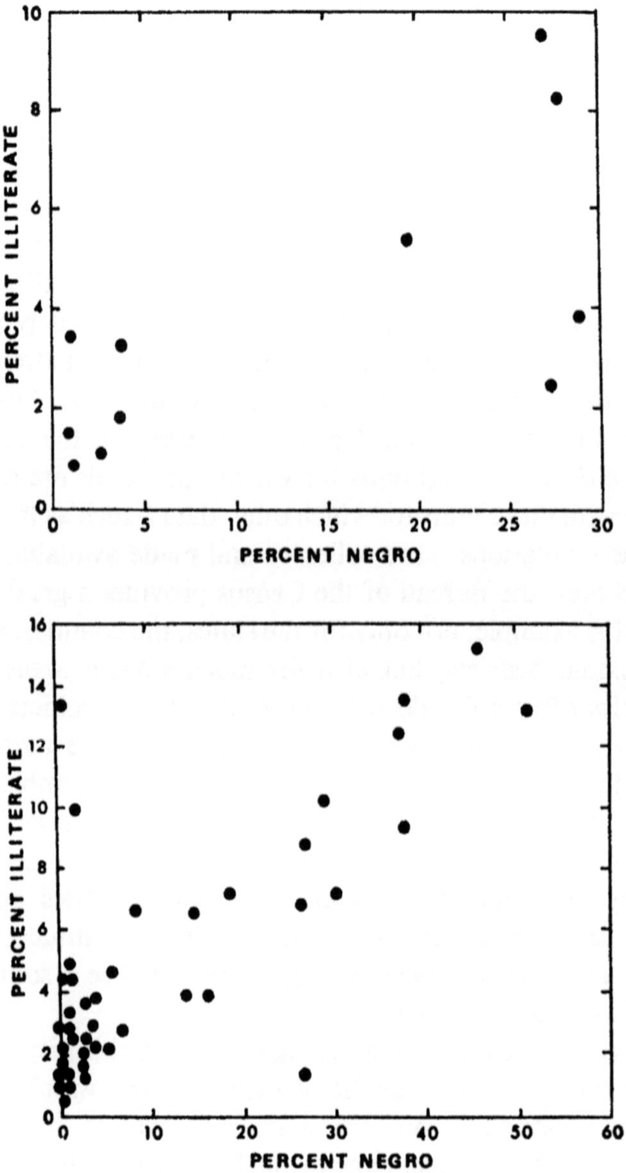

Figure 2.6 Regressions of illiteracy against percentage Negro by census divisions (top) and states (bottom). Source: Robinson, 1950, Figs. 1 and 2

This is indeed so, and data for all individuals aged over 10 in 1930 showed:

	Negro	White	Total
Illiterate	1·512 m	2·406 m	3·918 m
Literate	7·780 m	85·574 m	93·354 m
Total	9·292 m	87·980 m	97·272 m

with 16 per cent of Negroes illiterate compared with only 3 per cent of whites. Yet the correlation obtained at the individual level (0·203) was less than one-third of that (0·773) obtained at the ecological level of the states, indicating the considerable danger of inferring that just because Negroes were disproportionately represented in the states that had high illiteracy rates, they themselves had very high illiteracy rates.

In electoral geography, it is impossible to check the similarity between individual and ecological correlations because we lack data from which to derive the former. The lessons to be learned from Robinson's work are crucial, therefore, including: (1) not to make inferences about individuals from ecological correlations, unless they are based in logical hypotheses and are backed up by other information; and (2) to realize that any ecological correlation is relevant only to that particular set of population aggregates. To illustrate the latter point, we will again use data on voting for Nixon (Y) and rural-farm residents (X) in 1960. Remember that for the ten New Hampshire counties we obtained the regression and correlation:

$$Y = 43{\cdot}40 + 3{\cdot}53X \quad r_{YX} = 0{\cdot}55$$

For the nine census divisions, the results are:

$$Y = 45{\cdot}63 + 0{\cdot}24X \quad r_{YX} = 0.44$$

in which the b parameter is substantially lower than that for New Hampshire and the correlation coefficient is much smaller ($0{\cdot}55^2 = 0{\cdot}30$; $0{\cdot}44^2 = 0{\cdot}19$). This indicates that trends within New Hampshire are not the same as those across the census divisions. Of even more interest, however, are the results when we use the four census regions (of which the nine divisions are components)

$$Y = 51{\cdot}79 - 0{\cdot}10X \quad r_{YX} = -0{\cdot}22$$

which is another amalgamation of the same data used for the divisions and not a selection from it. Here we see that at the regional level the inference is that Nixon fared worse in the more rural areas, whereas at the divisional level it would be inferred that he fared best in the more rural groups of states. There is no question that one result is right and another wrong. Both are right. They differ because they refer to different ecological aggregates and so we must always ensure that all ecological correlations refer only to that particular set of areas. Clearly, choice of the set of areas is a crucial stage in the design of an analysis.

The fallacy which we have just illustrated is termed the *cross-level fallacy* (Alker, 1969). In addition to this, and to the *ecological fallacy* which we have already defined, others can be identified. Most important is probably the *individualistic fallacy*, which involves making inferences from individuals to aggregates. Are populations merely sums of their parts, or do they have characteristics of their own? Because labourers within a country are politically more radical, does this mean that the higher the proportion of labourers in any country, the more radical its politics will be? Given the nature of electoral data, the relevance of this fallacy in the present context is slight, although it could arise when survey data are used to predict ecological patterns.

Factor analysis

Our description of methods of analysing electoral data has focused so far on investigations which have involved the comparison of one map with another. But what is done when we want to compare three or more maps? A number of possible methods is available, but only one of these will be referred to in this book.

'Factor analysis' means a family of related techniques which seek for general patterns in a number of statistical distributions (in our case, maps) referring to the same set of observations; this is done by creating new patterns (maps) which are composites of the originals and which can be correlated with them (Johnston, 1978). In brief, a factor analysis takes the matrix of correlations between all the patterns and from this creates an average pattern: the *factor loadings* on this new pattern are the correlations between it and each of the original patterns, while the *factor scores* are the values for each observation on the new pattern. Having extracted this first factor – pattern, a second factor is then obtained, as the average pattern in the residuals from the regression of the factor scores on the original variables. Further factors can be obtained, up to as many as the number of original patterns, but usually only a few are extracted, to show the more general patterns among the variables.

Factor analysis can be used on electoral data in a variety of ways. One of these involves taking data for a set of successive elections, and seeking the general patterns of spatial stability in voting behaviour. To illustrate this, we have taken the percentage of votes which were cast for the Republican party candidate at each of the United States presidential elections since 1952. Our observation units are the nine census divisions. The first stage of the analysis (we use the principal components option; Johnston, 1978a) involves comparing each map with every other, including itself, giving a matrix of 49 correlation coefficients (i.e. all pairs of correlations for the seven maps, 7×7). From this matrix we extract general patterns which are averages of the correlations reported therein. The first factor is the average of all seven maps, and the loadings represent the correlations between those maps and the average – i.e. the closeness of the individual map to the average. The residuals from those correlations are then correlated with each other, producing a new correlation matrix from which a second average pattern – the average of the residuals from the first – is extracted. This procedure continues until we are satisfied that we have identified all of the general patterns; identification is aided by interpretation of the factor loadings.

Table 2.6 gives the factor loadings on the first three factors from our analysis of Republican voting in the United States. Inspection of the column of loadings for the first factor indicates

Table 2.6 Factor analysis of Republican vote percentages by census division: 1952–1976

	Loading on factor		
Variable (Year)	I	II	III
1952 (Eisenhower)	0·96	0·13	−0·14
1956 (Eisenhower)	0·91	−0·30	0·19
1960 (Nixon)	0·43	0·82	−0·34
1964 (Goldwater)	−0·67	0·72	0·02
1968 (Nixon)	0·88	0·39	−0·10
1972 (Nixon)	−0·76	0·52	0·18
1976 (Ford)	0·63	0·52	0·56

that the average pattern (drawn from all seven years) is closely correlated with the maps of Republican voting in 1952, 1956, 1968 and, to a lesser extent, 1976. These suggest a 'normal' pattern in the spatial variation of Republican support both at the end of the 'New Deal' period (see p. 125) in the voting for Eisenhower, and in later years in the voting for Nixon in the 1968 three-party contest, and to some extent in the voting for Ford against Carter. But the loadings for 1964 and 1972 are negative, indicating an inverse pattern of Republican voting to the average; whereas Republican candidates are usually weak in the South and strong elsewhere, Goldwater in 1964 and Nixon in his 1972 contest with McGovern reversed this position somewhat.

The loadings on the second factor in Table 2.6 indicate what we might term an early 1960s pattern. The main correlation with this 'first residual average' is with the 1960 pattern, that election being unusual both in its closeness and its providing the first victory for a Catholic. The 1964 pattern is also strongly correlated with it, indicating some agreement between the geography of Nixon's 1960 performance and Goldwater's in 1964. (Note that the 1964 pattern has substantial correlations with two of the factors, indicating that it lay between those two averages, having some components of both.) Finally, the third factor has no very large loadings; its main correlation is with Ford's performance in 1976 which, by its somewhat weak correlations with three separate factors, was clearly not typical in its geography of any other recent pattern of Republican voting (at least at the census division level).

With this factor analysis, therefore, we have been able to identify common patterns in a set of maps; the greater the number of maps involved, the less capable would we be of perceiving such commonalities by visual inspection. As a descriptive device, therefore, factor analysis is an important method for identifying the major trends, and at the same time reducing our information overload. It can be used not only with series of maps but with a range of other relevant variable sets; several researchers, for example, have used it to study voting patterns in various assemblies such as the United Nations (Russett, 1967), identifying groups of countries which tend to vote in the same way as well as the groups of issues on which they agree.

The example in Table 2.6 refers to general patterns in the *Y* variables – the voting distributions – but it may be that analysts are interested in general patterns among a set of *X* variables, those used to account for the voting patterns. Kirby and Taylor (1976), for example, assembled data on eight variables which they suggested might be related to the patterns of voting at the 1975 referendum on Britain's membership of the E.E.C. (Because of data availability problems, only 23 separate areas could be studied.) Factor analysis of the correlations derived from this 8×23 data matrix suggested that the eight independent variables could be replaced by two general variables (Table 2.7). The first of these – Factor I – has high positive loadings (correlations) for agricultural employment and 'other' votes (i.e. Liberal and nationalist) and high negative loadings for accessibility and population density; it can be interpreted as a core-periphery variable (see Chapter 3), reflecting spatial variations in protest against the two main parties. The second of these general variables – Factor II – has high positive loadings for Labour voting and unemployment and high negative loadings for owner-occupied housing and service employment; it is interpretable as an affluence variable, representing spatial variations in the quality of life within Britain and their reflection in the support given to the Labour Party.

It is possible to combine both *X* and *Y* variables (independents

Table 2.7 Factor analysis of independent variables: E.E.C. referendum study

Variable	Factor Loadings I	II
1. The ratio of Labour to Conservative votes at the last general election	−0·30	+0·86
2. Percentage of votes to parties other than Labour and Conservative at the last general election	+0·85	−0·16
3. The accessibility of the area to other parts of the country	−0·76	−0·52
4. Population density	−0·90	−0·05
5. Percentage unemployed	+0·25	+0·74
6. Proportion of households owning their homes	−0·03	−0·74
7. The ratio of agricultural to manufacturing and mining employment	+0·89	−0·35
8. Proportion of employment in service occupations	+0·36	−0·78

Source: Kirby and Taylor (1976, p. 188)

and dependents) in the same analysis (e.g. Busteed, 1975). This will produce general variables combining representatives from both sets, but interpretation is not always easy. More often, researchers use the factor scores from separate analyses of the *X* and *Y* variable sets in linear regressions, which provide clearer statements of the associations between voting and other patterns (e.g. Kirby and Taylor, 1976).

Survey Data and Opinion Polls

To counter the deficiencies of aggregate data and the problems of ecological analysis, social scientists have developed methods of collecting and analysing data by social surveys. In electoral work, this involves asking a representative sample of voters within a defined population which party they identify with, who they voted for at the last election, who they intend voting for at the next, and so on; other questions are also asked relating to various personal characteristics such as age, income and occupation, so that correlations can be derived similar to the map comparisons discussed in the previous section.

The aim of surveys and their analysis is to understand how voting decisions are made, but the methods of survey design and analysis have been developed from the older technique of opinion polling, the purpose of which is to monitor trends in opinions and attitudes. The first such poll was conducted in 1824 in Wilmington, Delaware to assess the outcome of the forthcoming presidential contest (Teer and Spence, 1973, p. 13); the main developments took place in the 1920s and 1930s in the United States and elsewhere after World War II. There are now many commercial organizations which conduct opinion polls. Some of these are commissioned by political parties (Rose, 1976; Blewett and Jaensch, 1972), either to report on the progress of a particular campaign or to predict the probable result of an early election; many are paid for by newspapers to form the basis for reports and opinions during an election campaign; and a few – such as Gallup and National Opinion Polls – produce regular (often monthly) soundings of public attitudes on a range of current issues, as well as voting intentions were an election to be called suddenly. Their tabulations differ from the type of electoral data obtained from published election results; instead of referring to how people voted (actual voting) they usually report people's preferred parties (how they would probably vote). This difference may or may not be crucial, depending on the nature of the analysis, but it is important to recognize its existence and possible influence on research results.

Opinion polls

Opinion polls are taken from samples of voters, selected according to established criteria in order to obtain a representative set of responses to the extent resources allow. Finance is an important constraint, but time is often of the essence. Polls must represent opinion at a certain time, and so sampling should be spread over a few days only, and the results of the questioning reported as soon as possible thereafter. In Great Britain, the average poll taken before a general election is based on the solicited opinions of about 2000 voters. These people are not randomly selected from the population at large, because of the difficulties of contacting them in a short period. Instead, a sample of about 100 constituencies will be taken, stratified to ensure equal representation of urban and rural, inner city and outer suburb, seaside resort and mining town etc. Within each, an interviewer may then be instructed to contact 20 people, 11 of whom should be female, 11 over 45, 11 in blue-collar jobs, and so on, the quotas being determined so that the characteristics of the final sample of 2000 closely match those of the whole British electorate. To achieve the necessary balance, the interviewer may have to contact more than 20 persons.

Quota or stratified sampling is not as accurate as random sampling, but it meets the pollsters' requirement of speed. In any case, all sampling is subject to some error; in general, the smaller the sample the larger that error is likely to be. Assuming that the samples are randomly taken, however, so that each individual in the population has the same chance of being selected, then it is possible to calculate the probable error associated with a particular result. Suppose that 2000 Americans were asked in September 1976 whether they would vote for Carter or for Ford in the forthcoming presidential election. For each possible percentage reply, one can calculate what is known as the standard error. One standard error tells us the area around the given percentage in which about 68 per cent of the possible samples are likely to lie; two standard errors enclose about 95 per cent of the probable responses. The calculations for one and two such 'standard errors' in the example we have taken give the following results:

Percentage who would vote for Carter	75	70	65	60	55	50	45	40	35	30	25
One standard error	0·97	1·03	1·07	1·10	1·11	1·12	1·11	1·10	1·07	1·03	0·97
Two standard errors	1·90	2·02	2·10	2·16	2·18	2·20	2·18	2·16	2·10	2·02	1·90

This means that if a pollster got an answer of 65 per cent favouring Carter, it is probable that 68 per cent of all random surveys of

2000 voters would give an answer of between 63·93 and 66·07 per cent (65±1·07), whereas 95 per cent of all surveys would provide responses ranging between 62·90 and 67·10 per cent.

Opinion polls are, therefore, estimates of voting proportions. Unfortunately, when they are reported in the media their probable margins of error are usually ignored, which is why when they prove to have been somewhat inaccurate people attack them rather too harshly. (There are other reasons for them being wrong, including both failure to get a truly random sample, changes of mind by the respondents, and straight misleading answers.) One important point to note is that the closer the answer obtained is to 50 per cent, the wider its error band. Assume a random sample of 2000 British voters asked in October 1974 whether they were going to vote Labour. The answer might have been between 45 and 55 per cent, and the error bands would be as follows:

Percentage who would vote Labour	45	46	47	48	49	50	51	52	53	54	55
One standard error	1·114	1·115	1·117	1·118	1·118	1·119	1·118	1·118	1·117	1·115	1·114
Two standard errors	2·183	2·185	2·189	2·191	2·191	2·192	2·191	2·191	2·189	2·185	2·183

Hence if a large minority, 49 per cent, replied that they intended voting Labour, in approximately 18 per cent of all samples there would probably, in fact, have been a majority rather than a minority favouring that party. Where margins are slight, therefore, the opinion polls may well predict the wrong victor, because they are based on surveys with inbuilt probabilities of error and not because of any faults inherent in them. (One other problem, as we have mentioned already and as we develop in Chapters 7 and 8, is the lack of proportional representation in most electoral systems, so that a prediction of the percentage of the votes which a party will win is not the same as its percentage of the parliamentary seats.)

Social surveys

Political opinion polls provide a lot of useful data for students of elections, but they are based on a few straightforward questions and not on detailed, in-depth interviews which can provide the necessary background information for an attempted understanding of voting behaviour. To obtain the sorts of data they require, therefore, social scientists have developed the wider field of survey research out of opinion polling. Pioneer work in this field was conducted by Paul Lazarsfeld and his associates at Columbia University, New York, in the 1940s, and some of their findings are discussed in Chapter 5. Large, regular surveys are now conducted by several organizations in the United States, such as the National Opinion Research Center at the University of Chicago and the Survey Research Center at the University of Michigan; in Great Britain, the Social Science Research Council developed its own Survey Research Unit and large, specially-designed surveys have been conducted in each general election year since 1964, formerly by Nuffield College, Oxford (Butler and Stokes, 1969, 1974), and now by the Department of Government at the University of Essex. Many of their data sets are available for re-analysis, through bodies such as the Social Science Research Council's Survey Archive at the University of Essex and the Inter-University Consortium for Political and Social Research at the University of Michigan.

The surveys in Great Britain conducted by Butler and Stokes illustrate the range of material collected. In 1963 they took a sample of 2560 electors of whom 2009 responded; 32 were selected from the electoral rolls of each of 80 constituencies, the latter being chosen so as to give proper representation to the following characteristics (Butler and Stokes, 1969, p. 538):

> The 618 constituencies of Great Britain were arranged into 40 strata (80 half-strata) on the basis of region, relative Conservative and Labour strength in 1959, the presence of a Liberal candidate in 1959 and of a prospective Liberal candidate in the forthcoming election, urban or rural character, and level of unemployment. Two constituencies were chosen within each stratum (one within each half-stratum) with probability proportionate to size of electorate.

Their estimate of the accuracy of the answers which they obtained, as representative of the attitudes and characteristics of the entire population of voters in Great Britain, was that in 95 out of 100 similar samples of about 2000 respondents they would get answers within the following ranges:

Reported percentage	*Probable range*
20	17·6–22·4
30	27·3–32·7
50	47·0–53·0
70	67·3–72·7
80	78·6–82·4

Regarding differences between groups, they suggested that if their sample was split into two sub-samples of 1000 each, then in 95 out of 100 similar samples they would get answers within the following ranges:

Reported percentage differences	*Probable range*
50	44·7–55·3
20	15·7–24·3
10	6·8–13·2
5	2·7–7·3

If, therefore, 20 per cent of their sample said that they intended to vote Liberal at the next election, then it was extremely probable that the intending Liberals *at that time* were between 17·6 and 22·4 per cent of all voters; if 30 per cent of female respondents had said they intended to vote Liberal compared to 20 per cent among males, then it was extremely likely that the difference between males and females in their intention to vote Liberal lay between 6·8 and 13·2 percentage points.

If samples are properly taken from a specified population, therefore, it is possible to make very accurate estimates of the characteristics and attitudes of the population from questioning only a very small proportion of the total. (The important factor is the *absolute* size of the sample, not its size *relative* to that of the population.) Of course, taking samples accurately is extremely difficult, and there are problems inherent in sample data which do not apply to the election returns discussed previously. The accuracy of responses is always far from perfect – usually a higher proportion of survey respondents will claim that they voted at an election than actually did, for example, and not all persons who voted Communist in a secret ballot will inform an interviewer that they did so; surveyed respondents in Belgium show higher support for religious parties than occurs in elections (Rose, 1974, p. 72), and respondents to surveys in Los Angeles in 1969 suggested greater support for the black candidate – public liberality – than was recorded in the final voting – private racialism (McPhail, 1971b – for further discussion of this phenomenon see Myrdal, 1969). Nevertheless the science of survey research has been very finely tuned in recent decades and it provides a great range of valuable data for electoral study. Butler and Stokes had 85 separate questions in their 1963 survey, for example, although because some were alternatives (depending, for example, on which party the respondent supported), no one person was asked them all. They covered not only the usual general background data of age, sex, occupation, religion, type of housing tenure etc., with statements about party preferences, but also a range of attitudinal probes, such as whether Britain should join the E.E.C., whether trade unions are too powerful etc., and the respondent's, and his/her parents', voting history.

There are many more possibilities for analysing survey data than for correlating voting returns with census or other information on population aggregates, because the individuals can be classified in so many different ways. Butler and Stokes, for example, could look at differences between the strength of support for Labour not only between age groups and between occupational groups, but also between age groups within occupational groups.

Survey data are usually analysed by the production of tabulations and cross-tabulations, with statistical assessment of the differences between the categories. In looking at the relationships between religion, class, and party preference, for example, Butler and Stokes produced the following one-variable tabulations:

Stated religion	*Percentage preferring Conservative*
Anglican	41
Church of Scotland	39
Methodist	23
Other Nonconformist	24
Roman Catholic	37
None	31

and then cross-classified religion with occupation (religions were grouped into four categories, with Methodists being added to the Nonconformist Group) to produce percentage preferring Conservative of:

Occupational Grade	*Stated religion*			
	Anglican	Church of Scotland	Nonconformist	Roman Catholic
I–III (high status)	72	74	41	55
IV–VI (low status)	30	25	22	18

The initial tabulation indicates some marked differences – notably between Roman Catholics and Methodists, on the one hand, and Anglicans and Church of Scotland on the other – in levels of Conservative support; the cross tabulation indicates that these differences, especially with regard to Nonconformists (including Methodists), are greatest in the higher status occupational groups (the 'middle class').

The possibility of combining the data in various ways to provide cross-tabulations allows for much more precise testing of the 'reality' of observed relationships than is the case with ecological analyses. In the example just quoted, for example, it may well have been that the differences between the various religious groups were spurious because if: (1) occupational groups differ in their party preferences; and (2) occupational groups differ in their religious affiliations; then (3) religious groups will differ in their party preferences. The latter relationship is not a causal one but a reflection of the first; its existence is denied once the variable 'occupation' is held constant (for a useful introduction to such analyses, see Davidson, 1976).

An example of a spurious relationship is given in Table 2.8. According to the results of a 1956 survey reproduced in part A of the table, rural voters in the Netherlands were much more likely than urban voters to support a religious party rather than a secular one. Of the city voters, however, only 32·6 per cent were practising members of a religious group, whereas most (65·0 per cent) of the rural voters were. Once this difference is held constant – in part B of Table 2·8 – the relationship between place of

Table 2.8 Religion, place of residence and party preference in the Netherlands

	Number of Respondents	*Percentage preferring a: Religious party*	*Secular party*
A. Party preference by place of residence			
Large cities	175	37	63
Smaller towns	495	56	44
Rural areas	269	70	30
B. Party preference by place of residence and religion			
(i) Practising members of a religious group			
Large cities	57	89	11
Smaller towns	261	87	13
Rural areas	175	97	3
(ii) Nonpractising members of a religious group			
Large cities	117	12	88
Smaller towns	233	22	78
Rural areas	94	19	81

Source: Lijphart (1974, p. 251)

residence and party preference is very much reduced; it was the spatial separation of religious groups which produced the pattern of party preferences varying by place of residence, and not the place of residence itself.

The range and depth of cross-tabulations possible gives great flexibility to the analysis of survey data, although the larger the number of variables used in a single cross-classification, the larger the sample must be to ensure sufficient representation of each group (e.g. over 45, Roman Catholics in occupational grades I–III who support the Conservative Party). In recent years this flexibility has been extended by the development of methods (notably one known as the Automatic Interaction Detector, or A.I.D.), which search the survey data for the major differences within the sample with respect to a particular variable. This generalized technique – known sometimes as 'data dredging' – enables researchers to identify patterns which require explanation, and it has been used in a large comparative study of party preferences in eleven different countries (Rose, 1974). In the Australian study, for example, the dependent variable was the percentage of the respondents who supported the Australian Labor Party (A.L.P.). The main difference, not surprisingly, was between occupational groups (Table 2.9); among the non-manual workers, religion and residence provided major differences in terms of A.L.P. support, whereas within the manual group trade-union membership, education, birthplace and religion all proved significant discriminators. In all, the analysis accounted for only 15 per cent of the variation in Labor voting in Australia, however; of the 16 analyses reported in the book, this Australian result ranked thirteenth in its success, the most efficient at accounting for variations in party preferences being the Dutch analysis, which 'explained' 51 per cent of the variation, mainly in terms of the respondents' religion (Rose, 1974, p. 17).

Survey data are used to test hypotheses at the individual level, therefore, in contrast to the ecological investigations possible with official voting returns. As we illustrate in the rest of the book, combination of the two often provides excellent insights into the various aspects of the geography of elections. For almost all research using either or both type of data, the information employed in electoral geography has been collected for other purposes. This imposes constraints on the range of analyses possible, yet already there is a great richness of completed work which we review in some detail in the following chapters.

Table 2.9 A.I.D. analysis of Australian voting preferences

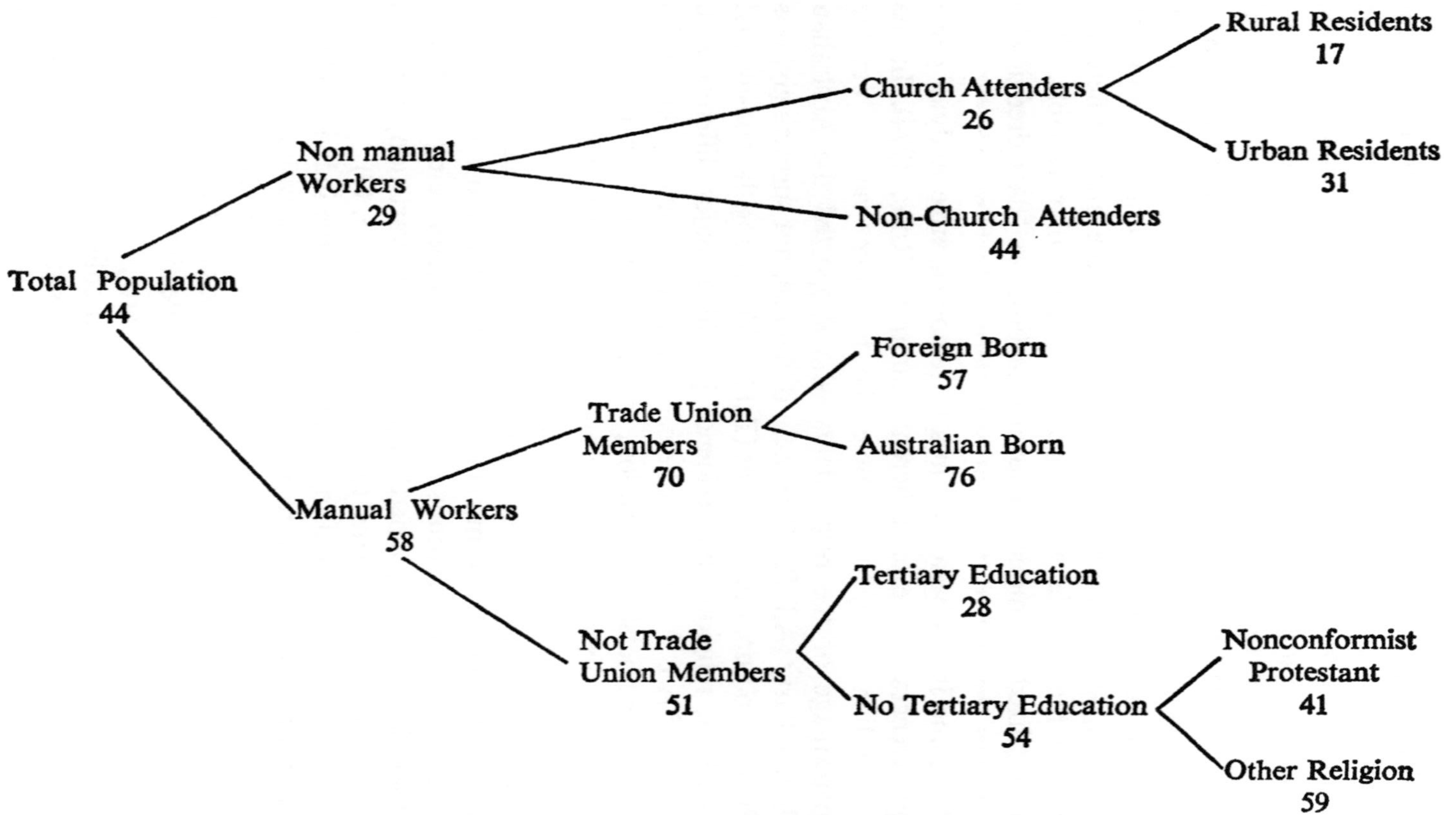

Source: Aitkin and Kahan (1974, p. 474) The numbers are percentage voting Labor.

Conclusions

The variety of methods for conducting elections is immense. We have dealt here only with those that have a major impact on most people's lives – those concerned with the election of national and local governments. The nature of the electoral system and of the published results strongly influences the ways in which elections can be analysed, but we have shown that even within those constraints the types of analysis possible are manifold, and that these are multiplied many times over by the collection of data sets specifically designed for electoral and political investigations. Following our discussion of the range of work in electoral geography in Chapter 1, therefore, we have now provided a statement of the methodology of such work: the rest of this book is concerned with the results.

Part Two

Geography of Voting

3 Political Cleavages and Geographies of Party Support

The geography of voting involves mapping the voting data described in the last chapter in order to try and understand the patterns revealed. There are two different ways of doing this. Some studies concentrate on the spatial pattern of the voting on the map; others attempt to compare the voting map with maps of other phenomena. The Siegfried study of voting in Ardèche in Chapter 1 is an elementary example of the latter approach. Clearly, the second type of study may build upon, and develop from, the first approach. In this chapter we shall deal with the patterns of votes *per se*, and in the next one with the various correlates of the voting maps. Before we consider these maps, however, we need to understand what the votes themselves represent. That is the subject matter of the first half of this chapter.

Until recent years, both types of study have lacked a general theoretical framework. This has meant that numerous empirical studies have remained isolated from each other. Studies have not usually been consistently linked together even within a single country, while comparisons between countries have rarely been attempted. Hence, despite the early studies of Siegfried and others, the geography of voting has lagged far behind survey analyses in comparative voting studies. Fortunately this situation seems, at last, to be coming to an end, largely through the historical and ecological studies of Stein Rokkan and his associates. We report on Rokkan's framework for comparative election studies in this chapter.

Cleavage Formation and Political Parties

Modern elections consist of competition between political parties for the support of the electorate. Although, in most voting systems, the actual voting decision taken by individual voters at the ballot box involves choosing between candidates, in practice the voter chooses between the parties they represent. Hence, the election of independent or non-party candidates is a very rare event in modern elections. This dominance of party over candidate in the voting decision varies from country to country. It is probably weakest in the United States, where the parties are less ideologically distinct, and strongest in countries using the list system, which explicitly promotes party voting. In all countries, however, party voting does have the property of making a potentially complex voting decision into a relatively simple matter of choice for the voter. Usually an election does not hinge upon just one or two issues but covers a wide range of topics of varying complexity. Each party represents a 'package' of responses to these issues. As such, they simplify the decision of the voter: instead of having to find out all the various positions each candidate takes on each issue, the voter simply has to find out which party the candidate represents (Lipset and Rokkan, 1967).

In order that a party label may have this property of simplifying the voting decision, it is necessary for political parties to be relatively stable groups of politicians with a relatively consistent basis to their responses to issues. Hence a party's treatment of 'new' issues in an election campaign should not be surprising but should be quite predictable, given the party's stand on related issues. This is possible because parties develop an image relating to a constellation of attitudes and values which they purport to advance. Any framework for studying the geography of modern elections must be based on an understanding of these political party images.

Rokkan's approach to studying political parties is historical. Party images are built up over time and can ultimately be traced back to particular events in the political development of a country. In the twentieth century, European and North American countries have all experienced increasing industrialization and urbanization, which has resulted in increasing similarities in their occupational structures. This economic uniformity has not been reproduced to anything like the same extent in the political field. There remains a great deal of variety in party systems among western countries. This means that citizens in different countries have different political alternatives offered to them in their elections: the voting decision is simplified for the voter in different ways. Let us consider this further.

Table 3.1 illustrates the variety of party labels. Seventeen major countries are included and we have divided them up into three geographical groupings, following Rose and Urwin (1970). These three groupings correspond to separate political traditions, reflected in voting systems as well as in political parties, and will be used in subsequent discussions. Despite the apparent variety of labels in the table, not all parties have been included. We have listed only major parties which have commanded substantial support since 1945. For instance, whereas most European countries have Communist Parties, these are only listed for France, Italy and Finland where they are a significant electoral force.

We have attempted to impose some order on the diversity of party labels by employing a right–left classification fo part of Table 3.1. This classification is loosely based upon the constellation of ideas on which each party bases its appeal. Left parties are identified as those parties having some links with a socialist philosophy, however tenuous. Of the remaining non-socialist parties, those with relatively explicit support of business interests are classified as right and the remainder appear under the central 'other' column. Whether they are politically 'central' is another matter. It is this rather mixed group which makes the simple right–left dichotomy of parties inadequate as a comprehensive framework for studying the geography of voting.

What does Table 3.1 show us? The variety of party labels is very large. No two countries have the same set of parties although the Scandinavian countries do exhibit many similarities. The most distinctive country is the United States, whose two party labels are not found elsewhere. Otherwise there is some overlap, with

Table 3.1 A selection of party labels

Country	*Left*	*Other*	*Right*
(A) *Anglo-American Countries*			
Britain	Labour	Liberal	Conservative
U.S.A.		Democrat	Republican
Canada	New Democrats	Liberal	Progressive Conservative
Australia	Labor	Democratic Labor	Liberal-Country
New Zealand	Labour	Social Credit	National
Ireland	Labour	Fianna Fail Fine Gael	
(B) *Scandinavian Countries*			
Norway	Labour	Liberal, Agrarian (Centre)	Conservative
Sweden	Social Democrat	Liberal, Agrarian (Centre)	Conservative
Denmark	Social Democrat	Radical	Conservative
Finland	Communist, Social Democrat	Liberal, Agrarian (Centre)	National Coalition
(C) *Other European Countries*			
Germany	Social Democrat	Free Democrat	Christian Democrat
France	Communist, Socialist	Radical	Gaullists (M.R.A.), Christian Democrat
Austria	Socialist		Peoples (O.V.P.)
Italy	Communist, Socialist	Liberal	Christian Democrat
Belgium	Socialist	Liberal	Christian Social, Catholic
Netherlands	Socialist	Liberal	Christian Historical, Catholic Peoples
Switzerland	Social Democrats	Radical	Catholic, Conservative

'Labour' and 'Social Democrat' being common labels of the left, 'Liberal' and 'Radical' dominating the 'centre' and 'Conservative' and 'Christian Democrat' appearing most often in the right column. Even where two or more countries use the same label, however, there will normally be distinct differences between the parties. Cross-national comparisons are fraught with difficulties because of this simple fact. The Conservative Parties of Scandinavia are very different from the Conservative Party in Britain, for instance. The Scandinavian parties are very much urban-based whereas in Britain Conservatives have long enjoyed rural dominance over most of the country. This type of contrast is hidden from view when we employ a simple right–left approach to considering political parties. What is required is an approach which goes beyond the current right or left wing images of parties and looks at how their political position has evolved. Only in this way can we begin to do justice to the 'other' parties in Table 3.1. This is the approach adopted by Rokkan. His message is a simple one – the variety of party political alternatives presented to voters can only be understood through knowledge of political party evolution within the different countries.

Dimensions of conflict

Why does one country in Table 3.1 have one particular mix of political parties while another has an alternative mixture? In this section we present Rokkan's answer to this question, which is based upon the European countries in Table 3.1. In this context different party systems reflect different patterns of state development evolving out of medieval Christendom. We consider the non-European party systems of Anglo-American countries, in the light of Rokkan's ideas, at the end of the section.

Modern political parties reflect conflicts from the past. These conflicts produce cleavages in society which reflect the two sides of the argument. A religious conflict over the supremacy of the Papacy, for instance, has led to marked cleavages in many countries along Catholic/Protestant lines. Such cleavages can be of several types. One way of viewing them is shown in Fig. 3.1. Conflicts and associated cleavage patterns in society may be

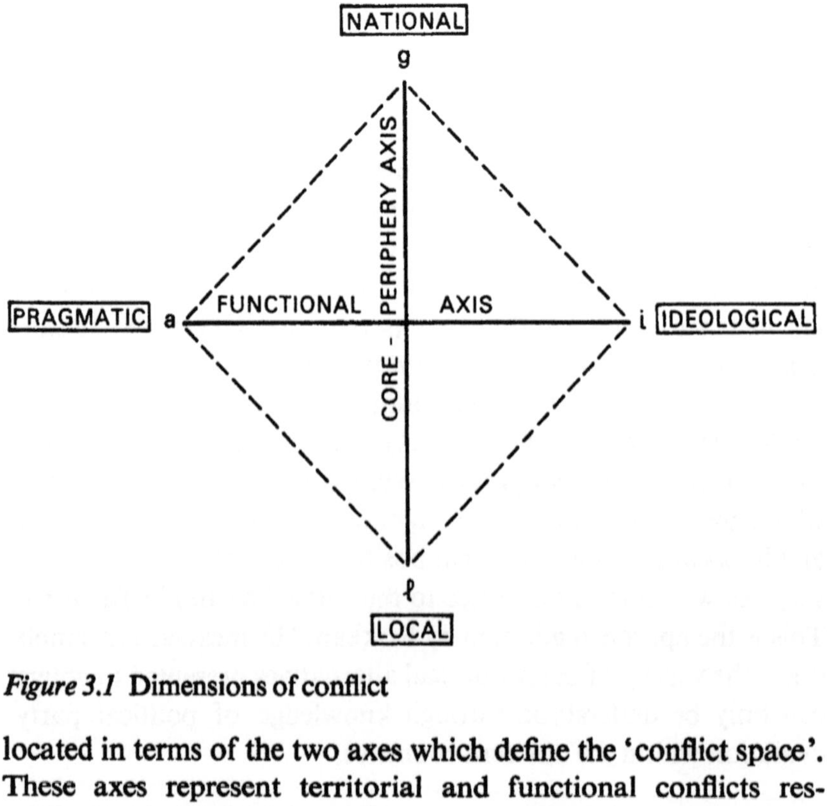

Figure 3.1 Dimensions of conflict

located in terms of the two axes which define the 'conflict space'. These axes represent territorial and functional conflicts respectively. A territorial conflict has a distinctive geographical basis to it. This is conflict between places and produces a cleavage in society along regional lines. This cleavage is in turn reflected in political parties whose basis of support is regional or 'sub'-national. The overwhelming support for Irish Nationalist candidates in southern Ireland before 1920 is a classic example of a territorial conflict with its social cleavage reflected in party terms.

The functional axis, on the other hand, concerns conflicts based upon different interest groups across the whole country. Such conflicts are socio-economic in nature and produce cleavage patterns based upon different group-functional roles in society. These cleavages are translated into party terms when, for instance, a Labour party exists and gains the support of working-class voters to the same degree throughout the country.

Rokkan defines four poles of conflict at the four corners of his quadrant. At *g* there is conflict among the elite on national goals and ideals, such as what sort of country are we building? At *l* there is conflict between the dominant culture of the national elite and the local and regional oppositions resisting incorporation. At *a* the conflicts are largely pragmatic relating to specific economic interests. At *i* conflicts are still functional but they take on an explicit ideological flavour; pragmatic disputes give way to moral debates with more tightly defined conflict, such as religious and communist conflict. Actual conflicts rarely fall at the poles of the two axes. The four 'poles of conflict' are a heuristic device defining a grid within which we can locate the original alliances of interests which lie behind the development of modern political parties.

The four basic cleavages in Europe

Core–periphery cleavages, located at the *l* pole of conflict space, inhibit the process of nation-building and may even lead to civil war and secession as in the Irish Nationalist case. Functional conflict at a national scale can only develop after some initial consolidation of the national territory in terms of physical and socio-economic integration. Where secession is avoided cultural-territorial conflicts may remain and be of varying importance. In Switzerland, Finland and Norway, for example, language-based cultural differences have been much less of a threat to national unity than similar conflicts in Belgium and Spain. We can attempt to explain such differences in terms of different national experience as functional conflicts have grown in importance at the expense of territorial conflicts.

Rokkan traces this development through four major conflicts which he terms the *critical cleavages* in the development of modern European states. Two of the cleavages are the product of the *National* Revolution and two are the product of the *Industrial* Revolution. Much of the political history of the European countries in the last couple of hundred years reflects the interaction between these two revolutionary changes, which largely diffused out of France and Britain respectively.

The four cleavages are as follows:

1. *Subject v. dominant culture*

This is the cleavage we have briefly described above. It represents initial conflicts as the nation develops and has been the subject of extensive writing by Karl Deutsch (1953, 1969). His work has been concerned with the success or failure of the nation-building group's interaction with, and eventual control of, surrounding cultures. Two processes are identified: the rate of *assimilation* which is reflected in the expansion of the dominant culture's language (Carvalho, 1962), and the rate of *mobilization* which concerns the incorporation of a subject area into a larger scale pattern of social communication and economic interaction beyond the locally-bound traditional society and economy. Knowledge of the proportions of a state's population that are assimilated and/or mobilized at any one point in time can then be used to assess the potential for nation-building or nation-fragmentation. Some states, such as the Austro-Hungarian Empire, failed and fragmented while other states survived to become modern nation-states. However, even in these 'survivors' the effects of this early cleavage can still be found in separatist parties such as the Basque Independent Party and the Scottish Nationalists. In fact the modern trend of increasing assimilation and mobilization has not led to the disappearance of the core–periphery dimension, which seems to have been resurrected in several countries in recent years. The recent rise of Scottish Nationalism, for instance, is totally unrelated to the current status of the Scottish Gaelic language but seems to have had its major impetus from Scotland's possible new role in the world economy as an oil-rich state. Deutsch's ideas represent a simple model which usefully identifies core-periphery conflicts as a major element of national political development, but which is not able to encompass the complexities of modern separatist development. However there is always a link between modern separatism and early failures to dominate a subject culture completely; Scotland *had* maintained its identity before the discovery of North Sea oil.

The continuing existence of the concept of a Scottish nation was the necessary condition for the subsequent success of Scottish Nationalism based upon modern economic issues.

2. *Church(es) v. government*

Rokkan sees the conflict between the aspirations of the mobilizing nation-state and the corporate claims of the churches as producing a decisive cleavage underlying many modern political parties in Europe. The fundamental issue was one of the control of community norms, most explicitly reflected in conflict over state or church control of education. Where established national churches were incorporated as agents of the state the issues were far less sharply drawn, but in religiously mixed communities and Catholic countries the secular ideas stemming from the French Revolution proved to be particularly divisive. Politically this cleavage led to parties of religious defence which were able to obtain the loyalty of church-goers of all economic classes.

The best example of this 'vertical' cleavage pattern is to be found in the Netherlands. For over one hundred years Dutch society has consisted of three major 'sub-cultures' – a general group (national/liberal/secular), a Catholic group, and an Orthodox Protestant group. By the 1920s all three groups were reflected in the national party system as Liberal, Catholic and Protestant parties. These groupings are reflected today in the Socialist and Liberal parties, Catholic party and Christian Historical party respectively, as listed in Table 3.1.

3. *Primary v. secondary economy*

The Industrial Revolution also set up conflicts which helped mould modern party systems. The initial conflict was between agrarian and industrial interests. The growth of a world economy in agricultural and industrial commodities led to differences of interest between countryside and town. Industrial interests favoured free trade to enable them to sell their new products, often in exchange for agricultural products, throughout the world; while agricultural interests sought tariff protection for their products. Whereas in southern Europe the religious cleavage dominated politics, in northern Europe this rural-urban cleavage has played a major part in the development of modern parties. In the five Nordic countries the cities have traditionally dominated political life and hence generated distinctive rural oppositions at the periphery. This is the basis of the difference between the Scandinavian and British Conservative parties referred to above. Scandinavian countries developed distinctive Agrarian parties which have not been able to assimilate easily with urban Conservatives. In contrast, whereas the dominant cleavage underlying British Liberal-Conservative politics until the 1880s was a rural-urban one, these conflicts softened as business-owners moved into the countryside to live alongside the country gentry and away from their workers. The result has been that rural-urban differences play only a minor part in modern British politics. In fact distinctive European agrarian parties have only evolved where this basic economic conflict has been combined with strong cultural opposition as we show below.

4. *Workers v. employers*

This latest fundamental cleavage has had by far the most uniform effect. Conflicts over work conditions and wages led initially to a variety of labour unions and then to the development of nationwide socialist parties. The nature of these latest parties of the 'left' varies from rather 'domesticated' pragmatic Labour or Social Democrat Parties to Communist Parties with varying levels of commitment to revolution. In general, the more domesticated and successful workers' parties are in northern Europe, whereas southern Europe and its Catholic culture has spawned more revolutionary and generally less successful working-class parties, the French and Italian Communist Parties being the classic examples.

A model of alternative alliances and oppositions

Modern party systems, as alliances and oppositions, derive from these four conflicts. The differences in the timing and the character of the National and Industrial Revolutions with their associated critical cleavages in different countries have produced the striking differences in party systems that exist today. In particular, the first three cleavages have produced most of the variety in party systems stemming from conflicts that developed before major extensions of the suffrage and the mass politics of the twentieth century. These latter events have led to the rise of the fourth cleavage in importance throughout Europe resulting in the variety of 'left' parties shown in Table 3.1. This development has tended to make party systems more alike as elections come to resemble the simple choice between 'left' and 'right' parties. This is why it is on the right and in the centre of the political spectrum that the main elements of variety in parties and party labels are to be found. It is this latter variation that Rokkan has attempted to explain as ordered consequences of decisions and developments from interaction of the first three critical cleavages in the history of each European country. The result is a *model of alternative alliances and oppositions.*

The nation-building group, the dominant governing elite in a country, can make alliances on either a religious or an economic front or both. Depending on national circumstances alliances can be either with a national church or the Catholic church, or alternatively a secular position may be held. In economic terms the alliance may include landed or urban-industrial interests. The nation-builders' alliances determine the peripheral group's response, again depending on national circumstances.

Using this system of alliances and oppositions Rokkan identifies eight basic party system types described in Table 3.2. The empirical examples are only approximate but in every case the cleavages represented in the alliances and oppositions are discernible in the existing party system, especially on the centre and right. Here we can see the source of the continuing difference between the British Conservative Party and its Scandinavian namesakes. While British Conservatives have never made headway in the Celtic fringe, this is far less important than the failure o Scandinavian Conservatives to win many votes from any rural areas; they remain an essentially urban party.

Table 3.2 A typology of European party systems

Type	*Nation-Builder's Alliance*	*Periphery's Opposition*	*Empirical Examples*	
I	National church and landed interests	Dissenters and urban interests	Britain Con. v. Lib.	Celtic fringe dissenters industry
II	National church and urban interests	Dissenters and landed interests	Scandinavia Con. v.	'Left' Agrarians Christians Radicals
III	National church (despite strong Catholic minority) and landed interests	1. Secular and urban interests 2. Catholic	Germany Con. v.	Liberals Bavarians
IV	National church (despite strong Catholic minority) and urban interests	1. Dissenters and landed interests 2. Catholic and landed interests	Netherlands Lib. v.	Calvinists Catholics
V	Secular and landed interests	1. Urban interests 2. Catholic	Spain Lib. v.	Catalan Corbists
VI	Secular and urban interests	Catholic and landed interests	France } Lib./Rad. v. Italy }	Con.
VII	Catholic and landed interests	Secular and urban	Austria Chr. v. Lib.	Pan-German Industry
VIII	Catholic and urban interests	Landed interests	Belgium Chr./Lib. v.	Flemish separatists

Source: Rokkan (1970)

The same picture set out in Table 3.2 may be viewed as a simple tree diagram of the nation building group's alliances:

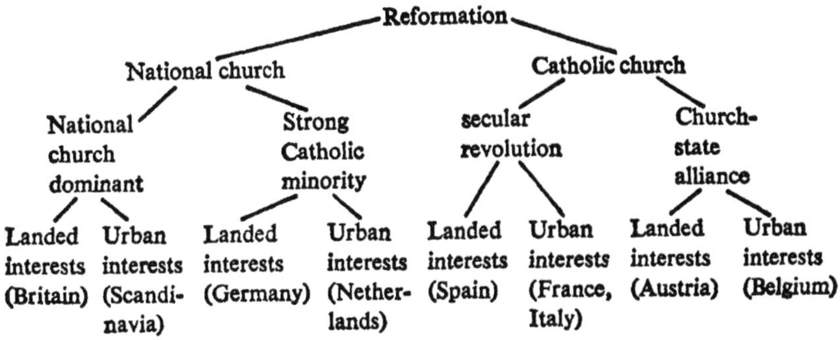

This diagram emphasises the wide sweep of Rokkan's ideas from reformation through to industrial revolution.

This model presents the party systems that had developed in Europe at about the turn of the century. These were the choices offered to the early voters as the suffrage was extended and mass participation originated. This was therefore the political environment within which the products of the mass participation, the working-class parties reflecting the fourth and final cleavage, had to find their position. This new opposition was a threat to all old parties, Liberal or Conservative, Protestant or Catholic. In most countries working class parties have grown to become a major force in the political scene and this has usually necessitated a reformulation of the original pattern of alliances and oppositions. In Britain, for instance, the Conservatives have incorporated the Liberals' urban-industrial interests while Labour have taken-over much of the Liberal strength in the Celtic fringe and among dissenters. The result has been the decline of the Liberals as a major party as British elections have evolved into a simple choice between 'right' and 'left'. The 1974 elections suggest this may be changing but the electoral system based on pluralities ensures that Parliament continues to be dominated by a two-party division involving Labour and Conservatives.

By contrast in Nordic countries the rise of the Social Democrats has not led to a coalition of the old parties under a single label. The proportional representation electoral system has not 'forced' a simple response to the Social Democrats so that the

Conservatives have remained urban and middle-class, alongside a separate Agrarian Party and a Liberal Party. The Social Democrats have taken over much of the 'old left's' support in the peripheral north. Hence, in this case, the present party system more clearly reflects the alliances and oppositions of the past. Elsewhere secular socialist parties have stimulated conservative alliances around the label 'Christian Democrats', which have effectively squeezed out the original 'Liberals'. However, the new parties of the left have not always forced a realignment of old parties in response to their common threat. In the Netherlands the threefold division of society based on the religious cleavage still dominates, to give a party system which reflects more than any other the alliances and oppositions of previous centuries.

Rokkan's work on political cleavages and party systems provides an ordered framework within which the geographies of political choice may be set. Geographical patterns of support and associations with other socio-economic patterns may be investigated in the light of this theoretical structure. However, the framework does relate only to Europe, and we need to consider non-European party systems as they relate to Rokkan's scheme before we concern ourselves with actual studies of the geographies of party support.

Fragments of Europe and cultural pluralism

Perhaps the simplest way to consider the new societies founded by Europeans (Latin America, French Canada, U.S.A., English Canada, Dutch South Africa, Australia and New Zealand), is as 'fragments' of Europe scattered across the globe. Louis Hartz (1964) has argued that the political developments within these new societies depended upon their 'date of departure' from Europe, since the settlers took with them only the traditions and values of the Europe they left behind. The significance of the fragmentation process is that the new society loses the momentum to change inherent in Europe as a whole. Hence, only part of the history underlying Rokkan's model will be represented in any one of the new European-settled societies. For instance, new societies founded before the National Revolution in Europe are identified as 'feudal fragments' (Latin America and French Canada), whereas those founded after this revolution are 'bourgeois (or liberal) fragments' (U.S.A., English Canada and Dutch South Africa) (Horowitz, 1966). Furthermore it is only in the most recently settled countries (Australia, New Zealand and western Canada) that stable left parties have emerged to reflect the class conflicts of the Industrial Revolution.

This interpretation of the new societies as taking off from Europe with just that part of Rokkan's cleavages available at the time of departure is useful in helping to explain the ideological range of parties in a party system – the lack of a left party in the U.S.A., for example (Table 3.1). It does not explain, however, the particular mixes of parties that emerged in the countries formed from the new societies. Although the original cultural origins of these countries are important, so also is the fact that they attracted further European settlers from all parts of Europe. The result has been that these countries have been culturally more diverse than emphasis on their original settlement implies and it is this cultural pluralism which has often been a distinctive influence on the evolution of the party systems. We concentrate our discussion on the four Anglo-American countries beyond Europe listed in Table 3.1.

In Europe the nation states that evolved were normally based upon one dominant culture. This was usually reflected in a common language in the core of the country. Where language differences existed these were on the peripheries of the states and the decline of peripheries and their languages is an integral part of Rokkan's framework. The theoretical end-result of this process is a set of single-culture nation states. In Europe the main exceptions to this process are in states that straddle major language boundaries, notably Switzerland and Belgium. In the new countries, on the other hand, exceptions to this cultural uniformity are the rule.

The transplanting of European populations out of their separate cultural territories in Europe to new lands in North America and Australasia inevitably led to cultural mixing in a new plural situation. Hence, although the dominant culture is British in all four cases, so that most of the population are English-speakers, other cultural groups have settled in the new countries. Furthermore, these other cultural groups are not conveniently located in peripheries but have settled in concentrations throughout many different parts of the rural and urban regions of the new countries. The end result of this process is a cultural pluralism that is not represented in Rokkan's framework. When we come to consider the party systems of the new countries, therefore, we need to consider their degree of cultural pluralism. We can order them – U.S.A., Canada, Australia, New Zealand – in terms of degree of pluralism and this will be reflected in their similarities to the British political system. We will consider each new country in turn but with additional emphasis on the party system of the U.S.A. where the cultural pluralism factor has had much the most influence.

New Zealand and Australia have the most homogeneous populations in cultural terms and have evolved party systems very similar to the British one. In both countries there are Labour parties in competition with a right-wing party to win control of Parliament. Both have economies which are much more agriculturally based than the British economy but this is only partially reflected in the party systems. In New Zealand a rural party, Social Credit, first fought in the 1954 election and since that date it has won only one seat. In Australia, the much older Country Party only survives as an ally of the urban-based Liberal Party. Australia's Democratic Labor does reflect the additional cultural or ethnic factor discussed above. This party broke away from Labor in the 1950s and is based largely upon Catholic Italian immigrant support. Although Democratic Labor have never won any seats in the Federal House of Representatives, the alternative vote electoral law allows their supporters to influence elections by their deflection of a proportion of the working class from Labor to Liberal in their lower preferences, as illustrated in Chapter 2.

In Canada the ethnic factor is far more important. Its most obvious influence can be seen in the existence of separatist parties for the French-speaking Québec. Both the Parti Québecois and the Créditiste party can be interpreted as rural periphery parties representing a subject culture in a manner not unlike that envisaged by Rokkan in European countries. Elsewhere in Canada later immigration has produced a more complicated mixed cultural pluralism. The two main parties are the Liberals and Progressive Conservatives, and although these labels suggest a party system like the British one of the nineteenth century, they are in fact very different. In Canada these parties are based on a variety of economic and ethnic interest groups with different alliances sometimes occurring in different provinces. We look at the bases of support for these two parties in the next chapter. Canada has one further major party, the New Democrats, who are a 'Labour' party and reflect the last of Rokkan's conflicts. Unlike the situation in all the previous party systems we have considered, this is a party of the left that is not a major competitor in national elections. It is in this respect that Canada is similar to the U.S.A. which has not developed a party of the left even of the size of the New Democrats.

We have already noted in Table 3.1 that the U.S.A. has developed unique party labels for its party system. In fact, the U.S.A. had developed political parties appealing to a large electorate before equivalent developments in Europe. Hence although the U.S.A. is European-settled, its party political evolution is a separate and independent case. As such the American party system has been intensively studied and deserves particular consideration (Chambers and Burnham, 1967).

The U.S.A. developed the very first party system based upon mass mobilization. By 1840 a system had emerged with two parties competing for the popular vote on a nation-wide scale (McCormick, 1967). This involved party organization, linking national leaders to local party workers, all helping to win the presidency for 'their' candidate. It included such disparate 'modern' features as a partisan press, door-to-door canvassing and the existence of personal party loyalties. In 1840 these party activities were so successful that over eighty per cent of the voters, two-and-a-half-million white adult males, actually cast their vote. It was three decades before any equivalent mass-mobilization by organized parties developed in Britain (McCormick, 1967).

The parties which competed in the 1840 election were the Democrats and the Whigs, the latter label reflecting some British influence. This two-party system evolved in 1828 and lasted to 1852. Its major claim to fame is its creation of nationwide party organizations, epitomized by the setting up of the first Democratic National Convention in 1848. However, the underlying conflicts reflecting each party's electoral support are much more difficult to discover. Burnham (1967, p. 294) remarks that 'each party was put together piecemeal from a bewildering variety of local cleavages and ethno-cultural hostilities'. Thus it would seem that the national party organizations produced weak, rather fragile coalitions. This was especially true of the Whigs who incorporated support ranging from New England urban liberals to wealthy, southern, rural slave-owners. The party floundered on the slavery issue and disappeared as a national force after the 1852 election.

Since the development of the first party system there have been three further party systems, all using the Democrat and Republican party labels. These party systems are separated from one another by what Key (1955) has termed *critical elections*. These are elections at which, in Key's words, 'the decisive results of the voting reveal a sharp alteration of the pre-existing cleavages within the electorate'. The realignment of alliances then persists for several subsequent elections so that 'new and durable electoral groupings are formed'. Thus, between critical elections there is a sequence of 'normal' elections when group alliances underlying party support are maintained. Sometimes these non-critical elections are classified further as 'maintaining', 'reinstating' and 'deviating' (Burnham, 1974). Our interest, however, focuses on the critical elections, since it is these which have determined the sequence of party systems in the U.S.A. (Clubb and Allen, 1971).

The first critical election is usually identified as occurring in 1856. It led to the Whig party being replaced by the Republicans in the lead-up to the civil war. Subsequent critical elections are identified as those of 1896, and 1928 and 1932. The realignments can be identified by correlating the party votes for successive pairs of presidential elections. Two 'normal' elections should exhibit similar patterns of support and hence will produce high positive correlations. A critical election, on the other hand, should exhibit a change in the pattern of support so that it should have a low correlation with the previous election. Such realignments are illustrated on Figure 3.2 where the correlations between votes for Democrat presidential candidates are shown for successive pairs of elections from 1880 to 1960. The deviating election of 1948 is ignored because the existence of a split in the Democrat ranks adds particular features to the election which are not of concern to us here. Figure 3.2 shows two clear breaks in the generally high correlations, identifying the critical years of 1892, and 1928 and 1932.

The identification of these critical elections gives us three sets of normal elections with their own particular party systems since the fall of the Whigs. From 1856 to 1892 the Republican versus Democrat elections revolved around the Civil War and its aftermath. This resulted in a Republican north dominating the scene until the re-entry of the south produced a rather evenly balanced but regionally based contest. This 'Civil War party system' was replaced in 1896 as the Democrats declined, after the collapse of the urban strength of the party in the north. The 1896 election can be seen as an attempt by the Democrats to ally the disadvantaged farmers with the industrial workers, but they succeeded only in producing a firm industrial alliance that defeated this combination. This 'industrial party system' which followed 1896, survived through the party-boss/progressive era in which party politics was largely based upon ethnic alliances at the local level, usually leaving the Democrats out in the cold as the second party. All this was changed in 1932. This election was fought during the Depression and involved Democrat party commitment to the economic policies in terms of employment, welfare and public borrowing that came to be known as the New Deal. This enabled the party to combine its rural strength with urban working-class

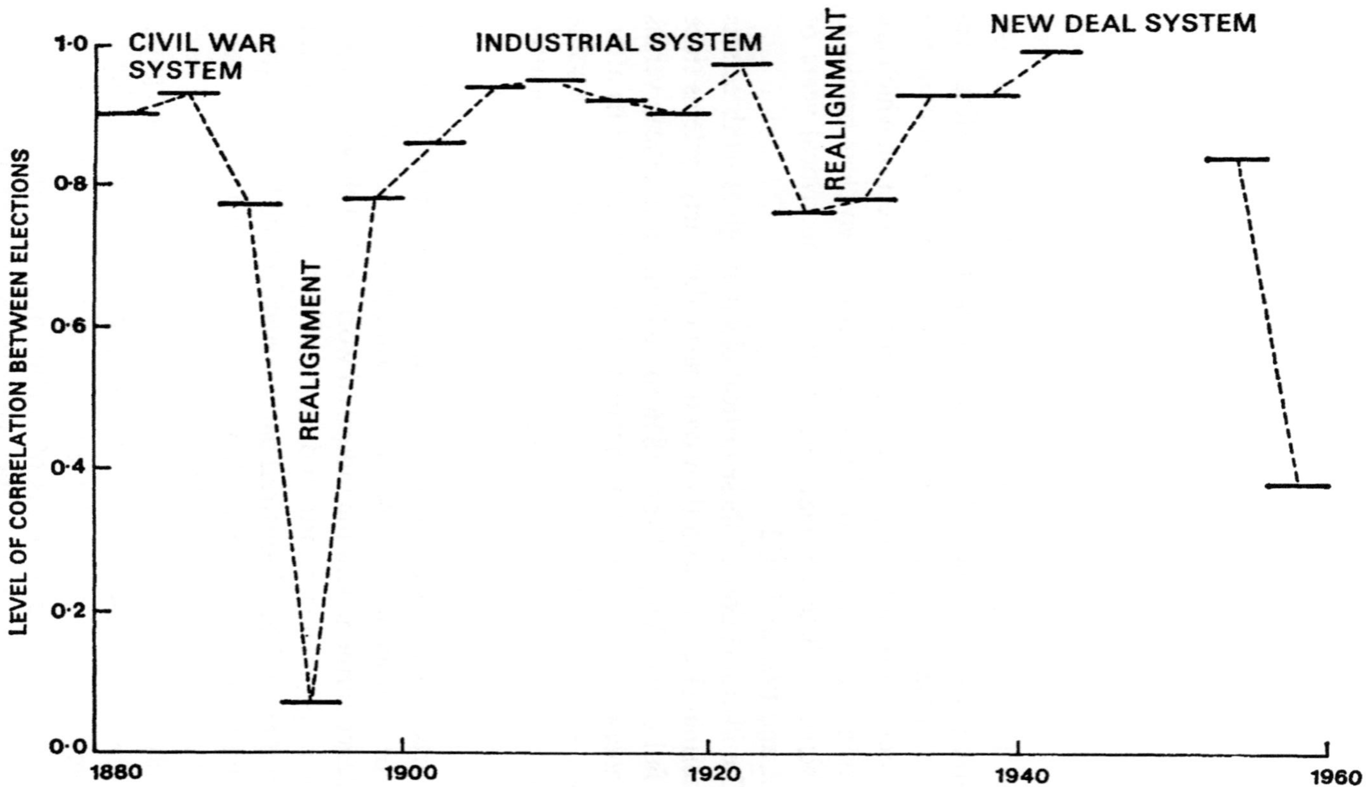

Figure 3.2 Levels of correlation between Democrat presidential voting by states, 1880–1960

support in a new alliance. It is sometimes debated whether this party system has continued to operate through the 1960s and into the 1970s. Figure 3.2 shows a low correlation between the 1956 and 1960 party votes, and since 1960 there have been three deviating elections with the Republicans (Goldwater) winning in the south but nowhere else in 1964, with a three-party contest in 1968 and a landslide victory for the Republicans (Nixon) in 1972. In 1976, however, the old Democratic alliance seemed to operate once more as Carter was able to build upon solid southern support and evenly split support elsewhere to form a presidential election majority. Hence it seems that since 1960 there have been no critical elections to cause major, permanent realignments of the cleavages, although the electoral situation has become much more fluid, so that the alliances that do exist are not as stable as in the past.

The contrasts and similarities between these four party systems, divided by the three critical elections, can be shown in the geography of their support. Figure 3.3 shows the average presidential vote for Democrat candidates by states in selected triplets of elections in each of the four systems. The first system is the most distinctive in the evenness for support of the parties over the country. The lack of any north-south division in the years before the Civil War is quite remarkable. In the second system the north-south division appears, with the Democrats totally dominating the south and being competitive in the north. In the third system the Democrats' northern strength has disappeared and the north-south contrast is at its maximum. In the final system the Democrats are competitive again in the north and as solid as ever in the south.

How does the modern American party system compare with its European counterparts whose contrasting origins we traced earlier? In fact the differences are not as great as is sometimes imagined. Although the distinctive regional component of the south remains, and particular ethnic cultural influences survive locally, since 1932 the party cleavage has been much more class-based than previously. Hence although the U.S.A. does not have a genuine left party in our Table 3.1, labour union endorsement

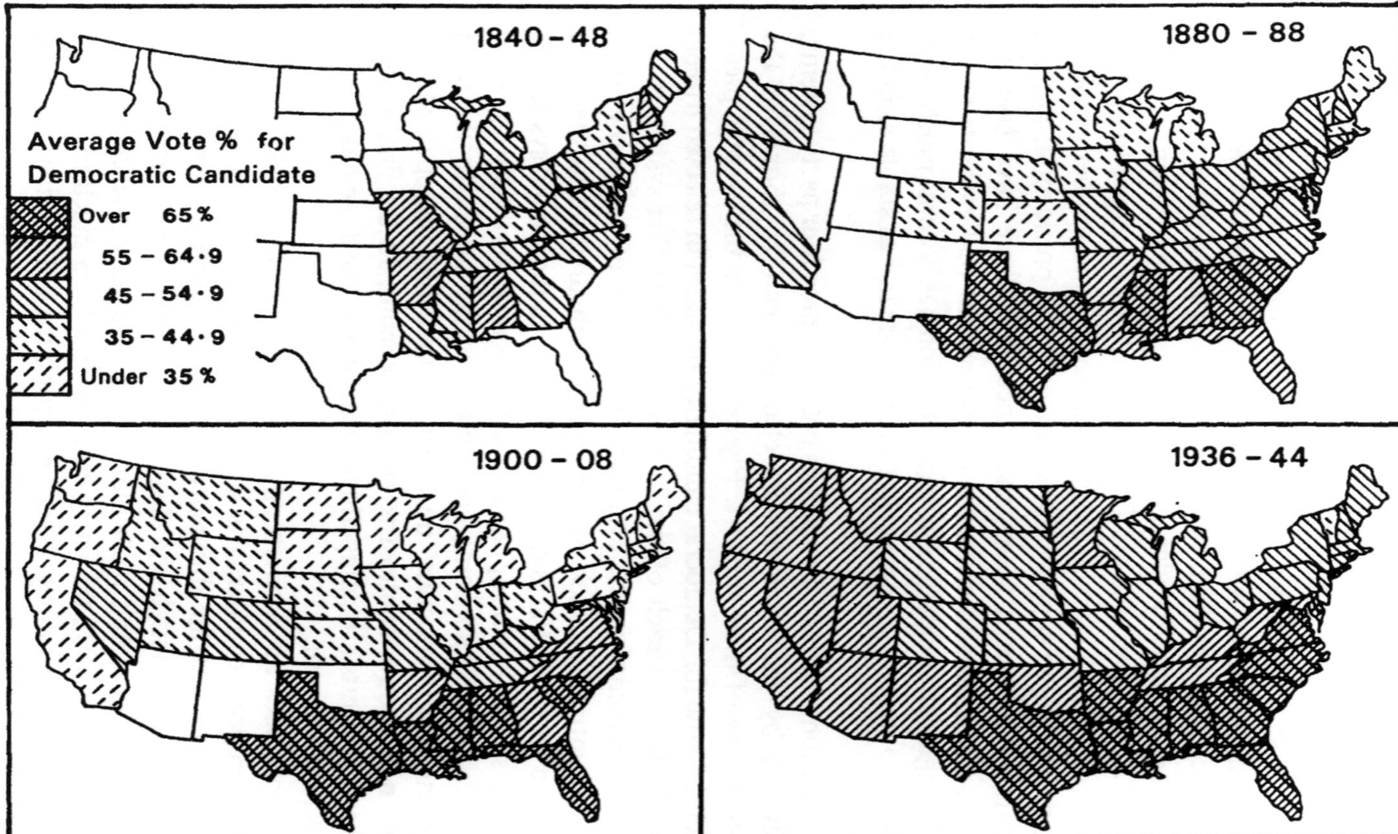

Figure 3.3 Voting patterns for Democrat presidential candidates in four party systems

is an important aspect of the Democrat Party's appeal to voters. This is entirely consistent with Rokkan's ideas on the way party systems in different countries become more similar as conflicts relating to the labour market form the basis of party differences. The Americans never developed a major socialist party, but they have produced an alternative in the 'New Deal Democrats'. In the next section we consider why the Americans do not have a major socialist party.

Mobilization of Peripheries

We introduced political parties at the beginning of this chapter as being a device whereby the electorate is presented with a relatively simple choice between alternative 'packages'. Individual voters can avoid detailed consideration of each issue by merely selecting the overall party 'package' they prefer. Of course political parties are much more than commodities that are advertised and sold at election time. Our discussion of the development of political parties has shown that parties have had a crucial role in the resolution of conflicts within the modern state.

The word 'party' comes from the same root as 'part'. Party systems are first and foremost outlets for divisions in society (Lipset and Rokkan, 1967). They are, as we have seen, expressions of these divisions or cleavages. They reflect a history of alliances against alternatives, and may still represent one choice in a conflict situation. However, they also have an integrative role. Participation in an election bestows a legitimacy on the particular political system (except where the party supported is separatist in nature). Thus the political party is both an agent of conflict *and* an instrument of integration. The previous section emphasized conflicts; in the second section of this chapter we consider the integrative role and the attempts of peripheries to resist integration.

The political party as an instrument of integration has been faced with two major tasks. In many countries peripheral areas have maintained distinctive traditions and it has been the role of national parties to incorporate these areas into the mainstream of the country's politics. Such peripheral areas are normally relatively inaccessible from the main central core of the country and it is this feature that has enabled distinctive traditions to survive. The political parties have to overcome this inaccessibility and spread their message across the whole of the country's area. The process envisaged is one of the spatial diffusion of a party's ideas from the centre out to the periphery.

A major second role of the political parties has been to bring new voters into the political system as the suffrage has been extended. In most countries suffrage reform has led to large jumps in the numbers of voters and the political parties have had the task of channelling the political aspirations of the newly enfranchised groups into the national political system. As we have seen, outside North America the extension of the franchise to further voters usually led directly to the rise of new left parties, allowing the workers v. employers cleavage to be explicitly represented in the party system. In contrast the enfranchisement of women led to no major alterations in the party systems.

Several researchers have been interested in both of these integrative roles of political parties and particularly in their interaction – how new groups of voters have been incorporated into the political system in different parts of the country. We would expect, *a priori*, that new groups of voters would be more easily incorporated into the political system in the central areas than in the more inaccessible regions of the periphery. Studies of the process, which is usually termed *mobilization of the periphery*, have found this is normally so.

The mobilization of the peripheries will be illustrated in three contrasting contexts. The first example discussed is a classic study of 'normal' nation-building processes in a Scandinavian context and uses Rokkan's work on Norway. We then move to the third ('other European') group of countries in Table 3.1, and consider the mobilization of a completely new province in Austria after the disintegration of the Austro-Hungarian Empire. Finally we deal with an Anglo-American example, considering some political responses of that most famous of peripheries, the American West.

Norway's two regional peripheries

The integration of Norway's peripheries can be viewed as taking place in four related steps (Rokkan, 1970). The first step is a purely legal one – the formal incorporation into the political system of citizens formerly kept out. This involves extending the suffrage and making facilities available for mass registration of voters. This extension of the legal-political rights of the citizens does not ensure their participation in the electoral process. The second step is the specific mobilization of the citizens in the election contests. This may be viewed as minimum participation. The third step involves the *activation* of the newly enfranchised citizens into direct participation in public life as candidates. This is closely related to the fourth step of *politicization*, whereby traditional systems of local rule are broken down through the entry of nationally organized parties. All four steps have been carefully documented by Rokkan (1970) using detailed ecological analyses.

It has been shown for several countries that when the suffrage is extended, the level of turnout – the percentage of registered voters casting their ballot – falls dramatically in the subsequent election. This shows the measure of the problem of mobilizing new groups of voters and is very clearly shown for Norwegian elections. The first election with adult male suffrage was in 1900 and the vote was only extended to women for the 1915 election. Figure 3.4 shows turnout levels for elections from 1897 through to 1924. Both extensions of the franchise are marked by a drop in turnout levels and there is a time-lag before turnout reaches its pre-extension level. In Norway the 1897 level was not attained again until into the 1920s. This time-lag is accompanied by a 'space-lag': mobilization of new groups is more rapid in some areas than in others. The spatially fragmented nature of Norway's settlement pattern has made the mobilization particularly slow and sometimes quite irregular. Figure 3.4 partially shows this effect in the contrast between cities and rural areas. The latter areas consistently have lower turnouts and are slower in catching up with their pre-extension situations. Although the rural areas include much more than the periphery, these findings do imply

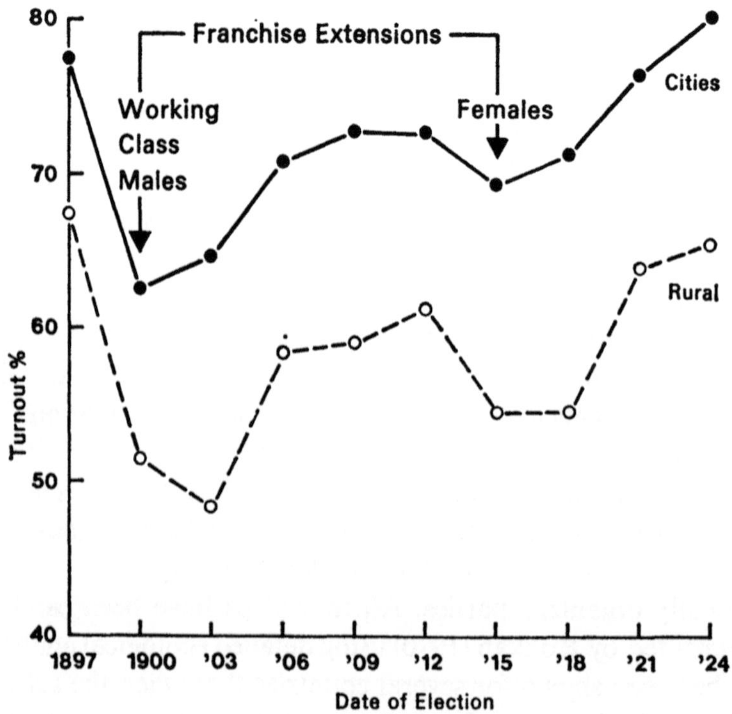

Figure 3.4 Turnout levels in Norwegian elections, 1897–1924

that mobilization is more difficult in more peripheral areas. This can only be fully illustrated, of course, by using a much more detailed ecological breakdown than a simple city/rural one.

Rokkan (1970) has shown that mobilization processes have not been able to overcome fully the problems of physical access in the more peripheral parts of Norway. An index of accessibility has been constructed for every commune, based on the existence of 'house clusters', children having to attend boarding school or attending schools with two or less classes. Table 3.3 clearly shows how turnout was appreciably lower in less accessible communes in the 1957 election within rural areas. This pattern of turnouts is repeated in analyses of other post-war Norwegian elections.

In order to define a more general concept of periphery, Rokkan (1970) adds cultural and economic elements to his classification of communes. Periphery scores are produced for all Norwegian communes by combining together measures of employment in the

Table 3.3 Differences in turnout in the Norwegian election, 1957

Type of area	*Accessibility*	*No. of communes*	*Turnout %*
A. Rural			
Fisheries	Low	62	64·9
	Medium	60	66·7
	High	48	68·8
Agriculture/	Low	46	72·4
Fisheries	Medium	110	75·8
	High	69	77·6
Mixed/	Low	81	73·7
Industrial	Medium	63	77·2
	High	79	79·5
B. Urban			
Mixed	—	15	77·3
Industrial	—	21	80·5
Suburban	—	26	80·2

Source: Rokkan (1970)

primary sector, population loss, farm size and income levels as well as isolation by transport. This allows communes to be designated 'extreme periphery', 'moderate periphery' and 'non-periphery'. In this typology, Norway's 674 communes were allocated as follows: 61 extreme periphery, 111 moderate periphery, with 502 classified as non-periphery.

The distribution of periphery communes varies by regions with half of the extreme periphery communes being located in the north. The breakdown of commune type by region is given in Table 3.4. The original core areas of the Norwegian state are usually identified as being located around Trondheim and Oslo (Pounds and Ball, 1964) which are found in the middle and east regions respectively. These two regions have the highest proportions of non-periphery communes, as shown in Table 3.4. This table also shows levels of turnout for the 1957 election. Notice hat in four of the five regions, turnout declines regularly with increasing level of periphery. In general, non-periphery communes have levels of turnout approximately ten per cent above

Table 3.4 Turnout levels in the 1957 Norwegian election

Region	*Peripheral type*	*No. of communes*	*Turnout %*
East	Non-periphery	176	80·2
	Moderate periphery	12	77·1
	Extreme periphery	1	71·4
South	Non-periphery	45	75·9
	Moderate periphery	16	77·0
	Extreme periphery	7	77·8
West	Non-periphery	163	73·8
	Moderate periphery	33	70·5
	Extreme periphery	11	65·6
Middle	Non-periphery	69	78·0
	Moderate periphery	14	72·8
	Extreme periphery	11	67·2
North	Non-periphery	49	68·7
	Moderate periphery	36	65·3
	Extreme periphery	31	60·8

Source: Rokkan (1970)

extreme periphery communes. This indicates that mobilization of the periphery had not been completed half a century after the suffrage reforms. However it is also clear that there are major differences between regions as well as within regions. Generally the east and middle regions have the highest turnout and the north the lowest. The south is the exception to the discussion above and has relatively high levels of turnout *irrespective* of the periphery typology. We return to this anomaly below.

If we compare the levels of turnout for 1957 (Table 3.4) with those at the beginning of the century (Figure 3.4) we find that the degree of mobilization has been quite effective. In fact the turnout level for cities in 1900 lies between the two lowest turnouts recorded on Table 3.4 (i.e. between the moderate periphery and extreme periphery in the north region). This directly reflects the success of the political parties in mobilizing the electorate throughout the country.

The process of politicization can be clearly traced in Norwegian local elections through the choice of voting system. In 1896 a law was passed which allowed any commune to petition for the replacement of the plurality system by a proportional representation list system for electing local councils. The use of a list system usually presupposes an organized party system and so the spread of P.R. through Norwegian local elections reflects the 'nationalization' of party conflict. It was the Labour Party which took the initiative in a national organization which promoted the P.R. system. By 1937 the Labour Party was presenting party lists of candidates in all but one town and in ninety-two per cent of all rural communes. In contrast at this same time the Agrarians had lists in only forty per cent of rural communes, the Liberals in thirty-seven per cent and the Conservatives in ten per cent. This procedure was initially related to the activation process as the party organizations increased their membership and recruited their members into local government service. All of these developments tended to occur earlier in non-periphery communes compared with periphery communes as we might expect, although once again there were distinct regional differences.

We can return to the 1957 election to illustrate the effect of this politicization process in terms of the nationalization of political conflicts. The degree of polarization in the election can be measured as the proportion of the total vote that was cast for the class-based parties (Communist, Labour and Conservative), the remaining vote going to the cultural/territorial parties (Liberal, Christian, Agrarian). Table 3.5 shows these polarization scores for three 'large' regions and for urban/rural/periphery (extreme and moderate) categories. The first two regions, east/middle and south/west, show a consistent trend with the cities being more polarized than the periphery. In this case it is the north which is the exception by having high levels of polarization for all types of category. Even the peripheral north has a higher level of polarization than the cities in the south/west regions.

Here we have two contrasting regional responses to the

Table 3.5 Polarization in the 1957 Norwegian election

Region	*Category*	*Polarization*
East/Middle	Principal cities	88
	Other cities	85
	Central rural	82
	Peripheral	68
South/West	Principal cities	75
	Other cities	68
	Central rural	61
	Peripheral	45
North	Cities	84
	Central rural	85
	Peripheral	80

Source: Rokkan (1970)

mobilization of the periphery (Rokkan, 1970). In the north the mobilization has been slower, as is clearly reflected in the turnout levels. In south/west turnout levels are not as low as in the north but these regions do not conform so closely to the major cleavage in Norwegian politics based on class. In fact both zones have similar levels of entry into the major class-based element of the Norwegian political system, the south/west's higher turnout merely involving additional voting for cultural parties who have maintained their appeal in this particular region, particularly in its peripheral communes.

In conclusion, we can identify two very different peripheral responses to the mobilization process in Norway: the highly polarized north has low turnouts in its peripheral communes, while the higher turnouts in the south/west reflect continuing support for earlier cultural parties.

Mobilizing a political vacuum: Burgenland, Austria.

The most extreme cases of political mobilization occur when a country's political parties have to start from nothing. This occurs where a new region is incorporated into a country with which it shares little or no political tradition. Such 'political vacuums' were formed in several instances with the creation of new states after the First World War. In these situations political parties had a key role in integrating the new areas into the country's political system. One such example has been studied in detail by Burghardt (1964) and we present part of his research here as a case study.

Burgenland is the easternmost province of Austria. It was transferred to Austria from Hungary after World War I. From being part of a centralized state, controlled by the Budapest parliament, it was transformed into a province of the new federal Austria. The new province was left with an almost complete dearth of politicians and civil servants and so presented the Austrian political parties with almost virgin territory. It was their task to mobilize this political vacuum and integrate it into the Austrian political system.

Burgenland was finally handed over to Austria in November 1921. By June 1922 there was a national election involving three major parties – the Christian (Catholic) Party, the Socialist Party and the Peasants' Party. Almost all party leaders and most candidates had to be imported from Vienna. As it was a largely traditional rural zone, the Christian Party expected to win the province in the election. However, in the event, the Socialists won thirty-nine per cent of the vote to the Christian Party's thirty-one per cent with the Peasants' Party winning a respectable fifteen per cent. This surprising result was almost certainly because of the lack of established loyalties in Burgenland. The Austrian party system was not yet established here, so that mobilization by particular parties was all important. It was the Socialists who were more successful in introducing their party apparatus into the province, based on the solid core of support from urban factory workers many of whom commuted to Vienna, the Socialist Party's national core. In the three subsequent elections before the Nazi take-over, the Christian Party managed to win its expected plurality.

The mobilization of the rural areas in support of the Christian

Party consisted of two processes. First the party had to establish itself as the National representatives of the interests of the traditional rural voters. This it was soon able to do as its major rivals, the Socialists, were restricted to the urban and commuter areas. Secondly the party had to compete with the much more limited appeal of the Peasants' Party. This party's strength lay in southern Burgenland, which was the most remote part of the province. Figure 3.5 shows those areas which supported the Peasants' Party in at least two of the four elections up to 1930. These areas are the

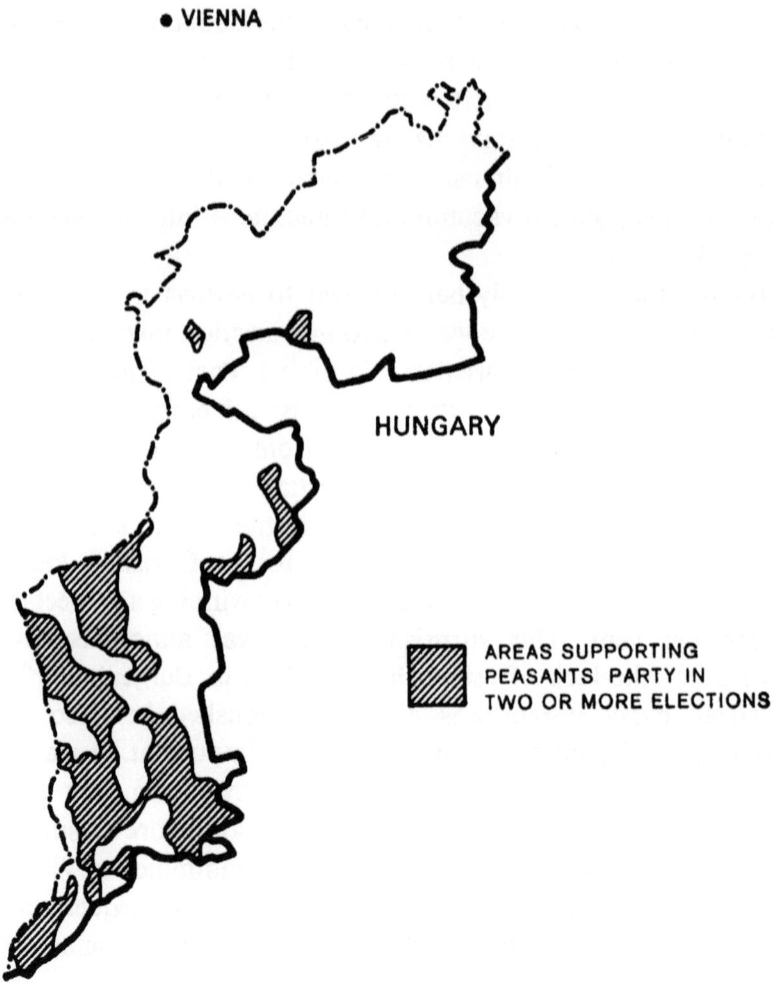

Figure 3.5 **Peasants' Party support in Burgenland, Austria, 1922–30**

more remote valleys, some of which had no direct communications with the rest of Austria at the time of the transfer in 1921. However, by 1926 a railway had been completed through to Vienna and bus routes established. Burghardt (1964) notes that on several occasions as valleys were linked into the rest of the province and Austria, their voting pattern changed from Peasants' to Christian Party. The process suggested is a mixture of Christian Party organization based on the new communications, plus the voters being more receptive to national appeal as they became more closely connected to the national economic life. The Peasants' Party did not completely disappear however. Their support was based on isolated Catholic peasants, plus the minority Lutherans. Whereas the Catholic peasants could be mobilized into Christian Party voters, this was not true of Lutheran peasants who would support neither Catholic (Christian) nor Socialist Parties. Hence, by 1930, when the last interwar election was held, the province was by no means totally mobilized into the Austrian party system. The Christian Party's level of support had increased to forty-one per cent, but it still did not dominate the Socialists (thirty-eight per cent) in this 'natural' Christian Party province, largely because of the Peasants' Party stubbornly holding on to its more peripheral support.

Mobilization of American peripheries

Like Norway, the U.S.A. has had two major peripheries. The most distinctive in political terms has been the southern periphery with its long history of conflict with the industria core of the north (Figure 3.3 p. 128). America's second periphery can be found in the west. This periphery is usually referred to as the American frontier and is associated with the writings of Frederick Jackson Turner (1920). In an idealized account of the frontier, Turner emphasized the influence of the gradual advance of American settlement westwards on American culture and institutions. In the hundred years to 1890, American society was continually incorporating new zones of settlement, first, as the frontier passed through the Appalachians, and later, as it crossed the Mississippi to the modern west. Turner argued that the frontier was a great 'seedbed' for the growth of American democracy (Mikesell, 1960), and Gould (1969) has shown how various electoral reforms such as women's suffrage began in the west and spread eastwards. There has been much debate over Turner's frontier hypothesis which need not concern us here. What we are interested in is the fact that there was a zone of the U.S.A. for a hundred years or so in which established party loyalties were missing. It was part of the task of the 'eastern' parties to mobilize this frontier into the American political system. This they managed to do by 1924, but not before some minor deviations had appeared only to die away.

The earliest indications of distinctive 'frontier' voting came with the ratification of the new federal Constitution from 1787 to 1790 (Fifer, 1976). The distribution of support for and against the federal system is shown in Figure 3.6. Although all thirteen states ratified the new constitution, support was not unanimous everywhere. Although the support for federalism was based upon complicated socio-economic considerations (Fifer, 1976), the spatial pattern of the support does suggest spatial influences of the sort associated with the periphery. Federal sympathies were strongest in the cities, the tidewater settlements and in the more accessible regions. Fifer (1976 p. 468) notes that 'the valleys of the Connecticut, Lower Hudson, Delaware, Potomac, Shenandoah and Savannah became important diffusion paths extending federal sympathies into the interior'. It was clearly in the less accessible rural zones of the early frontier that the anti-federalists obtained most support. This distinctive separate response of the frontier was to be repeated a hundred years later in other regions of the U.S.A.

All American party systems have been two-party affairs. However, at various times there have been minor third parties which have made some progress without being able to enter the political system fully. These parties have appealed to sections of the population who feel that their grievances are not being expressed through the existing political parties. We shall consider two examples here which relate directly to the increasing industrializa-

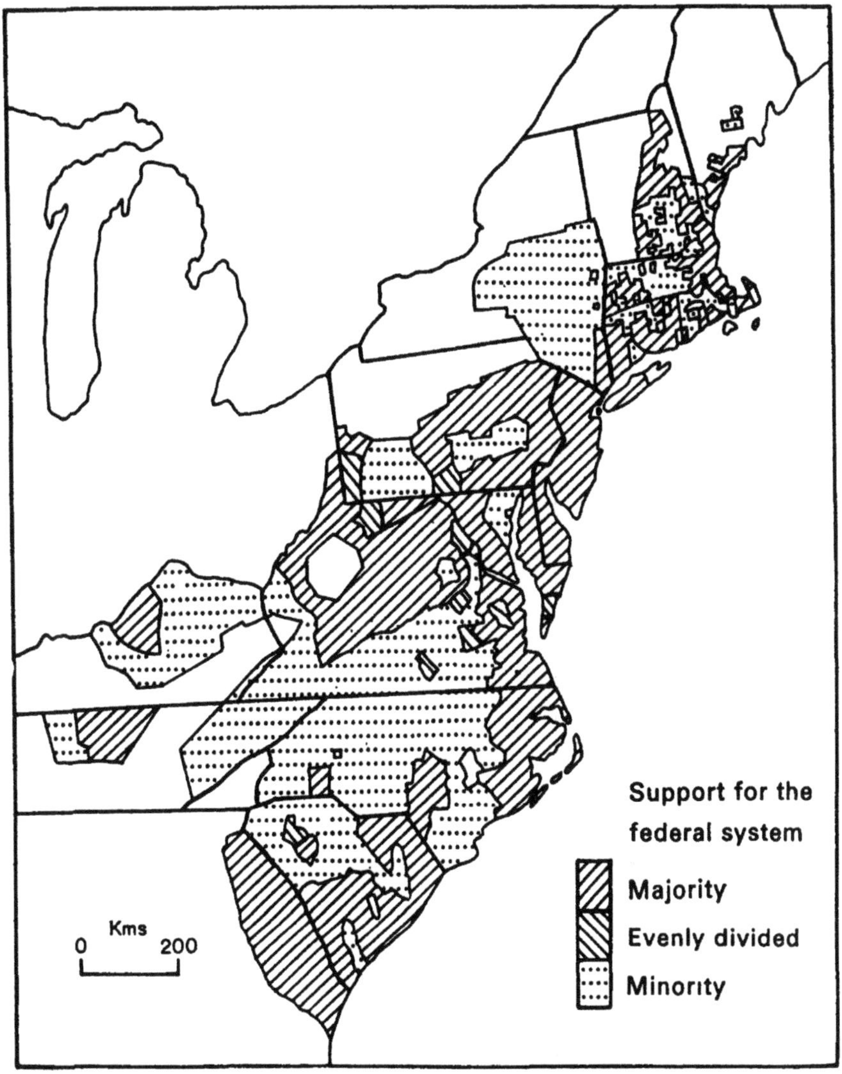

Figure 3.6 Pattern of support for the Federal Constitution, U.S.A., 1787–90

tion of the late nineteenth and early twentieth centuries. Both examples reflect Rokkan's two conflicts emanating from industrialization. Conflict in the commodity market produced an agrarian party, the Populists, for a short time, while conflict in the labour market led to the rise of a socialist third party. In both cases the major areas of state support were in the west, where established party loyalties were weakest, despite the fact that the conflicts represented by the parties were at least equally relevant in the south for the rural party and in the north for the socialist party.

In the presidential election of 1892 the Populists won over a million votes, consisting of eight and a half per cent of the total (Petersen, 1968). This was an extraordinary achievement for a completely new party although they were able to build upon a similar rural protest, the Greenback vote of 1880, which had recorded three per cent of the total vote. These were essentially protests by the primary production sector in the periphery (Wright, 1974). The classic interpretation by Hicks (1931) is of Popularism as the natural culmination of the frontier experience. The Populists were reacting against the new industrial system as they attempted to win a better deal for the small farmer in the new economic order. The old frontier zones were the periphery of the American state in both geographical and economic terms. As areas of recent settlement they had not been fully mobilized by the main parties. They had few established traditions or established elites to inhibit third-party development. In 1892 many of these areas were mobilized, not by the main parties, but by the Populists in a massive rural protest movement.

Figure 3.7 shows the distribution of the Populist vote in 1892 by states. Notice that four trans-Missouri states actually recorded Populist majorities. In fact if we extend the line of the Missouri north to the Dakotas and south to Texas we produce the main boundary of Populist support. This is the party of the recent frontier *par excellence*. In fact, by far the lowest western Populist vote occurred in California, which by 1892 was the longest settled and was quite urban in character (Rogin and Shover, 1969). Elsewhere the Populists won appreciable support in the south, especially around Alabama. However in the north their support was negligible.

The Populist success was clearly the result of America's western periphery in the late nineteenth century refusing to be fully mobilized into the existing party system dominated by northern industrial Republicans and southern Democrats. In 1896 they

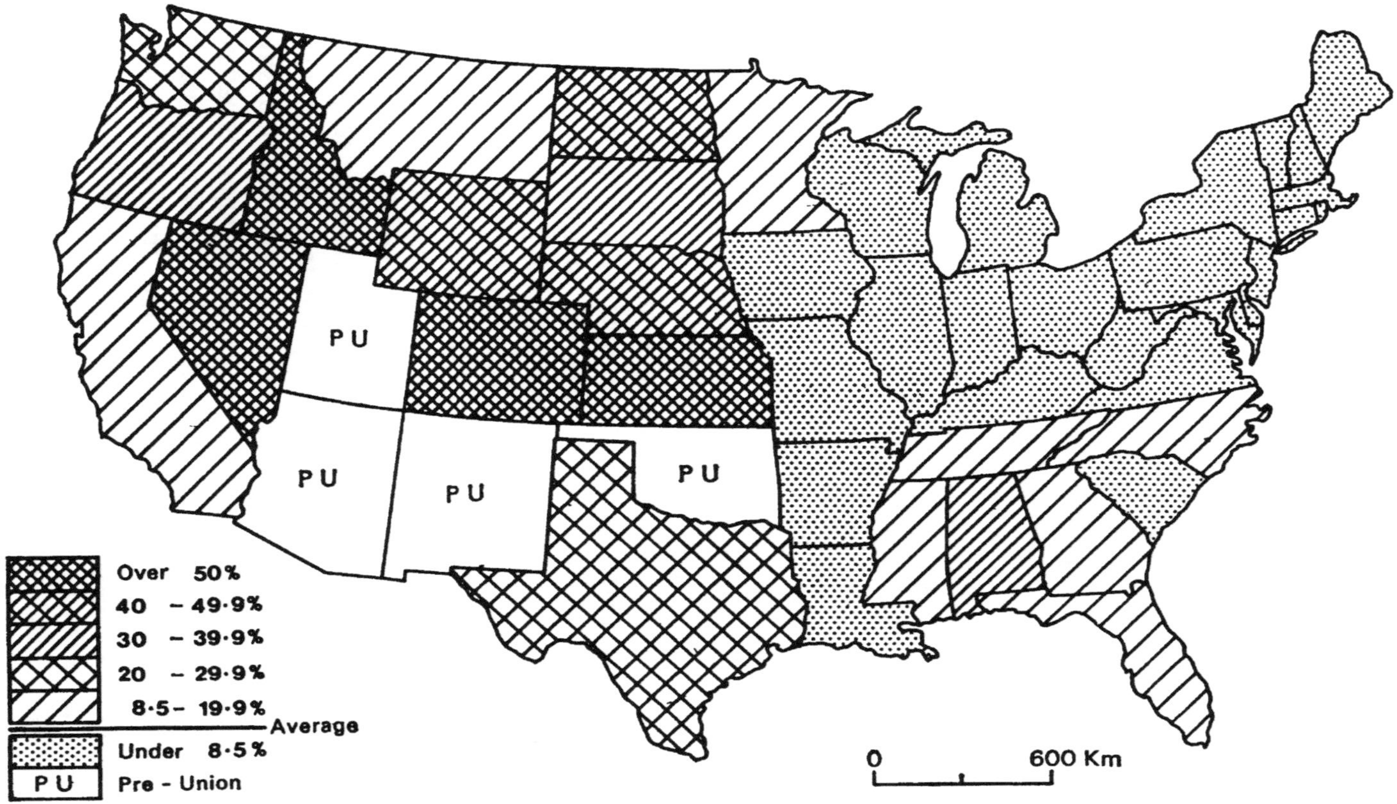

Figure 3.7 Voting pattern for the Populist presidential candidate, 1892

supported the Democratic candidate and largely fused with the Democrats. Their mobilization into the national party system at this point was to little effect, since the 1896 election was the critical one which established Republican dominance in the third of the American party systems. The Democrats' alliance with the Populists resulted in the party losing its northern supporters. The periphery became mobilized into the losing side.

In 1901 the Socialist Party of America was organized. This was just one year after the establishment of the British Labour Party and it is worth comparing their early fortunes. By 1912 the Socialist presidential candidate was winning nearly a million votes, six per cent of the total (Peterson, 1968). This performance is as good as the British Labour Party's early electoral history. At its peak the American Socialist Party had 118,000 members and had 1200 public officials elected across America. By 1922 they hardly existed, whereas the British Labour Party had become the official opposition and were within one year of forming their first government. Let us consider the American party in the light of this rather massive contrast in fortunes.

Many explanations of the lack of a major socialist party in America suggest that socialism is incompatible with the American way of life, or, at least, is less attractive to the more affluent American voter. Such arguments do not do full justice to the electoral achievements of the Socialist Party of America. Figure 3.8 shows the pattern of their vote in 1912. They managed to win support in the periphery, particularly the far west as well as in the industrial states. In this case they won some of the Populist support outside the south and combined it with some support in industrial states of the north. This represents a mobilization of primary voters (lumbermen and small farmers) and industrial workers. In Oklahoma, for instance, the earlier Populists had not allied with the Democrats in 1896 and many Populists formed the basis of the Socialist organization in the state. By 1912 Oklahoma was a major Socialist centre with 12,000 members in 961 branches (Weinstein, 1967). However, notice that even here levels of support nowhere reach the heights of Populist success in 1892 (Figure 3.7). Socialist strength was, however, far more evenly spread

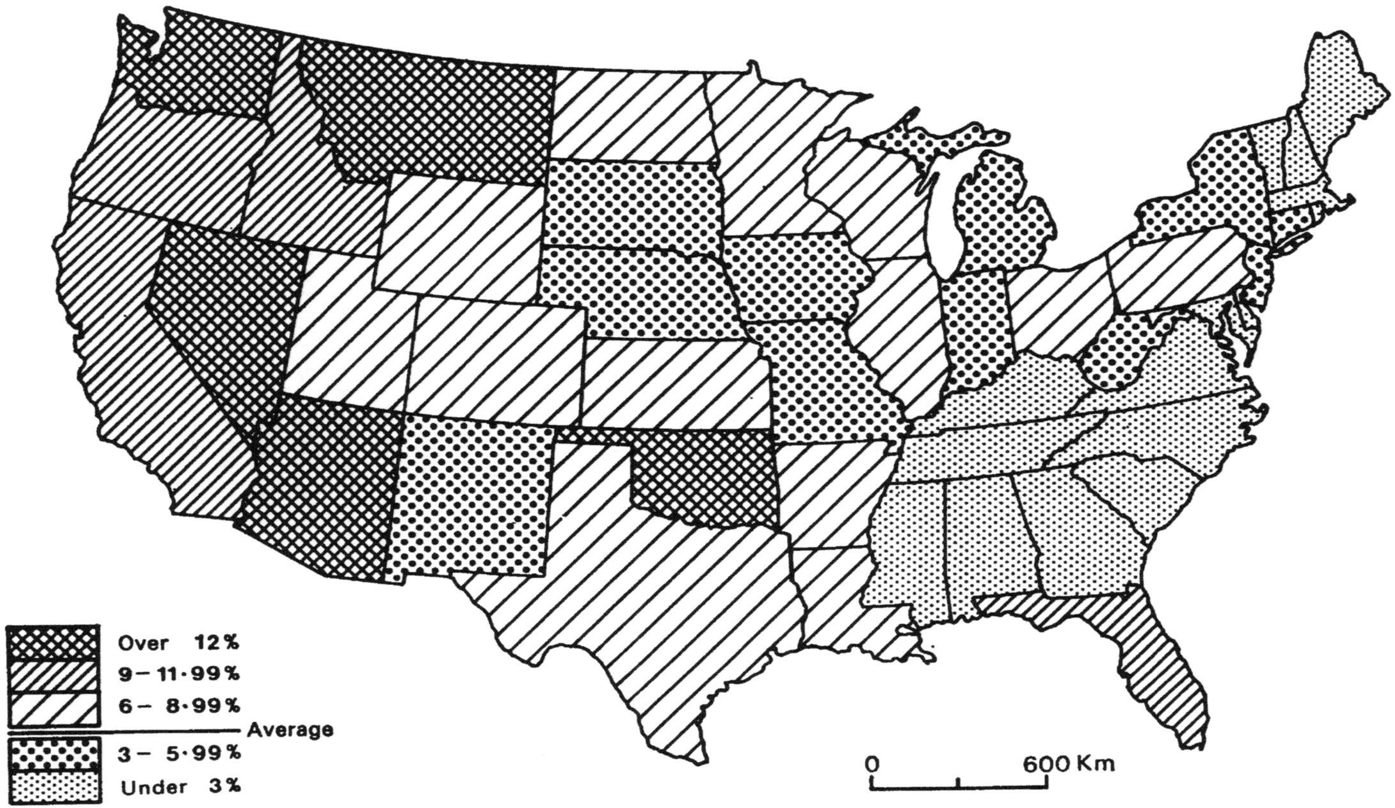

Figure 3.8 Voting pattern for the Socialist presidential candidate, 1912

among states, although they failed to make any impression on the south and New England.

Figure 3.8 emphasizes the western support for the party, although the industrial east played a far more important role in the growth of socialism than the 1912 election suggests. If we briefly turn to local government elections, we find that Socialist success in electing mayors and other major municipal officers illustrates this point. Between 1910 and 1920, for instance, Socialists became mayors in 32 Ohio towns, 19 Illinois towns, 13 Minnesota towns and in 12 towns in Wisconsin and Pennsylvania (Weinstein, 1967).

This list is quite impressive and largely reflects the massive successes of the Socialist Party as the only anti-war party after Wilson's Democrats changed their minds – 1917 was a year of very rapid Socialist successes, with the party regularly winning between thirty per cent and fifty per cent of the vote in local elections. In Chicago, for instance, the Socialist candidate won thirty-four per cent of the vote for mayor and was only overwhelmingly defeated because the Republicans and Democrats had united into a single anti-Socialist coalition. In fact the size of the Socialist vote led the Chicago Democrat leader to propose a national Republican-Democrat amalgamation to combat the new party (Weinstein, 1967, p. 157–8). Quite simply, as the New York *Evening Post* commented after a high Socialist vote in the city, 'The Socialists have won admission, as it were, to the family of political parties' (Weinstein, 1967, p. 159).

In 1917 it would seem that America had a three-party system with the Socialists as one of the main parties. At this stage they certainly were keeping up with their Labour comrades in Britain. However, they had no national successes, with only one congressman in Washington at any one time. There were no national elections in 1917. By 1920 they had lost momentum, partly due to persecution resulting from their anti-war stance. In 1917, for instance, the Oklahoma Socialist Party dissolved itself after threats of persecution. In 1919 a three-way split in the party helped its decline. In any case, the American Socialist Party never developed a concentrated core of support equivalent to Labour's coalfield strongholds in Britain. Hence, despite comparable support levels, the American Socialists never won the same representation at the national level as their Labour comrades (see Chapter 8). Nevertheless, in the 1920 presidential election the party's candidate conducted his campaign from gaol and again won nearly a million votes. This was a swan-song however. The high levels of support of 1917 were never regained and large numbers of the urban working class remained outside the political system until partially mobilized by the New Deal Democrats in 1932.

Hence, we can conclude that, unlike the south, the western periphery and the industrial inner city 'periphery' have not had any major lasting effect on the American party system. At times they still seem to be outsiders in the perennial north-south struggle. This was true of the 1976 presidential race where the Democrats took all the south (except Virginia) and enough of the north to win a majority of electoral college votes even before the largest state in the Union, California, declared its results. California voters might just as well have stayed at home, as in fact very many voters did across the country. The fifty-seven per cent turnout for the election was high by recent American standards but still represents a very low poll on a world-wide comparison. Compared with Figure 3.4 (p. 132), for instance, American mobilization in 1976 was only about equivalent to Norwegian rural areas at the beginning of the century. There still seems to be a large periphery, somewhere in American political life, available for mobilization. It is probably in this aspect that the American political system is most distinctive among western countries, rather than the nature of its political parties and the bases of their support.

The Distribution of Party Voters

The core-periphery dimension in Rokkan's framework is of particular interest to geographers since it closely relates to other topics in geography concerning the concept of accessibility and the spatial diffusion of ideas (Abler, Adams and Gould, 1971).

The geography of voting, however, is concerned with more than merely geographical manifestations of peripheries in voting patterns. Most voting in modern elections does not reflect a distinctive territorial cleavage but relates instead to the functional cleavages that Rokkan identifies. Such voting patterns are of no less interest in the geography of voting and they form most of the subject matter of the next chapter. Before we turn to correlates of voting patterns, however, we will briefly consider different patterns of voting that relate to Rokkan's alternative cleavages.

Voting patterns can be viewed in terms of the degree of spatial concentration in a party's support (Cox, 1969). At one extreme we can envisage a 'checker-board pattern' with an evenly mixed distribution of a party's supporters neatly alternating with a rival party's supporters across all parts of the country. At the other extreme the supporters of one party are completely restricted to just one part of the country. All actual patterns of party support can be arranged on a continuum of varying degrees of spatial segregation between these two extremes.

Figure 3.9 shows three hypothetical geographies of voting which correspond to the stages in the evolution of national voting patterns identified by Cox (undated). Figure 3.9(a) shows the territorial phase with a core–periphery pattern of votes producing segregation between supporters of different parties. In Figure 3.9(b) the first functional phase produces far less segregation of voters, since the cleavage is less explicitly territorial in nature. This may relate to the urban–rural cleavage in Rokkan's scheme. Finally, in Figure 3.9(c) a second functional phase produces party voters who are far more integrated, although segregation may still exist at a very small scale. This is the type of pattern we expect from class-based cleavages, where the voting pattern will only reflect different local residential areas.

As noted in Chapter 2, no countries report individual voting records, so that these geographies of voting are only made available as aggregate voting records for some given set of areal units. Analysis of voting patterns is therefore dependent on the areal units employed. Gross patterns may be studied by using large regions, as in the factor analysis example in Chapter 2 which

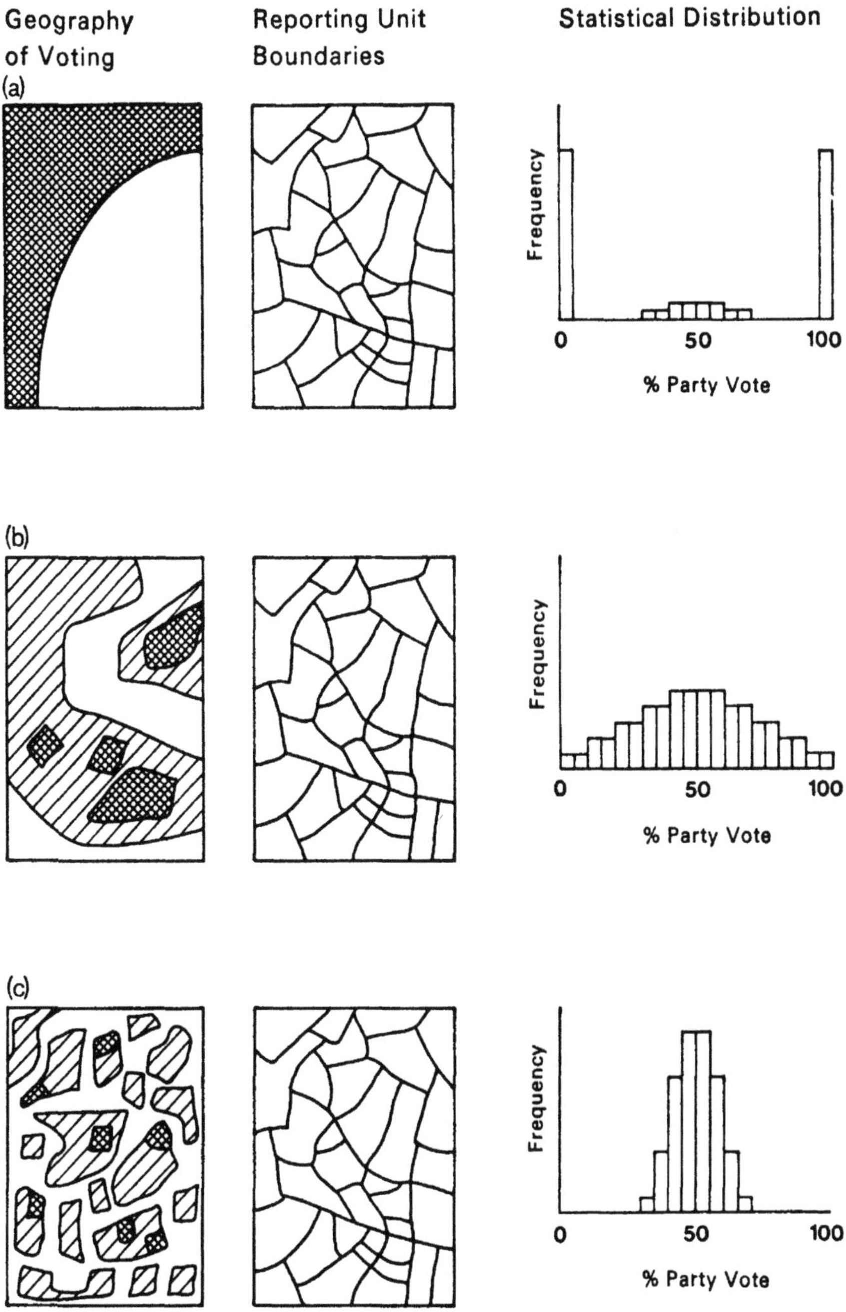

Figure 3.9 Geographies of voting and statistical distributions

employed U.S. census divisions; the fine details of a voting map may be studied by utilizing small areal units such as city precincts. Such detailed data are usually required to identify the geographical influences on voting which we describe in Part III. In Britain, most analysis occurs at the constituency level because this is the smallest unit for which data are made available. This scale is also important because it is the level of aggregation at which seats are won and lost. Hence this is the scale of analysis employed in our consideration of the geography of representation in Part IV.

The areal units used in an analysis of voting can be arrayed in terms of their frequency of occurrence at different levels of party support. In Figure 3.9(a), for instance, most areal units record either zero per cent or a hundred per cent votes for the party, while a few straddle the core–periphery voting boundary and hence produce levels of support between zero per cent and a hundred per cent. Such mixed areal units at this stage are rare, however, and the main feature of the statistical distribution of the frequencies is its U-shaped nature. As the geography of voting becomes less segregated, more areal units become of the mixed type, with their boundaries straddling the more complicated pattern of voting boundaries. In Figure 3.9(b) and (c) we find that the decreasing segregation is reflected by increasing numbers of areal units falling in the middle of the range of possible vote proportions. In fact the 'spread' of the frequency distribution about the mean vote for the party in these statistical distributions may be used as a measure of the segregation of the party voters *at the scale of the areal units being used.* Obviously the larger the areal units used, the more mixing of party voters is recorded and hence the statistical distribution is less spread out. In Britain, for instance, we would expect the spread of the Labour vote to be much greater over the 623 constituencies than over the twelve standard regions, on a much larger scale.

The usual measures of spread in a statistical distribution are called the *variance* and the *standard deviation.* The variance is simply the average squared deviation of the areal units (constituencies, regions etc.) from their mean value, the average vote. In a simple two-region example where a territorially-based party wins all the votes in one region and none in the other, then the two deviations from its average vote of fifty per cent are each 50, giving a variance of $(50^2+50^2)\div 2 = 2500$. The standard deviation is the square root of the variance, which in this case is 50. With a distribution of percentage values such as we are dealing with here, 50 is the maximum standard deviation and represents total separation of party supporters. If both regions had identical percentages of party voters, fifty per cent in each region, then there are no deviations from the average vote so that both variance and standard deviation are zero. This is obviously the minimum value and corresponds to total integration of party votes at the scale of the areal units of observation. It is possible, of course, to have very little variation between large regions concealing large differences between individual constituencies within them. In the final sections of this chapter we use standard deviations to monitor changing levels of segregation between party voters and we employ techniques based on the variance to monitor changes in voting patterns at different scales.

The nationalization of party voting

The evolution of party systems described in previous sections, and the stages in the development of national patterns of party support which we have presented in Figure 3.9 both imply a reduction in territorial or place-specific voting. As core–periphery cleavages give way to functional cleavages 'they produce alliances of ... similarly orientated subjects and households over wide ranges of localities and tend to undermine the inherited solidarity of the established territorial communities' (Lipset and Rokkan, 1967, p. 10). This development should be reflected in decreasing measures of spread of a party's statistical distributions, particularly at a regional scale. (Stokes (1967) and Cox (undated) term this process the *nationalization* of party voting.)

Rose and Urwin (1975) have used the standard deviation of regional percentages of party votes for all parties listed in the seventeen countries in Table 3.1 (p. 110) to assess the degree to which a nationalization of party voting has occurred since 1945.

For each country they measure the standard deviation of each party's vote over regions in the country for the two national elections nearest to 1945 and 1970. The 'regions' used range in number from the states of the U.S.A. (48 in 1945, 50 in 1970), to just five units, the four provinces plus Dublin, in Ireland. Other regions used are the standard regions for the United Kingdom, Australian states, Canadian provinces, Norwegian counties and German Länder. We will return to the obvious variations in regional size between countries when we interpret Rose and Urwin's results.

Before we consider the set of standard deviations that Rose and Urwin produce, we should note, with them, a particular limitation of the measure. Because the standard deviation is computed from deviations from the party's mean vote, small parties with low overall levels of support are likely to record only small deviations in most regions. Consider a distinctive regional party which obtains *all* of its support in one of two regions but is only a minor party even in its own region. Suppose its overall mean vote is five per cent made up of ten per cent in its region and zero per cent in the other region. Such a party has a standard deviation of 5, which is very small compared with a maximum of 50, especially considering the party is totally regional in its support.

This property of the standard deviation, of being related to the mean, occurs in many fields and there are numerous statistical methods of overcoming the problem. Rose and Urwin (1975) choose to employ a simple measure which they term the *cumulative regional inequality index*. This is obtained by computing the difference between the percentage of a party's vote in a region and the percentage of total voters in the region. All such differences are summed and divided by two to produce the index. In our hypothetical example above, for example, if both regions have the same numbers of voters, then, since the party wins all its votes in one region, the differences are (100–50) and (50–0) which sum to 100 to give a cumulative regional inequality index of fifty per cent. Clearly, the larger the index the more regional the basis of a party's support, irrespective of its overall level of support. We can illustrate the use of this index in the context of the breakdown of America's first party system before the Civil War, using states as our areal units. We have previously noted (Figure 3.3 p. 128) that the Whig/Democrat contests were not regionally based and this is shown in Table 3.6 with indices of only 4 and 3

Table 3.6 The eruption of regional voting in America

Parties	*Cumulative regional inequality*		
	1852	1856	1860
Whig	4	—	—
Democrat	3	9	27
Republican	—	29	26
American	—	30	—
Democratic (southern)	—	—	53
Constitutional Union	—	—	60

Source: Rose and Urwin (1975)

in 1852. In 1856 and 1860 the Whigs disappear, the Democrat index rises to 27 and three other regionally based parties emerge. In this case the result was the Civil War.

Rose and Urwin (1975) have used both the standard deviation, and the index of cumulative regional inequality, to assess the changing regional bases of the parties from the seventeen countries listed in Table 3.1. Their results are set out in Table 3.7. In general, as we would expect, levels of regional voting are relatively low. This presumably reflects the predominance of functional cleavages in modern elections. There are wide variations between countries, however. Among the Anglo-American countries, Canada has higher levels of regionally-based party support, in Scandinavia the highest levels are found in Norway and Finland and in the other European countries the Netherlands and Switzerland stand out as having high levels of regional voting. Whereas such findings are quite consistent with other studies of these countries, we must be careful in interpreting these results, because the regions used for different countries are themselves different in scale between countries. Hence cross-national comparisons are not strictly legitimate.

Table 3.7 Regional differences of political parties

Country	Party	Standard deviation c. 1945	Standard deviation c. 1970	Cumulative regional inequality c. 1945	Cumulative regional inequality c. 1970
(A) *Anglo-American Countries*					
Britain	Labour	12·1	11·1	7	7
	Conservative	6·7	7·4	5	6
	Liberal	4·5	3·4	15	16
U.S.A.	Democrat	19·9	10·2	4	6
	Republican	20·7	10·4	4	6
Canada	New Democrats/ C.C.F.	13·2	11·4	28	25
	Liberal	9·9	8·0	8	7
	Progressive Con.	12·0	11·1	23	15
Australia	Labor	4·5	4·3	4	25
	Dem. Labor	—	1·6	—	17
	Liberal	8·2	5·3	8	6
	Country	7·5	6·3	16	17
New Zealand	Labour	5·7	6·0	3	4
	Social Credit	—	4·0	—	12
	National	5·7	3·6	5	4
Ireland	Labour	5·9	8·4	16	18
	Fianna Fail	3·0	4·0	2	3
	Fine Gael	6·0	5·2	8	10
(B) *Scandinavian Countries*					
Norway	Labour	8·6	8·7	7	7
	Liberal	8·6	5·2	27	23
	Agrarian (Centre)	5·9	6·8	27	33
	Conservative	7·3	7·2	20	19
Sweden	Social Democrat	6·2	5·6	6	5
	Liberal	4·8	4·3	14	12
	Agrarian (Centre)	7·9	5·9	21	12
	Conservative	4·1	3·0	12	13
Denmark	Social Democrat	5·2	4·3	7	4
	Radical	4·5	2·5	21	6
	Conservative	5·7	4·0	19	10
Finland	Communist	5·3	6·2	13	26
	Social Democrat	6·6	7·3	10	12
	Liberal	2·4	2·2	17	18
	Agrarian (Centre)	12·1	7·8	27	27
	National Coalition	2·4	4·9	10	12

Table 3.7 – cont.

Country	*Party*	*Standard deviation* c. 1945	*Standard deviation* c. 1970	*Cumulative regional inequality* c. 1945	*Cumulative regional inequality* c. 1970
(C) *Other European Countries*					
Germany	Social Democrat	4·9	5·9	7	5
	Free Democrat	6·4	1·6	21	7
	Christian Democrat	10·5	6·9	12	6
France	Communist	6·9	6·3	4	13
	Socialist	4·2	4·8	11	11
	Gaullist	—	6·2	—	7
	Christian Democrat (M.R.P.)	9·4	—	13	—
Austria	Socialist	9·0	6·9	8	5
	Peoples (O.V.P.)	9·5	5·8	7	6
Italy	Communist	8·9	8·6	20	11
	Socialist	7·9	1·9	19	8
	Liberal	6·4	1·5	34	17
	Christian Democrat	8·0	10·1	7	6
Belgium	Socialist	9·8	7·2	8	11
	Liberal	1·9	4·9	5	8
	Christian Social	16·2	10·0	16	14
Netherlands	Socialist	8·6	6·5	10	9
	Liberal	4·1	2·6	18	10
	Catholic	24·8	16·0	27	26
	Christian Historical	5·1	3·7	24	22
Switzerland	Social Democrat	11·9	7·8	17	13
	Radical	15·0	7·3	17	13
	Catholic Conservative	28·9	17·8	36	35

Source: Rose and Urwin (1975)

Comparisons between 1945 and 1970 *within* countries are possible, however. In most countries there has been little change in the level of regional voting. Examples of reduced regional voting are more common than examples of increased regional voting, but usually the effect is small. Denmark, Germany and Italy seem to show definite signs of a trend towards elimination of regional voting and both Canada and the Netherlands, while maintaining regional bases to their voting patterns, do show evidence of some reduction. In contrast Finland is the only country where the statistics suggest increasing regional differences.

How can we interpret Rose and Urwin's results in the light of our previous discussion? The trend towards nationalization of party support is not a widely apparent force in the period since 1945. The main reason for this is that the breakdown of most regional voting in the countries analysed occurred before 1945. Rose and Urwin's findings can therefore be interpreted as illustrating the final stages of a nationalization process that had been largely completed by 1945. We should not fall into the trap of assuming that all regional voting will gradually disappear, however. Nationalization of the voting pattern has had only partial success in countries such as Canada where regional voting remains a major element of the party system (Campbell and Knight, 1975). Even in other countries, regional voting shows no sign of dying but may even be increasing, as in Finland. Table 3.7 is only based on the major parties listed in Table 3.1 (p. 110). Regionally based parties do exist which are not considered in Table 3.7 and these are shown in Table 3.8. All the parties in the table show extremely high levels of regional voting and they represent important territorial/cultural cleavages which remain as elements of the party system in the countries concerned.

Table 3.8 Regional differences and regional parties

		Standard deviation		*Cumulative regional inequality*	
Country	*Party*	*c.* 1945	*c.* 1970	*c.* 1945	*c.* 1970
Britain	Scottish Nat.	—	3·2	—	90
	Plaid Cymru	—	3·2	—	95
Canada	Social Credit	11·0	7·0	49	59
Norway	Christian People's	9·0	5·4	42	27
Finland	Swedish People's	8·0	6·9	54	58
Belgium	Volksunie	—	8·6	—	35
	Flemish Democratic	—	10·7	—	48

Source: Rose and Urwin (1975)

It seems that we need a longer time period than that since 1945 in order to monitor the nationalization of party support in most countries. Cox (undated) has done this for U.S.A. using presidential voting data for 1912 to 1964. Table 3.9 shows standard

Table 3.9 Nationalization of the Democrat presidential vote 1912–64

	Standard deviations	
Election series	*U.S. states*	*Iowa-Illinois-Indiana counties*
1912–28	15·6	9·4
1916–32	15·0	8·5
1920–36	14·7	7·6
1924–40	14·0	6·4
1928–44	12·2	5·9
1932–48	9·5	6·1
1936–52	8·4	6·3
1940–56	7·3	6·5
1944–60	5·7	6·3
1948–64	5·3	6·2

Source: Derived from Cox (undated)

deviations of the vote for the Democrat candidates for states and for counties within Iowa-Illinois-Indiana. Each row contains the mean vote for states or counties over the five elections in the years indicated. The first row, for instance, refers to variations in average state or county votes for the elections of 1912, 1916, 1920, 1924 and 1928. In contrast to Rose and Urwin's results, these standard deviations show a clear decline, especially at the state level, as the Democrat vote has become more nationalized. These data straddle the 1928–32 critical elections discussed previously and the results reflect the rising fortunes of the Democrats in the northern states at the national scale and also in the urban regions at the county scale after 1928. Cox's findings are entirely consistent with our previous discussion of the New Deal party system which, in effect, nationalized the Democratic party vote.

The nationalization of electoral swing

The changes brought about by the nationalization of party voting culminate in nation-level parties competing for support across the country. Electoral contests become essentially national events. This is reflected in some countries by the phenomenon of the uniform swing.

Electoral swing is a simple measure of change from one election to another. In a two-party situation it simply represents the percentage change in each party's vote as their fortunes fluctuate in unison. If in a particular constituency two parties win sixty per cent and forty per cent of the vote respectively at the first election and fifty-five per cent and forty-five per cent at the second election, we would identify a swing of five per cent against the leading party. Such swings can be computed where there are more than two parties but these produce different percentage changes in the vote for each party. This is not normally a problem in American elections with its predominance of two-party contests and in British elections where there are more than two parties in the contest the average percentage swing is used as a measure of change between the two main parties.

If elections are truly national contests then we might expect similar voting changes over all regions. This is typically found in British elections but is less evident in American elections. Stokes (1965, 1967) has been concerned to measure these differences by identifying separate components in the swings recorded at constituency level. A totally uniform swing over all constituencies would mean that every constituency would swing the same as the national average. The variance of constituency swings would be zero. This would reflect a complete nationalization of forces producing electoral change. If, on the other hand, forces producing change were solely local, every constituency would have a different swing and the variance of the constituency swing about the national average would be relatively high. In between these two scales we can envisage other influences of a regional nature where constituencies in a single region 'swing together'.

Stokes (1965, 1967) has attempted to measure these hypothesized influences on constituency swings by employing a technique known as *analysis of variance.* He states that the total variance of swing in the ith constituency of the jth region [$Var(s_{ij})$] can be calculated as

$$Var\ (s_{ij}) = Var(n) + Var\ (r_j) + Var\ (c_{ij})$$

where n is the overall common national component, r_j is the distinctive swing behaviour in region j and c_{ij} is the remaining specific variation in swing in the ith constituency of the region j. Formulae for computing the variance components are given in Stokes (1965). For our purposes here we can note that this technique allows us to assess the relative importance of the three geographical scales on the patterns of voting change.

Stokes (1967) has applied this approach to the five congressional elections in the U.S.A. from 1952 to 1960 and to the six British general elections between 1950 and 1966. His results are shown in Table 3.10. In both countries the intermediate geographical scale, state and region, is the least important. Here the similarities stop, however. In the U.S. elections the most important influences were found to be at the constituency level, in Britain they were national level influences. This difference probably reflects, in part, the contrast in size of the two countries.

Table 3.10 Components of variance in electoral swings, U.S.A. and Britain

U.S.A. 1952–60			*Britain 1950–66*		
Geographical Scale	*Variance Component*	*% of total Variance*	*Geographical Scale*	*Variance Component*	*% of total Variance*
District	13·98	49	Constituency	4·45	40
State	5·32	19	Region	1·42	13
National	9·32	32	National	5·13	47

Source: Stokes (1967)

A national component of swing variance similar to Britain's has been found by Barnett (1973) in his studies of the Communist Party in Denmark. He uses Stokes's approach on a whole series of election triplets from 1920 to 1964 and the components are shown in Table 3.11. His results allow us to trace a changing

Table 3.11 Components of variance in the changing Communist vote, Denmark, 1920–64

Election series		*Geographical scale*	
	National	*Regional*	*Constituency*
1920–26	1·76	7·10	91·14
1924–29	3·16	19·72	77·12
1926–32	31·18	17·30	51·52
1929–35	42·64	6·92	50·44
1932–39	39·56	11·96	48·48
1935–45	65·12	12·32	22·56
1939–47	64·74	11·66	23·60
1945–50	67·70	9·38	25·92
1947–53	56·88	11·46	31·66
1950–57	51·84	13·90	34·26
1953–60	57·04	14·68	28·28
1957–64	55·36	13·44	31·20

Source: Barnett (1973)

pattern of scale components with the growth of party support. In the 1920s the party obtained less than one per cent of the vote and its support was dependent on small local influences. At the end of the war the party's resistance to the German occupation led to it achieving its highest ever vote of twelve per cent. This was a general national move towards Communism, not a local phenomenon, and this is reflected in the high national variance components for the three election triplets which include 1945. The subsequent decline of the Communist vote to two per cent in 1964 has also been a 'national' rejection of the party so that the importance of the national component has only been slightly reduced despite the massive fall in the absolute level of the vote.

Barnett's (1973) results suggest that Danish politics are more similar to Britain's than they are to the U.S.A.'s in terms of the influences on electoral change. The dominance of the national component in Britain will not surprise observers of British politics. In fact the only surprise is that the national component accounts for merely half of the variation in swings. In another study of British electoral change using an alternative approach a very different result has been found.

Green (1972) has employed a factor-analysis approach (p. 88) to the problem of identifying different scale influences. Using ward-election statistics for two British cities, Leeds and Sheffield, wards have been correlated with one another in terms of their swing to and from Labour for council elections between 1951 and 1966. Two wards which always swing in a similar manner will record a high common correlation. If all wards in both cities tend to swing together this can be interpreted as the national pattern of swing and will be represented by the first factor in a factor analysis. Such a factor reflects the most common pattern in swing over all wards. A city-scale influence on swing, on the other hand, should be reflected by two separate patterns of swing, one for wards in Leeds and another for Sheffield's wards. Any local influences should relate only to particular wards. Green's results are shown on Table 3.12. Clearly, the first factor dominates the

Table 3.12 A factor analysis of swings in Leeds and Sheffield, 1951–66

Factor	*Proportion of Variance*	*Range for Leeds*	*Range for Sheffield*
1	73·25	0·112 to 0·165	0·102 to 0·167
2	6·12	(−0·066) to 0·260	(−0·399) to 0·073
3	4·44	(−0·394) to 0·258	(−0·102) to 0·287

Source: Green (1972)

swings, accounting for nearly three-quarters of all the variation. The range of factor loadings enables us to interpret this as a national component, since all wards have similar loadings in both cities. In contrast the second factor reflects separate patterns for each city, with Leeds having nearly all positive loadings and Sheffield having negative loadings in all but one ward. This city-scale factor only accounts for six per cent of the total variation and is therefore insignificant compared with the national-scale factor. Finally, the third factor is one which has a wider variety of loadings than factor one, but shows no separate city pattern. This is the first of several factors which reflect different local patterns of swing. Such factors are of even less importance than the city-scale factor.

Using a factor-analytic approach, Green has been able to find a much higher level of national influences on British voting changes than Stokes was able to find using national election swings. This paradoxical difference in findings is almost certainly because of their using different approaches for identifying influences at different geographical scales. The implication of this situation is that, despite quite sophisticated quantitative analysis, we still cannot satisfactorily separate out different scale components.

Katz (1974) has been particularly critical of Stokes's approach for identifying different scale components in swings. He argues that since each constituency or district has a different mixture of socio-economic groups, a national-scale influence will result in different swings in different constituencies. If the Democrats, for instance, pursue national policies which gain them additional support of union members across the country, this national swing will vary from district to district depending on the numbers of union members in each district. Stokes's model of nationalizing influences assures an equal force in each district; Katz's replaces this with a model that adds parameters to enable non-uniform influence at different scales to be measured. By concentrating on uniform swings, Katz argues that Stokes has under-estimated the nationalization of swing. He has reworked Stokes's data for the U.S.A. and finds that the proportion of variance attributable to the national level is 54·6 per cent compared with Stokes's estimate of thirty-two per cent. This change is compensated for by a district level variance component of only 26·2 per cent compared with Stokes's forty-nine per cent. Katz's approach clearly allocates more of swing variation to national forces than Stokes's original model. We may infer from this that Stokes's national component estimate of only forty-nine per cent of British swing variance would be found to be higher if Katz's approach were employed on the data.

The nationalization of electoral change is not easy to measure. The evidence we have presented, however, does suggest that it is greater in Britain than in the U.S.A. and that in both countries it is an important component in swing variance. Certainly it is more important than intermediate geographical scales – state, region, city – in all the analyses we have presented. There are very many remaining problems associated with electoral swing and its spatial pattern which are beyond the scope of this book (Berrington, 1964; Maclean 1973). In particular, it is not clear why a relatively uniform pattern of swing is produced in Britain, given the wide variety of socio-economic compositions of British constituencies. We return to this question in Chapter 5 where the uniform swing is interpreted as reflecting particular local geographical influences on elections.

4 Social Bases of Geographies of Voting

In this chapter we continue to employ Rokkan's model of party evolution as a framework for studying geographies of voting. This is because we continue to be interested in cross-national comparisons. In the last chapter this framework was used to make some sense out of election results from the American frontier to Austria's Burgenland. All the analyses in that chapter, however, were concerned with the voting data alone. Either the patterns of votes for single parties were used or else party votes were combined to form measures of polarization and turnout in the periphery studies. In this chapter we move on to consider the relationship of these voting patterns to a variety of social characteristics. These 'social bases' of voting will relate directly to the cleavages that Rokkan has identified plus the particular ethnic bases of much voting behaviour in North America.

We can illustrate the relationship between Rokkan's cleavages and voting behaviour by using the work of Lijphart (1971). He uses indices of voting behaviour originally devised by Alford (1963), which we can illustrate in terms of class voting. The strength of class voting in a country is found as follows. From survey data on voting and occupations we find that x per cent of the non-manual workers vote for the party of the left and y per cent of the manual workers similarly vote for the left party. The difference between these two percentages $(y-x)$ constitutes Alford's index of class voting. If voting is unrelated to class $x = y$ and the index is zero. If all manual workers vote left and all non-manual voters vote right then the index is a hundred per cent, which signifies 'pure' class voting. Most countries will score between zero and a hundred depending on their degree of class voting. (Notice that negative values are possible where more non-manual voters support left parties.) Similar indices can be derived for religious voting, in terms of church attenders voting for right-wing parties, and urban/rural voting, in terms of rural residents voting for right-wing parties. In both cases, if these criteria are independent of voting behaviour, indices of zero will result, otherwise the relative strength of these two factors within countries will be indicated.

These indices of religious, urban/rural and class voting correspond to Rokkan's three major cleavages that succeed the 'pure' territorial conflicts – the religion, commodity market and labour market conflicts respectively. Table 4.1 shows these three indices

Table 4.1 Cleavages and the social bases of voting *c.* 1960

Country	*Religion**	*Rural/urban*	*Class*
A. Anglo-American countries			
Britain	7	10	37
U.S.A.	16	11	20
Canada	22	—	8
Australia	14	—	33
B. Scandinavian countries			
Sweden	16	—8	53
Norway	21	2	46
Denmark	—	—	44
Finland	—	—	59
C. Other European countries			
France	59	11	15
Italy	51	12	19
West Germany	40	17	27
Netherlands	73	10	26
Belgium	72	7	25
Austria	54	22	31
Switzerland	59	—	26

Source: Lijphart (1971)

* Religious affiliation is used for Anglo-American countries and religious attendance for other countries.

of voting for a selection of countries. The size of the indices within each country indicates the relative importance of Rokkan's cleavages in modern voting behaviour. In all cases the rural/urban cleavage seems to be the least important. We may conclude that this economic conflict over the commodity market has largely given way to economic conflict over labour market issues. These class-based issues have not invariably superseded religious conflicts, however. Class-based voting only dominates the pattern of indices in Britain, Australia and the Scandinavian countries. In the U.S.A. and Canada no one index dominates. In the other European countries, in contrast, it is religious voting that dominates. This is particularly true of countries straddling Europe's Protestant/Catholic divide, such as the Netherlands and Switzerland, but religious voting also dominates in the Catholic countries. This suggests that instead of the most recent cleavage (labour market) superseding the earlier religious factor, in these countries religion remains the most important social basis of voting.

Table 4.1 illustrates how Rokkan's cleavages are reflected in voting behaviour. This forms the starting point to our investigations into the social bases of geographies of voting. It is only a starting point, however. Table 4.1 treats each factor separately whereas it is highly likely that cleavages interact to produce great variety in the social bases of voting. In particular, Rokkan's model implies differences *within* countries as well as between them. This was discussed in the last chapter in terms of spatial lags in mobilization. Regional variations within countries may be far more complex than such simple core–periphery patterns imply, however. Regional differences in voting behaviour can include much more than the standard, extreme cases such as the Irish, in British politics, Quebec voters, in Canadian politics, or the stubborn southerners who refuse to conform to the American party system. Even in a relatively integrated nation state, the voters' reactions to party labels may vary from one region to another. These differences may be related to economic or cultural differences. Sometimes they are distinctively geographical and relate to the contrasting political experiences of different regions as the national political parties evolved. Such situations can lead to subtle differences in geographies of voting for parties between regions. These differences may be just as important to their respective national elections as the aforementioned extreme cases. The major purpose of this chapter is to describe such regional differences in the social bases of voting.

A second purpose of the chapter is to illustrate the variety of types of data and analyses employed in modern electoral research. In Chapter 2 we distinguished between actual voting records and survey data, and commented on their respective limitations. In this chapter we illustrate the complementary uses of different types of data and analyses to supplement and substantiate findings. The results of such comprehensive studies are far more useful than any single analysis of a single source of data. Hence a secondary purpose of this chapter is to illustrate, where possible, the integration of alternative sources and analyses to produce a more reliable body of knowledge on the geography of voting.

The chapter is divided into three main sections based on the simple typology of countries employed in Tables 3.1 (p. 110) and 4.1. These three sets of countries do seem to display some consistent differences in terms of voting systems, political parties and voting behaviour and hence form convenient categories within which to describe social bases of geographies of voting. Within each section, however, we do not attempt a 'complete' geography of the voting – the sources are just not available. Instead we concentrate on themes which are particularly relevant to that set of countries and we treat each topic in some detail in just one or two countries. Since the cleavage framework that we use is most explicity associated with Scandinavian countries, we begin with this group of countries and the emphasis falls, inevitably, on Norway once again.

Scandinavian Countries

Scandinavian countries are the most homogeneous group of countries that we deal with. In Rokkan's typology they all conform to his Type II, in which a national-church–urban-economic alliance competes with a left coalition of landed interests, dissenters and urban radicals. The most distinctive legacy of this party system's development is the separation of urban conservatives from rural agrarian parties. Both of these interests now compete with socialist parties in modern elections. In fact Table 4.1 suggests that it is in Scandinavia where the fourth critical cleavage based on the labour market has been most successful in dominating the electoral situation. This is reflected in the high success rate of Labour and Social Democrat parties in Scandinavia. To dominate is not to eradicate, however. Old cleavages survive and in Scandinavia they are explicitly represented in the party system.

Scandinavia has become a major world centre for ecological/geographical electoral studies and we cannot possibly do justice to the whole range of work covering Scandinavian elections in this one section. Our strategy is to treat the Norwegian case in some detail because it relates directly to our framework in that the research reported is by Rokkan and his associates. We complement this example with a brief consideration of regional patterns of voting in Finland. Details of other survey and ecological analyses can be found in the journal *Scandinavian Political Studies*. For specific discussion of the Swedish and Danish party systems reference may be made to Sarlvik (1974) and Stehouwer (1967) respectively.

Cross-cutting cleavages in Norway

Opposition to central authority has been a fundamental theme in the evolution of the Norwegian party system (Rokkan, 1970). The first partisan election of 1882 was a direct right v. left confrontation with the king's government being challenged by an alliance of rural interests, urban radicals and dissenters. The result of the election was a victory for the left. This election contest incorporated four of the five major dimensions of conflict to be found in Norwegian politics:

(1) Territorial conflict. This centre v. periphery conflict has two geographical dimensions – north v. east and south; and west v. east, which are described in the previous chapter.

(2) Socio-cultural conflict. This involves the nationally orientated peasants versus the educated, European-orientated urban dwellers and is reflected in language disputes.

(3) Religious conflict. The secular, liberal urban population conflicts with the Lutheran rural population over such issues as prohibition.

(4) Commodity-market conflict. Rural land interests compete with urban business interests.

(5) Labour-market conflict. This conflict was not reflected in the 1882 election line-up since the working class was not mobilized until the twentieth century.

The present-day Norwegian party system reflects the interaction of these dimensions of conflict over almost a century of disputes and alignments. These conflicts may be located on Rokkan's schematic diagram of cleavages as shown on Figure 4.1. The specific location of each conflict is not precisely derived but merely represents Rokkan's personal view of the content of each conflict in terms of the dimensions of the grid. Nevertheless, the pattern on Figure 4.1 does illustrate the alternative alliances available for the development of political parties in Norway. The election of 1882 arrayed almost all mobilized forces of the time against the urban right. They were a mixture of geographical and cultural forces ranging from radicals through to agrarians. The subsequent history of the Norwegian party system largely consists of the break-up of this left coalition. The first split came along the religious cleavage as the orthodox fundamentalists of the south and west broke away to form the Moderates in 1888. However, this split became unimportant after the dissolution of the union with Sweden in 1905 when the left championed causes such as the defence of the rural language (*nynorsk*) and the protection of the young from alcohol. This kept the counter-culture v. centre socio-cultural conflict in operation for a generation or so. However splits on the economic axis soon occurred. A National Liberal party broke away in 1906, and was eventually incorporated into the Conservatives. This was an explicit attempt to produce an anti-socialist front. On the other wing of the party, a Workers Democrat party formed, although it was never able to

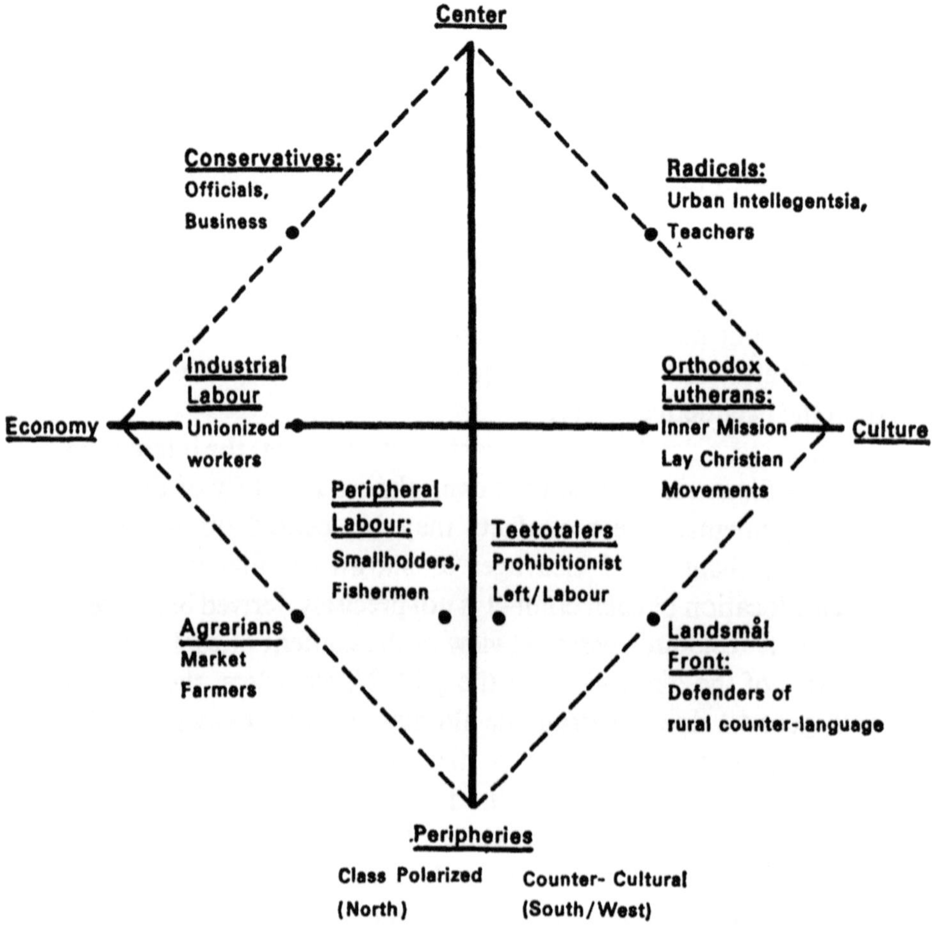

Figure 4.1 Political conflicts in Norway

compete with the new Labour party and soon disappeared. The united cultural front began to break up because of economic causes in 1917, with the organization of the Agrarian party. In 1933 the left was further split, again along the religious dimension, with the establishment of the Christian People's Party. Hence the old left has come down to us as three parties – Agrarian (since 1958 the Centre Party), Christian, and the remainder (including urban radicals) forming the modern Liberals. The old right has been converted from an establishment party, with little electoral appeal, into a party of urban business interests. The

Labour Party has emerged with the extension of the franchise. Although originally organized in the east, it had its first electoral successes in the northern periphery and has continued to include a major non-urban component in its support pattern. In terms of the commodity-market conflict, Agrarians ally with Labour against Conservatives. In the labour-market conflict, Agrarians ally with Conservatives against Labour. This three-way economic pattern of conflict has been added to the original geographical and cultural cleavages to produce today's five-party system. The relationship of these parties to the conflicts are set out in Table 4.2.

Table 4.2 Conflicts and parties in Norway

	Parties				
		Old left			*Con-*
Conflicts	*Labour*	*Liberal*	*Christian*	*Agrarian*	*servative*
A. *Geographical*					
South/west v. Centre		O	O		D
North v. Centre	O				D
B. *Cultural*					
Language opposition		O			D
Teetotal opposition			O		D
Religious opposition			O		D
C. *Economic*					
Rural v. Urban				O	
Rural class conflict	O			D	
Urban class conflict	O				D

Source: Valen and Rokkan (1974)

O = Opposition to status quo
D = Defender of status quo

The evolution of Norway's party system neatly illustrates the links between societal conflicts and the evolution of political parties, but how far do these links remain as part of the modern political scene? Today's party system had certainly fully evolved by 1936 when Labour first took control of government. Are the cleavages that were reflected by the 1936 election still important bases to modern voting decisions? In Chapter 3 we argued that parties need to be stable alliances with predictable policies in order to fulfil their role in elections. If this is true then we would expect to be able to predict each of the five main parties' pattern of support from our knowledge of their evolution.

We can begin by considering the two geographical factors of region and accessibility in rural communes. We have previously shown (pp. 131–6) that mobilization of the periphery varied by region and accessibility, and this was partially reflected in the level of polarization (support for class-based parties). Table 4.3

Table 4.3 Party strength by regions and accessibility: rural Norway, 1957

		% Votes cast for:				
Regions	*Accessibility*	*Lab.*	*Lib.*	*Chr.*	*Agr.*	*Cons.*
East and Middle	High	43·4	4·4	6·3	9·0	14·1
	Medium	41·0	4·9	6·7	14·9	7·6
	Low	32·7	7·2	10·8	14·7	5·1
South and West	High	30·6	13·8	13·0	7·4	9·7
	Medium	24·2	12·7	15·1	13·7	6·3
	Low	17·8	12·7	17·0	18·6	6·1
North	High	37·7	4·6	5·0	4·6	11·9
	Medium	37·6	4·9	6·6	5·9	8·6
	Low	35·3	4·5	7·2	6·6	7·9

Source: Rokkan and Valen (1970)

illustrates this by giving actual party vote percentages for the 1957 election. In all regions Labour do best in the more accessible communes. However, regional differences mean that even in the most accessible communes of the south and west Labour's strength is below low-accessibility communes in other regions. The Conservatives have a very similar pattern of support. By contrast the 'middle parties' of the old left tend to have hung on in the least accessible communes, particularly in the south and west. These simple geographical variations are obviously important in understanding Norwegian elections but they must be combined with the other critical conflict topics to provide a fuller explanation.

The cultural conflicts have generally centred on the distinctive nature of the south and west and therefore interact with the geographical factors considered above. The south and west have distinctively higher rates of church attendance, have higher proportions of people who are teetotal, have traditionally voted for prohibition in larger numbers than elsewhere and have more primary schools using the counter-culture rural dialect (*nynorsk*) for teaching purposes. Furthermore the south has higher proportions of Dissenters than other regions. All these features combine together to inhibit the expansion of Labour and Conservatives into the region. This is the region where the old left survives as a viable political force in the form of the three 'middle' parties. This is shown in Table 4.4. Here communes are divided among

Table 4.4 Language, church attendance and voting by region: Norway, 1957

Region	*Language*	*Church attendance*	*Middle Party % vote*	*Christian % of Lib.+Chr.*
East,	Bokmal	High	27·0	64·1
Middle		Low	21·0	55·6
and	Nynorsk	High	39·6	44·4
North		Low	30·4	51·8
South	Bokmal	High	45·3	47·5
and		Low	37·9	37·9
West	Nynorsk	High	61·4	57·0
		Low	49·7	56·2

Source: Rokkan and Valen (1970)

those that use *nynorsk* or *bokmal* (urban) dialects in schools, and by their levels of church attendance. Vote percentages for the middle parties are given separately for the south and west and the rest of Norway. Notice that it is the language factor which most influences middle party support within both areas. Differences due to church attendance have only a marginal effect. However, in *bokmal* communes, support for the Christian party is related to church attendance, but this relationship is not apparent in the *nynorsk* communes, where Liberal support on the language issue counteracts the religious-based support for the Christian People's Party.

The cultural distinctiveness of the south and west, illustrated above, means that this region will need to be separately considered in all subsequent analyses so that this cultural influence is not confused with economic characteristics. What of the economic conflicts? First we can consider the commodity-market conflict. If we concentrate simply on rural communes these can be divided between inland and coastal. Rokkan and Valen (1970) have calculated correlation coefficients (p. 84) between levels of party votes and employment proportions within rural communes. Table 4.5 shows correlation coefficients calculated for regions as indicated. Notice that the highest positive correlation is +0·85 between employment in agriculture and Agrarian Party vote in coastal rural communes outside the north. This is as we would expect and signifies that communes with high levels of employment in agriculture tend to record high levels of votes for the Agrarian Party. By contrast, in these same coastal communes in the east and middle regions, the correlation between Labour vote and agricultural employment is −0·59, indicating that communes with high levels of agricultural employment tend to have low levels of Labour voters. Again this is as we would expect.

Let us consider Table 4.5 more generally. First the Agrarian's vote is consistently highly related to agricultural employment, although the relationship is weaker in the north. Labour voting is consistently negatively related to agricultural employment, but again the relationship is weaker in the north. These findings are consistent with the north's more polarized nature, illustrated in the last chapter. The only evidence of positive support for Labour in Table 4.5 is with forestry workers, particularly in the south and west, although the relationship is not strong. Like Labour, the Conservatives are generally related negatively to these employ-

Table 4.5 Correlations between primary economic activities and party voting: rural Norway, 1957

Region	*% employed in*	*% voting for:* *Lab.*	*Lib.*	*Chr.*	*Agr.*	*Cons.*
A. *Inland rural communes*						
East and Middle	Agriculture	−0·49	+0·17	+0·18	+0·76	−0·51
	Forestry	+0·26	−0·16	−0·16	−0·01	−0·24
South and West	Agriculture	−0·59	−0·07	+0·02	+0·82	−0·39
	Forestry	+0·34	−0·10	−0·14	−0·05	+0·18
North	Agriculture	−0·14	−0·02	−0·02	+0·60	−0·06
	Forestry	+0·04	−0·09	−0·20	+0·22	−0·16
B. *Coastal rural communes*						
East and Middle	Agriculture	−0·55	−0·07	+0·30	+0·85	−0·54
	Fishery	−0·19	+0·02	+0·16	−0·42	+0·04
South and West	Agriculture	−0·43	−0·12	−0·03	+0·85	−0·18
	Fishery	−0·14	+0·22	+0·26	−0·52	−0·04
North	Agriculture	−0·20	−0·04	+0·04	+0·73	−0·16
	Fishery	−0·07	−0·05	+0·19	−0·46	−0·11

Source: Rokkan and Valen (1970)

ment ιypes. In contrast the Liberal and Christian parties apparently show no relationships with them, their correlations being consistently close to zero. Since these parties base their support on cultural factors we would expect them to fail to correlate with economic occupation factors.

Finally, let us consider the economic conflicts based on the labour market. This can best be illustrated using survey data involving some 1500 respondents grouped by occupation and our twofold division of Norway, distinguishing the south and west from the rest. Table 4.6 shows these sub-samples and their party preferences. Labour's support is clearly class-based, with the highest proportion of preferences from primary workers, fishermen (particularly in the north) and other non-primary

Table 4.6 Regional contrasts in party preferences by major occupation groups: Norway 1957

			Intended vote		
Sub-sample	*Lab.*	*Lib.*	*Chr.*	*Agr.*	*Cons.*
A. Primary					
farmers					
EMN	19	6	7	37	8
SW	7	15	11	40	10
Smallholders/fishermen					
EMN	42	2	8	8	10
SW	13	8	18	24	0
Workers	56	4	5	6	3
B. Non-primary manual					
Manufacturing					
EMN	65	2	3	1	5
SW	58	7	8	3	0
Craft					
EMN	60	1	5	0	8
SW	41	3	7	3	10
C. Non-manual					
public salaried					
EMN	40	10	12	0	20
SW	5	30	14	5	27
Private salaried					
EMN	27	1	9	1	38
SW	20	14	6	4	20
Employer					
EMN	11	5	5	0	50
SW	8	19	0	0	35

Source: Rokkan and Valen (1970)

EMN = East, middle and north
SW = South and west

manual workers. However, even within these occupational groups, levels of support are lower in the south and west, reflecting the cultural factors previously discussed. Notice the relatively high level of support for Labour in the publicly employed middle classes outside the south and west. Nevertheless, within this region it is the Liberals who have most support from these occupations. The Liberals are consistently more strongly supported in the south and west among all occupations and this is also true of the Christian People's party. In both cases, this reflects the general independence of their voting support from occupation types. In contrast, the other middle party, the Agrarians, have a distinctive occupational base, as we have seen, although once again the predominance of the south and west is noticeable even within the primary occupations. Finally, the Conservatives are very like Labour in being explicitly class-based, although in this case it is the middle class which gives them support. Apart from the publicly employed middle class, the Conservatives win most middle-class votes, with a level of support which is again lower in the south and west.

We have presented only a small part of Rokkan's electoral studies (Rokkan, 1970; Rokkan and Valen, 1970), and have used both ecological and survey analyses to illustrate our arguments. In Rokkan's work, the two types of analysis are used to complement each other and thus avoid either the ecological or individual fallacies discussed in Chapter 2. More recent survey work is presented in Valen and Rokkan (1974). However, the little we have presented clearly shows how the identification of crucial past conflicts in a society can be used to make sense of the country's political party system and the social bases of its support. Interacting geographical, cultural and economic cleavages are clearly discernible in the geography of voting in modern Norway.

Regional patterns of voting in Finland

Scandinavian party systems correspond to one type in Rokkan's framework, but this does not mean that they are all identical.We will briefly consider a second geography of voting, for Finland, to illustrate the variety that can exist within the single type. Finland has a similar recent history to Norway in that it only finally became independent this century. Since 1917 there have been six, major, political parties. Four of these parties have direct affinities with the Norwegian parties discussed above. These are the Social

Democrats, Liberals, Conservatives (National Coalition) and the Agrarians, who became the Centre Party in 1965. However, in Finland there is no religious party and the cultural dimension is represented by the Swedish People's Party for Swedish-speakers. Finally, Finland is distinctive among Scandinavian countries in having a major Communist Party. Table 4.7 shows the social

Table 4.7 Ecological comparisons of party preferences, Finland 1966

	Parties					
Cleavage	*Comm.*	*S.D.*	*Cent.*	*Lib.*	*Cons.*	*SPP*
Finnish-speaking	21	30	22	7	15	0
Swedish-speaking	13	11	2	0	2	72
Rural	20	23	34	4	9	6
Urban	21	36	3	10	21	5
Farmer	9	8	60	2	7	10
Farm labour	25	45	24	6	0	0
Worker	34	42	6	5	6	3
Middle class	6	29	8	15	28	9
Executive	4	10	9	15	53	8
South/west	19	34	15	8	16	4
Central	21	23	23	4	11	11
North/east	27	22	35	6	9	0

Source: Pesonen (1974)

bases of support for these parties, using survey data. The language cleavage is very clear-cut resulting in the Swedish People's Party consistently obtaining about ten per cent of the total vote since 1917. Less extreme, but nevertheless important, is the rural/urban cleavage, which produces a viable agrarian Centre Party, leaving the Conservatives with their typically Scandinavian urban base. Class differences, however, are most important outside the Swedish People's and Centre Parties. Social Democrats and Communists receive more support from lower classes, Liberals and Conservatives from middle and upper classes. In each case the more extreme examples of class voting can be found in Communist and Conservative support. Finally, we can consider regional differences. Finland can be divided into three zones – the core areas of south and west; central Finland; and the north and east periphery. In Table 4.7 an interesting contrast occurs. The Social Democrat and Conservative levels of support consistently decline from core to periphery, while the Communist and agrarian Centre Party support increases towards the periphery. How far these regional differences simply reflect the distribution of the other cleavage patterns, and how much they represent alternative party arrangements in different regions is a topic we will return to below.

The regional patterns of party support in Finland have been treated in some detail by Rantala (1967). He identifies five major zones. The coastal areas of the south and west contain most of the country's urban and industrialized population, and it is here that the party system is most competitive, largely reflecting residential areas by occupation. Behind this area is a wide belt, reaching the Russian border, where the Social Democrats have dominant support. Either side of this zone are areas of Agrarian support in the extreme south-east and in the north and east. The north is an area where the Communists compete with the agrarian Centre Party for support. Rantala identifies core areas for each party and shows how support for a party declines with distance from its cores. In essence the pattern that emerges is one of two contrasting zones. In the south and west the main election contests are between the Social Democrats and the Conservatives, the Liberals or the Swedish People's Party. In the north and east the agrarian Centre Party dominates but its main rival is the Communist Party. This division of the country into two broad zones is clearly illustrated in Figure 4.2 which shows the Communist vote in 1958. The Communists obtained twenty-three per cent of the total vote and the map shows communes recording above average Communist vote. Although the Communists are a major force in some southern communes, the contrast between north and south is quite striking. This northern bias in the Communist pattern of support is also found in Norway and Sweden,

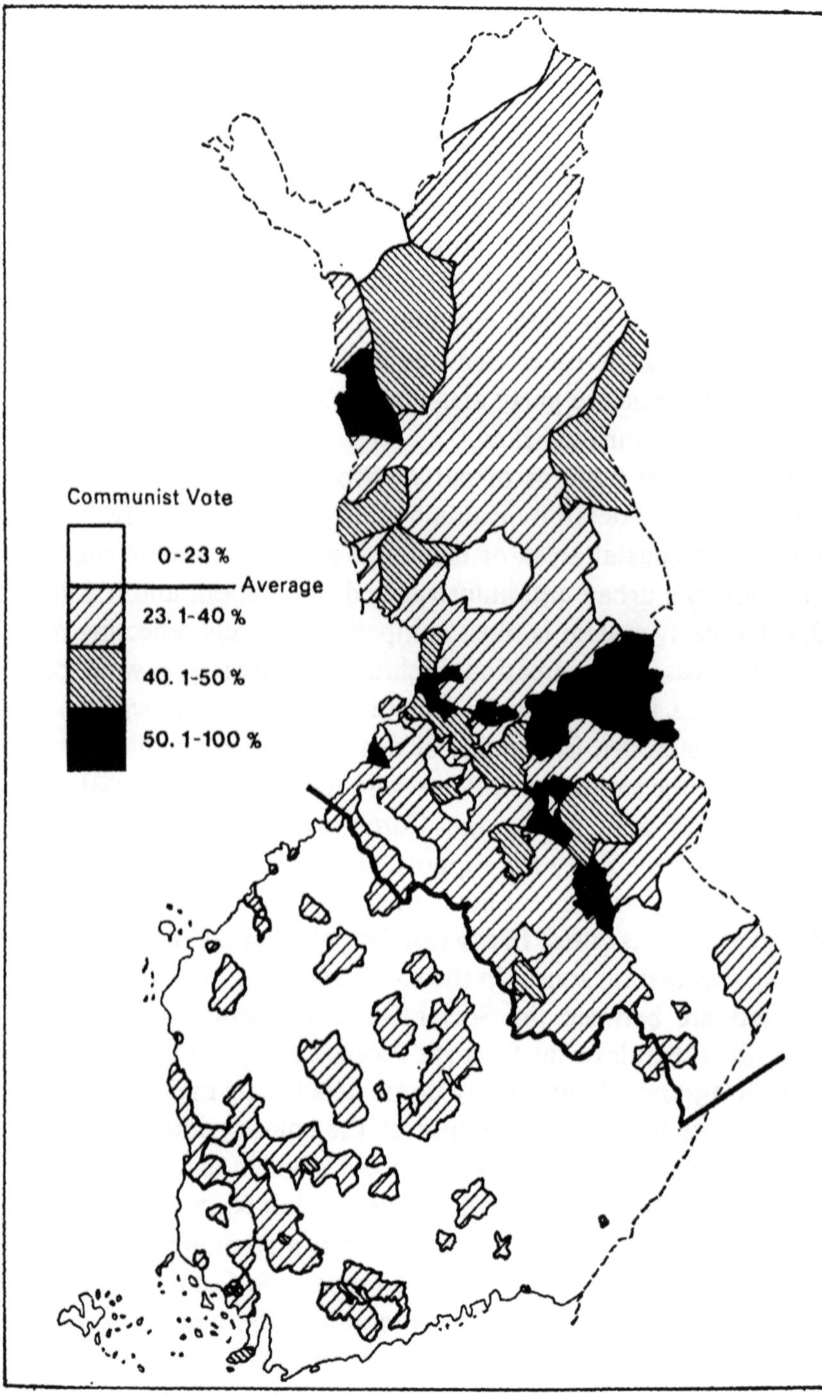

Figure 4.2 **Voting pattern for Communists in Finland, 1958**

the main difference being that in Finland the Communists have become a major party.

Allardt and Pesonen (1967) have used this division of the country as the basis of an analysis into the differences in social bases of support for parties. They used factor analysis (p. 88) to condense a set of forty-one political and social variables into six new composite variables or factors. Variables included ranged from proportions of votes for various parties in each commune to social variables, such as Sunday-school attendance and proportion of manual workers. The analysis was carried out for communes in the south/west and north/east separately.

The three, main, composite variables or factors produced by these analyses are shown on Table 4.8; loadings have been

Table 4.8 Selected factor loadings for Finland study

South/west		*North/east*	
	Factor I		
Socialist traditions		Communist traditions	
Comm. vote 1945	+0·89	Comm. vote 1945	+0·80
S.D. vote 1916	+0·63	S.D. vote 1916	+0·09
Comm. vote 1929	+0·69	Comm. vote 1929	+0·78
S.D. vote 1939	+0·71	S.D. vote 1939	+0·11
Prop. in industry	+0·33	Prop. in industry	+0·16
	Factor II		
Modernization		Modernization	
Prop. in agriculture	−0·79	Prop. in agriculture	−0·84
Income per capita	+0·63	Income per capita	+0·63
Prop. of homes electrified	+0·78	Prop. of homes electrified	+0·76
Prop. in retail	+0·77	Prop. in retail	+0·71
	Factor III		
National Conservatism		Rural Traditionalism	
Vote for largest party 1958	−0·45	Vote for largest party 1958	+0·58
S.D. vote 1916	+0 16	S.D. vote 1916	−0·81
S.D. vote 1939	+0·05	S.D. vote 1939	−0·86
Fascist vote 1936	+0·83	Fascist vote 1936	−0·07

Source: Allardt and Pesonen (1967)

selected for inclusion to help interpret the meanings of the factors. These meanings are indicated by the names given by Allardt and Pesonen (1967) to these factors, which are also included in the table. Their interpretation is as follows. Both Factor Is reflect the tradition of left-wing voting, but in the south/west this includes voting for both Communists and Social Democrats at the earlier elections; in the north/east only voting for Communist at the earlier elections has high loadings. Hence they are termed 'socialist' and 'communist' traditions respectively, the latter being much less based on industrial workers. The Factor IIs are very similar and relate to the less agricultural communes with their higher standards of living. The name modernization seems very appropriate in both cases. The Factor IIIs, on the other hand, are quite different. In the south/west the highest loading is with the Fascist vote. In the north/east the Fascist vote is not highly loaded though there is evidence of an anti-social democratic element. Allardt and Pesonen interpret these factors as reflecting different aspects of conservatism which they term 'national conservatism' and 'rural traditionalism' respectively.

How do post-war patterns of party support relate to these three basic dimensions? Table 4.9 shows the loadings for five of the six main parties on these three factors. (The Swedish People's Party vote is not included because they only present candidates in a restricted part of Finland.) The first thing to notice about the table is that in *both* regions it is the Communist vote which most closely mirrors the traditional left-wing support represented by the two Factor Is. In the south/west they reflect the general socialist tradition; in the north/east they reflect the communist tradition and this difference is made particularly clear by the negative Social Democrat loading in the north/east. In both regions the Social Democrats' highest positive loadings are with modernization (Factor II) and they do particularly poorly in areas that reflect Factor III's rural traditionalism in the north/east. This factor is particularly related to the Agrarian vote as we might expect. In the south/west the national conservatism of Factor III still relates to the Agrarian vote but here it is the Conservatives who most closely mirror this factor. This shows how parties can have different bases of support in different regions since in the north/east the Conservative vote is related to the modernization pattern. As an urban party they are unable to recruit support of conservatives in the rural areas of the north/

Table 4.9 Factor loadings for 1958 party votes in the Finnish study

A. South/west		Factors:	
Party support for:	I	II	III
Communists	+0·89	+0·16	+0·13
Social Democrats	+0·17	+0·25	+0·20
Liberal	+0·19	+0·32	+0·41
Agrarian	+0·09	−0·49	+0·49
Conservative	+0·17	+0·17	+0·81
B. North/east			
Party support for:	I	II	III
Communists	+0·88	+0·02	−0·05
Social Democrats	−0·44	+0·28	−0·67
Liberals	−0·08	+0·47	+0·03
Agrarian	−0·08	−0·49	+0·67
Conservative	−0·40	+0·64	+0·16

Source: Allardt and Pesonen (1967)

east. The pattern of support for the other bourgeois party, the Liberals, is similar to that of the Conservatives although their loadings are generally lower, indicating less clear-cut relationships. Finally, it can be noted that the Agrarian vote is consistently negatively related to the modernization factors.

This ecological study supplements the survey data presented in Table 4.7 (p. 178). The survey data clearly illustrated the operation of the main cleavages; the ecological study locates these cleavages on the ground and illustrates regional differences. These differences do not merely reflect different social patterns between south/west and north/east but suggest that the parties themselves may have different regional bases of support. This certainly seems to be true of the Conservatives and is also apparent in the relationship between the Social Democrats and

Communists. The only consistent party support over both regions would seem to be for the highly distinctive Agrarians.

Our two studies of Scandinavian party systems illustrate two major points. First, the evolutionary approach to understanding party labels through cleavages is clearly reflected in the social bases of modern voting behaviour. Secondly, the relationships between these social bases and the voting are quite subtle, with different regions sometimes having distinctive electoral contests within the overall national framework. To what degree these two points can be substantiated beyond Scandinavia will be shown in the rest of this chapter.

Other European Countries

In Table 4.1 (p. 165) the other European countries consistently show religion to be the most important social basis of voting. We should not, of course, interpret this to mean that these countries have only progressed to the second of Rokkan's four critical cleavages, so that economic conflicts do not exist or are of only minimal importance. From the last section we have come to understand that cross-cutting cleavages can exist to produce several interacting bases of voting. We can illustrate this by briefly considering the country in Table 4.1 which exhibits the highest level of religious voting, the Netherlands.

Dutch society consists of three main groups – Catholic, Protestant and secular – which are reflected in five main political parties: two secular, two Protestant and one Catholic (Lijphart, 1974). The religious basis of voting indicated in Table 4.1 is illustrated more fully in Table 4.10. Although religion dominates, it does not eradicate class voting. This can be seen when we consider party preferences among the two secular parties (Table 4.11). Although socialist parties dominate through all classes their support very clearly varies with social class. Labour has replaced the Liberals as the major secular party, especially among working-class voters, but it has experienced severe restrictions on its growth because of the dominant religious cleavage.

Similar examples of the rise of socialist parties finding resis-

Table 4.10 Church affiliation and party preference: Netherlands, 1956

	Party				
Religion	*Catholic People's*	*Anti-Revolutionary*	*Christian Historical*	*Labour*	*Liberal*
Catholic	90	1	0	5	1
Dutch Ref.	0	10	29	41	13
Orthodox Ref.	0	85	3	6	0
None	1	1	1	72	12
Other	8	5	5	69	10

Source: Lijphart (1974)

tance along religious, as well as class, lines have been documented in the geographical literature. In Burgenland, Burghardt (1963, 1964) has shown that once this periphery had been fully incorporated into the Austrian party system after 1945, the Christian Democrats were able to dominate the province and restrict the socialists to industrial and commuter regions. In West Germany, Laux and Simms (1973) show that the Social Democrat vote is related to two separate social variables. On the one hand, the more industrial a province is, the more votes the party wins – this is the class effect which we would expect for a socialist party. Secondly, however, there is a distinct religious effect – the more Catholic a province is the lower the Social Democrat vote. Hence,

Table 4.11 Class and secular party preference: Netherlands 1956

	Party	
Class	*Socialist*	*Non-Socialist*
A (High)	57	43
B	60	40
C	89	11
D (Low)	97	3
Total	82	18

Source: Lijphart (1974)

the old division of Germany into Protestant north and Catholic south is still reflected in the pattern of party votes, even after the rise of the socialist addition to the party system.

These examples are suggestive of cleavages old and new underlying the social bases of voting within the various countries. However, they remain general, national-level findings which omit the rich variety of responses to parties that exist within countries. This variety can only be obtained through detailed studies of the internal pattern of votes of individual countries as we illustrated for Norway and Finland. In this section we will deal with geographies of voting in France and Italy.

Social bases of voting in Italy and France

Southern Europe's two, established, parliamentary democracies both have Type VI party systems in the Rokkan model. This involves a secular, nation-building, élite, allied with urban interests, in conflict with a Christian (Catholic) rural alliance. Hence, prior to the mobilization of the working class into the system, liberal/radical republican parties competed with Catholic right-wing parties. On the left, the liberals have again been largely superseded by socialist parties and in both France and Italy the major socialist party is the Communist Party. Hence, today, the Type VI party system has its major contest between secular Communists and the Catholic-supported right.

Let us consider the Italian party system in some more detail. The nation-building groups after 1860 were secular élites, in direct conflict with the Papacy which objected to parts of central Italy under its authority being incorporated into the new Italian state. In the early years of the state the conflict with the church was reflected in the fact that the Catholic élites were forbidden from participating in the affairs of the state. The absence of the urban working class from the early political scene left the state firmly in the hands of the liberal élite. However, the extension of the suffrage, and the rise of votes for the left, led to a change in the church's strategy, so that even before 1914 the process of mobilizing the rural Catholic masses into the electoral system had begun. This produced three traditions – secular/liberal, Catholic and left – and these remain the basis of the modern party system despite the Fascist interlude from 1923 to 1945 (Barnes, 1974).

Barnes (1974) identifies nine parties which have gained some degree of nation-wide support in post-war elections. However, only three of these parties can claim to be major parties. On the right, the Christian Democrats dominate the scene, while on the left, there is a split between the Communists and Socialists. No other parties have gained appreciable support, the best fourth party performance being the Liberals' seven per cent of the vote in 1963. Hence the socialist parties have taken over from the Liberals as the secular opposition to the church. This means that the religious cleavage remains an important basis for voting, despite the rise of the explicitly class-based socialist parties.

The interaction of religious, class and urban/rural cleavages on Italian party preferences is shown by the survey data in Table 4.12. For the regular church attenders, support for the Christian Democrats is dominant, irrespective of class, and is reinforced

Table 4.12 Religion, class and rural-urban residence in party support, Italy 1965

	Urban		*Rural*	
Party	*Working class*	*Middle class*	*Working class*	*Middle class*
A. *Regular church attendance*				
Communist	5	0	3	0
Socialist	8	9	11	7
Christian D.	61	54	68	69
Liberal	1	7	0	1
B. *Non-regular church attendance*				
Communist	24	7	39	5
Socialist	21	22	29	26
Christian D.	22	28	54	33
Liberal	1	5	3	5

Source: Barnes (1974)

by rural residence. For the non-regular church attenders, the combined Socialist/Communist support is far greater than the Christian Democrat support among workers and roughly equivalent to it among the middle class. Hence, in this 'secular' group, the religious cleavage works against the Christian Democrats, who do not do as well as a major Conservative party might expect amongst a middle-class group. The Liberal Party has not really benefitted from this situation, however. Although it clearly has more support from the middle class than from workers, its level of support remains negligible. Two further points should be noted from Table 4.12. First, the Socialists are supported far more than the Communists among middle-class groups, and, secondly, there is a relatively high level of Communist support among the *rural* working class. We will return to both points later.

Although the particulars of the political history differ somewhat, the French party system has evolved into a pattern similar to that in Italy. Although there is no explicitly Catholic party as in Italy, the major voting cleavage is the secular/religious one which dominates the class cleavage, especially in rural areas (Dogan, 1969). We can illustrate this by comparing the three maps in Figure 4.3. Communist support is concentrated into three zones and these directly correspond to areas of low religious observance and not to the pattern of industrialization. Hence in the industrial east, with high religious observance, the Communists fare badly, while in the agricultural central departments, where religious observance is low, the Communists do very well. Here, as in Italy, the Communists are heir to an anti-clerical tradition.

Regional contrasts in Italy and France

This lack of a clear-cut relationship between left voting and the working classes has been used by Dogan (1974) in his ecological study of French and Italian party systems. The graphs in Figure 4.4 show the scatter of Italian provinces and French departments when plotted against Communist plus Socialist vote and per-

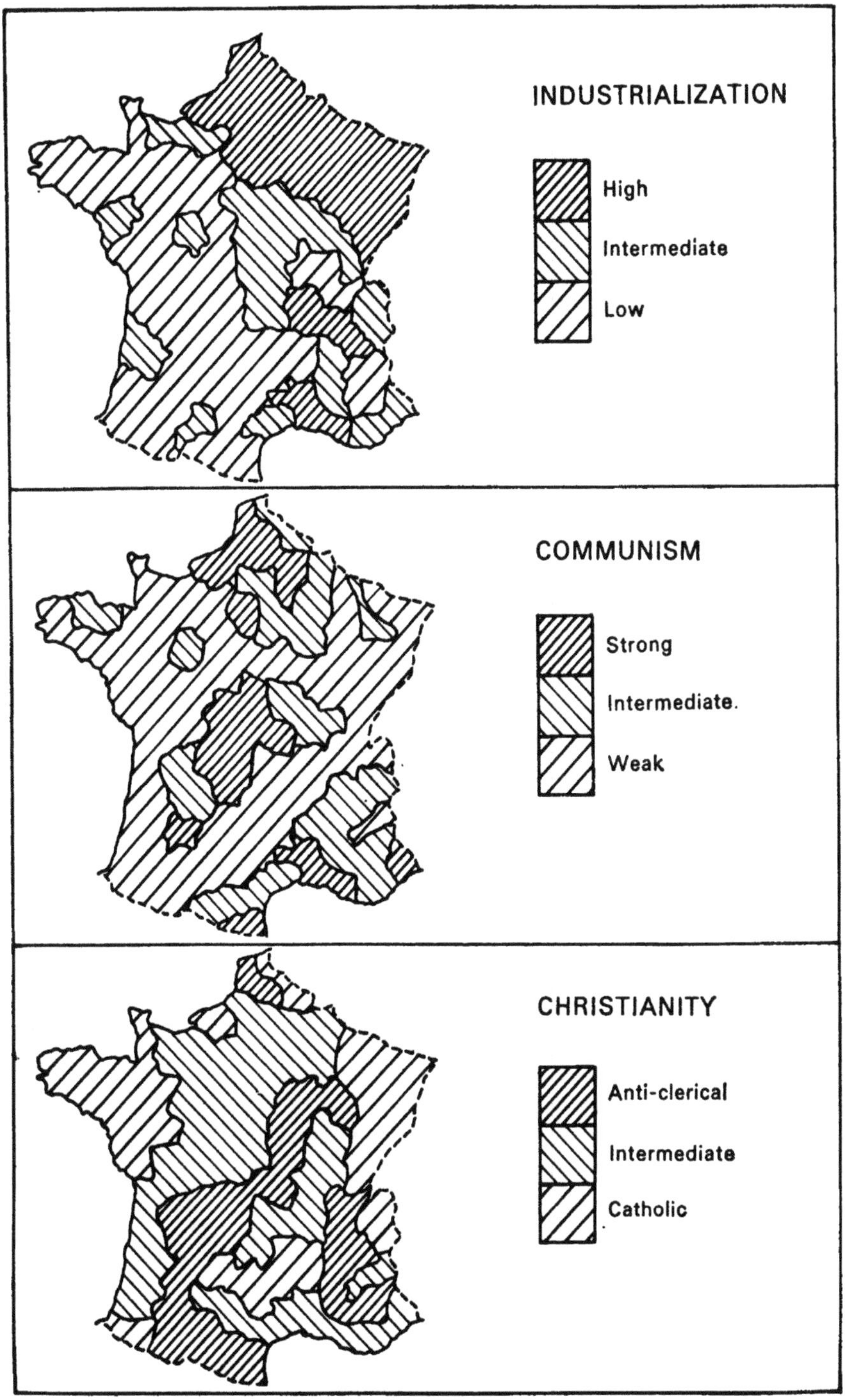

Figure 4.3 Industrialization, Communism and Christianity in France

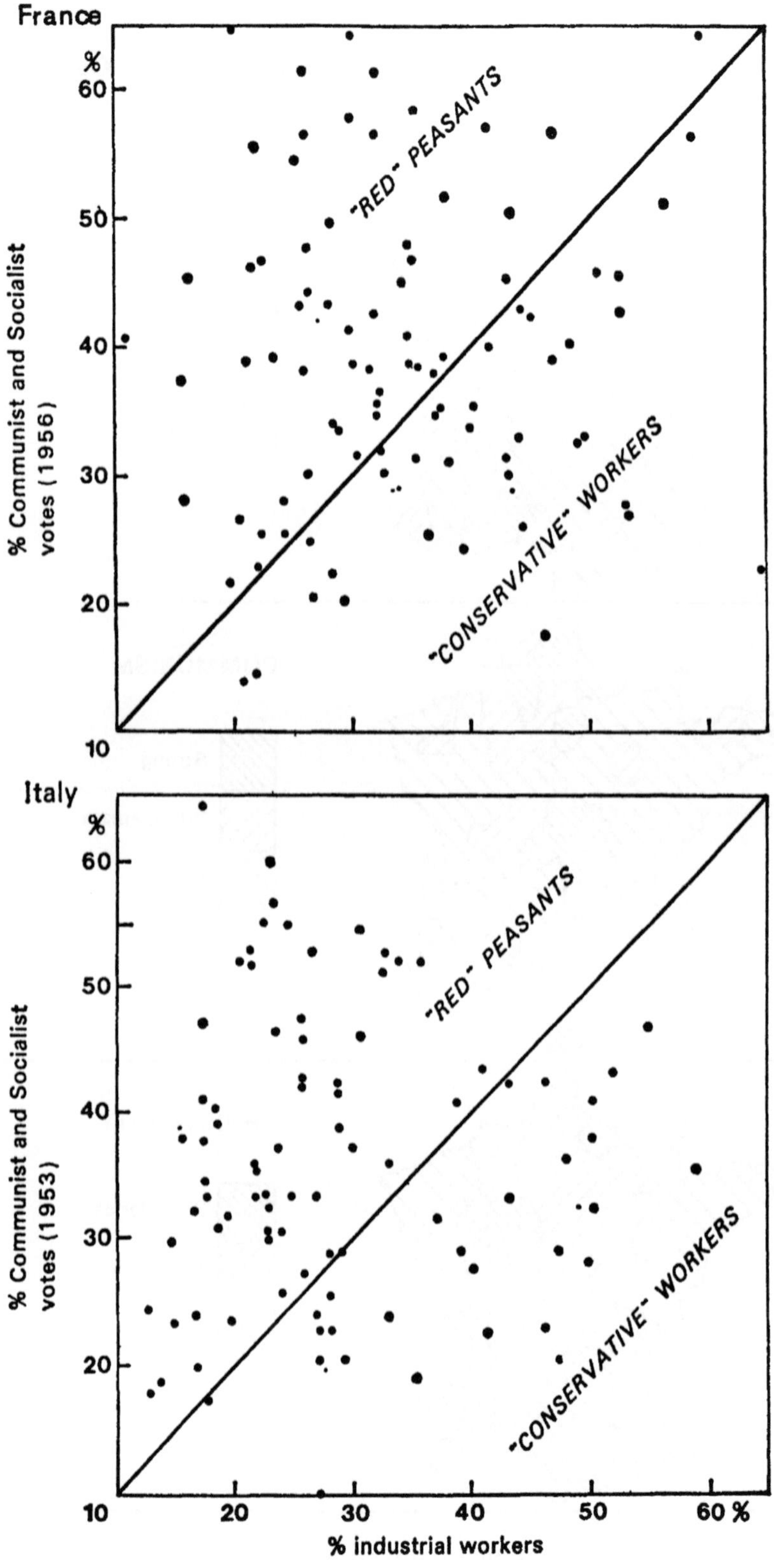

Figure 4.4 Red peasants and Conservative workers in France and Italy

centage industrial workers. The diagonal line defines a situation in which the proportion of left votes equals the proportion of industrial workers. Thus above the line there are more left-voters than industrial workers and below the line the opposite is true. Dogan identifies these as areas of 'red peasants' and 'conservative workers' respectively. The distribution of 'red peasants' in Italy is shown in Figure 4.5, which shows those areas in the 1953 election where the Communists alone obtained more votes than the number of industrial workers. The main area is a continuous block of territory between Rome and the industrial

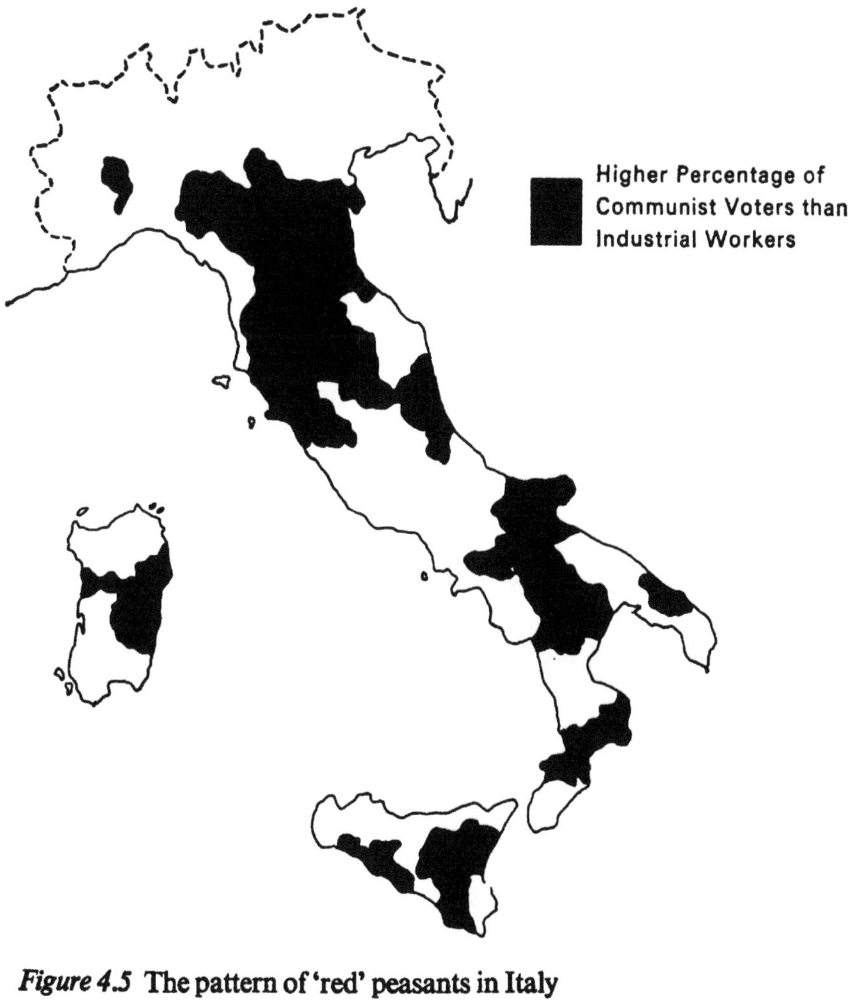

Figure 4.5 The pattern of 'red' peasants in Italy

north. Other zones in the south and in the islands actually represent quite small Communist vote proportions, though higher than the even sparser industrial workers. The central Italy zone, however, does represent a solid core of Communist strength in a rural area. Such Communist support is based upon agricultural workers and tenant farmers, with the latter being particularly concentrated in central Italy. In fact this area is a traditionally radical and secular zone, having supported agrarian socialism in the late nineteenth century and having been anti-clerical since at least the eighteenth century when the church owned great estates in the region.

In France the rural Communist support is quite different. Here there are fewer tenant farmers and they tend to be concentrated in the west which has remained an area of traditional religious observance and low Communist vote. In north-east France agricultural labourers vote Communist, but less so elsewhere. The core of rural French Communist support is the small farmers (land owners) of central and southern France with its low religious observance (Figure 4.3). Dogan (1974) writes of such areas as being 'dechristianized'. These are traditional secular/radical areas. As Williams (1970, p. 18) so neatly puts it – 'The peasants of these areas are voting not for the revolution of 1917 but for that of 1789'. Hence, the common ground between French and Italian rural Communism is not to be found in the economic or social structure but in regional traditions of anti-clericalism.

Dogan emphasizes the regional dimension that has underlain much of our discussion so far. He writes: 'In France and Italy, political cleavages do not take on their complete meaning if they are not observed in regional contexts, varying with the focus peculiar to each region. Political problems are often seen from an altered perspective in different parts of the country . . . Parties tend to adapt themselves to their milieu . . . In each type of party we can discover at least two varieties' (Dogan, 1974, p. 179).

In essence Dogan contrasts the urban and rural bases of the various political parties. We have already identified rural Communism as being separate from the 'normal' industrial Communism. Dogan emphasizes the point that the 'red peasants' support the party for very different reasons from Communist industrial workers. Similarly, the Christian Democrats have a left wing that is reformist and liberal and wins support in poorer urban areas while the right wing is conservative and wins the support of the peasantry and bourgeoisie. The Christian Democrats of Lombardy are very different from their namesakes in Sicily. In France, the Popular Republican Movement (Social Democrat) has traditionally been working class orientated and 'progressive' in the east and has been peasant orientated and reactionary in the west. In France, of course, this party has been replaced as the main anti-socialist party by the Gaullists. Even this new party has evolved at least two faces, ranging from a modern liberal reformist wing, through to a traditional conservative nationalism. According to Dogan (1974) the regional distinctiveness of these two Gaullisms is not as well-developed as for the older parties.

Capecchi and Galli (1969) present ecological analyses of party voting in Italy, which allow us a glimpse of these regional contrasts within party support. In Table 4.13 we have abstracted from their analyses selected correlations above $\pm 0{\cdot}2$ for the two main parties. In each case, the level of vote for the party was correlated by communes for Italy as a whole and for the four main regions – the more industrial north-west and north-east regions and the more agricultural central and south regions. In the industrial regions the north-east is traditionally anti-left and in the agricultural regions the central area is traditionally pro-left. This produces a simple two-by-two typology of the regional framework:

	Agricultural	Industrial
Pro-left	Central	North-west
Anti-left	South	North-east

Dogan's arguments, presented above, should be reflected in different social bases of voting between the columns in the typology, despite different levels of voting being represented by the rows. Table 4.13 supports these arguments for both

Table 4.13 Ecological correlations of Communist and Christian Democrat votes by communes, Italy 1963

	Regions				
Variable	*North-west*	*North-east*	*Central*	*South*	*Italy*
A. *Communisl vote*					
Illiteracy	+0·393	+0·297	—	—	+0·203
Primary schooling	−0·292	−0·324	—	—	−0·249
Industrialization	—	—	+0·227	+0·208	—
Sharecroppers	—	—	+0·248	(+0·172)	+0·315
Republic vote 1946	+0·573	+0·355	+0·687	+0·533	+0·431
B. *Christian Democrat vote*					
Illiteracy	−0·224	−0·351	—	—	—
Primary schooling	+0·440	+0·428	+0·236	(+0·169)	+0·278
Industrialization	—	—	−0·229	(−0·163)	—
Sharecroppers	—	—	−0·234	(−0·126)	−0·230
Republic vote 1946	−0·487	−0·394	−0·719	(−0·026)	−0·399

Source: Capecchi and Galli (1969): — < ±0·2

parties. In the north-west and north-east the educational variables are important for both parties, though in opposite directions; in the central and south regions it is the two economic variables which are important. The final variable in Table 4.13 illustrates the continuity in the pattern represented. The vote for the Republic in 1946 is positively correlated with the 1963 Communist vote and negatively correlated with the Christian Democrat vote in all regions. In all cases, the south has lower correlations, indicating a less distinct pattern of social bases to voting. (In this case correlations below ±0·2 have been included in Table 4.13 to illustrate similarities in pattern with the central region.)

Capecchi and Galli's (1969) analysis extends these simple correlation findings into causal models of inter-relationships and may be consulted for further details. For our purposes here, it illustrates ecologically two types of Communist Party competing with two types of Christian Democrat. These findings have been verified using survey data (Barnes, 1974).

Both Italy and France have an amazing variety of social geographies within their borders, which are reflected in many contrasting geographies of voting. The analyses we have presented here only scratch the surface of the regional diversities that have evolved and remain as stable features in their political make-up. Despite the fact that French geography was a pioneer in electoral studies, and cartographic studies continue to be produced (Goguel, 1970; Leleu, 1971), much remains to be done to capture the full subtlety of the interaction of political cleavages within the different milieux of France and Italy.

Anglo-American Countries

The British party system is designated Type I in Rokkan's model of European party systems. This consisted of nation-builders, involving established church and landed interests, competing with an opposition alliance of dissenters, urban interests and the peripheral Celtic fringe. This Conservative–Liberal system has given way to a Conservative–Labour system, with the modern Liberals normally squeezed out in the largely class-based political conflict. This British system provides a link with the party systems outside Europe which we deal with in this book. In the last chapter we noted how the Australian and New Zealand party systems are similar to the British system, whereas the Canadian and American systems are more distinctive. Table 4.1 (p. 165) confirmed these differences, with Canada and the U.S.A. recording relatively low levels of class voting. These contrasts in the social bases of voting in the Anglo-American countries have been explored in detail by Alford (1963).

Alford's comprehensive study involved deriving indices of class voting based on a total of fifty-three surveys between 1936 and 1962, covering the four major Anglo-American countries, Britain, Australia, U.S.A. and Canada. Lijphart's findings for these countries reported in Table 4.1 confirm Alford's earlier ordering in terms of class voting. Alford's analyses, however, are based upon far more data and this enables him to break down his national samples by regions. When regional differences within countries are considered the clear-cut ordering of the countries becomes somewhat blurred.

Table 4.14 Indices of class voting by regions

Britain (1957–62)		*Australia* (1946–61)		*U.S.A.* (1944–60)		*Canada* (1945–61)	
North	44	South Aust.	38	West Central	27	Ontario	17
Wales	42	Queensland	38	Mountain	22	Atlantic	13
Midlands	40	Tasmania	37	East Central	21	British Col.	12
Scotland	38	N.S.W.	35	Pacific	20	Québec	−1
South	35	Victoria	33	New England	19	Prairie	−5
		Western Aust.	27	Middle Atlantic	14		
				South	11		

Source: Derived from data presented in Alford (1963)

These regional patterns are shown in Table 4.14, and overlaps between regions in different countries can be seen. Thus, although British regions show a uniformly high level of class voting, the level recorded for Scotland and the south is matched by South Australia and Queensland. Similarly, west central U.S.A. has class voting on a par with Western Australia, and Ontario has a higher index than either middle atlantic or the south in the U.S.A. These regional variations may give clues to alternative cleavages underlying the party preferences. In the U.S.A., for example, it is the protagonists of the Civil War who record the lowest class voting, especially in the south. Similarly, in Canada the two regional cleavages, one cultural – French Canada v. English Canada – and the other economic – agricultural Prairies versus the industrial east – produce *negative* class voting indices. In Québec and the prairies there seems to be no relationship at all between class and voting.

We begin our detailed investigation of geographies of voting in this section by further analysis of the regional factor in Canadian elections, since this country seems to contradict the underlying arguments of Rokkan's approach more than any other. Secondly, we consider ecological analyses of voting in the U.S.A., where class voting is severely distorted by ethnic factors. Finally, we consider correlates of British voting patterns, which Alford considered nearest to 'pure' class voting.

The regional factor in Canadian elections

When we turn our attention away from European elections towards North American elections, the first feature we need to keep in mind is the massive change in geographical scale. Both Canada and the U.S.A. are far larger in areal extent than any of the countries of western Europe. On these grounds alone, therefore, we might expect regional differences to be more persuasive. Quite simply, peripheries can be far more remote from the political centre at this scale. In Canada this has resulted in the regional factor having a dominant role in attempts to understand the voting pattern in national elections. Both survey data (Simeon and Elkins, 1974; Schwartz, 1974) and voting records (Blake, 1967) have been used to analyse this regional factor; we concentrate on the latter source here.

The regional factor in Canadian elections can be viewed as the expression of three distinctive voting cleavages, each with a specific territorial basis. The first consists of a cultural cleavage with French speakers v. English speakers. In 1976 this resulted in a separatist party winning control of the Québec provincial government. The second cleavage is based on the commodity market, and pits the industrial east (Ontario) against the primary west (particularly the prairies). Finally, Canada has vast differences in wealth between regions, with Ontario and British Columbia having the highest standard of living, and the Maritime Provinces and Québec being the poorest. Blake (1967) considers that given these differences and the vast scale of Canada making frequent communications difficult, it is hardly surprising that a working-class party has not been able to evolve on the national scene to represent interests ranging from Ontario factory worker, through Maritime fisherman to British Columbian pulp-mill worker. Even the minor working-class party, the New Democrats, have a regional origin and maintain a regionally restricted support pattern.

Regional variations in party voting may reflect two different influences (Blake, 1967). First, there are historical associations between parties and certain regions which may still be reflected in modern elections. Secondly, there may be variations in the types of social groups which support a given party in different regions. Blake has attempted to measure both of these direct and indirect regional effects on Canadian voting for 1963 (excluding Québec) using a multiple regression model incorporating fourteen social variables covering ethnic, religious and class topics. Added to these were eight 'dummy' (0–1) regional variables using all the English-speaking provinces except Ontario. They are to allow for direct comparison of each province's voting pattern with that of Ontario. Finally, the regression model allows for the estimation of interaction terms, that is the joint effect of social and regional influences. Overall the model consists of three functional relationships:

party voting $= f$ (social variables)$+f$ (regions)$+f$ (joint social/region effects)

Each variable, region, or joint effect has a coefficient which indicates its importance in effecting a change in the level of voting. These regression coefficients are shown in Table 4.15 for the Liberal and Progressive Conservative vote in the 1963 election. The most striking feature of this table is the domination of the regional variability despite the omission at the outset of the most extreme regional voting in Québec.

Interpretation of the coefficients in Table 4.15 is as follows. The first coefficient is 0·03 between the German ethnic group and Liberal vote. This means that a 1 per cent increase in the proportion of Germans from one constituency to another is reflected by only a 0·03 per cent increase in the Liberal vote. This change is not significantly different from zero and so is not underlined in the table. Generally, changes in the social variables lead to only small changes in the Liberal vote compared with the regional 'dummy' variables. A constituency in Newfoundland, for instance, tends to have over 31 per cent more Liberal voters than an equivalent constituency in Ontario further west (after the

Table 4.15 Regression coefficients in an analysis of the 1963 Canadian election

Variables	*Liberal*	*Progressive Conservative*
Social		
German	0·03	0·34
Italian	0·20	−0·01
Dutch	0·26	0·68
Scandinavian	0·07	−0·27
East European	0·31	−0·22
Anglican	−0·16	−0·03
Baptist	0·11	0·36
Jewish	−0·11	−0·41
United Church	0·19	0·26
Roman Catholic	0·24	−0·15
Managerial/prof.	0·91	−0·05
White collar	−0·40	−0·03
Blue collar	0·39	0·31
Primary	−0·02	0·25
Regional		
Newfoundland	31·43	−32·12
Prince Edward Island	17·28	−21·61
Nova Scotia	19·72	−28·70
New Brunswick	20·38	−36·79
Manitoba	−7·14	−26·15
Saskatchewan	−14·79	−14·77
Alberta	−22·46	−15·87
British Columbia	−14·35	11·78

Table 4.15 – cont.

Variable	*Liberal*		*Progressive Conservative*
Interactions			
Maritimes/white collar	−1·42	Maritimes/white collar	1·59
British Col./white collar	0·95	Prairies/Italian	−4·86
Maritimes/Scand.	−7·36	Maritimes/Scand.	12·36
Maritimes/East Eur.	−5·06	British Col./Dutch	−1·82
Prairies/East Eur.	−0·23	Prairies/Anglican	1·34
British Col./East Eur.	−0·96	British Col./man./prof.	0·58
Maritimes/Anglican	0·58	Prairies/East Eur.	0·59

Underlined coefficients are significant at the 5% level.
Source: Blake (1967)

effects of social variables have been allowed for). There is a clear east/west contrast here: east of Ontario the Liberals do better, west of Ontario they fare worse. Finally, the interaction coefficients are generally larger than those for the social variables but smaller than the regional coefficients. For instance, although the Liberals do well in the Maritime Provinces as we have seen, where there are Scandinavian groups in these provinces they do far less well.

The relative importance of the three sets of coefficients is basically the same for the Conservatives in Table 4.15. Social variables are generally least important and the regional effects most important, with the Conservatives tending to do worse than in Ontario although less so in the west. In the interaction set of coefficients the Maritime/Scandinavian effect again stands out, this time increasing the party's vote appreciably.

Table 4.15 illustrates clearly that regional influences provide important bases to voting in Canada. Although there are important social bases such as managerial/professional support for the Liberals and Dutch support for the Conservatives, these effects are overshadowed by the regional influences. Both direct influences (regional 'dummy' variables) and indirect regional influences (interactions) are important for both parties in accounting for the pattern of their votes over Canada. This illustration of regional effects in Canada is all the more impressive when we consider that the major territorial cleavage, French–English, was not incorporated into the analysis.

Blake (1967) extended his analyses to elections from 1953 to 1965 and found no major differences in coefficients for either party. This suggests that the regional bases of support in Canadian elections are relatively stable and show no evidence of evolution into a more national basis along economic functional lines as implied in the Rokkan scheme of development. The territorial (McCready and Winn, 1976), cultural (Gingras and Winn, 1976) and social class (Chi, 1976) cleavages in Canadian politics are discussed in more detail in the collections of essays edited by Thorburn (1972) and Winn and McMeneny (1976).

The ethnic factor in U.S.A. elections

Burnham (1974) argues that ethnic patterns had an overriding importance in American elections, from the founding of the Republican Party in the 1850s at least until the rise of the 'New Deal' Democrats in 1932. Although this latter party system added a social-class dimension to American politics, there still remained the problem of finding viable coalitions from among competing ethnic groups. This is particularly true at the state and city level, where because of the uneven distribution of certain groups their local importance will often far outweigh their national standing. The classic example is the Jews, who constitute only about 3 per cent of the total U.S. population but nevertheless make up one quarter of New York City's population. We will concentrate on the city level in this section to illustrate ethnic bases of American voting.

Ethnic cleavages in the U.S.A. are of three basic types (Burnham, 1974):

(1) Racial – black v. white, with Indians and Mexican-Americans also locally important in some areas.

(2) Immigrant – established groups v. new immigrants.

(3) Religious – Protestant versus Catholic, with Jews also locally important.

Both major political parties have attempted to exploit these cleavages for their own ends. Furthermore, the cleavages themselves interact with each other and with other cleavages, notably those based on class. For instance, Converse and his associates (1954) found that ethnic groups were ranked in the following order in their support for Eisenhower in 1952 – German (74 per cent), Scandinavian (71 per cent), British (60 per cent), Poles (51 per cent), Italian (44 per cent), Irish (41 per cent). This ordering also reflects a religious cleavage, however, with Eisenhower winning more of the Protestant vote. Furthermore, it is highly likely that the rankings also reflect a class cleavage, with Eisenhower winning more middle-class voters, who are very often both Protestant and from North European backgrounds.

The 1960 presidential election is of particular interest for studying the ethnic dimension, since it involved an Irish Catholic candidate in John F. Kennedy. Dawidowicz and Goldstein (1963) have attempted to ascertain the importance of this ethnic characteristic in detailed studies of voting returns and census data for five American cities. We will present some of their results for Boston here.

Boston is a Democrat stronghold controlled by Irish Catholic politicians but with sizeable minorities of Blacks, Jews, Italians and Yankee Protestants. In 1956 the Democrat, Stevenson, won 54 per cent of the presidential vote; in 1960 Kennedy won almost 75 per cent. How far this resounding victory was based on selective ethnic factors can be seen from Table 4.16. This shows eight groups of precincts classified by census data into four Irish and four non-Irish groups. Each group is also characterized by income type, so that the class dimension may be identified. In 1956 this class factor certainly did operate within the Irish precincts, with Stevenson consistently losing votes at higher income levels. This effect is almost wholly obliterated in the 1960 voting in Irish precincts, where Kennedy wins massive victories in all precinct groups, the class effect being apparent only with the slightly lower Kennedy vote at the highest income level. In the

Table 4.16 Presidential voting in selected Boston precincts, 1956 and 1960

Ethnic group	*Income group*	*Democrat % vote 1956*	*1960*
Irish	Low	67·8	89·4
	Low/middle	55·2	78·8
	Middle	53·6	82·9
	Middle/upper	38·8	69·9
Italian	Low/middle	57·8	84·6
Black	Low/middle	49·4	55·2
Jewish	Middle	78·6	77·4
Yankee	Middle/upper	33·5	42·1

Source: Dawidowicz and Goldstein (1963)

non-Irish precincts, equivalent size swings are found only in the other Catholic precincts of the Italian group. Black and Yankee areas show smaller swings to Kennedy. The Jewish area shows no swing at all, but this partly reflects the fact that it had the highest Stevenson vote for 1956. Nonetheless, the consistently solid Democrat Jewish area was overtaken by every Catholic area in terms of Democrat vote in 1960. We can conclude from this table that the remarkably large victory of Kennedy in Boston in 1960 was based to a large extent on massive gains in Catholic areas.

Similar ethnic influences on voting patterns at the urban scale can be seen at other elections since 1960, often overriding class differences. Jews of all income levels, for instance, tend to be heavily biased in their support for the Democrats in all American cities. Burnham (1974) reports that in Baltimore, middle-class Jewish areas polled 79 per cent for Humphrey in the 1968 presidential election, while similar middle-class non-Jewish zones gave him only 31 per cent support. Conversely, in Miami, Salter and Mings (1972) report that traditional working-class areas which supported the Democrats very strongly from 1948 to 1960 became very pro-Republican after the influx of Cuban exiles into the area.

The major ethnic division in American cities in the last few decades has been the racial one. The influx of blacks into major cities, especially in the north, has radically changed their electoral geography. Although they have settled in inner-city areas which had usually been Democrat, the black population has been distinctive in the high level of support for the party of its choice. Lewis (1965) has traced the impact of black immigration on voting patterns in Flint, Michigan. His cartographic analysis shows that from being initially pro-Republican in 1932 (voting for Abraham Lincoln), the black area of Flint has increasingly become solid Democrat territory. From the 1940s onwards the black residential areas have consistently recorded the highest Democrat vote percentages (usually over 75 per cent) and the area of Democrat dominance has increased as the black ghetto has expanded.

As the proportion of blacks in northern cities has increased, so the Democrat party has fielded black candidates. This has sometimes polarized the voting in an extreme fashion. Burnham (1974) notes that the black Democrat v. white Republican contests for mayor in Cleveland in the late 1960s resulted in very high correlations ranging from +0·95 to +0·99 between ward percentages of non-white population and the Democrat percentage vote. This cleavage was represented by a division of the city where 80 per cent to 90 per cent of working-class whites were voting Republican and 95 per cent to 99 per cent of blacks were voting Democrat. Here clearly the racial–ethnic cleavage was overriding all other cleavages. In more general terms, this inner-city black dominance has produced a new territorial cleavage between city and suburb. As the more affluent leave the central city and its problems to an increasingly black population, city–suburb conflicts arise, mirroring both racial and class cleavages. This territorial cleavage is often very important in local referenda on issues such as local government consolidation and services. Brunn and Hoffman (1970) have studied one such referendum on open housing and illustrate the operation of the racial cleavage. We consider voting on such local issues in Chapter 6.

So far, we have presented several examples of particular cases of ethnic voting. We conclude this section with a description of a detailed study of one election contest, whose sophisticated ecological analyses enable the interacting cleavages alluded to in our previous examples to be partially exposed. The study is by McPhail (1971) and relates to the mayoral election in Los Angeles in 1969. This was a non-partisan election (not formally contested by parties) with 26 candidates in a primary contest, from which the two leading vote winners contested the final election. It was the nature of the major candidates which aroused national interest in what was formally only a local election.

Although 26 candidates contested the primary there were, in fact, only four main competitors – a black liberal Democrat (Bradley); a white conservative Democrat (the incumbent, Yorty); a Republican (Bell); and a local T.V. personality (Ward). In the primary they received 41 per cent, 25 per cent, 12 per cent and 16 per cent of the vote respectively. However, in the final run-off Yorty defeated Bradley by winning 53 per cent of the vote. It seems that most of Bell's and Ward's votes were transferred directly to Yorty.

McPhail's study involved a factor analysis of 41 variables over 632 census tracts, with a view to finding the underlying dimensions of the social geography and the voting patterns. The variables involved various social indicators and 12 measures of voting in the primary and final election. The three most important factors are shown in Table 4.17, with selected factor loadings (correlations) shown for both social and voting variables. Three cleavages can be identified. By far the most important is the racial cleavage. The only social variable which is highly related to the voting variables is the percentage of blacks in a census tract. The *less* blacks in a census tract, the higher the vote for all three white candidates. The class cleavage emerges as Factor II and is related to the Republican candidate's vote. Finally Factor III highlights the city–suburb cleavage which loads moderately high on the increase in the Yorty vote between primary and run-off. This voting variable loads slightly higher on Factor I, and this suggests that while Yorty's increase in vote came from white areas,

Table 4.17 Major factor loadings in the Los Angeles study

Factor I *Black-white cleavage*		*Factor II* *Class cleavage*		*Factor III* *City–suburb cleavage*	
Social variables:					
% Blacks	−0·89	Housing units over $20,000	+0·86	Pop. increase 1960–68	+0·76
		Professional occup.	+0·75	% commercial land	−0·84
		% foremen, operatives	−0·85	% owner-occupiers	+0·83
Voting variables:					
Final Yorty %	+0·93	Primary Bell %	+0·56	% Yorty increase	+0·36
Primary Bell %	+0·65			Primary Ward %	+0·34
Primary Ward %	+0·80				
% Yorty increase	+0·49				

Source: McPhail (1971)

this effect was particularly prevalent in suburban white areas, where Ward had gained some primary support.

We have only presented a part of McPhail's analysis here but it should be clear that this careful ecological approach can unravel the various cleavages behind urban voting patterns. Although the racial cleavage has come to dominate many electoral contests, other cleavages may operate and may be vital in the final result, as Yorty's successes in suburban Los Angeles illustrate. This study has been followed up by a cartographic analysis of subsequent mayoral elections involving successful black candidates (O'Loughlin and Berg, 1977).

We have concentrated on urban voting patterns in this section in order to highlight the ethnic bases of much American voting. We should not, however, leave the impression that ethnic patterns are unimportant as social bases for voting outside the cities. Dawidowicz and Goldstein (1963), for instance, show how the religious factor was important in selected rural areas in patterns of support for Kennedy in 1960. Even in the context of Wallace's overwhelming support in the south in 1968, Birdsall (1969) has been able to uncover numerous subtle differences in the effect of the racial factor in different parts of the south. Wright (1977) has taken this topic much further by combining use of ecological voting data with survey results. This brings us back to the point made at the beginning of the chapter – that complementary use of both types of data constitutes the most powerful strategy for empirical research. We can substantiate this assertion by moving away from North American studies and reporting on recent analyses of British elections.

Ecological models of British voting patterns

Blondel (1963) noted some time ago that there were very few ecological studies of British elections. He contrasted the situation with that obtaining in France with its long tradition of electoral geography. A simple explanation was that British voting patterns lacked the subtle regional contrasts found on the continent and hence an electoral geography approach had far less to offer in the British political context. This argument is related to other views which emphasize the dominance of class voting in British elections (e.g. Pulzer, 1967). Alford (1963) described British elections as the example of 'pure' class voting among the four Anglo-American countries he studied. We have already noted that using Alford's measure of class voting Lijphart (1971) has shown that Britain trails behind Scandinavian countries in levels of class voting (Table 4.1). It can still be argued, however, that class is more dominant in Britain. In the Scandinavian countries the multi-party system has allowed earlier cleavages, such as religion, to continue to be represented in modern voting. In Britain the largely two-party nature of modern elections has enabled the class voting to override other potential cleavages (Table 4.1 p. 165). If maps of voting merely reflect social class patterns then we must agree that electoral geography has little utility in British electoral studies beyond confirming what everyone knows.

The situation is not as simple as this argument suggests, however. Conservative electoral successes over more than a century have been based on their obtaining a substantial proportion of working-class support (Mackenzie and Silver, 1967). Furthermore, this 'deviant' class voting seems to have a geographical basis (Blondel, 1963). At the beginning of this section we noted that Alford (1963) had found different levels of class voting in different parts of Britain (Table 4.14 p. 196). Butler and Stokes (1969) in their analysis of survey data support Alford's findings. They classify their respondents by region of residence and show that the propensity of the working class to support Conservatives varies by region. In Table 4.18 we have combined their regions to illustrate the basic north/south dichotomy which emerges.

Table 4.18 Party support by class in two regional groupings, Britain 1963–6

		% Party support	
Regional grouping	*Class*	*Conservative*	*Labour*
North of England,	Middle	70·3	29·7
Scotland and Wales	Working	29·5	70·5
South and	Middle	74·7	25·3
Midlands	Working	37·0	63·0

Source: Butler and Stokes (1971)

Analysis of survey data collected on a national basis can only scratch the surface of the geographical variations that occur in British elections. Quite simply, sample size restricts the detail of areal variation that can be described. What analyses such as those by Butler and Stokes (1969) do is to suggest that the perceived lack of regional differences in British voting is incorrect and therefore it does not constitute a valid explanation for the lack of an ecological tradition in British voting studies.

It seems that we have to find an explanation for this omission elsewhere. Blondel suggests a rather simple practical reason. Voting records for British general elections are only available for constituencies, as we noted in Chapter 2. This set of areal units does not normally coincide with the administrative units for which most socio-economic data are reported. Hence, comparison of voting with social data is not as straightforward as in France where administrative units have usually also been constituencies. In the British context, researchers have had to combine constituencies to match administrative areas before analysis can begin. Roberts and Rumage (1965), for instance, compare voting in 157 towns with the towns' social characteristics. Miller, Raab and Britto (1974) have considered this problem of data comparability between voting and census returns for analyses going back to the 1920s. The point is that data comparability has not been a simple matter for ecological analyses of British elections and this has undoubtedly contributed to the lack of an electoral geography in Britain.

Fortunately, this is a problem with historical significance only. The 1966 census reported socio-economic variables by constituencies and this has been repeated for the 1971 census. Hence, for the first time, British voting patterns can be directly related to the socio-economic characteristics of the constituencies, and this has led to a belated development of an ecological approach to British voting patterns. Ironically, the late arrival of British electoral geography on the scene has not been without its advantages. Although the simple cartographic approach is represented (Kinnear, 1968), recent developments have incorporated relatively sophisticated ecological analyses which confront the problems of ecological inference described in Chapter 2. In this section we describe this ecological modelling and show how it can be related to survey analyses. In relatively few steps British ecological studies have caught up with and in some ways overtaken the French electoral geography with its very long cartographic tradition. Let us see how this reversal has come about.

The first attempt to build national scale models of voting in British elections was by Roberts and Rumage (1965). They employed data for 157 English and Welsh towns which had been collected for a study of British towns by Moser and Scott (1963), including socio-economic variables from the 1951 census and voting records for the 1951 election. Moser and Scott used the data to classify British towns. Roberts and Rumage, on the other hand, separated out the percentage Labour vote and then attempted to relate this to several of the variables from the census. They finally produced five models of urban left-wing voting using a multiple regression approach. Their study can be criticized on three important grounds. First, on geographical grounds, their areal framework is unsatisfactory since they include unlike units ranging from large cities such as Birmingham to small suburbs such as Surbiton. Furthermore, they do not cover rural constituencies. Secondly, their models can be criticized on statistical grounds in that their inter-related socio-economic variables violate the assumptions of the linear regression model they use (Taylor, 1977). Thirdly, although they have carefully selected the variables they include, some of them may be queried on purely political grounds. One variable relates to overcrowding, for instance, and it is hard to see why this social phenomenon *per se* can influence voting. Although eleven variables are used in this modelling, it is not unreasonable to argue that those that relate to voting do so because they reflect the class cleavage underlying British voting. Hence many variables largely repeat one another in the modelling.

Roberts and Rumage's modelling has been criticized on geographical, statistical and political grounds, so that we will not present details here. It must be seen as a pioneer venture which has been successively improved on all three grounds. In 1971 Crewe and Payne presented a much better model, albeit much simpler. They were able to match the 1966 census constituency tabulations with the 1970 election results to give a complete coverage of all of Britain at the same constituency scale. Hence the geographical problems of Roberts and Rumage were immediately overcome. Secondly, they did not attempt to build a large model of the voting but concentrated on what they viewed as the essential basis of the voting, social class. They therefore produced a simple regression model with two variables in which the percentage Labour vote was related to the percentage of manual workers in a constituency. Further influences on voting were found by an analysis of the residuals. The initial model enables the authors to produce a predicted Labour vote for each constituency on the basis of its proportion of manual workers. The difference between this prediction and the actual Labour percentage vote in 1970 is the *residual*. It measures that part of the Labour vote in the constituency that is related to factors other than the proportion of manual workers. In Rhondda East, for example, Labour obtained a massive 32·9 per cent more votes than would be expected solely on the basis of the manual workers. By contrast, in Cornwall North, Labour obtained 35·3 per cent less of the vote than expected. These are the largest positive and negative residuals respectively, and indicate examples where the model under-predicts and over-predicts the Labour vote.

Crewe and Payne (1971) list the top fifty positive and negative residuals, some of which are given in Table 4.19. Notice how they fall into distinct types, which indicate the additional effects on the voting pattern beyond the simple class dimension represented by the percentage of manual workers. Labour seem to do poorly in agricultural constituencies and better in very heavily working-class constituencies such as mining districts. This is so of some of these latter constituencies, including London's East End, despite their being in the southern group of regions in Butler and Stokes's (1969) survey analysis. Clearly Crewe and Payne's ecological study is picking up a much finer pattern of variations in support than can be seen in broad regional contrasts. Even the West Midlands group in Table 4.19 is restricted to the conurbation and relates to the local influence of Enoch Powell. We consider this particular example in Chapter 6.

Crewe and Payne's initial model has the advantage of simplicity, but the disadvantage of poor predictions. It overcomes the geographical problems of the previous efforts, avoids the statistical problems and has substantive political meaning as it relates to the basic cleavage underlying the voting. It does, however, need to incorporate further variables suggested by the residuals in order to make better predictions.

Two modelling exercises on the 1970 British constituency results were reported in 1973 (Barnett, 1973; Rasmussen, 1973).

Table 4.19 Constituencies where Labour do better and worse than expected for 1970

Positive residual groups		*Negative residual groups*	
I *Mining and heavy manufacturing in south Wales*		I *Scottish agricultural constituencies (not crofting)*	
Rhondda East	+32·9	Kinross	−27·0
Caerphilly	+29·9	Angus, North	−26·5
Aberdare	+29·4	Galloway	−24·4
II *Mining and heavy manufacturing in north-east*		II *Major English agricultural constituencies*	
Chester-le-Street	+17·0	Howden	−20·3
Blyth	+16·1	Westmorland	−19·1
Easington	+15·0	Norfolk, South	−16·6
III *Other mining areas*		III *Other agricultural constituencies*	
Dearne Valley	+17·9	Chippenham	−16·3
Barnsley	+15·2	Dorset, North	−15·9
West Fife	+14·5	Berwick-upon-Tweed	−15·7
IV *London East End and docks*		IV *West Midlands*	
Bermondsey	+15·7	Wolverhampton S.W.	−18·8
West Ham, South	+13·6	B'ham, Handsworth	−18·8
Poplar	+13·3	B'ham, Sparkbrook	−17·8
V *Homogeneous working-class constituencies*			
Ince	+17·0		
Sheffield Park	+14·2		
VI *Council estate constituencies*			
Aberdeen, North	+20·6		
Glasgow, Springburn	+18·3		

Source: Crewe and Payne (1971)

Both presented multiple regression models. Crewe and Payne (1976) criticize both studies because they include variables which have no direct substantive interpretation in terms of voting behaviour. Barnett (1973), for example, initially includes a large number of variables in his models, many of which have only a very remote link with voting. In one model he relates the Labour vote to percentage exclusive use of toilet, percentage owning more than one car and percentage females over 65. Crewe and Payne (1976, p. 58) suggest that this model is 'unhelpful in that nobody would seriously wish to claim that three of the main reasons why people vote Labour are that they do not have at least two cars and the exclusive use of a toilet and that they are not old women'. Similarly, Rasmussen (1973) produces several models, including a housing density variable which again can be related to voting behaviour only indirectly – nobody votes on the basis of the distance between his neighbours' houses. What Barnett and Rasmussen are producing, of course, are general structural measures of constituency type which relate to affluence and hence social class. They claim to be dealing with constituency predictions in the aggregate and not voting behaviour *per se*. None the less their models remain trivial and substantively uninteresting if they cannot be given an interpretation which can be related back to individual voting decisions. Although they are technically superior to Roberts and Rumage's original model, they do not constitute much of an advance politically. In fact they are substantively less interesting than Crewe and Payne's (1971) simple two-variable model and its residuals.

Crewe and Payne (1976) have developed their 1971 analysis by building a multi-variable model based on the residual analysis presented previously (Table 4.19). They also attack the substantive meaning problem directly, by going beyond statistical neatness. They consider the relationships between aggregate modelling and individual behaviour in detail so that they are able to combat the problem of the ecological fallacy (p. 85) directly.

They express their final model in the following verbal form:

The Labour share of the combined Labour and Conservative vote in any British constituency in the 1970 election = 30·7 per cent
+0·24 x the constituency's per cent of manual workers
−4·5 per cent if the seat is agricultural
+23·0 per cent if the seat was 'very' Labour in 1966
+9·7 per cent if the seat was 'fairly' Labour in 1966

−7·3 per cent if the seat was 'fairly' Conservative in 1966
−16·2 per cent if the seat was 'very' Conservative in 1966
−3·3 per cent if a Nationalist contested the seat in 1970
+3·6 per cent if the seat is a 'mining' one
+2·3 per cent if the Conservatives lost in 1966 and captured less than 60 per cent of the total vote of the losing parties
−6·4 per cent if Labour lost in 1966 and captured less than 60 per cent of the total vote of the losing parties. (Crewe and Payne, 1976, p. 64)

This model explains almost 90 per cent of the variation of the Labour vote. It is therefore a successful statistical model and Crewe and Payne argue that it is also a substantively interesting political model.

The form of the model is perhaps a little surprising. Unlike previous models there are only three variables based upon census data, the initial manual workers variable and the two employment types, agricultural and mining. These were prominent in the residuals in Table 4.19 and may be considered to relate to areas of working-class 'deferential' behaviour and working-class solidarity respectively. A constituency is defined as agricultural where over 3·5 per cent of its labour force are so employed and as mining when 5 per cent of its labour force are in mining. All the other variables added to the model are further voting variables. These relate first to strength and intervention of a minor party, which obviously may upset the two-party balance by giving the voter additional choices. Secondly, the political variables measure previous levels of Labour and Conservative strength. This relates to processes which seem to cause voters to tend to favour local majority parties irrespective of their own social class. Sometimes this is referred to as the 'neighbourhood effect' and we deal with it in some detail in the next chapter. Overall, the model relates aggregate Labour voting to other aggregate constituency variables that do relate to accepted ideas on voting behaviour itself.

How far is this latest model compatible with individual voting behaviour? Is it merely another case of an ecological fallacy despite the well-developed argument upon which it is based? All inferences from aggregate data to individual behaviour must remain conjecture, but we can check that the aggregate predictions do produce results that are consistent with individual survey results. Consider the following hypothetical data for occupation and voting proportions:

	Proportion manual workers	*Proportion non-manual workers*	*Proportion all workers*
Proportion Labour voters	0·8	0·2	0·5
Proportion Conservative voters	0·2	0·8	0·5
Proportion all voters	0·5	0·5	

The election returns give us the totals in the final column and the census data provide us with the totals in the final row. It is these final rows and columns for constituencies which are modelled in the ecological research. If we are interested in the cells within the categories, we need to use survey data where it is available. In the above example, for example, we find that 80 per cent of manual workers vote Labour. If we express these proportions more generally by the following letters:

	Manual	*Non-manual*	*All workers*
Labour	p	r	L
Conservative	q	s	$1-L$
All voters	M	$1-M$	

and

$p+q = 1$

$r+s = 1$

we can write the following equation

$$L = pM+r(1-M)$$
$$= r+(p-r)M$$

The Labour vote is here expressed as a linear function of the proportion of manual workers M, with the two constants r, the proportion of non-manuals who vote Labour, and $(p-r)$, the difference between the proportion of manual workers who vote

Labour and the proportion of non-manuals who vote Labour. Interestingly enough, the latter constant is identical with Alford's index of class voting with which we began this chapter.

For our purposes here, however, the important point is that the aggregate two-variable model of Labour voting against manual workers over all constituencies can be written:

$$L = a+bM$$

Taking a and b as given from a plot of L against M, they can be seen as giving predictions for the individual cells; comparison of the two equations gives values for r, p, s and q, as follows:

$$\begin{aligned} r &= a \\ p &= a+b \\ s &= 1-a \\ q &= 1-(a+b) \end{aligned}$$

In our example, ideally the results should give as aggregate model the equation:

$$L = 0{\cdot}2+0{\cdot}6M$$

from which we read off, $r = 0{\cdot}2$, $p = 0{\cdot}8$, $s = 0{\cdot}8$ and $q = 0{\cdot}2$ as in our original survey data. In this situation our aggregate ecological model would be entirely consistent with the individual survey data.

Crewe and Payne (1976) discuss this approach towards linking ecological and survey research more fully; in the present context we can go forward and discuss their results. They use a technique which enables them to estimate the survey proportions by combining the manual-workers variable with levels of voting in 1970. Their results are presented in Table 4.20 alongside Butler and Stokes's survey data for the 1970 election. We must remember that the survey data are subject to sampling errors. All but one estimate from the ecological analysis is easily within the sampling error of the survey estimates. This is truly an impressive linking of the ecological model to survey data based on individual responses.

Finally Crewe and Payne (1976) consider residuals from their

Table 4.20 A comparison of survey and ecological estimates of Labour proportions

	Survey estimates		*Ecological estimates*	
	Manual	*Non-manual*	*Manual*	*Non-manual*
Very Labour seats	0·82	0·38	0·80	0·39
Fairly Labour seats	0·68	0·38	0·67	0·33
Marginal seats	0·58	0·26	0·56	0·29
Fairly Conservative seats	0·43	0·26	0·44	0·24

Source: Crewe and Payne (1976)

final multiple regression model presented above. They hope that, at this stage, residuals relate to merely local effects which cannot be incorporated into a national scale model, unlike the residuals from their first two-variable model. The highest over-prediction is only 13·4 per cent for Cannock and the largest under-prediction is 20·8 per cent for Hamilton. Both reflect particular features – Cannock is in Enoch Powell country and Hamilton was the site of a famous Scottish Nationalist by-election win between 1966 and 1970. Most other large residuals can be similarly explained in terms of non-national factors. This is reflected in the fact that large residual constituencies typically experienced deviant swings from 1966 to 1970 away from the norm for the country. This is a clear indication of numerous local factors at work.

In this final section we have concentrated on ecological studies of British elections at the expense of survey studies. Even within the ecological category we have not considered smaller-scale studies such as those of London boroughs (Rowley, 1969, 1971; Cox, 1968, 1969). Our justification for considering only national-scale ecological modelling is that it illustrates neatly a sequence of studies which have become technically more competent and, even more important, substantively more interesting. By tackling the problem of ecological inferences, Crewe and Payne (1976) provide the most explicit example of how aggregate analyses and individual survey data can be related to one another for further understanding of the voting patterns. Their explicit recognition of residuals implies further factors which are not covered in aggregate modelling. Several of these particular local factors are the subject matter of the next two chapters.

Part Three

Geographical Influences in Voting

5 The Neighbourhood Effect

We make a multitude of decisions during our daily lives. Many are small and of little or no lasting consequence, but a few may have considerable long-term effects, both on ourselves and on others. Such decisions may be made on the spur of the moment, as instantaneous reactions to unexpected situations which frequently arise, for example, when one is driving. Most require some consideration, however, but little forethought, because we have developed stereotyped reactions to certain stimuli – such as choosing from the lunch menu in a cafeteria. A few may be made only after careful and time-consuming deliberation. These are perhaps relatively rare, for few of us spend much of our lifetime making important decisions. The act of voting – or of deciding not to vote – may be an example of this type of decision, though undoubtedly all people do not accord it the same amount of consideration.

Whatever the decision and the way it is reached, it is almost certain that it will be guided, if not governed, by a relevant personal theory. To many, theory is a concept of the pure sciences, comprising a set of rules which describes and explains certain phenomena, such as the reactions when two chemicals are mixed. This theory is probably derived from previous experience (experiment in the chemistry example), and so it can frequently be stated very succinctly in algebraic form. If there is no direct previous experience, however, the rules will be derived from related experiences (other experiments using slightly different chemicals), and will be phrased as a set of probable consequences requiring empirical verification.

But theories are not just sets of formulae which describe chemical reactions; they are sets of propositions – statements of relationships among phenomena – which form the contexts for interpreting any information or stimulus. All of our actions are governed by theories, therefore. Whether we allow our children to see a certain film at a cinema will be influenced by our theories of the effects of such films on behaviour, of the susceptibility of our children to react in certain ways, and of their safety while at the cinema. Similarly, who we choose to vote for in a general election will be guided by our theories of our own self-interests and of the various political parties and personalities involved, as well as the inter-relationships between those two sets of theories. Few such theories are as formalized as those of the chemist. Most are probably very informal and imperfectly developed; they almost certainly conflict with those of others (as with the children forbidden to visit the cinema). Each of us has many theories to guide our daily lives. Some of them are independent of the others; some are grouped in constellations of higher-order theories. Our reactions to the need to vote are undoubtedly related to our theories, for example, of the operation of international money markets, of the costs and benefits of the various faces of capitalism, of individual greed and selfishness, and so on; they form our political philosophies.

It is with the constellation of political theories that we are concerned here. As we have shown in the preceding two chapters, much of the decision-making process about voting is inter-related with class position and individual theories of class relationship. Yet not all people with the same apparent class position vote in the same way, which suggests either a variety of theories being used to process the available political information, or some selection from it. And so here we look at the reasons why different people in the same place vote in the same way while similar people in different places vote in different ways.

The Social Context

A simple answer to the question 'why do people develop certain attitudes and behaviour patterns?' may be teleological; they are born with them as part of some grand design. The importance of heredity is a topic of continuing, sometimes virulent, debate among social scientists, but it is clear that many of our theories are not with us when we are born. They are learned. How? And from whom?

Socialization

Childhood is the major period of learning, and so the major sources of our theories come from contacts established during that period – from parents, siblings and other kin, from local playmates and adults who are encountered frequently, from school teachers and clergy, and, increasingly, from mass media personalities and advertising ('propaganda'?). Each of these sources acts as a model, as an idealization either to be admired and emulated or to be rejected and shunned. All of the child's reactions to the many stimuli of everyday life have to be learned, and theories developed accordingly. Sometimes trial and error is involved – as in seeing how hot a fire is – and most children conduct their own behaviour experiments. But the bulk of learning is guided, explicitly or not, by the teaching and example of others.

Learning is a never-ending process, though it perhaps tails off after a certain age. Much of it is crammed into the period of formal education, which now lasts until the age of at least sixteen in many of the countries we are concerned with here, during which time a mass of information, not all of it structured into theories, is passed on to the child. Presentation of such material is usually, although most probably only implicitly, value-laden and reflects the attitudes of the models. In this way, children develop attitudes and aspirations, behaviours and beliefs that are consonant with those of their 'teachers' of whom by far the most important are usually the parents (Herbert, 1976). Beyond the home, the school, and the playground, is a large industry also aimed at 'teaching' attitudes and at getting us to teach others. There has been a great deal of academic interest in advertising, communications, and personal influence, as illustrated by the works of Katz and Lazarsfeld (1955) and their followers (e.g. Klapper, 1960).

Overt political attitudes are rarely learned in the early years of socialization, in part because of a general belief that some maturity of years is needed to appreciate the complex arguments preceding the voting decision, which is why people are not allowed to vote in most countries until they are at least eighteen. But since political attitudes and culture are very much related to general social attitudes, and as politics are usually closely allied to class structures, children certainly learn much about politics – often implicitly – as they become socialized into their class situation. Their early political preferences are closely allied to those of their parents: Butler and Stokes (1969) found that of people whose parents were Conservative supporters, 89 per cent said that as children their first party preference was for Conservative, with 92 per cent as the corresponding figure for children from pro-Labour families. (If parents were divided in their loyalties, their children tended to adopt their fathers' preferences.)

School and neighbourhood provide other relevant political information for the child, which may be in line with the parents' view, or may conflict with it. In the latter situation, the child then has to reconcile the conflicting information, and form an attitude. At the high-school level in America, Levin (1961, pp. 600–601) found that, 'the climate of political opinion in the high school community appears to be exerting an influence on all the students within the community to choose the political party that *had already been chosen* by the majority of the adult members, regardless of the party preferences of their own parents'. This does not suggest a wholesale anti-parent revolt, however (Hyman, 1959, p. 115); it has been found that those most likely to remain loyal to their parents' view are the children neither dominated nor left alone by those persons (Macoby et al., 1954).

As the child moves into adulthood, so the range of information sources widens, involving both mass media and personal friends and acquaintances, many of the latter encountered either at work or around the home. Much of this information may confirm attitudes already learned, especially if the child remains in the same social stratum and milieu as his parents, which will often effectively filter out conflicting information. Others, especially the socially and the spatially mobile, may encounter very different information and models, leading them to revise their constellation of political theories. And so, whereas about 90 per cent of respondents in Butler and Stokes's survey recalled initial party preference consonant with their parents', the level of agreement at the time of the survey was only 75 per cent for those from Conservative homes and 81 per cent for those with pro-Labour upbringings. Greatest changes were among those whose parents did not support the party that was the major choice of their class (i.e. Labour for the working class and Conservative for the middle class); of children from homes where parents supported 'their' class party, 85 per cent had remained loyal to their parents' preference, which was the case for only 58 per cent among the children of 'deviant' parents.

Some changes in political attitudes reflect general, national or regional trends, but even so they are not uniform through all groups within society. Most of them are made by the relatively young; age brings resistance to change and what is known as political immunization. But just as studies of migration identify 'stayers' and 'movers' – those who never move and those who move frequently – so in politics one can recognize committed and floating voters, the latter being much the more volatile in their preferences. Butler and Stokes (1969) studied such changes among their respondents over three time periods – 1959–63, 1963–4, and 1964–6: the percentages changing their party preferences in each were 30, 36 and 26 respectively. Much of the earlier change was later rectified. Of those whose preference was constant during 1963–4, only 15 per cent changed during 1964–6, whereas of those who changed during the first period 44 per cent changed again during the latter. Much of this change involved short periods of support for the Liberal Party, then a, relatively, very minor force in British politics. Of those preferring Liberal in 1959 only 31 per cent did so in 1966; the comparable figures for Conservative and Labour were 68 and 76 per cent respectively.

What causes such changes, which may be crucial to election results? A changed perception of a party's relevance; disillusion with a leader; dissatisfaction with government actions; a change in personal status leading to a reappraisal of political attitudes and preferences: all of these are involved. Many are of no concern here, since their geographical context is irrelevant. Some are, because they are associated with inter-personal influence, usually either at work or in the home neighbourhood. Both of these are clear geographical locations, spatial milieux within which socialization occurs, leading perhaps to a particular type of political conversion – the neighbourhood effect.

Structural effects

Social structures impose constraints on the behaviour of individual members. Within these constraints – the norms and values of the society – actions are influenced by two sets of forces, the personal norms of the individual, and his knowledge of those of the groups and communities among whom he lives. Since individuals wish to remain part of the various groups to which they belong, they behave in ways which will be approved of, and rewarded by the group, rather than in those ways which could bring disapproval and sanctions. In other words, we choose to behave in ways which will not leave us feeling guilty that we have offended the norms and values of our chosen peers.

Structural effects occur when the individual's norms and values point him one way, whereas those of group or community suggest an alternative course of action, and the latter are 'victorious' in that the individual follows the guidelines of the external forces rather than those of his own predispositions (Blau, 1960). He has decided that social approval is more desirable than freedom from a personal feeling of guilt. Such decisions are made in a wide range of situations. An adolescent, for example, may feel impelled to join in the vandalism being perpetrated by a local gang, despite his feelings of guilt while doing so, because he fears their sanctions if he fails to participate. The structural effect is thus a type of social influence; it is often referred to as a contextual effect, for obvious reasons.

Individuals act out their various roles in society as members of a number of groups and communities. In each, it may be that their personal values and norms, and hence decisions, conform to those of the other members. Complete conformity is very unlikely, however. Among the majority who share the same orientations, views are likely to be reinforced by conversation, so that, unless they are presented forcefully, the minority views are probably rejected. Those in the minority may find the group climate of opinion strongly against them. They then have a number of options, of which Hirschmann (1970) has focused on three (for a discussion of these see Barry, 1974 and Birch, 1975): (1) *exit* occurs when the individual is unable to reconcile himself to the view of the group, and so leaves it; (2) *voice* is when he attempts to alter the group view to his own; and (3) *loyalty*, which may follow a period of voice, occurs when he accepts and adopts the group view. The latter is the structural effect. Many groups do not insist on complete conformity of action on every issue, of course, so that deviant behaviour is always possible and is accepted, but the more an individual deviates from group norms, the greater the probability that he will eventually take the exit option.

In studying one particular type of behaviour – voting – as an example of structural effects, we focus here on several milieux which impinge strongly on most individuals in society – those of their workplace and home neighbourhood. By far the greatest emphasis is accorded to the latter. The importance of the home neighbourhood to the individual results from a well-known pattern, which itself is a consequence of a geographical influence. Because of the costs, in time as well as in money, of moving from one place to another, for very many people social contacts are restricted to the immediate area of the home. This is attested to by a large volume of empirical studies of friendships and acquaintanceships (there are good summaries in Michelson, 1970 and Mercer, 1976), which show that for most people the greater the distance another dwelling is from their home, the less likely they are to have a friend or acquaintance living there. (This occurs even in short culs-de-sac of only a dozen or so homes: Johnston, 1974b.) In part, this pattern of local contacts reflects the operations of intra-urban housing markets, which we discussed in Chapter 1, and the desire of people to live among those with whom they prefer to develop social relationships, yet within these constraints it is still clear that distance strongly influences the pattern of contacts, both informal – via chance meetings, common friends etc. – and formal – e.g. social clubs and churches. Different groups may be more restricted than others – non-car owners compared to car owners; old compared to young; mothers with young children compared to childless couples, etc. – but the variations in dependence on the neighbourhood are relative rather than absolute. Those very much dependent on the home area are often known as localites, with those who range much more widely to meet friends being termed cosmopolites.

Interaction in the confines of the workplace is even more restricted spatially than it is in the area of the home, because of time constraints. Within a large factory, most workers only get to know their immediate workmates, with whom they share journeys to and from work, lunch and other breaks, and perhaps attend union or other meetings; within a large office, a majority will know only those they work alongside, or come into frequent contact with; and so on. For some, home and workplace are virtually synonymous, but the factory system and the large city centre office blocks, plus the ethos of the planning profession in most cities, have ensured a clear spatial divorce between residence and job for almost all employees in the last few decades. For most people, therefore, the workplace contains a small group of friends and acquaintances, many of whom will have similar social backgrounds and attitudes, even if they do not come from the same areas.

In all, we can suggest a total of six possible social contexts which have a spatial form:

(1) The home, within which members of the family interact.

(2) The neighbourhood, within which all family members, but particularly those who do not go out to work – the children and the housewife, plus the retired – very probably develop social contacts.

(3) The school, which is a major socialization environment for

children and sometimes for parents too, if they become involved in administering this local institution in some way.
(4) The workplace, which may be a small office, one shop in a large factory, a tradesman's round etc. and in which close acquaintanceships often develop.
(5) The place for leisure activities, such as a local pub or sports club, where neighbours meet on an informal basis.
(6) Formal organizations, such as Womens' Institutes and trade unions, where individuals gather and talk – many of these organizations have a *de facto* if not a *de jure* spatial organization.
In most of this chapter, our main attention is on the second of these, although the relevance of all will be discussed.

The workplace and structural effects

Politics may well be a topic of conversation among people who work together, particularly during election campaigns. Issues and personalities may be to the forefront in the mass media, and discussion of them prolonged, perhaps even heated. A workplace where trade union activity is considerable almost certainly would have such discussion taking place, but conversations revolving around political issues are common in many situations. Some workers may be immunized from any influence that such discussion might have on their own attitudes and preferences, perhaps because it is in conflict with those being learned elsewhere, but others may well be affected and in their turn may influence others still.

One workplace at which political discussion is extremely common is a university. This was studied in the United States by Lazarsfeld and Thielens (1958) during the McCarthy era, when academic freedom in the universities was under serious threat. Each respondent in a large sample of social scientists was classified according to the degree to which he held permissive views on such topics as whether communist professors should be sacked, whether student Young Communist Leagues should be prohibited, and whether radical teachers were a luxury that could not be afforded. The older respondents tended to be the more conservative, and those with more permissive views were concentrated among the more eminent social scientists in the recognized higher quality institutions. Within these workplaces (Lazarsfeld and Thielens, 1958, p. 163):

> Next to the creative leader comes the competent teacher and productive research scholar. Even if he might be by nature more amenable to the general currents of public opinion, he is more directly in communication with the leaders of his profession, and his thinking is shaped by the process of mutual interaction among primary groups ... Thus he too will add to a permissive climate when appointed to a distinguished institution.

This is a very clear structural effect.

Another workplace studied in some detail is the printing industry shop in the United States, whose workers are organized into the International Typographical Union. This union has two clearly defined political factions which differ in their views on the best policies for improving their members' conditions; the Progressives favour each 'local' (district branch) conducting its own negotiations with employers, whereas the Independents are for nationally organized, more militant action. In voting at union elections and referenda members face three sets of influences: (1) their own political predispositions – liberal or conservative; (2) the general sentiment in their workplace; and (3) the current policy of the union as a whole, which depends on whether the Progressives or the Independents are in control. Looking at the first two only, the percentage of members voting according to their personal predispositions was (Lipset, Trow and Coleman, 1956, p. 345):

Personal Predisposition	Conservative	Liberal	Conservative	Liberal
Workplace Orientation	Independent	Progressive	Progressive	Independent
	87	68	55	38

Conservatives in a Progressive-dominated workplace were subject to conflicting influences and much more likely to vote against their personal feelings than were those in Independent-dominated workplaces, where the general climate of opinion reinforced their own views.

British sociologists and political scientists have also looked at the effect of workplace on voting behaviour, basing their analyses on theories of differences in attitudes and life-styles within classes, particularly the working class. Thus Piepe *et al.* (1969) identified three types of worker: (1) the deferential, who works in small service-industries, has frequent face-to-face contact with his employer, and is politically both isolated and conservative: (2) the proletarian, who works in large plants, has little personal contact with 'bosses' and whose political attitudes are based on conceptions of trade union solidarity; and (3) the privatized, who lacks either community or political ties. Their hypothesis was that deferential workers are more likely than their proletarian counterparts to vote for the Conservative Party, and study of groups of towns whose Labour Party voting was either more or less than predicted from knowledge of their class structures, indeed indicated that the negative residuals (greater Conservative voting) tended to be in resort, administrative and commercial centres – which have concentrations of deferential workers – whereas the positive residuals (greater Labour voting) were concentrated in the heavy industrial, proletarian towns.

The nature of the industry in which working-class voters are employed has also been associated with their political tendencies, notably in the embourgeoisement thesis (Goldthorpe *et al.*, 1968) which holds that affluent workers in boom industries – such as car manufacture – are less likely than members of the traditional working class to vote for the Labour Party. To test this hypothesis, Crewe (1973) identified three groups of constituencies: (1) those with concentrations of affluent workers – more than 40 per cent of the workforce being manual workers while rates of home ownership and car ownership are substantially greater than the national average – 15 constituences; (2) those with concentrations of traditional workers – more than 15 per cent of the labour force are employed in mining – 17 constituencies; and (3) those with concentrations of affluent tenants, similar to the constituencies in the first group except for the home-ownership levels. Again using residuals from equations predicting voting behaviour from class structure, he found that constituencies in the first and third groups had higher Conservative voting percentages than expected and had been swinging more towards the Conservatives over the preceding decade, whereas those in the second group were more solidly Labour than expected. The embourgeoisement thesis was validated, therefore; affluent workers in 'growth industries' are apparently becoming politically conservative.

The Neighbourhood Effect

Of the various structural effects, from our point of view the most interesting is that produced by the neighbourhood, the local environment within which much social contact occurs. We showed in Chapter 4 how a great proportion of the geography of voting can be related to the spatial division of labour. This geographical separation of people performing different economic roles within society occurs at a variety of scales. The richest and most powerful families are almost invariably congregated into a few settlements – London and Paris, New York and Toronto etc. – as are many of the senior bureaucrats of the public and private sectors of industry and commerce. The working classes are clustered elsewhere, in the manufacturing towns and the seaports, on the coalfields and, to some extent, on the land; the retired are often in major concentrations at inland and coastal resorts.

Spatial segregation at this scale is far from complete. Every parliamentary constituency in Great Britain and congressional district in the United States will contain some white-collar workers – bank managers and clerks, school teachers and social workers, medical officials and municipal bureaucrats – as well as others in blue-collar jobs – fitters and turners, mechanics and motormen – and young as well as old, immigrants as well as locally-born, and so on. Despite this, the general complexion of districts varies considerably, as shown by a classification of the 623 parliamentary constituencies in England, Scotland and Wales (Webber, unpublished). Forty different characteristics of the constituency populations (including households and their dwellings) were analysed (using factor analysis), with the results suggesting thirty different constituency types, many of which were clearly identifiable as particular areas, such as the coal-mining districts which have above average percentages of skilled manual workers and of homes without an inside W.C. and below average rates of car ownership. Each of these constituency types is a different socio-political environment, comprising a characteristic social structure with which certain social and political attitudes will be associated (see Chapters 3 and 4).

The countries we are focusing on here are highly urbanized, and within the cities and towns the various social, economic and demographic groups are usually to be found in different areas (Johnston, 1971). This is partly through choice, particularly for the wealthier groups who wish to live in relative seclusion from their 'social inferiors', and partly through the operation of the private and public sector housing markets which, if they do not actually allocate households to particular areas, at least very much constrain the range of available choice. At the extremes of the class scale, spatial segregation is especially marked, but most areas have some social mixture, with people from different economic backgrounds and birthplaces living nearby, if not next door to each other or in the same street. Webber's classification of constituencies also illustrates this segregation pattern in the larger cities and conurbations. Among the thirty constituency types were those identified as: peripheral council housing areas, characterized by high percentages of persons aged 45–64 and 15–24, and of semi-skilled workers; high status central London, with above average concentrations of professional and non-manual workers, and also of young people living alone; high status outer London, with high percentages of households in owner-occupied homes; and low status Clydeside, whose populations included above average percentages of unskilled and unemployed persons, and also of households living in cramped conditions.

These different milieux are those which confront their residents, both those raised and socialized in them and those who move into them from other environments. As neighbourhood contexts, they act as structural effects in many cases, offering conflicting political attitudes to some individual predispositions. Constituencies, wards, ridings, congressional districts; all these are relatively large areas in many countries – the average English constituency contained 64,908 voters at the October 1974 general election. Within each, the map of social areas is often complex and contains as much variety, if not more, as there is between constituencies. Thus, some high status London suburbs contain council-housing estates and most mining areas will have pockets of middle-class housing. Each of these social areas is a separate social milieu, with a dominant political ethos. But none is entirely independent of those surrounding it. They may be grouped together to form catchment areas for schools, churches, and various social organizations, within which are brought together people from different backgrounds. And so each little part of the country has its own dominant social ethos and political orientation. But no local population, however small, is entirely homogeneous in all of its attitudes, in part because the segregation processes are far from complete, in part because people move from place to place or from social group to social group and carry their learned attitudes with them, and in part because there are always mavericks, people whose attitudes are not consonant with the majority of their 'type'. And so in every social area a variety of views and opinions is held and discussed, which might act as the basis for a structural effect for some of its residents.

Operation of the neighbourhood effect

The neighbourhood effect comes about because some people in an area convert others to their viewpoint, as a result of discussing various political issues with them. The neighbourhood is a communications network in which, it is assumed, 'no man is an island'. Social problems in general and, in our present context here, various political issues are discussed in conversations with neighbours, friends and acquaintances (Cox, 1969a); there may be no overt intention to try and convert people to a different attitude from their current one, but it could be that as a result of conversation, maybe only one or maybe a number of similar ones, some people change their minds and their voting intentions. At least one geographer has indicated his doubts about this proposal (Prescott, 1972, p. 87):

> My own experience in talking to individuals about the way they voted in particular elections, is that many did not know exactly why they voted as they did. Certainly in rationalizing their decision, no one has ever explained their votes in terms of the flow of information or the political complexion of the area in which they live.

The cynic could respond that people who have been swayed by conversation with particular individuals might be unprepared to admit it, even if they were aware of it. In any case, it is only expected that a relatively small proportion of the electorate is affected in this way, and their conversion may be the result of a slow period of acculturation (political osmosis) rather than by the sort of instantaneous reaction which happened on the road to Damascus. (And of course, the large advertising industry has proved that some people can be convinced of almost anything!) However unlikely the process might seem, there is a large body of circumstantial evidence, which we shall discuss here, whose characteristics are very much in line with what one would expect of a neighbourhood effect.

Logical models based on assumptions that people mainly converse with those who live in their neighbourhood, and that such conversation influences attitudes and behaviour, require validation of the assumptions as well as of the deduced consequences. The former can only be based on anthropological research, looking at the details of social networks and political conversation (Sheingold, 1973). One such study was undertaken by Fitton (1973), who was interested in whether people responded to the same political stimuli in an area, whether these were the majority stimuli in those areas, and what the size of the area was. To achieve his goals, he interviewed all of the electors living in three streets of terraced houses in the Manchester area of England, involving a total of 87 respondents, most of them from working-

Table 5.1 Voting in three Manchester streets in 1970

Street	*Number of voters*	*Labour*	*Percentage voting Conservative*	*Liberal*	*Percentage not voting*
Caesar Street					
Middle class	2	50	0	0	50
Working class	24	46	29	12·5	12·5
Archer Street					
Middle class	4	50	50	0	0
Working class	21	38	38	5	19
Nelson Street					
Middle class	7	71	29	0	0
Working class	29	55	38	0	7

Source: Fitton (1973, p. 453)

class backgrounds. Voting in the three streets was predominantly for the Labour Party at the 1970 general election (Table 5.1) but during the campaign period preceding the voting 15 of the 87 changed their mind about which party to support.

Fitton first discovered that most of his respondents were not aware of the political complexion of the wards in which they lived, and among those who changed their minds during the 1970 campaign there was no indication of a clear swing towards the ward majority view. If the neighbourhood effect was operating, therefore, it must have been at a finer spatial scale than that of the ward (see also Cox, 1972) and Fitton (1973, p. 456) argued that: 'If the neighbourhood environment is to provide a source of control over members of groups within it, there needs to be evidence that friendships and contacts exist within the streets, that these contacts are important for individuals, and that they have political saliency for them.' The three streets, despite their external similarities, were very different. Although more than half of its residents had lived there for more than twenty years, Caesar Street was the least friendly and contained many antagonistic relationships. It was also politically the most stable; only three voters changed their party preferences between the 1966 and 1970 elections. Residents were not aware of their neighbours' political opinions in most cases, and rarely discussed political issues. The seven Conservative voters did form a very tight social cluster, however, whereas there was little social cohesion among the other nineteen residents. The opportunities for political conversion through conversation were few, therefore, but the three who changed their preferences in the 1970 campaign did swing towards the majority view among their friends.

Nine of Archer Street's twenty-five residents changed their party preference prior to the 1970 vote, and as many as fifteen reported political discussions with others in the street during the campaign period. It was a much friendlier area than Caesar Street, although supporters of the two main parties tended to be in separate cliques. Nevertheless, of the nine vote-changers, six were apparently influenced by the local discussions.

In Nelson Street, the friendship groups were much more heterogeneous in their political attitudes compared to those in the other two. This may be a reason why residents were not very aware of their neighbours' politics, for they seemed to fear the feelings of 'social disharmony' which political discussion might produce. Twelve of the thirty-six reported such discussion prior to the 1970 election, however, and five of the six who changed their preferences did so to come into line with those of their main friends.

With regard to these three streets, therefore, Fitton (1973, p. 471) was able to conclude that: 'In so far as change took place it was predominantly in the direction of the street sub-group to which the individual changer was attached', which is in line with the hypothesized role of the neighbourhood as a source of contagious effects. It was not the only locale playing that role, however, nor was it of equal importance in each street. For some people, local political discussion was to be avoided because it was likely to arouse feelings and disturb the social equanimity. Thus the nature of the local environment in terms of its degree of friendliness and trust, as well as the personalities of the individuals (their openness to contagious influences etc.), are all important potential determinants of the likelihood of neighbourhood effects. In addition, some people are less oriented towards their immediate neighbourhood in their social contacts than are others. Excluding the 'loners' or isolates, who have no contacts, we can identify two main groups. The localites are those who, often because of external constraints, are very much tied to their local area; they include the old and the immobile poor, and many young parents, especially mothers with no employment outside the home. The cosmopolites, on the other hand, are more mobile and are not tied to a particular locality for their social life. Households with cars (especially those with two), non-family households (childless couples; single adults etc.), and to a lesser extent those who work some distance from home, may all meet others in different milieux from the neighbourhood and so be less influenced by the local climate of opinion. The relative size of these groups, where they live, and the effects of interaction on their political behaviour, are all topics as yet virtually unresearched, and few have emulated Fitton, and also Burstein (1976), in conducting detailed field investigations of the contagious process.

Empirical Studies Suggesting Neighbourhood Effects

All settlements comprise a series of interlocking communications networks through which information is transmitted. Every individual resident is potentially a receiver, a processor, and a transmitter of information, much of which is received from the mass media. Which information is received in this way depends on the sources tapped, which are very much a function, as is the next stage of processing or evaluating it, of partisan attitudes and values – the theories discussed earlier. After processing, much information will be rejected; the accepted pieces may be modified, with some parts amplified and others played down, and are then ready for transmission, should the individual participate in discussion of a relevant topic.

Fitton's detailed study suggests that people vary in their activity rates as information receivers and transmitters with regard to political information. In every neighbourhood there are likely to be at least a few transmitters, however, and because of the relative socio-economic homogeneity there, the information which they relay will probably be similarly oriented towards one political view (Robinson, 1976). It is from them that other receivers, initially of another persuasion, are likely to receive contrary views to their own, which may lead to their conversion. They will not be obliged to follow; with the secret ballot the sorts of obligations to employers and religious leaders which were typical of nineteenth-century Britain (e.g. Cox, 1970a) have now disappeared. Appeals to the conscience are occasionally made by religious leaders – against Mintoff's Socialist Party by the Archbishop of Malta in 1962, for example, and by the Pope against the Italian Communist Party in 1976 – but the vast majority of voters are free agents. Many are firmly committed to one party but, as we saw from Butler and Stokes's data (p. 225), there are many floating voters too. If the neighbourhood effect operates, then those floating voters who are liable to change their preferences should follow the lead of the majority view in their home area.

As we have shown, full testing of this model demands exacting and time-consuming field work. In its absence, how can we test the hypothesis, which is that party support is even more polarized spatially than one would expect if all individuals were not in contact with their local social environment. Geographers, in particular, are interested in patterns at aggregate scales, often involving many thousands of voters. At this level the hypothesis can only be tested through sensible collection and sensitive analysis of data, from which inferences are made regarding the likelihood that observed patterns indicate a neighbourhood effect. Three procedures in this vein are reviewed here; their findings are only suggestive of neighbourhood effects but, as we shall show, the circumstantial evidence is strong.

The repeated survey

Beyond a very small area, it is impossible to study all members of a social network, and so the next best alternative must be employed. This is the repeated survey of a large sample, a procedure developed by three Columbia University sociologists – Paul Lazarsfeld, Bernard Berelson and Hazel Gaudet (1944) – in an investigation of how people decided which way to vote in American presidential elections. Their interviewing involved 3000 residents of Erie County, Ohio, chosen because its voting patterns tended to be typical of the results in the country as a whole. Six hundred respondents were interviewed once a month from May until after the election in November, providing a large bank o data on the evolution of preferences between Roosevelt, the incumbent Democrat, and his Republican challenger, Wilkie.

The usual American party preferences were apparent at the aggregate level: higher socio-economic status residents tended to support Wilkie, whereas the working class preferred Roosevelt, but within each economic class, both younger voters (under 45) and Catholics were more likely to support Roosevelt than were their elders and the Protestants. Many were not fixed in their preferences, however: the percentages making their decisions at various stages of the campaign were:

May 48 June–August 31 September–November 21

The early deciders were generally the politically-committed; the floating voters of September–November were for the most part the relatively apathetic.

A source of delay for many lay in conflicts of interest; they were subject to opposing views in their main information sources. Table 5.2 identifies three of these conflicts showing, separately for the politically-interested and the politically-apathetic, the effects of a conflict on the timing of the decision. Among the politically-interested whose family was disunited in its views, eleven times as many delayed in their decision until the last months compared with those for whom the family environment was politically united. Of particular interest to us is the similar effect for those whose friends changed their minds, although of course there is no indication that these are local friends. These conflicts of interest also characterized different types of late deciders; those who changed their preferences from one party to another were more

Table 5.2 Conflict of interest and timing of voting decision

Percentage deciding in Conflict source	*Politically interested* May	*Politically interested* June–August	*Politically interested* September–November	*Politically apathetic* May	*Politically apathetic* June–August	*Politically apathetic* September–November
I Between religion and economic status						
Conflict	56	30	14	36	28	17
No conflict	68	21	11	48	37	24
II Within family						
Family divided	48	29	23	29	28	43
Family united	75	23	2	56	38	6
III Friends						
Changed their minds	65	21	14	38	37	25
Were static in views	67	31	2	55	42	3

Source: Lazarsfeld *et al.* (1944, pp. 58–9)

likely to have experienced conflicts than were those moving to one party from an initial 'don't know'.

For many respondents, the reason for their uncertainty in May was because at that time the parties had not yet held their nominating conventions, and once the candidates were known the decisions were soon made. Among the others, the researchers suggested that decision-making was influenced by a 'two-step flow of communication'. It was the politically-committed who were likely to listen to radio programmes and read in the papers about the campaign. The waverers, many of them politically apathetic, were not; most of their information came from the locally committed and, as Cox's (1969a) model suggests, this was biased towards the local majority viewpoint through selective evaluation (see Klapper, 1960, p. 95). If these waverers can be persuaded which way to vote by the local information transmitters then, as Lazarsfeld *et al* conclude (1944, p. 158): 'The side which has the more enthusiastic supporters and which can mobilize grass-root support in an expert way has great chances of success'. This, unless the transmitters are atypical of the local population, is a neighbourhood effect as hypothesized. The nature of the 'persuaders' was discovered by asking the waverers whom they were influenced by (Table 5.3). Relatives clearly had greater influence on females than on males, suggesting that wives – in 1940 at least – depend heavily on husbands for political leadership. Friends and neighbours were far from major influences; it is of interest to note that they were of much greater importance to blue-collar workers, to farmers, and to women, all of whom are more likely to be localites than cosmopolites.

The methodology developed in Erie County was used eight years later in the small town of Elmira, New York, to study the Truman-Dewey contest. Again, a major finding was that voters subject to conflicts of interest tended to swing towards the local majority view. This was termed a 'breakage effect' and was described as follows (Berelson, Lazarsfeld and McPhee, 1954, p. 100): 'When the voter's close associates do not provide him with a single clear political direction – when instead they offer him an alternative – then wider associations in the surrounding com-

Table 5.3 Type of voter and source of persuasion

	Type of voter				
	Male	*Female*	*White collar*	*Manual worker*	*Farmer*
Percentage who were influenced by					
Relatives	5	33	5	8	8
Business contacts	33	8	38	41	8
Friends and neighbours	14	23	8	17	25
Non-personal sources	56	52	57	47	70
Percentage who were most influenced by					
Relatives	0	14	3	1	3
Business contacts	19	5	17	28	5
Friends and neighbours	4	6	1	4	10
Non-personal sources	77	75	79	67	82

Source: Lazarsfeld *et al.* (1944, pp. 171–2)

munity reinforce one position over the other.' In Elmira this meant a resounding victory for Dewey.

Similar studies were conducted in England in the 1950s. In the London constituency of Greenwich, for example, Benney and Geiss (1950) found that in families which were united in their political views, 89 per cent of those who initially intended to vote Labour eventually did so, whereas the corresponding figure for disunited families was only 71 per cent. Comparing Greenwich, a strongly Labour seat, with the pro-Conservative constituency of Hertford, Martin (1952) identified different types of voting patterns which could be ascribed to local environmental variations. Amongst those who considered themselves middle class, for example, nearly three times as many voted Labour in Greenwich as in Hertford (Table 5.4) and similarly many more working-class residents in Hertford voted Conservative than did their contemporaries in Greenwich. Other tables showed that of those who voted 'with their class' (e.g. working class for Labour), many fewer changed their party preferences between the 1945 and 1950 elections than was so with the 'class unfaithful'; for example, of the professional middle class, 96 per cent of those supporting Conservative in 1945 voted the same way in 1950 but this was so for only 57 per cent of those opting for Labour in the first contest.

Single surveys

The repeated surveys are very productive of research data but difficult to design and maintain (keeping the interviewees happy!) and increasingly expensive to mount. As a consequence, many researchers interested in the strength and nature of the neighbourhood effect have had to rely on what they can glean from single surveys. One of these was designed jointly by a geographer (Kevin Cox) and a political scientist (John Orbell) working in Columbus, Ohio. They analysed the data separately, but produced similar conclusions.

Orbell (1970) suggests that the clearer the cues (the politically-relevant information) circulating in an area, the more likely that an individual resident would respond to them, so that majorities

Table 5.4 Socio-economic status (perceived) and voting in Greenwich and Hertford

Occupation	*Perceived Status*	*Greenwich*			*Hertford*		
		Labour	*Liberal*	*Conservative*	*Labour*	*Liberal*	*Conservative*
Professional	Middle class	16	1	78	6	11	78
Salaried	Middle class	22	6	62	8	14	70
Salaried	Working class	44	6	44	18	15	48
Manual	Middle class	58	3	32	41	12	29
Manual	Working class	72	2	12	54	14	17

Source: Martin (1952, p. 235)

for one party should be enhanced in areas where it was already predominant rather than those where its lead over an opponent was slight. Four factors were thought to operate as influences on political conversion within the neighbourhood:

(1) the content of the cues – which party they were biased towards; (2) the clarity of the cues – the degree to which leaders in the 'two-step' process disagreed; (3) the receptiveness of the receivers; and (4) the responsiveness of floating voters to the cues. From these, Orbell hypothesized:

(1) That people who were politically committed and motivated would have the most accurate political information.

(2) That the politically apathetic are 'most likely to conform to whatever cues they receive from the district' (Orbell, 1970, p. 335), but because of their low involvement these cues might be both few in number and selected randomly, and so might be unrepresentative of the district and not necessarily lead to conversion to the majority view.

(3) That people with just a moderate involvement are 'most likely to conform to the *objective* political structure of their districts', because they receive more cues than the apathetic and are less resistant than the committed.

The Columbus data verified these hypotheses, indicating that it is the middle-of-the-road responsible citizens who are, nevertheless, not avidly interested in politics who are most likely to be the subjects of neighbourhood effects, in areas where the cues predominantly favour one party.

Cox's (1969b) analyses were built around four hypotheses suggesting who would be the most open to neighbourhood effects: (1) those whose informal social contacts mainly took place around their home; (2) those whose formal social contacts – through membership of various voluntary organizations – were mainly local; (3) those who had recently moved into an area, and were thus more likely to be at odds with the local political climate (see also Cox, 1970b); and (4) those who were located in the middle of a scale measuring degree of political involvement. Of the first two, the second received the greatest endorsement from the Columbus data, indicating that political conversion is more likely to occur in formally-constituted groups than during informal conversations; this is because formal organizations are likely to bring residents into contact with a representative selection of local views, in which the neighbourhood majority should be dominant, and in which those inclined to change may have their leanings reinforced by the majority (Klapper, 1960, p. 68), whereas in their choice of friends and acquaintances people are more likely, as Fitton's work showed, to select those with similar views to their own. Not all voluntary associations may be as effective, however, for Freeman and Showel (1962) interviewed respondents who were much more prepared to take advice from members of some organizations than of others; the Parent Teachers Association, the various churches, and organizations for service veterans were all favoured by members, but the churches were not by the non-members.

Cox's third hypothesis was also confirmed with recent immigrants to an area being apparently more influenced by the local milieu than were long-time residents, especially if the former joined local voluntary organizations. And finally, in agreement with Orbell's finding, it was those with moderate political involvement who were the most susceptible to neighbourhood conversion. Cox's (1969b, p. 182) conclusion was that formal social contacts in the area around the home are the main channels along which locally-biased political information is transmitted to the receivers.

Neighbourhood effects, mediated through local communication networks, may be a function of other variables and thus only occur because of the operation of additional influences. To test whether the effects occur independently of other variables, Segal and Meyer (1969) looked at a sample of nine towns stratified into three groups according to their general political leanings. Individual respondents were then classified by their own socio-economic status and by that of their neighbourhood, and the percentage voting Republican in each class was tabulated (Table 5.5). Neighbourhood influence was clearly strong in all types of town. Among the low socio-economic status respondents, for example, in every type there was a greater percentage voting

Table 5.5 Class, neighbourhood and urban context: Republican voting patterns

Political characteristic of town	*Strong Democrat*		*Mixed*		*Strong Republican*	
Neighbourhood socio-economic status	*Low*	*High*	*Low*	*High*	*Low*	*High*
Respondents' socio-economic status						
Low	16	29	20	43	49	67
High	22	36	37	65	65	89
(entries are percentages voting Republican)						

Source: Segal and Mayer (1969, p. 225)

Republican among those living in the higher status neighbourhoods, with the greatest difference occurring in the towns with a mixed political complexion, suggesting to Segal and Meyer (1969, p. 226) that 'the local community most effectively directs the partisanship of its members where neither party commands the party allegiance of the town' (which is somewhat in opposition to Orbell's conclusion). This assumes not only that the operative process is the neighbourhood effect but also that there is marked spatial segregation of the socio-economic classes within the towns. The effects of variations in segregation have been highlighted in Almy's (1973) study of voting on five non-partisan issues – fluoridation of water supplies; education; parks; civic improvements; and public works – in eighteen U.S. cities. He proposed that the greater the spatial segregation of classes, the greater the cohesion within classes in their attitudes to the issues, because of neighbourhood effects; and also that the more segregated towns would show greater polarization between classes in attitudes to the issues. Both were found to be valid hypotheses, presenting more strong circumstantial evidence favouring the neighbourhood effect.

One of the features of urban neighbourhoods is that their characteristics tend to remain constant, despite often rapid rates of change in their populations (about one in every five American residents moves home each year, and one in every six or seven British residents does likewise: Johnston, 1971). Do political attitudes display such constancy also, suggesting a continuous neighbourhood effect operating on new arrivals? This should be so, especially if there is a strong local organization for the initially dominant party, and it has been demonstrated by Key and Munger (1959) for southern Indiana from 1868. There the counties are strongly Democrat, having been peopled by post-Civil War migrants from the southern states who were very anti-Republican, as most of the south still shows today.

A similar continuity, long after the decline of the original reasons for the partisanship and the death of its originators, has been isolated in rural Wales (Cox, 1970a). Respondents to a large survey were categorized as living in one of two types of area: (1)

Traditional Wales, mainly rural areas with strong Welsh language and non-conformist religious roots and with a tradition of liberal radicalism reflecting opposition to English, Anglican landlords; and (2) *Modern Wales*, the coalfield and manufacturing areas where anglicization has been more extensive and politics are based on the British class-system. Cox put forward the hypothesis that social class would be the main determinant of voting patterns in the latter context, but that in 'Traditional Wales' radicalism would be more closely related to variables other than class, reflecting the liberal tradition. This turned out to be so. In 'Modern Wales' the Labour Party's strength was among the lower-class, urban residents; in 'Traditional Wales', it drew its support mainly from males, from those in trade unions – and thus in a national information network – and from rural areas. (Interestingly, the revival of Welsh nationalism in the 1970s, through the Plaid Cymru party, has been strongest at national elections in 'Traditional Wales'.)

In rural areas, neighbouring communities may develop opposing patterns of partisanship, despite their apparent similarities in social and economic structure, because of the continuity of a neighbourhood effect. Occasionally, however, a community may undergo a rapid transition from one dominant view to another, as Scheuch (1969) discovered in some small Saarland communities where the whole population tended to follow their leaders when the latter changed their views (see p. 284 below on similar patterns in Japan). National politics are not the only issues on which such local polarization may develop, as illustrated by some non-survey data. Members of the British National Union of Miners vary considerably in their 'militancy' on various issues, depending on the coalfield in which they work and the nature of its leadership. At present, Yorkshire, Scotland, Kent and South Wales in particular have reputations for being left-wing, and are led by militants such as Arthur Scargill (Yorkshire) and Mick McGahey (Scotland); other fields – such as North Derbyshire – are known to be more middle-of-the-road and are the 'marginal constituencies' which have to be won if any issue is to be carried nationally (see Chapters 7 and 8). The extent of these variations comes out in the percentages of miners voting in favour of the Labour Government's pay policies in 1975 (£6 per week maximum) and 1976 (4½% maximum, plus tax cuts). The miners were generally more receptive to a pay policy in 1976 (Table 5.6) but inter-coalfield variations changed relatively little. A variety of reasons for the differences can be suggested, going back into the history of working conditions and labour relations on the various fields and into the origins of the miners, as well as the nature of the current leadership: militancy is also greater 'down the pit' than among surface workers.

Aggregate patterns

Studies of aggregate patterns are usually based on published data collected for other reasons, notably censuses (Chapter 2), which can be spliced with election results and, in some cases, extended by comparable survey data. Analyses of these can therefore only provide circumstantial evidence regarding neighbourhood effects. The validity of the inferences depends on the logic of the hypotheses and of the assumptions from which they are derived, on the value of the data for the particular test, and on the degree to which analysts can discriminate between conflicting hypotheses which purport to account for the same patterns.

An extremely successful example of this type of methodology is the work by Petras and Zeitlin (1967) on the spread of radicalism into Chilean peasant communities. In that country's 1947 presidential election, the Communist candidate won 18 per cent of the national vote, but he obtained 71, 63 and 55 per cent respectively among the coal-, nitrate- and copper-mining populations. The latter groups all live in concentrated areas; to what extent does the miner's sphere of influence spread outwards into surrounding peasant communities? Two processes have operated to generate such a spread – a neighbourhood effect around the homes of the radical leaders. The first was the effort of the miners' unions to radicalize the landless peasants: an editorial in the Communist daily *El Siglo* (20 February 1966) argued that (Petras and Zeitlin, 1967, p. 585): 'All the workers in all the

Table 5.6 Coalfield support for government pay policy in the National Union of Miners

Coalfield	*Percentage favouring policy in*		*Coalfield*	*Percentage favouring policy in*	
	1975	*1976*		*1975*	*1976*
Kent	35·75	52·00	Midlands	63·75	69·50
Scotland	36·25	37·50	Durham Mechanics	65·00	75·50
Scottish Engine Men	54·25	58·00	South Derbyshire	68·33	77·00
Yorkshire	38·00	51·00	Leicestershire	68·50	66·50
South Wales	45·67	47·00	Northumberland Mechanics	69·33	82·50
North Derbyshire	49·25	62·00	North Wales	70·00	74·00
Nottinghamshire	54·25	54·00	Yorkshire Surface Workers	73·50	83·00
Northwest	56·00	60·00	Durham Engine Men	77·50	86·00
Durham	57·00	63·50	Cokemen	79·00	82·00
Cumberland	61·50	60·00	Midlands Craftsmen	80·50	83·00
Northumberland	62·50	72·00	Colliery Officials and Staff	86·67	91·50
			Total	53·40	60·50

Source: *The Times* 8 June 1976, p. 14.

unions should unite with the peasants, wherever the unions are near agricultural properties in which the peasants are initiating struggles in defence of their interests. The miners' unions must be there to bring all their moral and material support to the peasants who are struggling for possession of the land'. Secondly there was contact between the miners and the peasants, with some of the latter joining the former in temporary employment.

The degree of support for Salvador Allende at the 1958 and 1964 presidential elections is indicative of the neighbourhood effect in voting for a radical candidate. Chile's 296 municipalities were classified as either mining or agricultural according to their occupational structures (they could be in both), and the agricultural municipalities were further subdivided into satellites (adjacent to a mining municipality) and others. Allende clearly got more support in the satellites at both dates than in the other non-mining municipalities – especially among tenant peasants rather than landowners (Petras and Zeitlin, 1968) – in addition to the greater strength of his following in the non-agricultural areas (Table 5.7).

Similar results, though the analysis was based on no logical rationale, have been observed in the pattern of Labour Party voting in England and Wales (Roberts and Rumage, 1965). One of the variables selected to account for variations among the 157 borough constituencies in 1951 was 'distance to the centre of the nearest coalfield', the validity of the choice being defended solely on the grounds that it was taken from 'the writings of political scientists'. About 15 per cent of the variation in Labour support was apparently related to this variable – the further from a coalfield, the less the Labour vote – but the statistical analysis is not sufficiently detailed to indicate whether this distance effect is not merely a result of spatial variations in, for example, the percentage of working class households.

In another study of voting at Britain's 1951 general election, Cox (1968) found that within Greater London there was more support for the Conservative Party in suburban areas than in the central city, even when the variation in the class structure of these areas had been allowed for, a finding parallel to an earlier one by

Table 5.7 The neighbourhood effect in Chilean peasant communities

Percentage strongly supporting Allende in[a]	*Non-agricultual municipalities* 1958	1964	*Agricultural municipalities* 1958	1964
Mining municipalities	93	93	100	100
Satellite municipalities	73	93	60	80
Other municipalities	45	67	31	51
Percentage giving Allende weak support in[a]	*1958*	*1964*	*1958*	*1964*
Mining municipalities	4	0	0	0
Satellite municipalities	7	0	20	3
Other municipalities	21	10	49	20

[a] strong support for Allende in a municipality is over 30 per cent of the vote in 1958 and over 40 per cent in 1964; weak support is less than 20 per cent in 1958, 25 per cent in 1964.
Source: Petras and Zeitlin (1967, p. 583)

Cornford (1964). Cox interpreted this as a neighbourhood effect in the more dominantly Conservative areas where a high percentage of the population are localites; both Taylor (1969) and Kasperson (1969) disagreed with this interpretation, but it has been confirmed by a re-analysis of the data (Biel, 1972: there are many inferential problems because of other possible influences, however; Rose, 1976, p. 35). Reynolds (1974) produced very similar results from an analysis of the 1967 mayoral election in Indianapolis.

Many other studies have inferred neighbourhood effects from aggregate data, such as those of Crewe and Payne (1976) and Miller, Raab and Britto (1974): the latter concluded (pp. 67–8) with 'the possibility that when Labour voters are in a small minority they are *less* loyal than Conservatives in the same situation and more prepared to defect to a Liberal or Nationalist'. This suggests variability in receptiveness (p. 238). More often, however, analysts have combined aggregate data with survey information, using the latter to predict what the aggregate pattern would be without a neighbourhood effect. This assumes that the survey data came from a random sample of voters; bias towards one type of neighbourhood would otherwise capture the neighbourhood effect in the survey. Butler and Stokes's (1969, 1974) major study of the British electorate exemplifies this. Using survey data alone, they first compared two types of constituency – the seaside resorts (long considered bastions of the Conservative party) and the mining areas (Labour strongholds) – and found that in the resorts the Conservatives received a high proportion of the votes from people who called themselves working class, whereas in the mining areas Labour won many votes from the self-assigned middle class (Table 5.8). The analysis was then

Table 5.8 Constituency type and voting in Britain

Type of constituency	*Mining*		*Resort*	
Perceived class of respondents	*Middle*	*Working*	*Middle*	*Working*
Percentage voting				
Conservative	64	9	93	52
Labour	36	91	7	48

Source: Butler and Stokes (1969, p. 183)

extended to the whole country, using opinion poll data for 120,000 respondents. Graphs of the percentage of middle-class and of working-class residents in a constituency against, respectively, percentage of middle class voting Conservative (Figure 5.1) and working class voting Labour (Figure 5.2) both show that the more dominant the class is in a constituency, the greater the proportion of its members who vote along the expected class lines, which is again circumstantial evidence favouring the neighbourhood effect hypothesis.

Butler and Stokes's data have been re-analysed by Garrahan (1977) to take account not only of the social milieu of the voter but also his housing class. The results (Table 5.9) show a similar overall level of support for the Conservative party among middle-

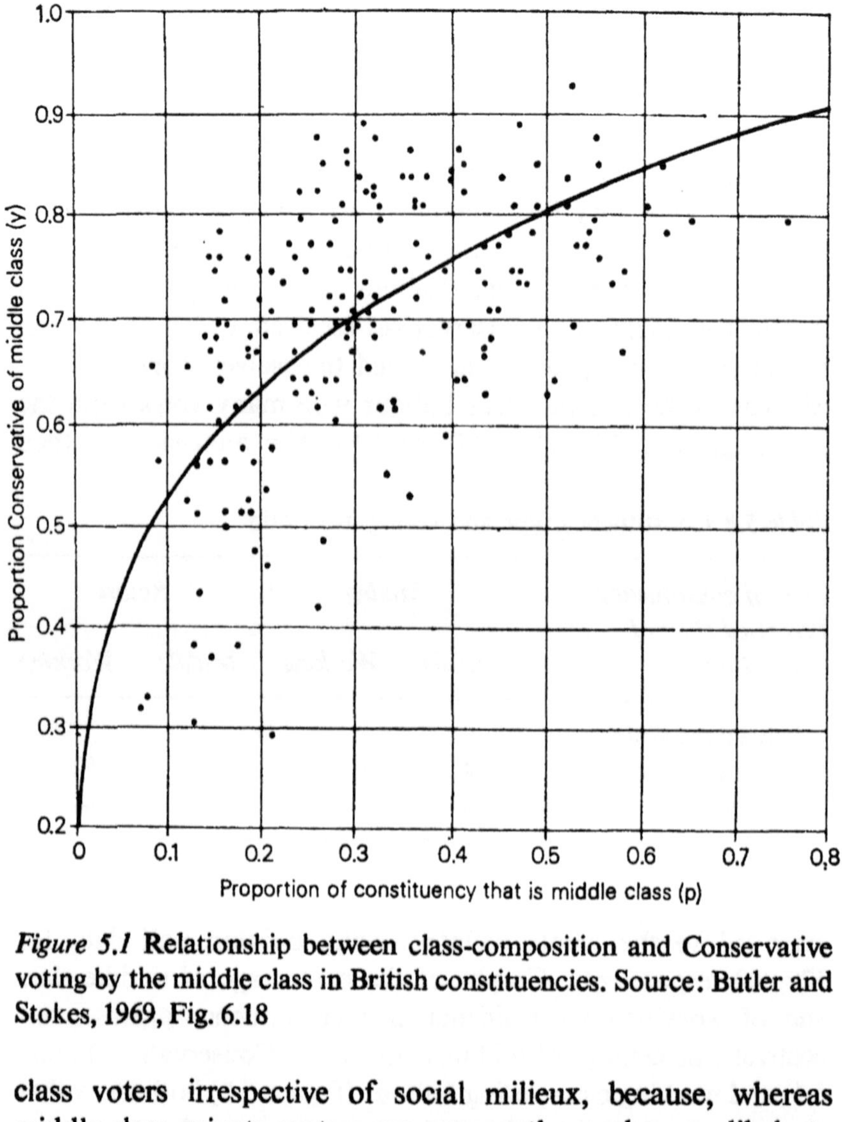

Figure 5.1 Relationship between class-composition and Conservative voting by the middle class in British constituencies. Source: Butler and Stokes, 1969, Fig. 6.18

class voters irrespective of social milieux, because, whereas middle-class private renters are apparently much more likely to vote Labour if they live in predominantly working-class districts (which is in line with the neighbourhood effect hypothesis), middle-class owner-occupiers are stronger in their Conservative support in working-class than in mixed milieux (perhaps because they feel they have more to defend in the former areas). Among the working class, on the other hand, the data clearly support the neighbourhood effect hypothesis, with lower levels of Labour

Table 5.9 Class, milieu, housing tenure and voting

	Council tenant	*Housing Tenure* *Private rental*	*Owner-occupier*	*All*
Living in mixed milieux (<66 per cent working class)				
Per cent middle class voting Conservative	39·6	63·3	68·4	65·4
Per cent working class voting Labour	65·6	48·8	33·8	48·9
Living in working-class milieux (>66 per cent working class)				
Per cent middle class voting Conservative	35·9	41·5	78·0	66·0
Per cent working class voting Labour	81·1	69·5	56·9	69·0

Source: Garrahan (1977, p. 126)

support for each tenure group in mixed as opposed to predominantly working-class milieux. Within the working class, however, owner-occupiers are least likely to support Labour, their equity in the capitalist system being a means of 'buying' their votes for the Conservatives.

In the second edition of their book, Butler and Stokes (1974, pp. 140–51) identify some of the implications of this neighbourhood effect in the light of an accepted British electoral regularity, the uniformity of the swing in votes between elections over the whole country. Data show that, for example, if the national swing is 10 per cent away from the Conservatives (i.e. their percentage of the poll is 10 points lower at the later election) then this same swing tends to occur everywhere. But this does not imply that the Conservatives are losing the same percentage of their support everywhere; if they lost 10 per cent of their votes in a constituency where they initially polled 80 per cent this would fall to 72, whereas in one where their first performance was 30 per cent the fall would be only 3 percentage points, to 27 per cent. For a uniform swing of 10 percentage points to occur, Conservative would lose one third of their support in the 30 per cent consti-

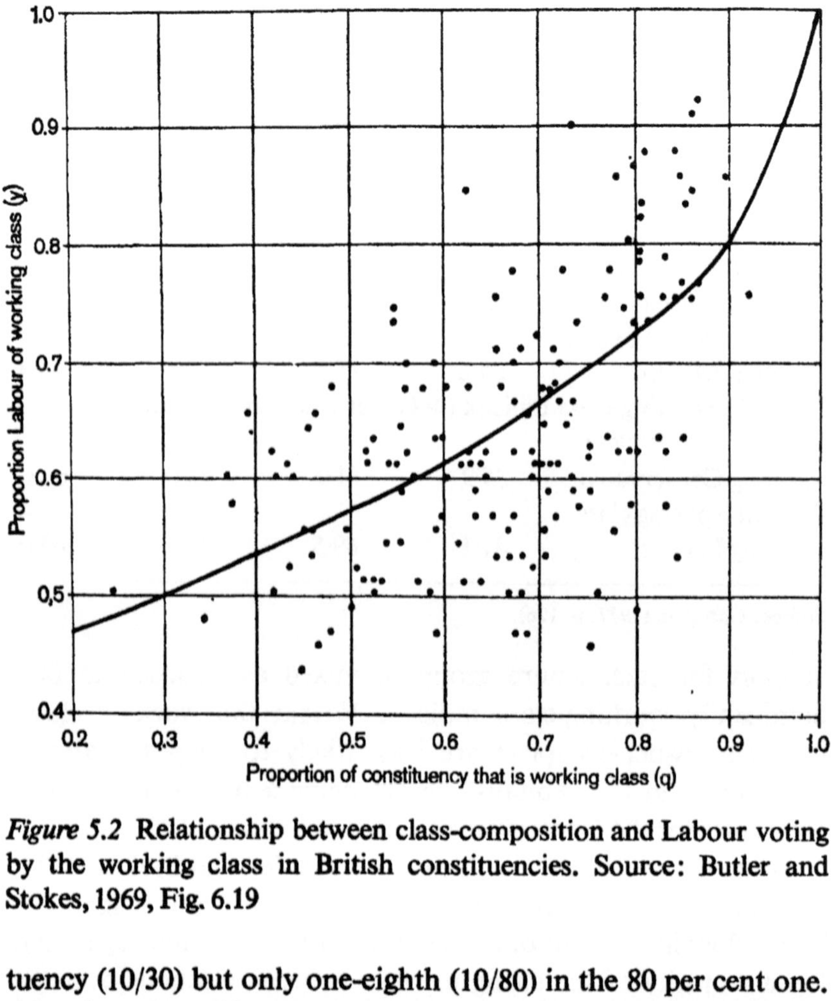

Figure 5.2 Relationship between class-composition and Labour voting by the working class in British constituencies. Source: Butler and Stokes, 1969, Fig. 6.19

tuency (10/30) but only one-eighth (10/80) in the 80 per cent one. Why does the uniform swing occur, therefore, with less vote-loss in the seats where a party is strong? Butler and Stokes suggest that it is because of the neighbourhood effect, with much less attrition of a party's support where the social ambience strongly favours it; this is particularly so, they show, among voters whose main sources of political information came from local conversation rather than from the national mass media.

The empirical regularities in Figures 5.1 and 5.2 can be accounted for by very simple models of political conversation and conversion. Assume a neighbourhood in which 12 residents support party A and 8 support party B. Assume further that whom individuals talk to there is solely a function of chance, so that for party A supporters there is a 42 per cent chance (8/19) that a person they meet will be a party B advocate; for the latter, there is a 63 per cent chance (12/19) that they will meet a supporter of A. Both are more likely to meet an A rather than a B supporter. If we now assume that after meeting one person, the other converts to that view, then: (1) of the 12 supporters of A, 5 (42 per cent of 12) shift their allegiance to B; and (2) of the 8 supporters of B, 5 (63 per cent of 8) shift their allegiance to A; which gives a final division of party support as A = 12−5+5 = 12 and B = 8−5+5 = 8. But one conversation is probably insufficient to cause a conversion, so let us now assume that two contacts, out of two, with somebody of the opposing opinion are necessary. For A's supporters, there is an 18 per cent chance of making two random contacts with B protagonists, and for the latter there is a 40 per cent chance of two meetings with A's supporters. Conversion then becomes (1) of the 12 supporters of A, 2 (18 per cent of 12) shift their allegiance to B; and (2) of the 8 supporters of B, 3 (40 per cent of 8) shift their allegiance to A; which gives A = 12−2+3 = 13 supporters and B = 8−3+2 = 7 supporters. Similar calculations can be made for any number of conversations, and the resulting patterns of support (Figure 5.3) indicate that the greater the number of conversations needed, the less is the neighbourhood effect (Johnston, 1976b).

Fitton's fieldwork and Cox's survey data indicated that people do not select their local friends and neighbours randomly and that they are more likely to be the objects of neighbourhood effects in formal organizations, and so this simple mode of conversion through conversation is somewhat unrealistic. It can easily be modified, however, to incorporate conversion through meetings in groups drawn at random from the population. Assume now that conversation in our population of 20 occurs in groups of 5. At the outset, 12 of the 20 support party A and it can be proved (Segal and Meyer, 1969) that of all the possible groups of 5 selected at random from the 20, 68 per cent of them will have a majority of members whose preferences are for A. In other words, the dominance of the major attitude in the area is

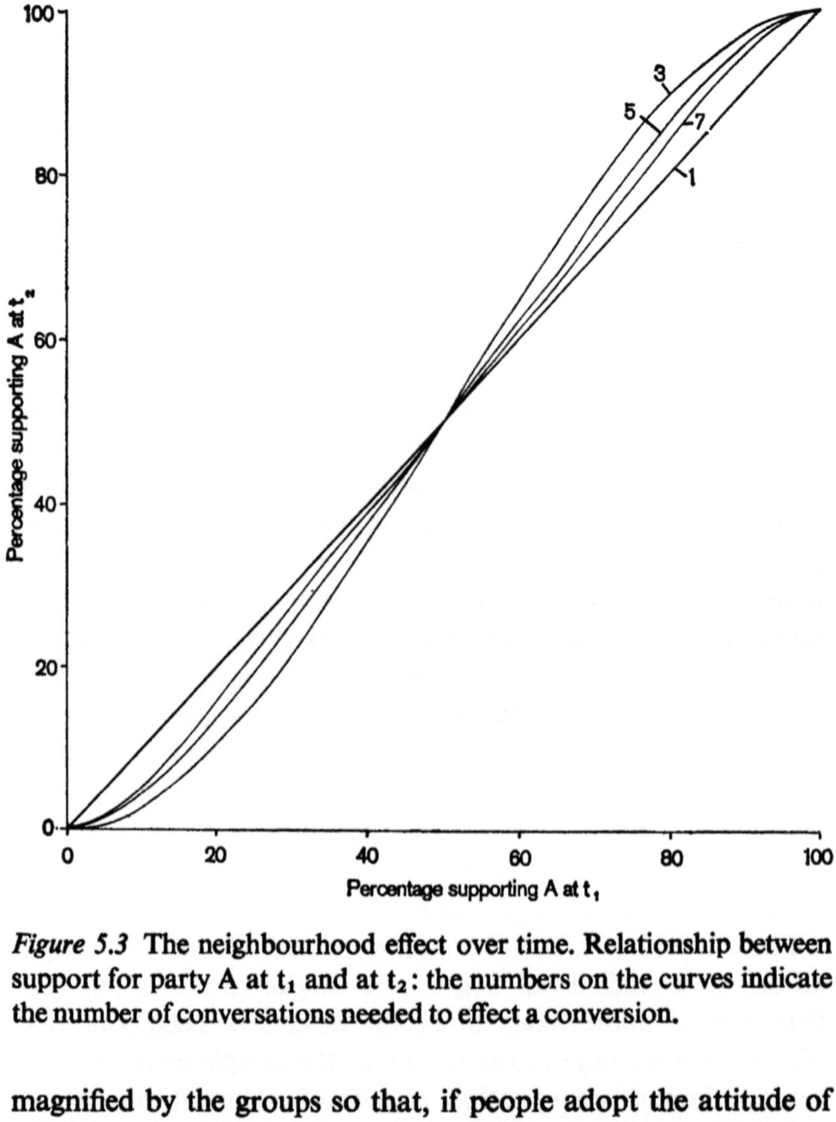

Figure 5.3 The neighbourhood effect over time. Relationship between support for party A at t_1 and at t_2: the numbers on the curves indicate the number of conversations needed to effect a conversion.

magnified by the groups so that, if people adopt the attitude of the group they belong to and group memberships develop randomly, then from an initial partisan division of 12 supporters for A and 8 for B, the neighbourhood effect will convert this to 14 and 6 respectively.

Predictions of the extent of the neighbourhood effect can be varied according to the size of the groups (and also whether they have odd or even numbers of members), the number of groups an individual joins in a given period, the importance of unanimity of cues in the conversion process, and the degree of resistance to conversion (Johnston, 1976b). The characteristic form of the neighbourhood effect curves shown in Figure 5.3 remains, however, suggesting that – unless supporters of the minority party B are much more resistant to conversion than are those of the majority, A – the result will always be amplification of the majority.

To test the general validity of these models, two methods have been adopted. Both use survey data to predict the voting pattern without a neighbourhood effect. In the first, the survey data indicate the party preferences of different social groups and data on membership of these groups are used to predict voting patterns by areas. Thus Cox (1971) had the following matrix for a sample of Paris voters in 1956:

	Percentage voting	*Communist*	*Non-Communist*
Social class	*Ouvriers*	34	66
	Non-*ouvriers*	18	82

and used it to predict the Communist vote in each precinct. If a precinct had 60 per cent of its population *ouvriers* its Communist vote should be $(60\times34)+(40\times18)/100 = 27{\cdot}6$. Comparing these predictions with the actual patterns, he found a trend which conformed to the theoretical curves of Figure 5.3, except that there were no extreme values which cause the curve to bend inwards near to the 0,0 and 100,100 coordinates (Figure 5.4). In line with the neighbourhood effect, therefore, the Communist Party was even stronger than expected where it was dominant, and weaker than expected where its potential supporters were in a minority.

Use of this method is problematical because the survey data probably already include some element of the neighbourhood effect, and it is difficult to design sampling procedures to avoid the difficulty. Butler and Stokes's (1969, pp. 178–9) data, for example, indicate that whereas 70 per cent of the lowest status group members vote Labour in the north-east region, only 56 per cent do in the south-east. This reflects the continuity of the neighbourhood effect, and hampers its study at any one date.

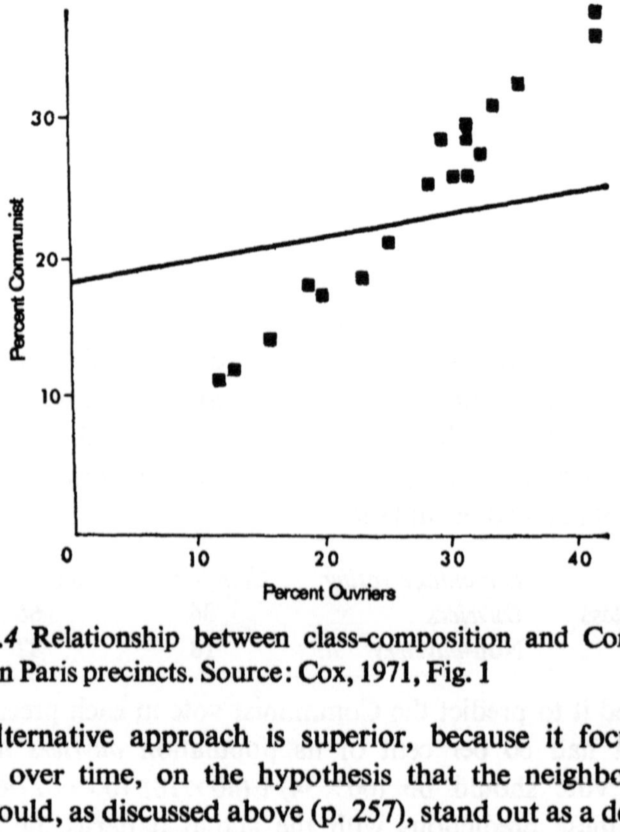

Figure 5.4 Relationship between class-composition and Communist support in Paris precincts. Source: Cox, 1971, Fig. 1

An alternative approach is superior, because it focuses on changes over time, on the hypothesis that the neighbourhood effect should, as discussed above (p. 257), stand out as a deviation from the uniform swing. Butler and Stokes (1969, p. 365) suggested that this was so, indicating that of the voters who said that they preferred Conservative in 1963 but who voted Labour in 1964, 62 per cent of those living in safe Conservative seats changed their preferences back in 1966 – i.e. swung back to conform to the local environment – compared to only 43 per cent of those who lived in constituencies held by Labour. The general method adopted is that outlined for the first approach. Using his Columbus survey data, Cox (1971, 1972) produced the following vote-change matrix:

	Percentage voting	*Democrat*	*Republican* in 1964
Voted in 1960	Democrat	84	16
	Republican	23	77

and used this and data on the 1960 voting pattern in Columbus to predict the Democrat vote in 1964, by precinct. The results

(Figure 5.5) clearly indicate that the swing to the Democrats was greatest in the areas of initial Democrat strength and that the Republicans more than held their own in their bailiwicks. Similar

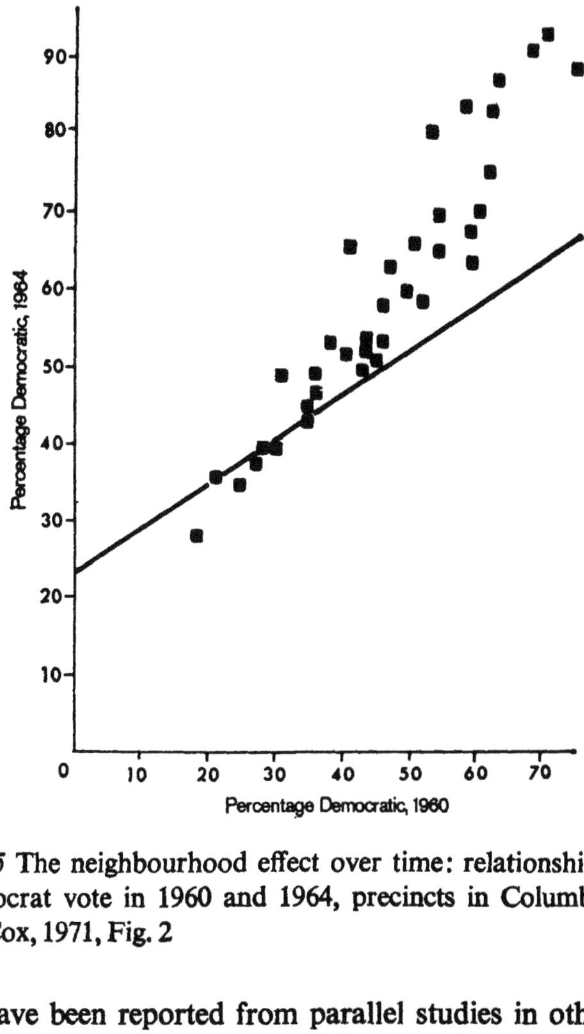

Figure 5.5 The neighbourhood effect over time: relationship between the Democrat vote in 1960 and 1964, precincts in Columbus, Ohio. Source: Cox, 1971, Fig. 2

results have been reported from parallel studies in other places (Johnston, 1977c), although Cox (1971) has shown, from a study of towns of various sizes, that the larger the place the greater the average neighbourhood effect, because of the greater social segregation in bigger settlements.

It is easy to be over-influenced by the results of the studies reported here into believing that the neighbourhood effect is a major factor determining voter behaviour. For this reason, a paper by Tate (1974) provides a salutary alternative view. Using the A.I.D. method (p. 101) he re-analysed Butler and Stokes's survey data, using both individual and neighbourhood contextual variables to discriminate between Labour and non-Labour voters. The individual variables accounted for over 32 per cent of the variation among the 1363 respondents, with occupation the best discriminator. The contextual variables accounted for only 6·4 per cent, with the main discriminator being the class composition of the electorate. Analysis, using both sets of variables together, suggested virtually no influence for contextual effects, with constituency class composition providing a very minor portion of the 'explanation'.

These findings contradict those of Butler and Stokes (reproduced here in Figs. 5.1 and 5.2). One inference to be derived from them concerns spurious relationships; do the patterns suggested by Figs. 5.1 and 5.2 occur therein only because of the operation of other, non-contextual variables which are held constant in the A.I.D. analysis? If this is indeed so, then the concept of the neighbourhood effect must remain open to considerable doubt. Other evidence is much more favourable to the concept, however, and raises questions about the suitability of different forms of analysis, thereby throwing down a major challenge to those who would provide a valid test of this interesting hypothesis.

Rival Hypotheses

Despite the volume of circumstantial evidence reviewed here, not all writers are convinced by the neighbourhood effect hypothesis. Prescott's views have already been cited, and Kasperson (1969, p. 409) has argued that: 'Cox's suggestion that increased communication, especially among suburban housewives, may facilitate political conversion in the suburbs is an attractive notion since it would open the door for analysis of the role of spatial interaction in attitude formation. Unfortunately for geographers, there is considerable evidence questioning such an interpretation'. The evidence Kasperson quotes includes some from the Elmira study (p. 242) that *most* political discussion is between people with the same partisan predispositions and that relatively few people will debate political issues because they can prove socially divisive in a close-knit community. It is not claimed that the neighbourhood effect is a major determinant of voting, however, and most evidence would support this (Tate, 1974; Rose, 1976), but if the processes described here do not operate, then it is necessary to find plausible alternative explanations for the patterns which we have described.

One possible explanation lies in the form of the data used. Both Hindess (1967) and A. H. Taylor (1973) have identified evidence for neighbourhood effects of the form suggested by Fig. 5.3 when using the percentage of votes for Labour as their variables, but not when they use percentage of the electorate who voted for Labour. Taylor suggests that this is because of an effect which he terms *safe seat apathy*; his argument is that in constituencies where voters believe a certain party is bound to win, probably by a large margin, they are more likely either to abstain or to cast a 'protest' vote for a minority third party. His tests of this were far from conclusive, however, perhaps because it is only the supporters of the party likely to lose who abstain. The idea demands further testing, but it is difficult to see its validity in, say, Australia where voting is compulsory but a neighbourhood effect still exists (Herbert, 1975; Johnston, 1976a).

Two further hypotheses have been advanced to account for the patterns that are consonant with the neighbourhood effect notion. One is that they result from differential campaign activity; this is discussed in detail in the next chapter, where no evidence is presented that campaigning is organized to accentuate local party strengths, although clearly this could be achieved. The other is that self-selection processes lead people to live among and act like those whom – on objective grounds such as census occupational classifications – they differ from.

Self-selection can be a characteristic of two groups of people. The first are those who live – often in small, socially homogeneous clusters – in environments not consonant with their own status. For example, most low socio-economic status settlements, such as coal-mining villages and towns, will contain some professionals such as doctors and schoolteachers. Some may adopt the political attitudes of their milieux, as a neighbourhood effect, but others may be socially mobile but spatially immobile people who retain their social and political roots. Surveys of medical and dental graduates have found, for example, that a lot of them tend to return to their home districts (Butler *et al.*, 1974; Coates and Rawstron, 1971), so many of the schoolteachers in mining villages may indeed come from mining-village stock, especially as such places are not particularly attractive to people from other environments and backgrounds. Similarly, in Britain many working-class people support the Conservative party, a pattern which is often explained as working-class deference to 'social superiors' or 'natural rulers' (McKenzie and Silver, 1967). This may be a fading relationship, however, as fewer people remain who were politically socialized before Labour became a major political party.

The other method of self-selection concerns the socially mobile working class who aspire to middle-class status (and, to a lesser extent, the 'objective' middle class who identify themselves with the working class). Inter-class boundaries are extremely blurred, of course, with income differentials frequently favouring the working class (Westergaard and Ressler, 1976), so that many of the would-be mobiles can afford homes in middle-class areas. If they do, their residence there will not so much lead to conversion to middle-class political attitudes as have been preceded by such conversion. There is little evidence of any large-scale movement of this kind, however (Berger, 1960; Laserwitz, 1960).

Other evidence favours the neighbourhood effect hypothesis rather than that of self-selection. The studies of voting changes, such as Cox's (1971), are unlikely to confuse the two processes, especially if the changes occur over relatively short periods, and this view is confirmed by careful analyses of other survey data. Putnam (1966), for example, concluded that it was the 'tyranny of public opinion' which dominated the patterns of changing political preferences, especially among voters who were members of local, formal organizations. And Foladare (1968) found that voting in particular contests was more likely to come under neighbourhood influence than were general political preferences. His data from Buffalo (Table 5.10) show that, for example, non-manual workers in manually-dominated neighbourhoods are more likely to be Democrats than are non-manual workers living elsewhere, but even more likely to have preferred Kennedy to Nixon in the particular 1960 election.

> The fact that voting preference is more affected by type of neighborhood than is party affiliation demonstrates the effect of clustering. Since party affiliation represents normal political predisposition, the larger vote for the candidate preferred in the neighborhood demonstrates the effect of contact with neighbors on political preferences. Clustering has more effect on the immediate decisions than it does on the more remote party identification (Foladare, 1968, p. 521).

The Nixon–Kennedy contest was influenced by other factors, such as religion (Kennedy was the first Roman Catholic to be elected president) but detailed analysis indicated to Foladare (1968, p. 522) that 'The more white Protestants are exposed to Catholic neighbours, the smaller is the likelihood that they supported Nixon over Kennedy', which again is strong evidence for the neighbourhood effect ('clustering' is Foladare's terminology).

Conclusions

The neighbourhood effect is of interest to many social scientists because it is a particular case of a general process, that of socialization. Further, it is intriguing to them because its existence and extent are difficult to isolate, requiring great technical tenacity in devising appropriate methods for its measurement. For geographers, it indicates an important output of the spatial segregation of different population groups, which has been a major research interest in the last decade. Within the whole field of the geography of elections, its impact may be negligible, since it is unlikely that it influences election results in many cases (because its basic finding is that anticipated majorities are exaggerated); it may be crucial in some constituencies which are

Table 5.10 The neighbourhood effect in Buffalo

Percentage manual workers in neighbourhood	*<65%*		*66–80%*		*81%+*	
Occupation of respondent	*Non-manual*	*Manual*	*Non-manual*	*Manual*	*Non-manual*	*Manual*
Party Affiliation (percentage)						
Republican	57	30	30	21	27	14
Democrat	34	35	37	51	64	63
Candidate voted for in 1960 (percentage)						
Nixon (R)	60	48	33	17	18	8
Kennedy (D)	40	48	67	82	82	88

Source: Foladare (1968, p. 519)

divided into several social areas of different complexion, however. But it does have implications elsewhere in the subject, with respect to the spread of new parties and ideas, for example (Chapters 3 and 4), to where parties should campaign to their best advantage (Chapter 6), and to the geography of representation (Chapter 7).

6 Candidates, Issues and Campaigns

In the preceding chapter we reviewed the evidence regarding the effects on the voter of the opinions of others among whom he lives and works. This is but one aspect of the inter-relationships between electors and their environments which might influence their voting decisions. It portrays the individuals discussing political issues with each other as voters, when many people in society are more than just 'other voters'; a few are candidates for office; many more are party workers, committed to winning the election for their organization. And so we turn now to an investigation of these particular individuals, on where they live and campaign, and how they influence the voting decisions of the electorate.

Much voting in partisan elections is habitual; the electors always cast their preference for the same party, on a continuing belief that only that party can best serve their personal self-interests. A considerable proportion re-determine their preference during each election campaign, however, surveying the policies of the competitors and passing judgement on the actions of the current government (and perhaps of past ones too). Where partisan politics are not as strong as in Britain, say, and campaigns are more personalized, as they frequently are in the United States, then the elector may be more swayed by the characteristics of the individual candidates and their positions on what the elector perceives as the key issues (interestingly, Ennis, 1962, pp. 196–205, has shown how candidates are often able to determine those key issues).

Voting decisions are based on a variety of criteria. As part of a survey conducted in four American states (Colorado, Iowa, Minnesota and Washington) prior to and after the 1960 presidential election, respondents were asked (Ennis, 1962, p. 189), 'when you vote for Senator, which is most important to you: the man himself, the stand he takes on public issues, or his political party?' With the Iowa respondents, who were not atypical, several features stand out from the answers (Table 6.1):

Table 6.1 Important determinants in voting for senator: Iowa, 1960

	Percentage giving the important determinant as:		
	The man	*The issues*	*His party*
Voters with high educational levels living in			
Large towns	23	71	6
Small towns	36	61	3
Rural areas	42	54	4
Total	38	58	4
Voters with low educational levels living in			
Large towns	33	61	6
Small towns	60	37	3
Rural areas	50	43	7
Total	49	45	6

Source: Ennis (1962, pp. 189–90)

(1) Voting for party, irrespective of the issues or of who the candidate is, is rare.
(2) Better-educated voters are more concerned with issues, and the senatorial candidates' positions on them.
(3) Small-town and rural residents are more likely to vote for the candidate as a person than are their contemporaries in the larger settlements. This could in part be related to the problems of mobilizing the periphery that we discussed in Chapters 3 and 4. Ennis (1962, p. 191) argues that: 'where social class cleavages are

pronounced in a community, class perspectives will ramify into political choices to a greater extent than in communities less sharply polarized ... traditional or personalistic forms of reference are more dominant in communities where a class orientation is minimized' – with the latter being the small towns and the rural areas. Of these three findings, the last is of the most general interest. That voters were not very party-oriented may be a peculiar feature of the American party system; that rural voters are more 'personal' in their politics may not.

Voters may use different criteria when voting for different offices, or the same criteria may lead them to vote for candidates from different parties because of personal characteristics or issue orientations. In many American elections, for example, people are voting every four years not only for a president and a congressman, but probably also for a senator and a state governor, as well as for a variety of state and local government legislators and officials. Most candidates are allied with a particular party and many electors vote, say, for a full Democrat slate, a decision which is particularly easy if voting machines are in use, since a single lever can then be pulled to cast all of their votes. Exactly how people make the decision to vote for a full slate, unless they habitually vote entirely for the one party, is not clear. A 'coat tails' procedure has been suggested, by which voters first make their decision on which candidate to support for a major office, such as president, and then decide to vote for all of the candidates for other offices from the same party. The 1960 four-state study, referred to above, found that as the election came closer voters were more polarized in giving all of their choices to either one party or the other, but there was no evidence that the major decision was taken on the important offices and all the others were consequent upon that (Meyer, 1962).

A recent marked change in American voting behaviour has been the shift away from the decision to vote a full party slate. Between 1940 and 1972, for example, Burnham (1975) found a considerable reduction in the correlations between the percentage of the relevant votes obtained by the Democrat candidates for four major offices in West Virginia (his observation units were the 55 counties). Clearly, West Virginians have become less partisan. A vote for Nixon in 1972 was probably associated with one for the Republican gubernatorial candidate, as the correlations show (Table 6.2), but not necessarily for that party's

Table 6.2 Democrat voting for four offices: West Virginia, 1940 and 1972

Correlations between votes for[a]	*President*	*Senator*	*Congressman*	*Governor*
and votes for				
President		+·988	+·980	+·991
Senator	+·734		+·992	+·994
Congressman	+·536	+·680		+·998
Governor	+·910	+·718	+·513	

[a]Correlations for 1940 are above the diagonal and for 1972 below. The square of a correlation coefficient indicates the proportional agreement in the two voting patterns over the 55 counties so that in 1940 0·976 of the vote for senator could be predicted from the vote for president (in a statistical sense) but in 1972 the proportion was only 0·539.

Source: Burnham (1975, p. 338)

Senate and House candidates as well. This suggests that the state's voters did not believe that their interests in the Congress would be best served by members of the same party as that of their preferred White House incumbent. One reason advanced to account for this is the immense power of senior (long-serving) members of both houses of Congress, in the committee positions they can obtain and the rewards this can bring, such as defence contracts, to their states. Voters are thus loath to remove an incumbent senator or representative without very good reason, leading to a growing institutionalization of Congress (Polsby, 1968) and 'split ticket' voting when a candidate from a different party seems a better prospect for the presidency. Such split voting may have been particularly marked in the southern states in 1948 and 1968 when third-party candidates – Thurmond and Wallace respectively – stood against the Democrat strength there (Burnham, 1975), but it was also a general feature in 1956 with

Eisenhower being returned to the White House when there was a strong swing to the Democrats in the House of Representatives (Campbell and Miller, 1957; Cummings, 1966). The extent to which voters do 'split their ticket' cannot be discerned easily from aggregate voting data, but inspection of individual ballots in Milwaukee has shown that whereas in 1960 some 68 per cent of all voters selected candidates from a single party, in 1970 the corresponding figure was only 32 per cent (Burnham, 1975, p. 319).

'Split ticket' voting is encouraged by the American electoral system in which many contests are decided simultaneously. Elsewhere it occurs over periods of time, which may account for the relatively large swings in opinion recorded at the Australian and New Zealand general elections of 1975. Both phenomena suggest that the electorate is responsive to a variety of stimuli in making its voting decisions. In some cases, more so perhaps in certain types of contest than in others, it may be the personal characteristics of the candidates, irrespective of party, which determine their success or failure and, as we suggested in Chapter 1, such personalized voting might have a very clear pattern in its geography. Other decisions may be made on specific issues; such issues may be national in scope, but others may be very localized, with candidates or parties taking up positions relative to local interests and receiving votes accordingly. Finally, contestants may decide that it is more beneficial to campaign for votes in some parts of the constituency than others. All of these determinants suggest a clear geography of influence on voting patterns and election results, and they form the foci of the remainder of this chapter.

Voting for the Candidate: The Friends-and-Neighbours Effect

Even if an election is being fought between parties, it is usually their candidates, often with no indication of party identification, who are placed on the ballot paper and who votes are given to. If an elector goes to the polling booth either completely undecided who to vote for or totally apathetic as to the outcome (probably he will only be apathetic if voting is compulsory or if he has somehow been cajoled into voting by others), then he may search the ballot paper for some cue as to whom he might support. If the only information available is a set of names, and one of the candidates is a local person known to him, then the local man may pick up his vote simply because he has been recognized (Stokes and Miller, 1962, have shown that voters for congressmen in the United States are much more aware of candidates from their own communities).

Voting for a local person simply because his name has been recognized on the ballot paper is almost certainly not a frequent occurrence, although it undoubtedly does occur, just as well-known names or 'odd' names – length, ethnic origin etc. – often seem to attract votes (Mueller, 1970; Blydenburgh, 1974). Two other reasons can be suggested for candidates doing particularly well in their home areas, however.

(1) The first is knowledge of the candidate, not simply of his existence but also of his qualities, and perhaps of him personally. Since, as we showed in the last chapter, people are more likely to know others in their home locality than residents of more distant settlements or suburbs, then the closer a voter lives to a candidate's home, the more likely he is to know him – or to know somebody who knows him, for many people like a little fame or notoriety to rub off onto themselves. Because of this personal contact, the voter may feel impelled, through some sense of loyalty, to support the local candidate (unless, of course, his knowledge leads him to a firm decision to vote for another!). This pattern of support has become widely known as the friends-and-neighbours effect, based on personal ties between candidate and constituent.

(2) We have already argued that self-interest is a major determinant, if not the major determinant, of voting decisions, and this revolves around how much the individual hopes to gain personally from political decisions which will be taken if certain candidates win. Thus the second reason for supporting a local candidate, irrespective of any personal links with him, is 'because he understands the problems of *our* area' (Reynolds, 1969, p.

186) and may thus be able to get the sorts of benefit that his neighbours want (and so win their votes again next time). Such 'pork-barrel' politics, as they are known in America, are perhaps not as strong in some electoral systems as in others, although this may have been less true in the past. Quaife (1969, p. 54) reproduces the following statement from an Australian local newspaper of the nineteenth century (*Kilmore Examiner*, 10 October 1856):

> we are not yet ripe for the full enjoyment of Responsible government – we do not yet understand what the exercise of the suffrage involves – we have no particular political opinions! . . . we know nothing about political principles abstractly considered. If a man will but promise to make us roads no matter how . . . then we shall consider him worthy of support – he is a good man and ought to be elected.

And it is not only to parliaments and congresses that such representatives are sent. State political parties often give their primary preferences to 'favourite sons' (frequently the state governor) at American presidential nominating conventions, hoping that they can thereby bargain local gains at the second ballot; the entire Mississippi delegation to the 1976 Republican convention was uncommitted and became a great focus of interest for the neck-and-neck Ford and Reagan campaign organizations.

Friends and neighbours in intra-party contests

The classic study of the friends-and-neighbours effect is Key's book on politics in the southern states of the U.S.A., parts of which we discussed in Chapter 1. Regarding Alabama, for example, he said (Key, 1949, pp. 37–8):

> A powerful localism provides an important ingredient of Alabama factionalism. Candidates for state office tend to poll overwhelming majorities in their home counties and to draw heavy support in adjacent counties. Such voting behavior may be rationalized as a calculated promotion of local interest, yet it also points to the absence of stable, well-organized, state-wide factions of like-minded citizens formed to advocate measures of common concern. In its extreme form localism justifies a diagnosis of low voter-interest in public issues and a susceptibility to control by the irrelevant appeal to support the home-

town boy. In some instances, of course, localism may reflect concern about some general state issue bearing in the area [as Key, p. 91 suggests for Florida] ... In well-developed two-party situations localism is minimized ... The classic case is that of Duchess County, New York, the home of Franklin D. Roosevelt, a Democrat of some note. The county, traditionally Republican, stubbornly held to its partisan attachments and repeatedly failed to return a majority for even its most distinguished son ... [But in the south] the harshest criticism that can be made of a politician is that he cannot win in his own beat or precinct. If his friends and neighbours who know him do not support him, why should those without this advantage trust a candidate?

His argument is supported by the voting in the Democrat primary for the Eighth Alabama Congressional District in 1946. Seven of the candidates lived in six different counties and each of these, except Twitty who lived in the same county as Jim Smith,

Table 6.3 Friends-and-neighbours voting: Alabama, Eighth congressional district, 1946

Candidate in Democrat primary election	*Percentage of total vote*	*Percentage of vote in home county*	*Percentage of vote to second candidate in home county*
Johnson	15·0	65·1	22·0
Jones	22·7	97·5	0·9
Meadows	8·5	47·4	24·7
Pounders	4·5	40·2	28·7
Jeff Smith	17·8	70·1	14·4
Jim Smith	19·5	62·1	2·9
Twitty	12·0	30·1	2·9

Source: Key (1949, p. 38)

polled his highest percentage in his home county, in some cases leaving very few votes for his opponents (Table 6.3).

Key's work on the friends-and-neighbours effect 'has gained the status of a political truism' (Tatalovich, 1975, p. 807). It was entirely based on his study of the southern states in which the Democrat hegemony is pronounced (Chapter 3) because of the relicts of the post-Civil War attitudes. The major elections there are not the final contests between Democrat and Republican, since the results of these are usually foregone conclusions, but the Democrat primaries, which are non-partisan and based more on intra-party factionalism, which may have strong local bases. Two primaries are common, to ensure that the winner of the run-off, and hence the likely victor of the final election, has majority support within the Democrat party. Such primaries are frequently characterized by strong friends-and-neighbours effects, which were identified by Key in each of Alabama, Arkansas, Florida, Georgia, Mississippi and South Carolina. But it is not only in the south that primary elections have this characteristic. Three New England states – New Hampshire, Maine and Vermont – are dominated by the Republican party to almost the same degree as the Democrat southern hegemony (Ranney, 1965), and Lockard (1959) found strong evidence of friends-and-neighbours effects in the Republican primaries of all three (Figure 6.1) as well as, to a lesser extent, in the more competitive state of Massachusetts.

All of Key's analysis was based on interpretation of choropleth* maps and tabulations, so recent workers have attempted more formal identification of the effect. Reynolds (1969a, 1969b, 1974), for example, has adopted Coleman's (1964) model of local influence (p. 230) to identify a decline in support away from his home for one candidate in the 1954 Georgia gubernatorial primary. Tatalovich (1975) has studied Mississippi, where the Democrat candidates won all of the contests for senator, governor, and lieutenant-governor during the period 1943–73. The primaries for these elections attracted 147 Democrat candidates in that time, and Tatalovich advanced eight hypotheses to account for the extent to which each of the 103 who received neither less

* In choropleth maps, shading (or colour) is used to depict subdivisions of geographical space (such as political units). Observations are allocated to classes defined by a certain range of values and different densities of shading are used to represent each class.

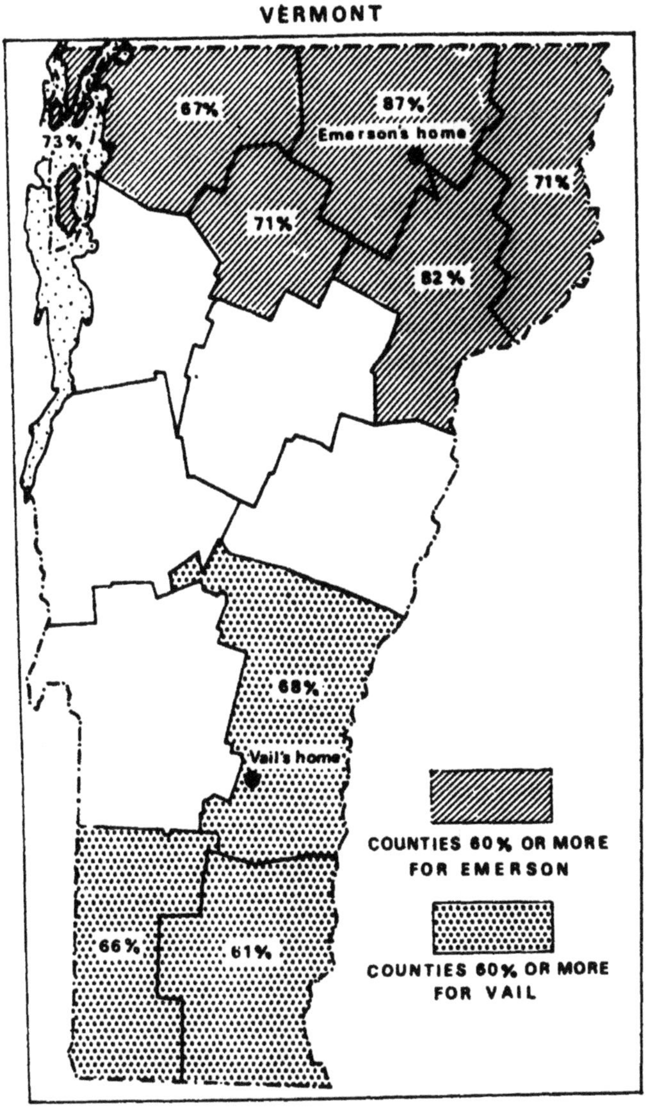

Figure 6.1 The friends-and-neighbours effect in voting for rival candidates for the Republican nomination for governor, Vermont, 1952. Source: Lockard, 1959, Fig. 2

than 10 per cent nor more than 90 per cent of the votes had a friends-and-neighbours effect:

(1) The effect should be most apparent in the first primary, because the weak candidates, who should have a local base only,

are excluded from the run-off, and it should be even less apparent in the final contest against the Republican and other party candidates.

(2) With the decline of sectional politics, the effect should be weaker in 1973 than in 1943.

(3) The effect is most likely when rival candidates live some distance from each other.

(4) The effect is most likely when the strongest candidates live in different parts of the state.

(5) The greater the number of candidates, the greater the likelihood of an effect.

(6) The effect is most likely in elections for the least prestigious office (lieutenant-governor).

(7) The effect is most likely for weaker candidates.

(8) Candidates standing for the first time are most likely to have a strong friends-and-neighbours base.

To test these, Tatalovich correlated a candidate's percentage of the poll in each county against distance from his home; a significant relationship was identified in 60 per cent of the contests, and only seven candidates displayed no friends-and-neighbours effect at some time during their political careers. Only one of the hypotheses – the sixth, regarding the prestige of the office – was not verified (Table 6.4): the candidates most likely to have strong friends-and-neighbours support were thus the weak ones, standing for the first time in the 1940s or 1950s, in contests against several others at the first primary, and with no local rivals.

Non-partisan elections in the United States are not the only ones in which the friends-and-neighbours effect has been observed. They might be less likely in plurality contests elsewhere, perhaps where partisan attachments are strong, but they have been identified, for example, in the pattern of voting for McCarthy as senator from Wisconsin (McCarty, 1952; Figure 6.2), in the support for Wallace within Alabama during his 1968 presidential quest (Black and Black, 1973), in the 1972 Toronto mayoralty contest, and among minor party candidates at New Zealand general elections (Johnston, 1976f): the absence of polling-booth, precinct, or ward data precludes any search for them in Great

Table 6.4 The friends-and-neighbours effect in Mississippi, 1943–73

Hypothesis	*Percentage of candidates with the effect*	*Hypothesis*	*Percentage of candidates with the effect*
(1) Type of election		(6) Office	
First primary	62·5	Senator	65·0
Run-off primary	58·6	Governor	60·0
General election	50·0	Lieutenant-governor	57·9
(2) Period		(7) Candidate's overall poll	
1943–58	64·9	10–29%	65·3
1959–73	54·4	30–49%	57·1
(3) Distance to nearest opponent		50–69%	61·9
0–99 miles	58·5	70–89%	20·0
100+miles	63·2	(8) Election attempt by candidate	
		First	75·6
(4) Distance to strongest opponent		Second	52·4
0–99 miles	47·5	Third	50·0
100+miles	68·3	Fourth or more	48·3
(5) Number of candidates			
2	57·6	Total	60·2
3	37·5		
4	57·9		
5+	67·4		

Source: Tatalovich (1975, p. 811)

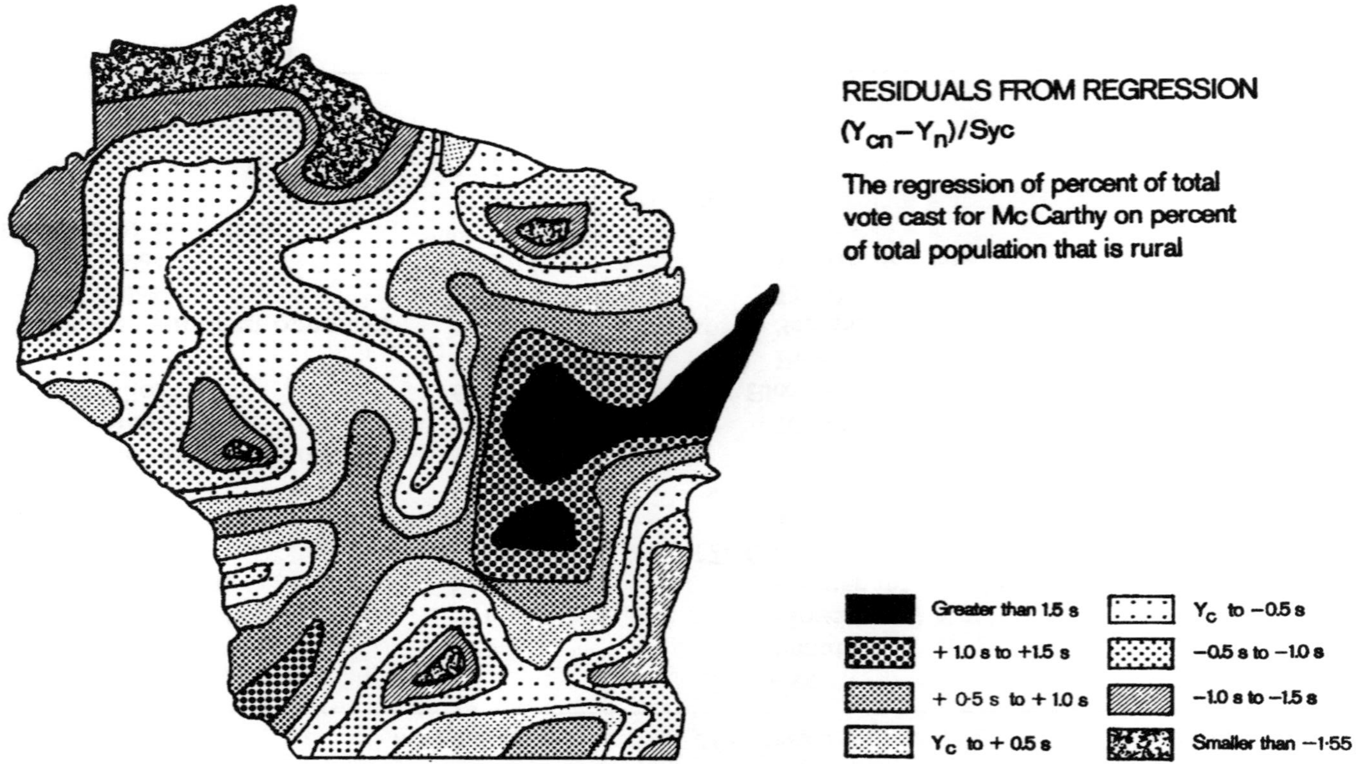

Figure 6.2 The friends-and-neighbours effect in voting for McCarthy as senator for Wisconsin, 1952. The values plotted are residuals for each county from the regression of McCarthy's vote on the percentage of each county's population classified as rural. Positive residuals – where McCarthy's vote was under-predicted by the regression – are clustered around his home at Appleton in the east. Source: Thomas, 1968, Fig. 4

Britain. Under the various list systems, such as Denmark's (p. 63), the likelihood of voting for local candidates is also strong.

Friends-and-neighbours effects have also been identified in the 'at large' multi-member plurality elections for New Zealand's city councils. In both Lower Hutt and Christchurch, parties put up a full slate of candidates for the vacancies (15 in Lower Hutt, three parties; 19 in Christchurch, 2 parties), and in each voting for party is dominant (Johnston, 1972, 1973, 1974a; Blydenburgh, 1974). Nevertheless, many electors clearly split their tickets, and a variety of factors other than party membership influence voting for candidates (in Lower Hutt – whether they are incumbents and party leaders, their general publicity, and their position on the ballot; in Christchurch – whether they are incumbents, their sex, their publicity, and their position on the ballot). Voting for local candidates irrespective of party is also frequent, either because they are literally friends and neighbours or because a local representative is considered desirable (party discipline is not always strong in voting by council members). A Labour Party supporter in Christchurch might choose to cast one of his 19 votes for a local candidate (either an independent or a member of the opposition Citizens' Association) without much fear that by doing so he will be harming his party's cause in terms of an overall victory; as a consequence he may get both a local representative and a Labour government. In choosing which Labour candidate not to vote for, he might use the above process in reverse, perhaps deciding to omit an unknown, standing for the first time who doesn't live in the voter's local area.

As a result of this voter decision-making process, it was hypothesized that each candidate would do better at the booths close to his home (the city has about 160,000 residents and there are 119 polling booths) than would the other members of his party. This was tested against the results of three elections (1968, 1971 and 1974), using a variety of methods. In 1968, of the 34 major party candidates living in, or close to the boundary of, the city, 26 clearly did relatively well in their home area (Johnston, 1972), and in 1971 a similar finding resulted from a slightly different type of analysis for all 43 candidates (Johnston, 1974a). In addition, it was found that:

(1) Independent candidates, who generally lack the finances for a city-wide campaign, tend to rely on strong local support – and, nevertheless, all lose.

(2) Candidates living in areas where the opposition is strong tend to get the strongest friends-and-neighbours support – those living where their party is strong will presumably get massive support in any case.

(3) Candidates not living close to others tend to poll stronger local support.

(4) Candidates standing for the first time usually have a stronger local base than do incumbents.

For the 1974 election, Christchurch was divided into five wards, one returning three councillors and the others four each. Of the 28 candidates living in the ward for which they stood, there was evidence of a friends-and-neighbours effect for 14 (Forrest, Marjoribanks and Johnston, 1977).

In Dunedin City, a smaller New Zealand urban area, the two main parties traditionally do not put up a full slate of candidates for the 12 vacancies; in 1971 Labour fielded 10 and the Citizens' Association 9. This would seem to invite voters to operate the friends-and-neighbours effect for their 'spare' non-party votes, but this did not appear to occur. Perhaps because of Dunedin's size (a population of about 87,000), a series of unique patterns was observed (recall Cox's, 1971, finding – see above, p. 263 – of lesser neighbourhood effects in small cities) and only 7 of the 19 major party candidates received a clear home-based friends-and-neighbours effect, although one other had one based on his workplace (Forrest and Johnston, 1973); interestingly, one candidate had what seemed to be a reverse-friends-and-neighbours effect, doing less well near to his home than he did further away!

A final example, that shows how candidates and parties often operate the friends-and-neighbours effect to their advantage, comes from elections to the Japanese Diet, at which each voter has only one vote, irrespective of the number of members to be returned from the constituency (p. 43). In the intra-party contest for votes there emerges what might be termed a 'two-tier friends-and-neighbours effect'. This is illustrated by a study of one candidate's campaign; Sato, a member of the ruling Liberal Democratic Party, stood in 1967 for the second time in the Oika Second District, which returned three members and for which three L.D.P. candidates fought one Socialist and one Communist (Curtis, 1971). Within rural areas, the aim is to build up a 'hard vote' by which the candidate obtains the support of local political leaders, whom the other residents follow as a form of obligation which is a hangover from feudal rural social organization: thus (Curtis, 1971, p. 39), 'A voter will cast his vote for a certain candidate in order to return a favour received from that person or to repay an obligation to a third party who is supporting the candidate'. In urban areas, candidates build up personal followings through *Koenkai* organizations created 'for the purpose of expanding and to some extent institutionalizing their support'; 5·8 per cent of adult Japanese were *Koenkai* members in 1967, another 1·8 per cent had been members, and 11·4 per cent had been invited to join at least one (there are also youth branches). Local support is sought by pushing particular issues; Sato emphasized that he was the only candidate from his home town of Beppu, for example, and he obtained 42 per cent of his votes there (Table 6.5).

As a consequence of this intra-party competition, the distribution of votes among the various candidates varies considerably from place to place within a district. Thus, within the Oika Second District (Table 6.5) there is the outstanding performance of Nishimura in the rural districts of Kunemi and Himeshima, and less so in Kogachi. That the third L.D.P. candidate – Ayabe – had only one very clear friends-and-neighbours effect, in Kitsuki, perhaps reflects the relative poverty of his local organization and resulted in his failure to capture the third seat from Nishimura.

Intra-party contests are rare in British politics, because of the widespread use of the plurality system. One recent example for which there is a spatial breakdown of the poll is the 1976 contest for the leadership of the Liberal Party between David Steel and John Pardoe. At the time of the poll, which involved all members of the party, in a system akin to the American electoral college, Steel held a parliamentary seat for southern Scotland and Pardoe

Table 6.5 Voting in Oika Second District in 1967

Party Candidate	Sato	L.D.P. Nishimura	Percentage of votes for Ayabe	Socialist Kumatsu	Communist Tsuru	Total votes
City districts						
Beppu	41	15	16	26	2	61,567
Nakatsu	21	20	22	34	4	28,599
Bungo Takeda	28	23	24	25	1	12,754
Kitsuki	25	7	42	25	1	13,232
Rural districts						
Kunemi	7	65	11	15	2	5290
Himeshima	0·1	97	0·3	2	0·1	2206
Kunisaki	15	46	17	20	1	11,778
Musasti	19	44	18	18	2	3411
Aki	27	27	24	21	1	7095
Hiji	21	10	30	38	1	10,490
Yamaga	26	18	19	35	1	6803
Ota	37	30	13	19	1	1950
Matama	18	29	32	19	2	3407
Kagachi	16	56	11	16	1	3260
Sanko	22	24	24	28	2	3561
Honyabakei	22	33	24	20	1	3615
Yabakei	13	31	26	24	6	4898
Yamaguni	34	19	21	25	1	3405
Innai	26	19	29	25	1	4371
Ajimu	22	17	26	34	1	6218
Ekisen	19	23	28	27	2	3574
Yokkaichi	18	23	28	29	2	11,564
Negasu	25	29	17	25	3	9110
Usa	21	14	30	26	10	4770
Total	27	23	22	26	2	226,629

Source: Computed from Curtis (1971, pp. 246–7)

Table 6.6 Voting in the Liberal Party leadership contest, 1976

Region	*Percentage of votes for* *Pardoe*	*Steel*
Birmingham	38·5	61·5
Devon and Cornwall	56·7	43·3
Eastern Counties	31·6	68·4
Home Counties	32·9	67·1
Manchester	37·2	62·8
London	31·9	68·1
East Midlands	42·8	57·2
West Midlands	43·3	56·7
Merseyside	34·7	65·3
Northern Counties	45·0	55·0
Western Counties	34·8	65·2
Yorkshire	36·0	64·0
North Western	35·5	64·5
Scotland	26·0	74·0
Wales	37·5	62·5
N. Ireland	10·0	90·0
Total	36·0	64·0

represented a Cornish constituency and, as Table 6.6 shows, each performed much better in his relevant 'home area' than in the country as a whole. As in the other elections studied here, therefore, this result presents strong circumstantial evidence which favours the general hypothesis of a friends-and-neighbours effect.

Friends-and-neighbours effects at preferential elections

After a dissolution of both Houses of Parliament, an S.T.V. election was held for the ten Senate seats for each of the Australian states in May 1974. In New South Wales, these places were contested by 73 candidates, 57 of whom represented formal parties or groupings. The Liberal–Country Party coalition nominated six candidates who attracted 987,711 first-preference votes, 982,136 of them for the candidate at the top of their list. The remaining

5575 first preferences might have been distributed among the other five, on a friends-and-neighbours basis, as votes for local candidates which would do little harm to the party's overall chances of success. (With virtually any distribution of those votes, four successes were certain; five were elected.) The votes for the five are shown in Table 6.7, and expressed as percentages of the non-Cotton vote (Cotton was the first elected). If each received a friends-and-neighbours effect in his home division (the constituency for a House of Representatives seat; there were 45 in the state), then, it is suggested, his percentage of the non-Cotton vote there should be twice his percentage of all non-Cotton votes; Table 6.7A shows that this was not the case for only one of the five, with the other four getting on average 2.7 times their overall percentage in the home division.

Australian electoral divisions are divided into a small number of subdivisions for reporting purposes. To test the friends-and-neighbours hypothesis further, it is suggested that each candidate should do twice as well in his home subdivision as did Cotton, relative to the performance of each in the division as a whole. This proved to be so for only two of the five Liberal–Country Party candidates studied (Table 6.7B), although two others – Anderson, an incumbent senator, and Baume, a general practitioner, both conceivably with broad local bases of support – are close to the threshold set.

The Republic of Ireland also uses the S.T.V. system, though with smaller constituencies than the Australian, but, as we showed in Chapter 2 (p. 61), voters there do not necessarily allocate their first preferences to the same candidate within the party of their choice. The two main Irish parties, Fine Gael and Fianna Fail, select candidates for each constituency to appeal to its various sections, such as the different religious groups. One of the most important sections is the local vote, which is very important in Irish politics because of the errand-boy role (representing the interests of constituents as a sort of ombudsman) demanded of the members by the electorate (see Chapter 9, p. 475). Thus the parties seek out the friends-and-neighbours effect by, whenever possible, selecting candidates from different parts of the con-

Table 6.7 The friends-and-neighbours effect in voting for the Senate: Liberal–Country Party, N.S.W., 1974

A. *By electoral division*					
Candidate	Carrick	Scott	Anderson	Baume	Moppett
Votes (first-preference)	732	1182	931	1516	1214
Percentage of non-Cotton vote	13	21	17	27	22
Divisions with at least double that percentage	4	3	3	3	1
Percentage of the non-Cotton vote in home division	17	74	38	55	69
B. *By electoral sub-division*					
Candidate	Carrick	Scott	Anderson	Baume	Moppett
Percentage of division votes cast in home sub-division for Cotton	9·5	6·0	5·9	11·5	6·9
Percentage of division votes cast in home sub-division for candidate	15·2	53·5	11·1	22·1	39·3

Source: computed from *State of New South Wales Statistical Returns showing the voting in each sub-division in relation to The Senate Election 1974.* Australian Electoral Office, Canberra, 1975. Data on candidates' home addresses were kindly supplied by the Australian Electoral Office.

stituency. This has been illustrated by Sacks (1970) for the Donegal North-East constituency, which returns three members, in 1969. Fine Gael and Fianna Fail both fielded two candidates, and both also delimited the parts of the constituency in which each candidate would canvass and where the party's supporters would be directed to vote for him. (This now happens in Ulster too; Laver, 1976.) The result was a sizeable relationship between each candidate's vote and the distance from his home, as illustrated in Figure 6.3 and 6.4 for the two Fianna Fail candidates, both of whom were elected. The top map in Figure 6.3 shows what we might call the 'true' friends-and-neighbours effect for Cunningham, as the booths where he polled very well absolutely (he obtained 24 per cent of the first preferences over the whole constituency); the lower map in Figure 6.3 which indicates where he polled well relative to the party vote, shows his extended area of friends-and-neighbours influence caused by the division of the electorate between himself and Blaney – the candidate of the western portion (Figure 6.4).

Voting on Issues

Most elections are fought on issues, usually only a few. These may be general, such as 'would party A run the economy better than party B has done in the last few years?' whereas others are more personal – 'would you buy a used car from this man?'. Attempts to crystallize debate on a particular issue often fail – the Australian Labor Party was unable to maintain interest in the Governor-General's dismissal of their government in December 1974 when the electorate wished to debate the wider issue of economic management. This is particularly the case in two-party systems; in multi-party contests and parliaments it is often the case that some parties are elected for their stands on particular issues only (see below, p. 465).

Within the general spectrum of issues relevant to an election campaign, however, it may well be the case that the overall voting patterns are modified in certain areas by voter reaction to candidate and party positions on relevant local issues. In the 1971

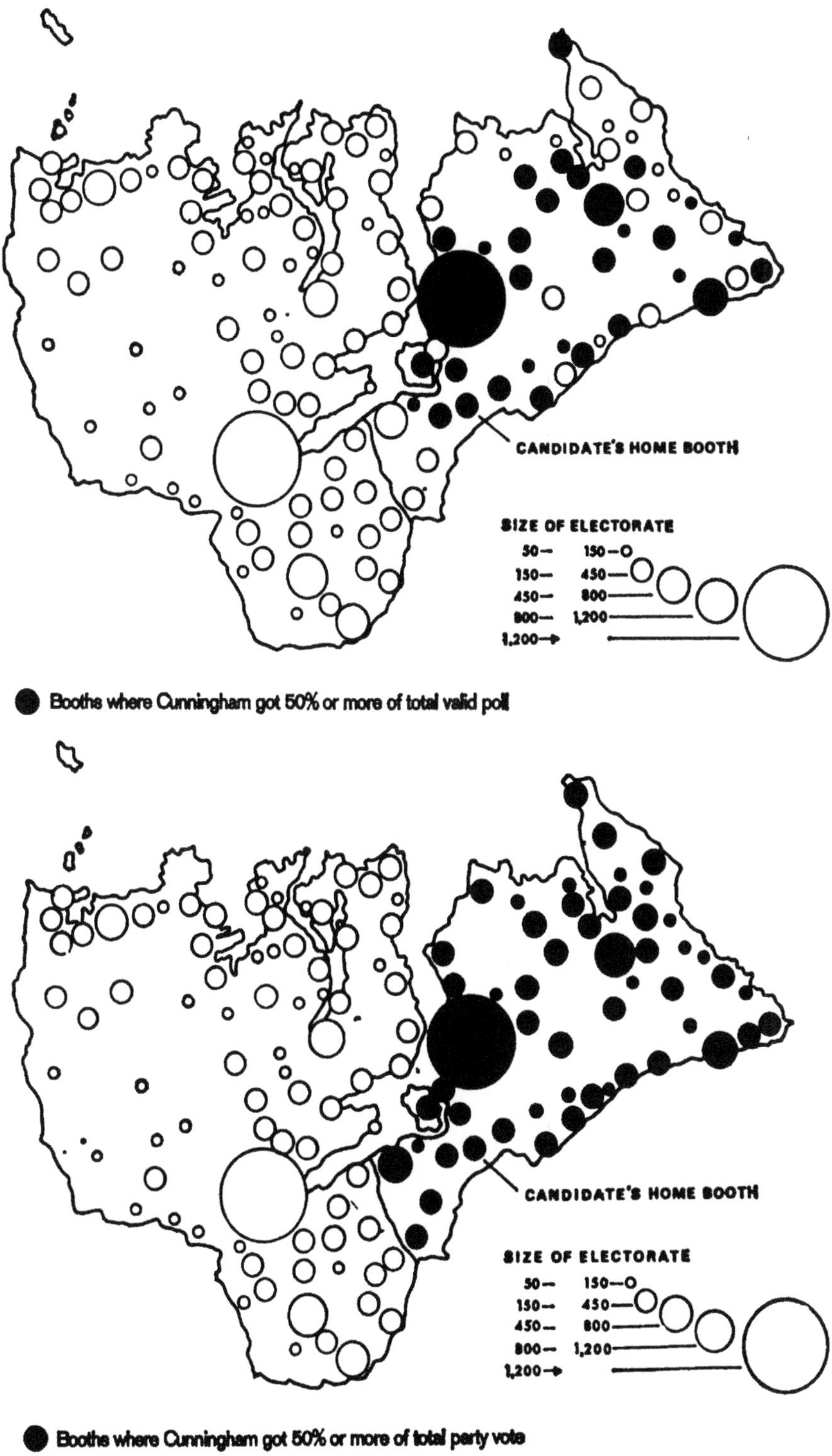

Figure 6.3 The friends-and-neighbours effect in voting for Cunningham, a Fianna Fail candidate in the Donegal North-east constituency for the Irish Dail, 1969. Source: Sacks, 1970, Maps 2 and 3

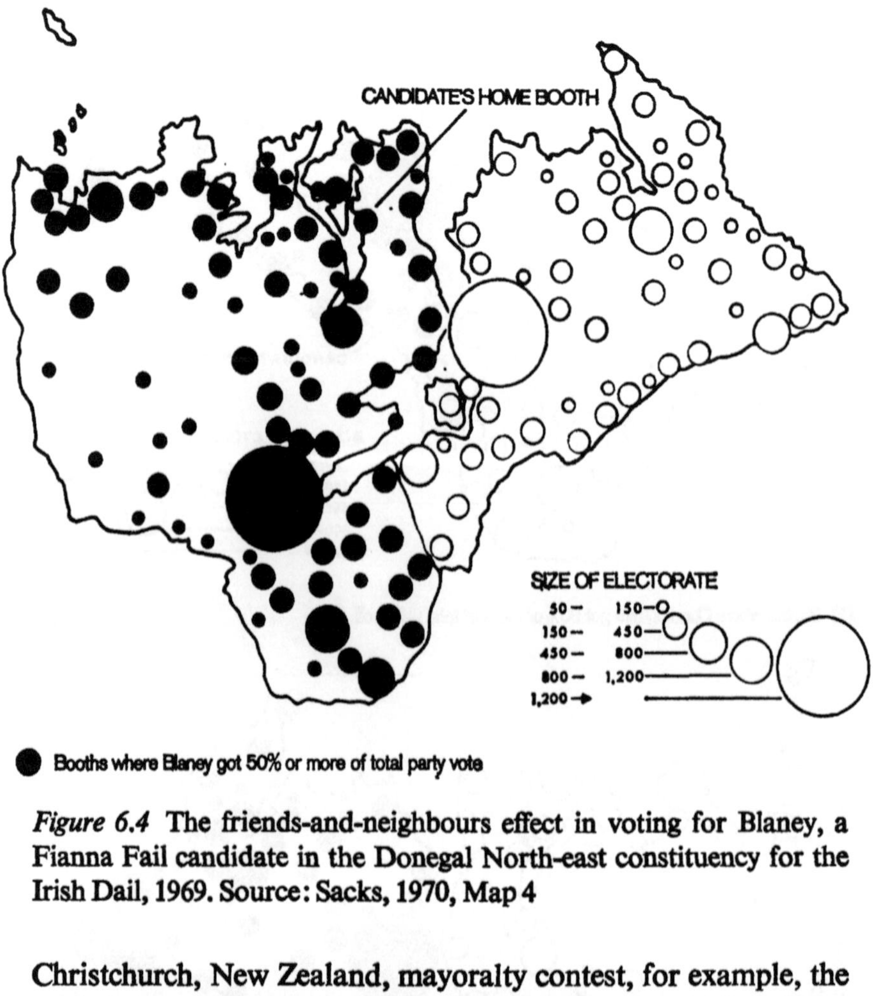

Figure 6.4 The friends-and-neighbours effect in voting for Blaney, a Fianna Fail candidate in the Donegal North-east constituency for the Irish Dail, 1969. Source: Sacks, 1970, Map 4

Christchurch, New Zealand, mayoralty contest, for example, the basic issues between the incumbent, Guthrey, and his Labour party challenger, Pickering, were the former's general credibility and his somewhat dictatorial methods. But there were local issues also, particularly concerning motorway proposals and whether the stadium for the 1974 Commonwealth Games should be built at Porritt Park (Guthrey) or Queen Elizabeth II Park (Pickering). Over the 119 booths there was about a 14 per cent swing away from Guthrey – who lost the election – but some areas deviated markedly from this trend. There was much less of a swing than average around Porritt Park, for example (the booths shown by open circles in Figure 6.5), and also in the area of the

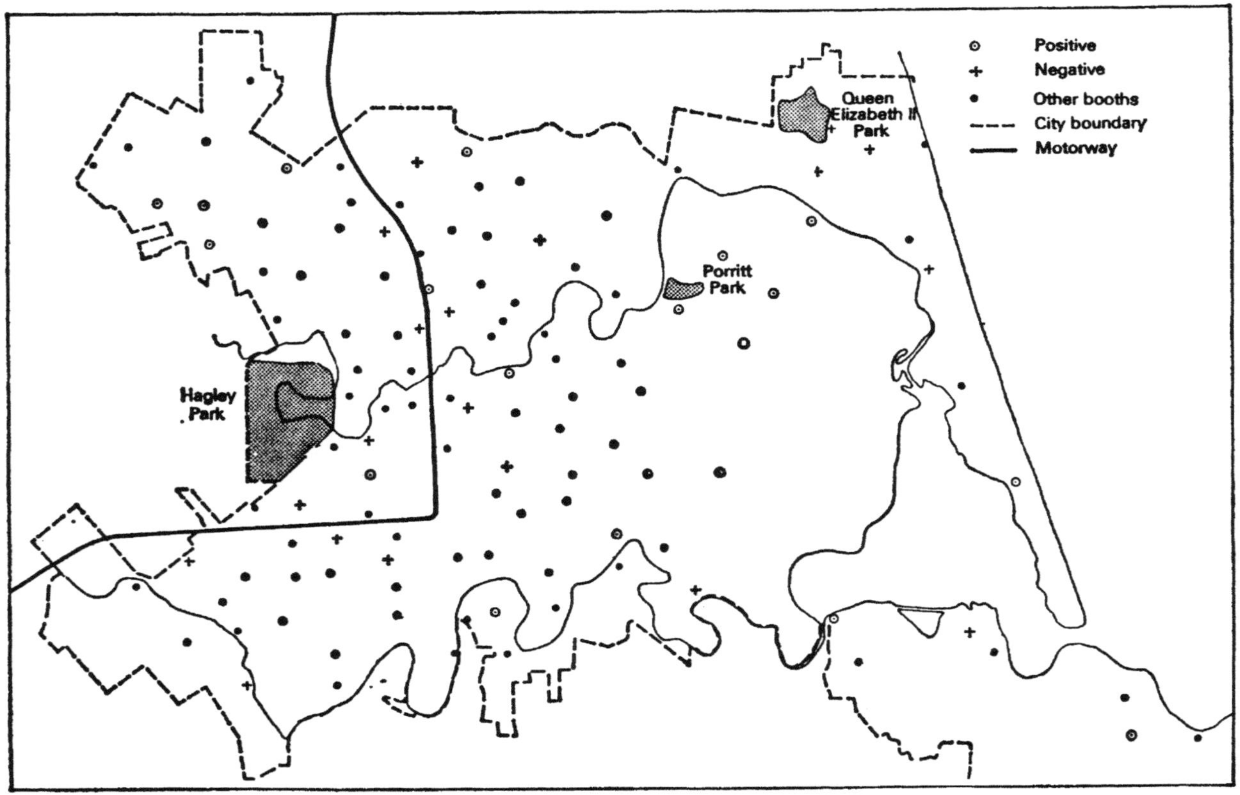

Figure 6.5 Residuals from the regression of voting for Guthrey in the Christchurch mayoralty contest, 1971 against voting for him in the 1968 contest. The residuals identified are those more than one standard error away from the regression line.

north-eastern part of the city around Guthrey's home (the latter was presumably a friends-and-neighbours effect). Conversely, greater than average swings against Guthrey (shown by a + in Figure 6.5) were recorded in the area of his opponent's proposed stadium, presumably indicative of their desire for the facility to be built there. (It was. See also Forrest, Marjoribanks and Johnston, 1977.)

Race as an election issue in Britain

Self-interest on local issues may cause people temporarily to abandon their usual party preferences, therefore, especially if politicians campaign on these issues. (There are several pressure groups in the United States which monitor congressmen's roll-call records and publish their interpretations of the outcome. Some of these ratings are published in the biennial *Almanac of American Politics*, Barone, Ujifusa and Matthews, 1972, and one of them was used by Ronald Reagan to show the 'liberalism' of his proposed vice-presidential running-mate for the 1976 election, Senator Richard Schweiker.) One such issue in Britain in recent years has been immigration. Busteed (1975), following Deakin (1965), has shown that there was a national swing to Labour in the 1964 election of 3·1 per cent but that in the West Midlands area, the home of many coloured immigrants whose movement to Britain had been curtailed by the 1962 Immigration Act, passed by the Conservative government, the swing was much less; Conservative actually won two seats from Labour, including one held by the prospective Foreign Minister, Patrick Gordon-Walker.

Deakin (1965, p. 158) urges caution in a wholesale interpretation of these results as anti-immigrant, and thus against the less hard-line Labour view of the time, for Labour were not affected significantly, relative to the general trend, in all seats with large immigrant populations (Table 6.8). In the Birmingham area, for example, one of the seats lost by Labour – Perry Bar – had a much smaller immigrant population than did others which the party either held or won from Conservative. Several factors

Table 6.8 Immigration and voting swings: selected English constituencies at the 1964 general election

Constituency		*Main immigrant group*	*Number of immigrants*	*Local swing*[a]	*Immigrant vote*[b]	*Regional swing*[a]
Birmingham	All Saints	West Indian	18,000	−0·8		−2·5
	Handsworth	West Indian	15,000	−6·3		−2·5
	Perry Barr	West Indian	1,000	+0·6		−2·5
	Sparkbrook	Mixed	6,000	−3·3		−2·5
Eton and Slough		Mixed	5,000	+0·1		−4·2
Smethwick		Indian	4,500	+7·2	0·7	−1·6
Southall		Indian	6,000	+0·2	9·1	−4·3
West Bromwich		West Indian	6,800	+2·3		−1·6
London	Deptford	West Indian	5,000	−4·7	8·4	−4·3
	Holborn/St Pancras S.	Cypriot	2,500	−5·8	(0·7)	−4·3
	Islington E.	Cypriot/West Indian	10,000	−4·4	7·6	−4·3
	Lambeth, Brixton	West Indian	10,000	−5·0		−4·3

[a] in percentage points of the two-party vote only; a negative swing is towards Labour.
[b] percentage of the vote won by an independent candidate standing on the immigration issue.
Source: Deakin (1965, p. 159)

influenced the variations. Most important was whether immigration was a local campaign issue. The majority of candidates avoided it entirely, but in Perry Bar the Conservative aspirant issued a 'notorious' anti-immigration leaflet and at Smethwick (the seat lost by Gordon-Walker) the Conservative candidate (who was a local resident) campaigned strongly on the immigration issue (Hartley-Brewer, 1965, p. 104). At Southall, Deptford and Islington East, independent and minority-party (e.g. the British National Party) candidates 'protected' the major parties by attracting the protest vote, although Labour still performed relatively poorly in Southall. Finally, there seemed to be some relationship between the degree of anti-immigrant feeling and both the economic status of the local host population and the origins of the immigrants. West Indians apparently produced much less hostility than did Indians; Pakistanis, too, did not create great voter antipathy, although Spiers's (1965, p. 156) concluding comment on Bradford – 'Is race likely to become a political issue in Bradford? In the opinion of the present writer it is not' – unfortunately has not stood the test of a further decade.

One of the Conservative members for a West Midlands constituency who became involved in the immigration issue was Enoch Powell. Initially, he played no major role in the campaign on this issue (Foot, 1965), and he was not involved in the major swings to Conservative in certain West Midlands constituencies in 1964. Immigration was not a major issue in the 1966 contest, when there was a swing back to Labour and the party regained the seat at Smethwick. Powell climbed onto the 'anti-immigrant bandwagon' in 1968 with some powerful oratory (Foot, 1969), which he maintained throughout the 1970 election campaign – despite clear unease about his views among the party leaders. Powell's popularity was demonstrable in that, whereas the national swing to Conservative in 1970 was 4·7 percentage points, in Wolverhampton (the town which he represented) the swing in the two constituencies was 9·1 and 8·7 percentage points.

Powell left the Conservative Party in 1974 (he later joined the Ulster Unionists and was elected to represent a County Down constituency). At the February 1974 election he counselled his supporters to vote Labour – as he did himself – because he was opposed to the 1973 British entry into the European Economic Community, which had been negotiated by the Conservatives. Having played a major part in the defeat of Labour in 1970 through his advocacy over the immigration issue, it seems that in 1974 he could well have been responsible for that party's victory. The swing to Labour in the Black Country constituencies (Fig. 6.6) was very much greater than the national trend. To some, this

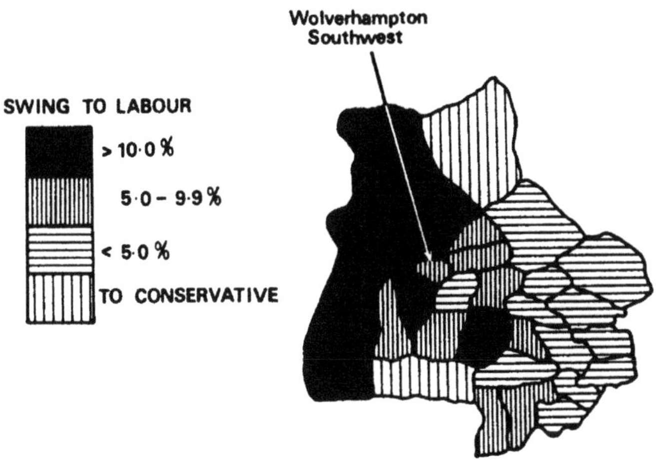

Figure 6.6 'Enochland' in 1974; the swing to Labour at the February election in the West Midlands, indicating the major trend in Wolverhampton and surrounding constituencies.

merely reflects Labour voters returning to their normal preferences after deserting the party over the immigration issue in 1970. To others, however, it represents the power of Powell in his West Midlands bailiwick. One week before his pronouncement, a Birmingham constituency was reported by pollsters as having a 13 per cent lead for Conservative; after Powell had counselled a Labour vote, however, that lead had fallen to only 2 per cent (Johnson and Schoen, 1976).

The role of the immigration issue and the influence of Enoch Powell are illustrated in the following statistics and in the maps of Fig. 6.7. In 1964, the national swing to Labour was 3.1 percentage points. In twenty-five constituencies there was a swing to

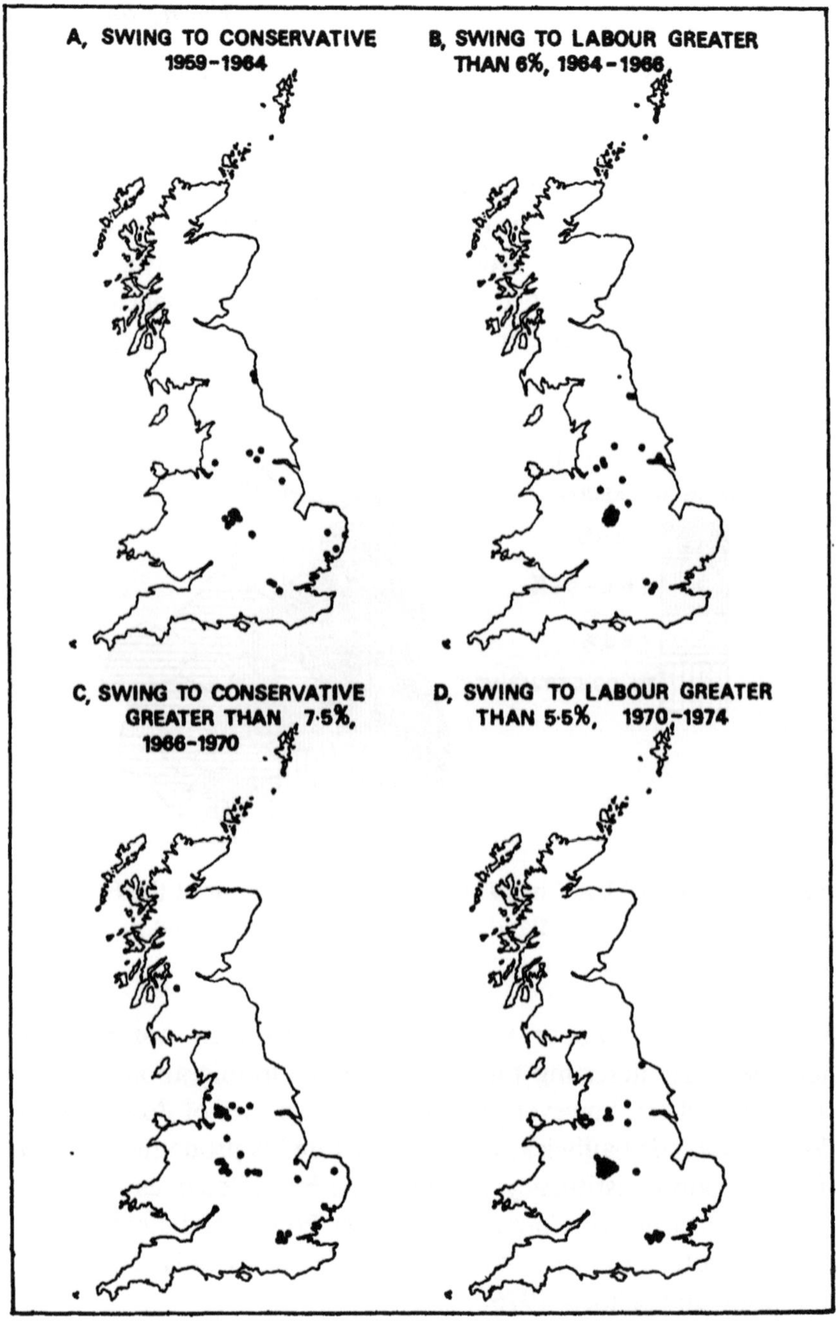

Figure 6.7 'Enochland' in Britain, 1964–74. Each of the four maps portrays the seats deviating most markedly (in one direction) from the national trend; the clustering of such seats in the West Midlands in each map indicates the effect of Enoch Powell on voter volatility in that area relative to the country as a whole.

Conservative, however; nine of them were in the West Midlands, and all twenty-five averaged 2·11 per cent of their population born in the New Commonwealth countries, compared to a national average of 1·7 per cent. (The immigrant figures refer to the 1966 sample census and are taken from Butler and Pinto-Duschinsky, 1971.) In 1966, there was a swing to Labour in Great Britain of 2·7 percentage points. Twenty-six constituencies recorded a swing to Labour exceeding 6 points; ten of these were in the West Midlands (Fig. 6.7B), presumably reflecting the swing back to Labour once the immigration issue had died down, and the average percentage of New Commonwealth born in all twenty-six was 3·78. There was one other notable regional grouping at this election. The three seats in Hull all reported more than twice the national swing, and the Humberside/North Lincolnshire area in general was characterized by above-average swings. This seems to be the result of increased local support for Labour following proposals for a New Town in the area (Steed, 1966, pp. 282–3) which included, as first indicated during the crucial Hull North by-election in 1966, a promise to build the long-awaited Humber Bridge (Crossman, 1975, p. 437).

The national swing to Conservative in 1970 was 4·7 percentage points; among the thirty-four which recorded a swing of 7·5 points or more were seven in the West Midlands (Fig. 6.7C) and in addition there were major swings to Conservative in both Derby and Leicester. The average percentage of New Commonwealth-born in these thirty-four was 2·15, again compared to the national figure of 1·7 in the 1966 Census results. Finally, in February 1974 the recorded swing to Labour was 1·1 percentage points. In twenty-nine constituencies, a swing of 5·5 points or more was recorded, and thirteen of these were in the West Midlands (Fig. 6.6; 6.7D); foı all twenty-nine the average percentage of the population with 'New Commonwealth roots' was 7·28, compared to the national figure of 2·41 (data from the 1971 Census, given by Steed, 1974).

There is a clear inference to be drawn from the data quoted here, that the more volatile of the British constituencies in the last twenty years, in terms of swings of opinion from one main party to another, have included many with above average percentages of immigrants among their residents. Many of these have been in the West Midlands area which was Enoch Powell's political home-base, and the maps suggest a very clear 'Enochland' which has been crucial in determining the result for at least two of the last five British elections. The reasons for this volatility are undoubtedly manifold but, as Steed (1974, p. 332) remarks, they include a remarkable tribute to the influence of Enoch Powell.

Individual politicians or groups galvanize an electorate to vote in a particular way on a local issue that much concerns them, therefore, so producing voting patterns which deviate markedly from wider trends. Powell certainly seems to have achieved this; the British Liberal Party achieved several by-election successes in the early 1970s by concentrating on local themes; George Wallace has been able to trade on right-wing sentiments in certain states of the American south. Wallace's recent performance mirrors a similar event in 1948. Then, the Democrat national convention adopted for its policy-platform several planks relating to civil rights and segregation issues. This angered southern Democrats (especially in Alabama, Mississippi and South Carolina), who put up a third-party Dixiecrat ticket, nominating Governors Thurmond (South Carolina) and Wright (Mississippi) respectively for president and vice-president. Within Mississippi, almost all of whose voters were white, support for this ticket was greatest in the counties containing most blacks and most farmers, suggesting that support for segregationalist policies was strongest in those areas where the whites had most to lose from civil rights legislation (Heer, 1958).

Referenda

Some votes, notably referenda, are taken on individual issues, and local interests should stand out in the pattern of results. An example of this is the 1974 Swiss referendum on whether the number of foreign workers in the country should be reduced to 500,000 by 1 July 1978 (at the 1970 Census there were 657,030, accounting for 21·9 per cent of the workforce), with the added proposal that they should account for no more than 12 per cent of the population in any canton except Geneva, where the limit was to be 25 per cent. (This was the second referendum on the subject; one in 1970 had been defeated by 54 to 46 per cent of the voters.) A variety of factors would influence how people voted on this issue, or even whether they voted. Given the general importance of foreign workers to the Swiss economy (37 per cent of all workers in Geneva, for example), we would expect that voter turnout would be greatest, and voting against the proposal also greatest, where foreign workers were considered most important. This is borne out by the two graphs in Figure 6.8. In graph A, the scatter of points for the 25 cantons, and the best fit linear regression, the line drawn to indicate the general trend in these points, confirms the hypothesis that turnout (the national figure was 70 per cent) was greatest in the cantons with most foreign workers relative to the total workforce – the line slopes up. In graph B there is even clearer confirmation that the percentage voting for the restriction (national figure, 34 per cent) was smallest where the foreign workers were most important in the total labour force. Neither relationship is particularly strong, however, but in both graphs, most especially that for percentage voting 'yes', the operation of another influence is suggested. Switzerland is a dominantly German-speaking country (approximately 70 per cent report that German is their first language), but in six cantons in the south-west (Fribourg, Ticino, Vaud, Valais, Neuchâtel and Geneva) German-speakers are in the minority (Italian is dominant in Ticino, and French in the other five), and in one canton in the south-east (Grisons), the German-speaking percentage, although still in the majority, is well below the national average (Romansch takes second place there). These seven cantons are separately identified in the graphs by squares, indicating in Figure 6.8B that, with the partial exception of Grisons, the non-German dominated cantons were much more favourably inclined towards the foreign workers, matching other trends in the pattern of Swiss voting (Kerr, 1974: for a further interpretation of these referenda see Johnston and White, 1977).

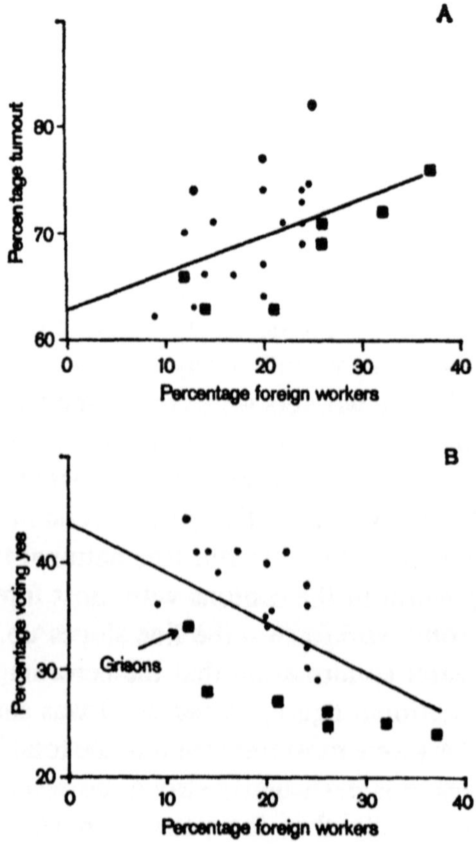

Figure 6.8 Issues and voting: immigrant workers in Switzerland. The upper graph (A) shows the regression of voter turnout for the referendum in 1974 on reducing the number of foreign-workers against the size of the foreign-born population in each canton: the lower graph (B) shows the regression of voting for restrictions at that referendum against the same independent variable. The larger symbols in each case indicate the non-German-speaking cantons.

As we pointed out in Chapter 2, referenda are frequently held by local governments in the United States. Analysis of voting at eighteen of these in the Wisconsin capital of Madison during the 1960s indicated great consistency in the pattern of results over the 41 precincts. In general, the higher the socio-economic status of the district, the greater its support for the referendum, whatever the issue, which Harmatuck (1976) suggests indicates the aware-

ness of the higher status groups of the need for 'good government' and their insensitivity to the extra tax burden it may impose. Suburban areas – those occupied by young families – are, however, consistently against proposals, other than those involving educational facilities, on the argument that suburban areas are underprovided with many basic facilities and will not benefit from extra tax cost on such issues as improving the airport. Despite this overall consistency, however, particular issues may produce peculiar voting patterns in certain areas; on a referendum about the purchase of the private bus company serving Madison, for example, as well as strong support from the élite and opposition from the poorly served suburbs, the areas whose populations provided most bus users were very much in favour of the purchase. (The referendum was held soon after a strike by bus company employees and a threat to withdraw the service.) Similar results were obtained from a study in six Illinois counties forming the Chicago metropolitan area, concerning a 1974 referendum on whether a regional transportation authority should be formed. Greatest support for the proposal (which was passed by a bare margin, with 50·48 per cent of those voting in favour) was in areas with high-income populations, where bus usage was great and large proportions of the workforce had jobs in the city centre, which the R.T.A. would probably serve best (Soot, Kortheiser, and Wojtkiewicz, 1976).

The traditional hypothesis regarding voting behaviour is that individuals cast their ballots in order to maximize their self-interest. On many local referenda this should involve them in a cost-benefit analysis, calculating what economic return they will get if they vote for a certain proposal that, if carried, will mean greater expenditure for them from their property taxes. On a referendum for the establishment of a local zoo, for example, the returns are the same for all – the benefit of being able to visit the zoo – but as property taxes increase with income for home-owners, the cost of the zoo will vary among the voters. The higher the income, the less the return to the voter relative to his costs, and the less likely that he will favour the expenditure. Thus, whereas renters – who pay no property taxes directly – should vote in favour of all spending referenda, home-owners should not, and the greater the value of their homes, the more likely they are to oppose the spending. In analyses of a large number of referenda, Wilson and Banfield (1964) found that only part of this self-interest hypothesis was valid: renters were indeed more generally in favour of spending referenda than were home-owners, but high-income home-owners were more likely to vote 'yes' than were their middle-income counterparts. This unexpected pattern, they pointed out, could be the result of the low marginal utility of dollars for high-income people, but the latter did not vote for spending on all issues – e.g. in Cook County they were in favour of a new state hospital for indigents but not in favour of a $300 bonus being paid to Korean war veterans. Instead, 'a more tenable hypothesis, we think, is that voters in some income and ethnic groups are more likely than voters in others to take a public-regarding rather than a narrowly self-interested view of things – i.e. to take the welfare of others, especially that of "the community", into account as an aspect of their own welfare' (Wilson and Banfield, 1964, p. 886). This public-regardingness hypothesis reflects cultural variations in the socialization process, and Wilson and Banfield's analyses showed that it was the upper-income groups, especially those of Anglo-Saxon stock, in American cities who were most likely to vote for certain spending programmes because they were in the public interest, even if relatively expensive to them personally.

Sometimes the pattern of voting on local issues does not turn out to be as expected. In 1964, the city of Flint, Michigan held a referendum on whether to introduce an open housing ordinance which would remove all legal restrictions on who could buy housing where (such discrimination was removed nationally in 1968). It was anticipated that householders living close to the edge of the black ghetto would be most against this ordinance, since they would perceive it as a generator of black invasion of their residential areas, with a consequent lowering of property values and production of an undesirable – to them – 'mixed' neighbourhood. In fact, it turned out that the further people lived from the ghetto edge – i.e. in the outer suburbs – the greater was their opposition to the ordinance (Brunn and Hoffman, 1970), suggesting that the suburban rich are not as liberal as they like to be thought.

The Campaign

The few weeks before a vote is taken, particularly in national elections, are a period of intense campaigning activity, with many people spending long hours at efforts to ensure that others vote a certain way. This period is now regulated in most countries, with laws specifying, among other things, how long it can last, how much each candidate can spend during it, and where and how he can raise that money. In many cases, however, the brief campaign period is merely the top-gear running of an organizational machine which is constantly operating to keep elector, elected and aspirant in contact with each other, and thus aware of feelings and opinions on various issues.

Campaigning takes place at a variety of spatial scales, from small local areas to the nation as a whole. In national elections, much of the effort involves projection of party policy and leadership image through the mass media to the electorate at large; a procedure which Rose (1967) claims is often far from rational. But where elections are determined in constituencies, and success nationally depends on the number of constituency victories, the major reinforcement of the national campaign and the detailed vote-winning efforts is at the local scale. Contestants, notably parties, must devise methods for winning votes where they are most needed (Johnston, 1976e), so that campaigning has a clear spatial component in its investment of resources, usually labour, time and, to a lesser extent, money.

The constituency campaign

Having determined its national strategy – which policies it will advance, which aspects of its record it will highlight, which elements of the opposition personnel and policies it will attack, etc. – a party must then decide where it will invest its effort in selling that strategy, given that time and money prevent it mounting an equally large and effective campaign everywhere. As we showed in Chapters 3 and 4, the spatial division of labour and the class-basis of much voting means that constituencies, especially those in plurality electoral systems, are not of equal importance to a party, given the realistic assumption that very large swings in voter preferences between elections are unlikely except in rare, and usually localized circumstances. Some constituencies are safe for a party; it has always won a large proportion of the votes there, and another electoral victory is a virtual certainty: others are hopeless; its support there is weak and there is undoubtedly no way in which it could win votes from enough electors to gain victory there. In between are the marginal constituencies; those which can be won and lost by a relatively small swing of voter preferences, or of turnout if one party's supporters tend to abstain from voting more than do another's.

In terms of campaign planning, it is clear that most effort should be concentrated on the marginal constituencies, ensuring that the party suffers no losses there and aiming for gains from the opposition. The safe seats should receive some attention, to keep the party faithful contented and to maintain the party's strength, which is often valuable in, for example, allowing leaders (and ministers if the party is in office) respite from the need to spend a lot of time 'nursing' their constituencies. As to the hopeless seats, the logical conclusion is that they should be ignored, sparing any wasting of resources on campaigns that are doomed before they start. This has been the case in the last few decades in South Africa, with a peak in 1961 when there was no contest in 67 of the 150 constituencies (Heard, 1974). The white South African electorate was very polarized between the right-wing Nationalist Party, which is Afrikaner-based, and the slightly more liberal United Party, which gains its strength from the English-speaking community (Peele and Morse, 1974). The former has always been strongest in the rural areas, winning over 85 per cent of all the constituencies there since 1958, and the latter was strong in the urban areas; each party has tended not to contest in the other's stronghold. (In 1961, the Nationalist party won 24 uncontested seats in the non-metropolitan areas and United won 17 in the urban areas. In all, the Nationalists fielded 104 candidates and 99 of them were elected; United fielded 99 and 49 were successful.) Since 1961, the numbers of uncontested seats have fallen drastically with only 18 and 10 in 1966 and 1970 but an increase to 43 in 1974. There are several reasons for this trend. The first is the movement of the Afrikaner into the towns (de Klerk, 1976), where in 1970 the Nationalists won 50 per cent of the constituencies compared to only 20 per cent in 1948; a large proportion of the urban seats are now contested, therefore. Perhaps of more importance, however, is the nature of the new contests. Two new parties have been formed in recent years. The Herstigte Nasionale Party (H.N.P.) was formed in 1969 by right-wing dissidents from the National Party, and it now competes in a large number of seats (77 in 1970; 43 in 1974). The Progressive Party split from the United Party in 1959. It won one seat in Johannesburg in 1961, which Mrs Helen Suzman has held ever since, and after the 1970 election was joined by another dissident group from the United Party, to form the Progressive-Reform movement. The impact of these two parties is indicated in Table 6.9. For both, a major aim was to replace the other party of that wing – the H.N.P. to replace the Nationalist, and the Progressive-Reform to replace United as the opposition (as it did in 1977) – so that in 1974 of the 122 contested constituencies, 42 (just over a third) were what we have termed 'intra-party' contests, since they did not involve Nationalist versus United. If these are added to the 43 uncontested seats, then just over half of all constituencies did not involve the voters in a choice between Government and Opposition.

The logic of the South African parties is not now followed in many other places, one major exception being the American southern states where Republican support has been very weak until recent years. A major reason for the fielding of candidates irrespective of their chances of success is that in countries such as Britain the electorate is not as polarized between sections who are also spatially segregated as it is in South Africa, partly because the average constituency contains many more voters in Britain. And so every constituency will have a fairly substantial minority

Table 6.9 Type of contest, South African general election, 1974

	Province				
	Cape	*Natal*	*Orange Free State*	*Transvaal*	*Total*
Unopposed candidates					
Nationalist	18	0	5	7	30
United	4	5	0	4	13
'Inter-party'					
United v. Nationalist	17	5	1	26	49
Three or more parties	3	2	3	17	25
'Intra-party'					
Nationalist v. H.N.P.	6	1	3	15	25
United v. Progressive-Reform	6	4	0	7	17
Other	1	3	2	0	6
Total	55	20	14	76	165

Source: computed from the official election returns, Republic of South Africa, *Government Gazette*, 17 May 1974, No. 4279.

for the party expecting to lose; those voters will want their party to field a candidate so that they can express their preferences, and the local branch of the party may be of wider value – in the transfer of funds, for example (Rose, 1976) – and perhaps of importance in a marginal seat after the next boundary revision. Further, many parties use hopeless seats as locales for grooming apprentice candidates. As the Liberal Party indicated at the 1974 elections, aspiration to be a party with national rather than local status implies fielding a candidate in every constituency. Also, for that party every vote counted in its attempts to build a case for electoral reform and the introduction of a system based on proportional representation.

This failure to contest hopeless seats was formerly a common phenomenon in British politics, even for the major parties (see Dunbabin, 1966, for late nineteenth century evidence). In Northern Ireland, where the community is politically very polarized and the two opposing groups are spatially segregated, large numbers of uncontested seats were the norm in the elections to the Stormont parliament during the period (1921–69) when the plurality system operated. Out of the 52 seats, the number uncontested at each election (Darby, 1976, p. 111) was:

Election	1921	25	29	33	38	45	49	53	58	62	65	69
	0	12	22	33	21	20	20	25	27	24	23	7

Although the parties now usually contest every constituency in Great Britain, they do not invest equally in each. There is a maximum amount which can be spent by the party (not by the candidate, who can spend his own money as much as he likes) during the campaign, set by Act of Parliament as: 'In a county constituency £1075 with an additional 6p for every six entries ... in the register of electors in use at the election and, in a borough constituency, £1075 with an additional 6p for every eight such entries' (Election Expenses ... 1975, p. 3). The greater amount that can be spent in county constituencies reflects the greater costs of contacting voters in low-density rural areas. None of the parties spends its full quota; the total expenditure in Scotland at the October 1974 general election was £268,551, whereas the maximum allowed would have been about £450,000, and no party spent the full allowance in any one constituency, although some came very close (83 per cent of the expenditure was on printing and stationery).

A logical hypothesis concerning the spatial variations in constituency expenditure would be that the greater the chance a party had of winning a constituency, the more they would spend of their allowance. This hypothesis was tested for the 71 Scottish constituencies at the October 1974 general election, relating the percentage of the allowance spent by the party (the vertical axis) to its distance in votes from the winning party at the previous, February 1974, election, expressed as a percentage of all votes cast then (the horizontal axis). For both Labour and Conservative, the best-fit regression lines in Figure 6.9 show that the hypothesis is valid, as it also is for Scottish Nationalist and Liberal, with the last two graphs referring only to the 34 constituencies which all four parties contested in both elections. Separate regressions are shown for the seats won and lost by each party indicating, for example, that if Labour had won a seat and been 20 per cent ahead of the next party in the previous February, in October it spent 8 per cent more on average of its campaign allowance than if it had been 20 per cent behind the winner. Thus each party, as expected, spends most money campaigning where there are greater chances of it either winning or losing the constituency, and, in addition, each spent relatively more in the seats it won in February than in those it lost. The slopes of the regression lines vary in their steepness, however, and in general the smaller the party the less it spent in the constituencies it had little hope of winning. Relative to what they would spend in a very marginal seat (e.g. one with a one vote margin), the four parties would be spending the following amounts when the gap between the winner and themselves was 20 per cent of the total poll: Labour 90%; Conservative 78%; Scottish Nationalist 78%; and Liberal 72%. The two larger British parties are more intent on making their presence widely felt, it would seem, while the smaller parties conserve their more meagre resources for the constituencies in which they are most optimistic of their chances (Johnston, 1977e).

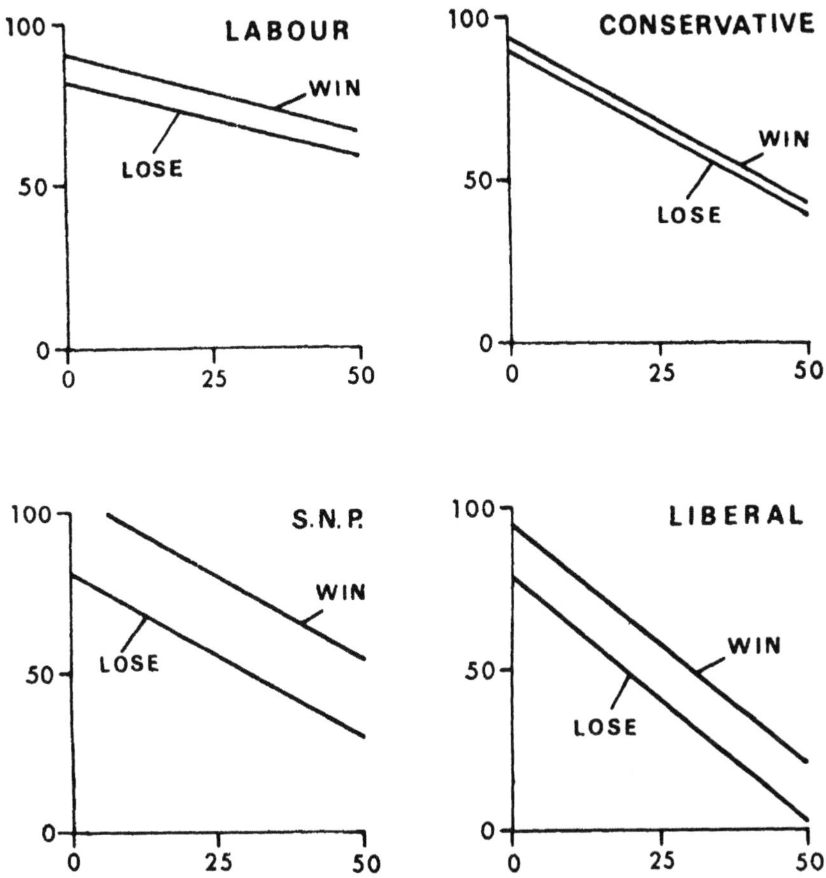

Figure 6.9 Regressions of party campaign expenditure against constituency marginality at the October 1974 general election in Scotland: the independent variable is the distance between the relevant party's candidate and either the next candidate (if the former won in February), or the winner in February, as a percentage of all votes cast; the dependent variable is the percentage of allowable expenditure spent. Separate regression lines are shown for the constituencies won and lost by each party in February 1974.

The main purpose of constituency canvassing in Britain is to increase voter turnout of one's party's supporters, and the bulk of the expenditure is on stationery and printing to get the message across (party workers who deliver the handbills etc. are unpaid). Turnout is higher in marginal constituencies (Fletcher, 1968;

Rowley, 1971), though it is not clear whether this is because of the party's expenditure. Taylor (1972) investigated changes between the 1966 and 1970 general elections, and found that greater expenditure was related to greater turnout, that both Labour and Liberal votes increased with an increase in the relevant party's campaign expenditure and a decrease in Conservative expenditure, but that the Conservative vote was poorly related to any expenditure changes; the latter finding suggests that Conservative voters are less likely to abstain if their party is not actively campaigning than are Labour and Liberal supporters (see Crewe, Fox and Alt, 1977). Overall, Taylor (1972, p. 331) concluded that the changed patterns of spending between the two elections were 'large enough to suggest that if local organizations had not changed since 1966 the election result would have been different'.

In United States presidential elections, the electoral college system (see p. 45) makes votes in some states more valuable than those in others. At first sight, the differences between the states seem different from what one would expect, since it turns out to be the larger states which are the most valuable. Yet the smaller the state, the less votes needed to win it; in 1976, for example, only 31,002 votes were needed to win Alaska whereas 3,773,509 were needed for success in California, so each vote won in Alaska would seem to be ten times more valuable than one in California, in terms of its importance for winning the state. Victory in California, however, was fifteen times more valuable, because the candidate winning that state received 45 electoral college votes compared to only 3 for the Alaskan victor. Thus, although victory may be more costly in the larger states, the potential benefits are greater. Detailed analysis of this cost-benefit appraisal, based on game theory (Shapley and Shubik, 1954), showed that in the 1960s each vote in New York was worth 3·312 votes in the District of Columbia (Banzhaf, 1968), and the general pattern is that the more populous the state, the more valuable each vote is (Figure 6.10). (Game theory is an algebraic form of analysis which suggests what should happen when two or more contestants are faced with a set of choices as to action, in this case political behaviour. Each contestant knows what the consequences of

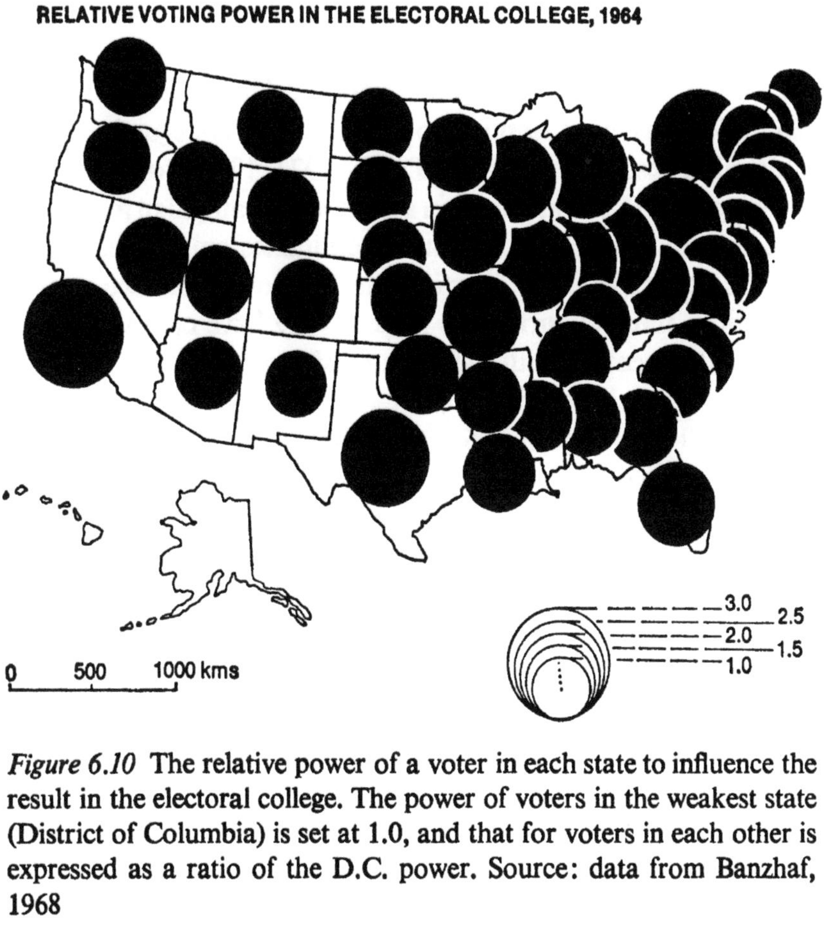

Figure 6.10 The relative power of a voter in each state to influence the result in the electoral college. The power of voters in the weakest state (District of Columbia) is set at 1.0, and that for voters in each other is expressed as a ratio of the D.C. power. Source: data from Banzhaf, 1968

each set of actions will be – e.g. if I do A and my opponent does B, I will gain £*x*, but if both of us do B, I will lose £*y* – but each has no intimation of what his opponents will do.) In the electoral college example, the power of a state is defined as the number of losing coalitions which it could transform into winning coalitions if it joined them – i.e. if it was won by the same party. Thus, if 270 votes are needed for victory in the electoral college and a party seems sure of winning enough states to get 250, Alaska with three votes will be much less important to it in its campaigning than will New York with 41 or Illinois with 26. These analyses assume that each state is equally likely to support either party, however, and so provide only a first approximation to the complex game-playing that goes on in presidential campaigns. Brams, 1975, provides a good introduction to such analyses.

A variety of alternative game-theoretical approaches (Coleman, 1972) has been applied to the electoral college situation, with similar results. Brams and Davis (1973, 1974), for example, have suggested that under certain assumptions campaign resources should be allocated by presidential candidates among the states according to a particular function (the 3/2 power) of each state's population, thus favouring the larger. They have compared this theoretical allocation with the amount of campaign time spent in each state by each presidential/vice-presidential ticket during the period 1960–72. Only in 1964 (the Johnson–Goldwater contest) was there not a reasonably close fit, and Table 6.10 shows how in general the larger states received much greater percentages of the campaigners' time than they had percentages of the electoral votes, because the votes were allocated in larger blocks to the large-state winners. In three of the four campaigns the Republicans paid more attention to the smaller states, which is as would be expected, since much of the party's strength is in the rural areas. The Republican candidates have a greater need to keep the faithful happy in these areas, leaving the Democrats free to campaign in the big states, where much of their strength lies in any case.

We have so far discussed campaigning in terms of spending money and time exhorting people to vote, but have paid little attention to how the campaigning might attempt to persuade them which person or party to vote for. It is a logical deduction from our arguments on where candidates ought to campaign, however, to suggest that this campaigning should include the orienting of policies – proposed or actual – towards those people and places whose votes are the most valuable. In a plurality system, therefore, governments would be expected to direct some of their policies towards the party faithful in their safe seats, but to expend their greatest political initiatives on 'buying' votes in the marginal constituencies (Tullock, 1976, gives an excellent introduction to the economics of vote buying); the hopeless constituencies will largely be ignored (Johnston, 1976e). Brams and

Table 6.10 Campaign appearances and electoral college votes in American presidential elections

	Size of state					
	Large (20+ electoral college votes)		*Medium (10–20 electoral college votes)*		*Small (3–9 electoral college votes)*	
Percentage of	*Campaign time*	*Votes*	*Campaign time*	*Votes*	*Campaign time*	*Votes*
1960 Democrat	66	38	21	34	13	28
Republican	56	38	25	34	19	28
1964 Democrat	45	39	24	32	31	29
Republican	38	39	29	32	32	29
1968 Democrat	61	39	26	32	12	29
Republican	52	39	21	32	16	29
1972 Democrat	60	39	24	30	26	30
Republican	63	39	17	30	20	30

Source: Brams and Davis (1974, p. 125)

Davis (1974, p. 131) – quoting in part from Scammon and Wattenberg (1970, p. 213) – have argued that it is no longer the case that, 'states can be pinpointed like military targets and, independent of nearby and faraway other targets, captured with a high probability by a concentration of forces superior to that of one's opponents . . . The day of the pinpoint sectional or statewide campaign is gone – if it ever existed – and the fact that votes cannot be garnered in bushels on specific street corners is of crucial significance when one looks at the arithmetic of the future'. Nevertheless, if votes in some places are more valuable than are those in others, parties and candidates are likely to recognize this, and to organize their campaigns accordingly.

There has been little detailed analysis of this proposition. United States data show that residents of the large states, particularly those of the north-eastern seaboard, have received disproportionate numbers of cabinet appointments. In analysing maps of where presidents have drawn their cabinets from during the present century, Brunn (1974, p. 91) argues that:

> when the president considers nominations . . . While he may consider the professional expertise or government experience as paramount, he also can weigh heavily the states these élites represent. His election may have been ensured by key states or personalities in those states. Therefore he may feel he 'owes' the voters and leaders of those states some representation in his cabinet. On the other hand, he may know that to handle problems dealing with agriculture he would prefer to have a cabinet member from an agricultural state that the nation's farmers and lobbies can readily identify with . . . A further reason that a president may select an individual from a particular state is to maintain his popularity or that of his party.

Thus, political considerations may give some states much more cabinet representation than others, over a period, as illustrated in Fig. 6.11: six states were represented in the cabinet appointments of both Kennedy (a Democrat) and Nixon (a Republican). The implication drawn from these appointments is that they are, in part, a recognition of the importance of votes from those states and that, in turn, the cabinet appointees will, to some extent, favour their home areas in various policy initiatives.

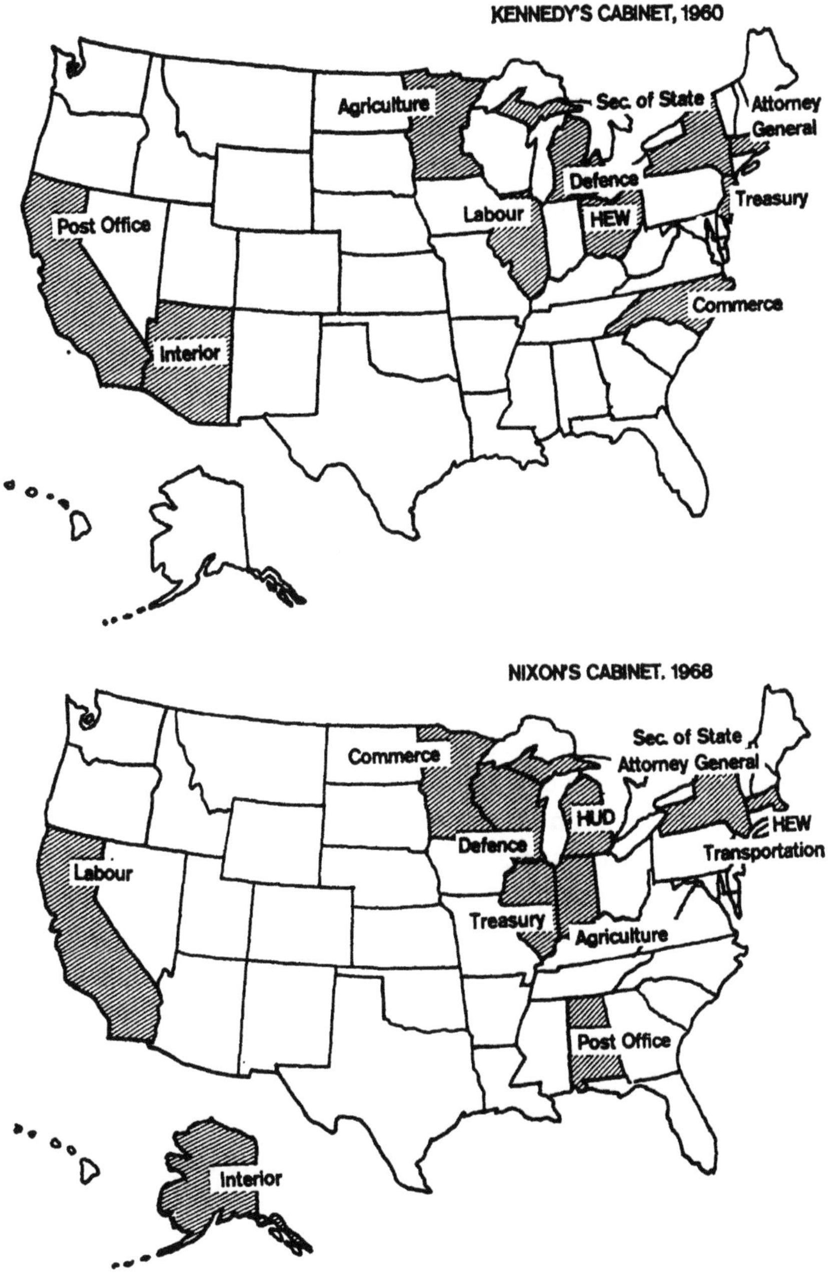

States represented: Cabinets of Presidents Kennedy and Nixon

Figure 6.11 State representation in two recent American Cabinets.
Source: Brunn, 1974, Figure 4.5

Members of the United States Congress, and also of the state legislatures, are able to exercise considerable power in the allocation of public resources towards those whose favours they seek – their constituents. This process – known as pork-barrel politics – is possible because major spending decisions are made by Senate and House committees, whose reports are usually accepted by their relative parent bodies. Representatives and senators strive to obtain places on those committees where they can best represent their constituents' interests – indeed some state delegations feel they have an automatic right to positions on certain committees. As the result of complex trade-offs between committee members – and links between members, the Bureau of the Budget and the professionals of the relevant spending department – states with representatives on committees tend to get a greater share of the allocations than would be predicted by any model of distributional equity. The most powerful, and best rewarded, positions on these committees are the chairmanships. Attainment of such status usually comes with seniority, so that it is the congressmen and senators with safe seats who are best able to achieve such power and influence (Ferejohn, 1974, gives an excellent introduction to one aspect of pork-barrel politics).

American federal and state politicians act much more as individual constituency representatives than do their counterparts in many other parliaments – such as the British – where party discipline is much stricter, and party membership and conformity are often necessary for electoral success. Whereas British parliamentarians act very much as ombudsmen for their electors, in terms of righting grievances about public administration, they are much less able to obtain tangible economic rewards for their constituents than are their American peers. Nor are they as likely to vote against their party in parliament over action that might be against local interests among their electorate; the stronger ties between parliament and executive in Westminster than in Washington ensures the general control of the party whip. Nevertheless, there is evidence that parties when in government in Britain do organize policies so as to maintain their electoral base and to avoid alienating voters in marginal constituencies (Johnston, 1978b).

Somewhat differently, Spilerman and Dickens (1975) have investigated the power of various population groups to influence election results under different electoral systems, and have concluded that (Spilerman and Dickens, 1975, p. 474), 'relative to the popular vote, the electoral clout of large states, metropolitan centres, Negroes, Catholics and, possibly, low-income persons is enhanced under the electoral college', thereby suggesting that policy initiatives which are successfully directed towards these groups could produce valuable returns, given the existing strengths of the two main parties among other groups (farmers for Republicans etc.). Finally, and more directly, May (1972, p. 251) has pointed out, with regard to the allocation of federal finances in Australia, that; 'In the Commonwealth elections of 1961 . . . the government suffered a heavy loss of votes and eight out of a total of fifteen seats lost were in Queensland electorates; subsequently in the period 1960–61 to 1962–63 specific purpose and additional assistance grants to the government of Queensland, per head of the state's population, almost doubled, while similar grants per capita to the other states rose only by about 40 per cent'. Most of our information about such electorally-oriented policies is at present in anecdotal form, although current work is providing a somewhat sharper focus. In the extraction (by taxation) and allocation (by grants and federal expenditures) of United States federal funds by states, there is a strong element of progressive redistribution of money from the relatively high-income states to those with lower per capita earnings. Holding this policy constant, however, it is also apparent that, in the 1970 tax appropriations and allocations (data are from Barone, Ujifusa and Matthews, 1972), residents of states which Nixon won in 1968 each paid $43 less in tax and received grants of $124 more per capita than in states that he lost (the mean per capita taxation by states was $867 and mean per capita grants was $927).

The relationship between electoral variables and spending by state governments in America on welfare programmes has been the focus of much more research, although the relevant literature is full of debate over problems of measurement and information (for example, Pulsipher and Weatherby, 1968; Fenton, 1966; Fenton and Chamberlayne, 1969; Dawson, 1975; and Wright,

1975). A major finding of many studies has been that the more competitive states – where control of the state legislature could change from one party to the other with a relatively small swing in voter preferences (Ranney, 1965; Fenton, 1966) – have spent more on welfare programmes as part of a 'vote-buying' exercise among the poor by the party in power; in states where a single party's hegemony is virtually assured, as in most of the south and parts of New England and the Midwest, the need to woo the poor voters is negligible so that, for example, in the Aid to Families with Dependent Children programme average payments are lower, more applications are turned down, and fewer poor families receive any aid at all in these states (Wohlenberg, 1976; Johnston, 1977b). Permanent campaigning, in the form of policies, is thus more intensive in the places where extra votes are most valuable, a proposition which also holds, to a lesser extent, among British local governments (Alt, 1971).

The local campaign

The types of campaigning just discussed are aimed at large blocks of voters, usually in relatively large areas, as measures intended to influence their party preferences the next time that they vote. At the local level, the purpose of campaigning is less to influence party preferences and more to ensure that the voters, especially those known to support the relevant party, exercise their democratic right. The functions of party organizations at local levels, therefore, are to identify the faithful who will support the party, to exhort them to vote, if necessary obtain special privileges for them (such as postal votes) and, again if necessary, see that they get to the polling booth. Conversion by conversation is much less important and probably too time-consuming; in most contests it is left these days to the party leaders through the mass media.

Much of the research on local campaigning has been undertaken in the United States, where the party organizations are legally recognized and are charged with overseeing the balloting in certain states (Rossi and Cutright, 1961). Each polling district or precinct has a captain from each party – in some states these captains are elected, in others appointed by the party machine – who appoints his own deputy. Some of these captains are paid, others are voluntary; those representing the party in power in the state/city/county may have a certain amount of patronage to disburse in the form of jobs; many are using such local positions as first steps in a political career. The role of the captain is to know his electorate and to mobilize support for his party within it.

The role of the precinct organization in one anonymous city in the Midwest ('Midwest City') has been studied in detail by Cutright and Rossi (1958a, 1958b). They assumed that there is such a thing as a 'normal vote' (Converse, 1966), in much the same way as many students of the neighbourhood effect do, in order to estimate, from the population structure of a precinct, what its vote should be. The Democrat vote at the 1956 Presidential election (the second Eisenhower–Stevenson contest) was estimated by a regression involving three independent variables (percentage of the population who were European immigrants, percentage of households who owned their own homes, and the median rental for homes), and they sought reasons for deviations from this expected voting pattern in the strengths of the party organizations. Precinct captains were categorized on such characteristics as their religion, their commitment to the party's candidates, their knowledge of their electors, their campaigning work rate, and so on, and these were tabulated against the average deviations from the predicted normal vote (Table 6.11). Thus the Democrat captains who talked to a lot of voters per day were likely to produce an above average vote for their party in the precinct, as were those who were Catholics (Midwest City was strongly Catholic) and those who were not opposed by an active Republican captain; elsewhere, Rossi and Cutright (1961) showed that Negro captains were very efficient at winning large voting percentages in their precincts. This activity by the local organization paid greatest dividends in the marginal precincts, where the two parties were relatively equally matched.

Cutright and Rossi (1958b) also studied the effects of the precinct organization on intra-party voting in primary elections in

Table 6.11 Precinct organization and its effect on presidential voting: Midwest City, 1956

	Average deviations from normal vote			
Number of voters precinct captain talks to per day	0–10	11–20	21+	
Democrat	−1·21	−0·24	+1·78	
Republican	−0·56	+1·91	+6·92	
Religion of precinct captain	Catholic	Protestant	Other	
Democrat	+0·25	−0·70	−1·01	
Republican	+0·39	+0·02	−1·02	
Rating of captain's activity	High	Fairly high	Fairly low	Low
Democrat	+2·34	−0·02	−0·52	−1·61
Republican	+1·44	+0·09	+0·05	−2·67
Activity of both parties				
Democrat	High	High	Low	Low
Republican	Low	High	Low	High
average Democrat deviation	+3·88	−0·91	−2·63	−1·58

Source: Cutright and Rossi (1958a, pp. 176–9)

Midwest City. No normal vote exists in such contests, and candidates are very dependent on their local representatives, which means that they compete for the endorsements of precinct captains, hoping that these will bring wider precinct support (as in the Japanese 'two-tier' friends-and-neighbours effect; p. 284). Data were collected for eight contests on the amount of captain endorsement, the number of local workers, the number of house parties attended ('house parties are financed by the candidates and conducted by his workers and are designed to bring the candidate face to face with voters in an informal context': Cutright and Rossi, 1958b, p. 204), and on local knowledge – the friends-and-neighbours effect – of each candidate. All except the number of house parties (on average 139 were held for each Democrat candidate over the whole city) proved to be excellent predictors of the result, again indicating the importance of the strength of local organization.

In primary elections within a fairly small city, the friends-and-neighbours effect and the neighbourhood effect will both probably be operating, in addition to the influence of local campaigning. For the friends-and-neighbours effect, Cutright and Rossi calculated the average deviation from the predicted vote for each candidate in his home precinct, and for all other candidates there, and found a very clear pattern in six of the eight contests (Table 6.12); irrespective of the efficiency of their local organizations, most candidates did very well in their home precincts. Regarding the neighbourhood effect – termed the majority effect by Cutright – later study showed that (Cutright, 1963, pp. 384–5): 'The effect of party activity on voting in Partisan City [renamed from Midwest City] seems to be about 4 to 5 per cent after we control for the majority effect . . . both the majority effect and the party worker act to guide the voter to his final voting choice'. Thus all three effects – neighbourhood, friends-and-neighbours, and local campaigning – were influential on the final distribution of votes in this intensively studied city. The methodology of the work has been criticized, for its lack of precision in measurement, but its findings have been replicated in more 'sophisticated' analyses (Crotty, 1973).

Table 6.12 Local organization and the friends-and-neighbours effect: primary elections in Midwest City, 1956

	Contest			
Democrat	1	2	3	4
Mean deviation in home precinct	+5·72	+2·29	+0·46	−2·55
Mean deviation for other candidates in that precinct	−0·76	−7·85	−4·36	+0·40
Republican	1	2	3	4
Mean deviation in home precinct	+8·16	+1·75	+11·90	−0·85
Mean deviation for other candidates in that precinct	−4·65	−5·33	−4·20	−3·06

Source: Cutright and Rossi (1958b, p. 268)

Although Cutright and Rossi were able to show that efficient local party organization increased the percentage of the vote obtained in a precinct, except where it was matched by the other party and no other effects were operating, they did not specify whether this increase was *a turnout effect*, i.e. the Democrat party workers ensured that Democrat supporters voted, *a conversion effect*, i.e. the Democrat party workers convinced some Republicans to vote for their man, or a combination of the two. In an analysis of survey data relating to all American presidential elections from 1952 to 1964, Kramer (1970) found that people were much more likely to vote if they had been contacted by a local party worker, but produced no evidence that canvassing influenced the way that they voted. Blydenburgh (1971) found in a study of campaigning for a county legislature in New York, however, that canvassing influenced preferences as well as turnout. The reason for this difference, he suggested, was that for a presidential election voters get their information from the mass media and so the only role of the local organization is to remind them of their obligation to vote; local elections may be ignored

Table 6.13 Ward voting in Harrow East

	Votes (percentages in brackets)					
Election	*1950*		*1951*		*1952*	
Party	*Conservative*	*Labour*	*Conservative*	*Labour*	*Conservative*	*Labour*
Safe Conservative wards						
Kenton	3533 (70)	1521 (30)	3474 (75)	1172 (25)	3380 (64)	1904 (36)
Belmont	3137 (70)	1370 (30)	2809 (73)	1422 (27)	2522 (63)	1513 (32)
Stanmore North	3449 (75)	1147 (25)	3225 (78)	931 (22)	3031 (66)	1561 (34)
Safe Labour wards						
Queensbury	2080 (42)	2894 (58)	2303 (47)	2632 (53)	2073 (36)	3645 (64)
Stanmore South	2017 (44)	2601 (56)	2230 (48)	2463 (52)	1740 (36)	3068 (64)
Marginal ward						
Harrow Weald	2555 (48)	2808 (52)	2850 (52)	2604 (48)	2657 (42)	3735 (58)

Source: Brown (1958, p. 176)

by the mass media, however, in which case the local party workers are sources of information about the election as well, making them much more powerful potential influences on how those that they contact vote.

The turnout effect of local campaigning has also been demonstrated in Great Britain. Brown (1958), for example, has shown how different strategies adopted by the Conservative Party in the former constituency of Harrow East affected both voter turnout and the election result at successive elections. The district comprised six wards; three were considered safe Conservative seats, two were safe Labour and the sixth was marginal, being won in 1950 by Labour (Table 6.13). In 1951 the Conservative agent (equivalent to an American precinct captain except that he organizes a very much larger area and, in the Conservative party at least, is usually a full-time, paid employee: Rose, 1976) decided to divert his party workers away from the safe wards and into the marginal and Labour seats during the evening of polling day. Some 350 canvassers with 65 cars were involved; the effect on turnout in the safe Labour wards was considerable and, even more important, the seat in the marginal ward of Harrow Weald was won for the Conservative candidate (Table 6.13). The strategy was not repeated in 1952, however; Labour regained Harrow Weald again and the Conservative vote fell in Queensbury and Stanmore South. (Part of this last trend represented the usual pattern in British local government elections of being anti- the national government – Newton, 1976, pp. 17–18; Conservative beat Labour in the 1951 general election.)

Similar findings were reported by two political scientists who acted as Labour Party agents in, respectively, a marginal ward in Dundee and a safe Conservative ward in Lancaster at the 1971 local government elections. Their tasks were to identify all of the Labour supporters and to exhort them, by frequent canvassing (including on polling day itself), to vote. In both cases, they were extremely successful in increasing Labour turnout relative to the average in their respective cities, so much so that Labour won the safe ward in Lancaster (where the Conservative campaign had been complacent) as well as the marginal one in Dundee

(Bochel and Denver, 1972). Clearly, it was suggested, party organization can increase voter turnout in these, usually low-turnout, local elections, and if one party is more active than another, its share of the vote can be influenced considerably. Newton (1972, p. 254) contested this with Birmingham findings that, 'turnout in marginal wards has little or nothing to do with the closeness of the party competition, the involvement of the electorate in a closely fought campaign, or the efficiency of local party machinery'. Denver and Hands (1972, p. 513) countered, following Rose's earlier argument (see above, p. 309) that: 'Our observation of local parties convinces us that they are rarely efficient electoral machines: they do not in fact usually concentrate workers and resources in marginal wards'. Rose (1976, p. 70) has gone further, with regard to national elections, and claimed that: 'Headquarters staff of the two major parties are unable to identify constituencies where organizational efforts will produce better or worse results than would be expected from the national swing'. In other words, wherever parties choose to invest campaign resources intensively they can usually influence turnout in their favour but, whether through irrationality or a lack of resources where they might be most valuable, they do not always do this where it would be most beneficial.

Campaigning, as we showed in the extracts from Cutright and Rossi's work, is difficult to isolate from the other geographical influences as an effect on voting patterns. To try and overcome this problem, several authors have conducted controlled experiments. Eldersveld (1956), for example, selected from an American city's electoral records 500 respondents who had not voted in recent elections. Some of these were then subjected to a variety of campaign techniques prior to the next election and their turnout compared to those of the control group within the 500 who were not canvassed. The results (in percentages),

	Personally contacted	*Contacted by mail*	*Not contacted*
Voted	25	10	6
Did not vote	75	90	95

clearly suggest the efficiency of campaigning, particularly by personal contact. In a more ambitious experiment, in a safe Republican county in New York, Blydenburgh (1971) persuaded the two main parties to adopt the following campaign procedure in four selected precincts:

(1) Democrat – 100 per cent door-to-door canvass: Republican – no canvass.

(2) Democrat – 100 per cent telephone canvass; Republican – no canvass.

(3) Republican – 100 per cent telephone canvass; Democrat – no canvass.

(4) Republican – 100 per cent door-to-door canvass; Democrat – no canvass.

The 'normal' turnout and Democratic voting percentages were predicted for these and other precincts in the same way as by Cutright and Rossi (see p. 321), and the deviations inspected for the effect of the canvassing. It was clear that turnout was increased in all four districts because of the blanket coverage of the canvassing (Table 6.14), and also that the general swing towards the

Table 6.14 Campaign strategy, turnout and Democratic vote: Monroe County

	District[a]			
	1	2	3	4
'Normal' turnout	80·9	83·0	91·7	83·3
Turnout after canvass	87·9	86·6	94·9	85·7
Effect of canvass	+7·0	+3·6	+3·2	+2·4
'Normal' Democrat vote	32·3	34·0	28·7	36·5
Democrat vote after canvass	31·1	32·0	22·8	29·0
Effect of canvass	−1·2	−2·0	−5·9	−7·5

[a] for key to districts, see text.
Source: Blydenburgh (1971, p. 368)

Republican party at the election was reduced in the two districts where only the Democrats canvassed (with the suggestion that door-to-door canvassing was more successful than were attempts at exhortation and persuasion by telephone).

Experiments in Britain have produced similar results. The two main political parties did not campaign in a safe Labour ward at the Dundee city council election in 1970, apart from distributing the usual candidate-identification literature to all households, and so two political scientists decided to canvass in one block of flats there, but not in another. Each block contained about 450 voters and was about three-minutes' walk from a polling booth. (The distance that people live from a booth is related to the likelihood of their voting. In a study of one ward in Swansea at the 1972 local government elections, A. H. Taylor (1973b) found that nearly 65 per cent of those living only one-minute's walk from a booth voted, compared with only 35 per cent of those living five to six minutes away. And in an investigation of a drive to register black voters in the Monroe district of Philadelphia, Ley (1974) found that it was propinquity not publicity which was crucial in determining whether people availed themselves of this basic democratic right; the further people lived from the registration office the less likely they were to register.) In the canvassed block, voters were visited three times by a pro-Labour worker, and all identified Labour supporters were contacted on polling day to ensure, if possible, that they voted. Finally, on the day after the election, all electors in both blocks were interviewed to discover whether they had voted; 64 per cent had in the canvassed block, compared to 54 per cent in the other. Of those canvassed, the campaign was most efficient in getting old people to vote, was particularly effective with males (turnout in the canvassed block was 14 percentage points higher for males than in the other block; for females it was only 1 percentage point), and was most successful among those it managed to contact on the actual polling day.

These experiments were conducted in safe constituencies in local elections, and their findings cannot be generalized very far. They do suggest that campaigning can be very effective at influencing turnout rates, however, and their implications for parties are considerable. As Price and Lopfer (1975) have realized, resources are best spent in marginal constituencies, and it may be that they are, since turnout is usually highest in those areas (Fletcher, 1968), although if all parties follow this advice, the result is likely to be stalemate. But given limited resources, where should parties concentrate their efforts within constituencies? Miller's (1956) advice is to invest where the party is already strong, rather than to fight the neighbourhood effect where it is weak, and this was confirmed by Blydenburgh (1976) in a hypothetical analysis based on game theory.

Transferring these arguments from local to general elections is more difficult. Several British analysts are very dubious about the electoral value of local campaigning and organization. After the 1955 general election, Butler (1955, p. 205) argued that: 'The evidence is inconclusive but it certainly gives no positive support to those who contend that the results were greatly affected by the efficiency of the local machine', although after a close contest the conclusion was more cautious (Butler and Pinto-Duschinsky, 1971, p. 336): 'The margin of victory was so small that we cannot exclude the possibility that in 1970 organization did tilt the balance'. Candidates certainly put a great deal of effort into personal campaigning, but a detailed study of the benefits of this suggested that (Grave in Kavanagh, 1970, p. vii), 'although many candidates and party workers derive considerable personal psychic satisfaction from the campaign, their efforts have little if any effect on the outcome'. Nevertheless, investigation of one campaign, at Barons Court in west London at the 1964 election, very clearly suggested that Labour won this marginal seat because of their superior organization. As we have shown, canvassing in Britain involves identifying one's party's supporters and then ensuring that they vote. The Labour Party in Barons Court identified 14,287 supporters and received 15,966 votes. The Conservatives identified 10,985, but received 14,800 votes, suggesting that they were inefficient in their initial canvassing and that better methods could have ensured greater Conservative turnout, and perhaps Conservative victory (Labour won the seat by 1166 votes and the election by a majority of four seats only).

And so debate, experiment and analysis will undoubtedly continue. In elections fought over very large territories, the likelihood that parties will be sufficiently well-organized everywhere to be able to identify where extra effort will be most valuable is slim, always assuming that central organizers can persuade local officials to redistribute party effort to ensure general as against local success. At closely contested elections, extra effort within particular parts of a constituency may be vital, however, not only in delivering that constituency to a party but also in determining who will form the next government. The main consequence of campaigning may be to make candidates feel good and local, voluntary workers feel useful; sometimes they may also be effective.

Conclusions

Elections are fought in places – in living rooms, in front of television sets, and behind newspapers; on doorsteps; in pubs, clubs and committee rooms. The geography of the contest leads to the geography of the result, and is influenced by the geography of the environments within which the debate and the decision-making proceeds. Many people, we know, habitually vote in the same way, but enough are at least prepared to change their minds for it to be worthwhile trying to influence them. In this and the previous chapter we have looked at some of the main geographical influences in this, at the effect of local environments and candidates, local issues and campaigns, on the wider issue of the election result.

The importance of the various geographical influences on voter behaviour varies over time, over space, and between different types of elections. From the examples quoted here, for example, it is clear that canvassing has a much greater effect in elections/referenda where turnout is generally low, which in most countries is at the local rather than the national level. But particular issues – such as immigration at the 1964 and 1970 British general elections – can become very important locally and have considerable impact at a much wider scale. Personal voting for candidates is also generally more apparent in local elections, but variations in party discipline (between the United States and the United Kingdom, for example) and in the nature of the contest (inter-party or intra-party) are also important in determining whether individual influences on the result are important. In brief therefore, geographical factors are always in operation, as social environments in different areas are manipulated by candidates and parties. Very often, the consequences of such manipulation are minor and indiscernible, but our review here illustrates the sorts of occasions and situations in which the geography of the contest takes on a major role.

Part Four

Geography of Representation

7 Electoral Abuses

The geography of representation is a product of the geography of voting. However it can never exactly replicate all the subtle details of the voting map. Millions of votes have to be condensed into just a few hundred representatives. The manner of the translation of votes into seats depends on the electoral law of a country, in particular its system of voting. Where the system involves multi-member constituencies, each area may be represented by members of each of the main parties to reflect a varied voting pattern. Where the system uses single-member constituencies, however, each constituency can be represented by a candidate of only one party. In this way, a varied voting pattern is very greatly simplified when translated in a pattern of representation. Such voting systems have been associated with *electoral abuses*, which are the subject of this chapter. Hence, we will be largely concerned with representation in countries with plurality voting systems (Britain, U.S.A., Canada, New Zealand and South Africa) and majority-type systems (Australia and France). The geography of representation in countries with other voting systems, which exhibit far fewer abuses, is left until the next chapter.

What do we mean by an electoral abuse? We can begin to consider this question by defining the concept of electoral bias. This can be measured as the difference between the percentage of the vote a party receives and the percentage of seats it wins in an election. For instance, if a party receives 45 per cent of the vote and wins 55 per cent of the seats then the bias is 10 per cent. This is a positive bias for that party at that particular election. If in the subsequent election the party only receives 40 per cent of the vote and wins 35 per cent of the seats, it would have suffered negative bias of 5 per cent. Electoral abuses obviously involve such biases but they imply more than a simple bias; they involve some intention to abuse the system. Electoral biases can, and do exist where no particular partisan manipulation of the voting system exists. This is illustrated and discussed in the next chapter. Here we concentrate on specific abuses of the voting system that involve intentional discrimination by some voters at the expense of other voters.

Where the voter lives determines who his representative is. This is because constituencies are areally defined. Hence, electoral abuses will involve some form of geographical discrimination among voters. The translation of votes into seats for single-member constituencies depends upon the location of constituency boundaries as they are superimposed upon the geographical pattern of party voters. The problem that emerges from this simple procedure is that different locations of constituency boundaries may produce different numbers of wins for the various parties *even if the underlying pattern of votes remains constant*. Hence, for a single pattern of votes there will be several alternative election results in terms of seats, depending upon how constituency boundaries are drawn. This has been termed the *districting problem* (Taylor, 1973) of single-member constituency systems. There will always be numerous alternative ways in which a country may be divided up into constituencies and so there will be numerous alternative geographies of representation which will produce different electoral outcomes.

The districting problem provides the environment within which electoral abuses have been able to exist. Particular constituency arrangements can be chosen which discriminate against particular voters. In this situation, voters will be discriminated against depending upon where they live; the geography of the voting is being used to produce a desired electoral outcome. This geographical discrimination has taken two basic forms. Constituencies can be drawn so that they enclose different numbers of voters. This is termed *malapportionment* and is designed to give one party or interest group more seats by defining small constituencies in areas of their voting strength. This electoral abuse is based upon different numbers of voters in constituencies and hence constitutes numerical discrimination. In contrast, boundary discrimination involves carefully drawing constituency boundaries so that one party or interest group is particularly favoured irrespective of sizes of constituencies. A slight change in the location of a boundary can easily change a marginal constituency into a safe one for the party controlling the boundary drawing. This electoral abuse is commonly termed *gerrymandering*. We will consider each type of geographical discrimination in turn.

Numerical Discrimination: Malapportionment

Let us begin with a simple example of malapportionment. We will assume a country with a very evenly balanced two-party system, with each party geographically concentrated in different regions. The East Party (EP) wins 50 per cent of the vote overall, but receives 80 per cent of the vote in its own region. The West Party (WP) has the converse pattern. Such a situation does not necessarily lead to a parliamentary stalemate. If this country has an odd number of parliamentary seats then one of the two parties must win an overall majority, because the voting tie cannot be translated into a representation tie. Which party wins can be controlled by malapportionment.

In Figure 7.1 (a) our hypothetical country is divided into five constituencies to elect five representatives. The eastern region is

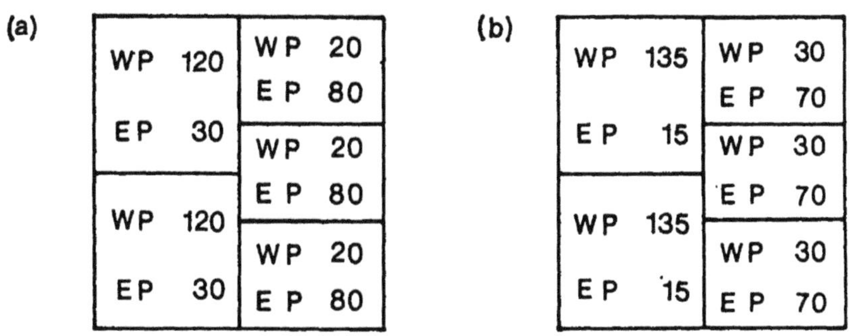

Figure 7.1 Malapportionment

divided into three constituencies of 100 voters each while the western region has only two constituencies with 150 voters in each of them. This simple exercise in malapportionment means that EP has three safe seats out of five and hence a stable parliamentary majority; with this particular constituency arrangement WP would *not* win a parliamentary majority even with a large voting majority. Suppose there is an even swing of 10 per cent from EP to WP. The new election result is given in Figure 7.1 (b). Now WP receives 60 per cent of the vote overall but EP still wins the election with its three safe seats. In fact it can be seen that WP needs a swing of over 30 per cent in order to win the election by prising EP's safe seats away from this highly advantaged party. Clearly, malapportionment can severely distort the translation of votes into seats. Before we treat actual examples of this electoral abuse, we consider its measurement so as to facilitate comparisons between countries and within countries over time.

Measuring malapportionment

There are very many different ways in which malapportionment may be measured. Perhaps the most obvious beginning is to compare the average sizes of constituencies won by different parties. In our hypothetical example for example, WP constituencies are 150 voters each and EP constituencies are only 100 voters each. The difference, 50 voters, is a gross measure of the malapportionment. Such simple differences between average constituency sizes have often been used in British studies of malapportionment (Butler, 1947; Rowley, 1970, 1975a, b).

In American studies, measurement of malapportionment has been developed much further. Alker and Russett (1964) identify three types of measures:

(1) Measures of extremeness. These measures are simple to calculate and concentrate on the major anomalies. The most-used measure is the ratio of largest to smallest constituency. This ratio may be interpreted as how many times more value the vote in the small constituency has. For instance in Figure 7.1 the ratio is 150/100 = 1·5; each vote in the east is worth one-and-a-half votes in the west.

(2) Measures of average deviations. A criticism of the extremeness measures is that they only consider a small number of constituencies. To overcome this problem we can compare *every* constituency with the average size. The average of these deviations produces the *mean deviation* which is a more comprehensive measure of malapportionment. For our hypothetical example the average size is 120 voters, producing two deviations of 30 and three of 20 so that the mean deviation is $120/5 = 24$ voters. Obviously with no malapportionment all constituencies are the same size and the mean deviation is zero.

(3) Measures using cumulative distributions. A very common way of comparing areas is to construct their cumulative frequency graph. In the case of constituencies, this involves ordering the constituencies from largest to smallest. Both the proportions of total representation and total population (or voters) are then added cumulatively and plotted on a graph. The line connecting these points on the graph is called a *Lorenz curve*. For our hypothetical example the ordering consists of the two western constituencies, followed by the three eastern constituencies. Each constituency has 0·2 (one fifth) of the total representation. The western constituencies have 0·25 of the total voters each, while their eastern counterparts have 0·17 of the total voters each. The resulting cumulative proportions describe the Lorenz curve in Figure 7.2(a). Figure 7.2(b) shows a typical Lorenz curve, based upon many more than five constituencies. Since it is based upon a large number of constituencies it describes a 'smooth' pattern from which various measures can be derived.

A Lorenz curve can be used to describe malapportionment in several ways. The *minimal majority* measures the smallest possible proportion of population who can elect a majority of the representatives. This can be read off the graph from the 50 per cent point on the representatives' axis (Figure 7.2(b)). From the population axis the *over-represented proportion* can be easily read from the graph. This is found at the point where the gradient of the Lorenz curve changes from under 45° to a steeper gradient of over 45° (Figure 7.2 (b)). These two measures have particular political interpretations, but they do not use very much of the information displayed on a Lorenz curve. A more comprehensive

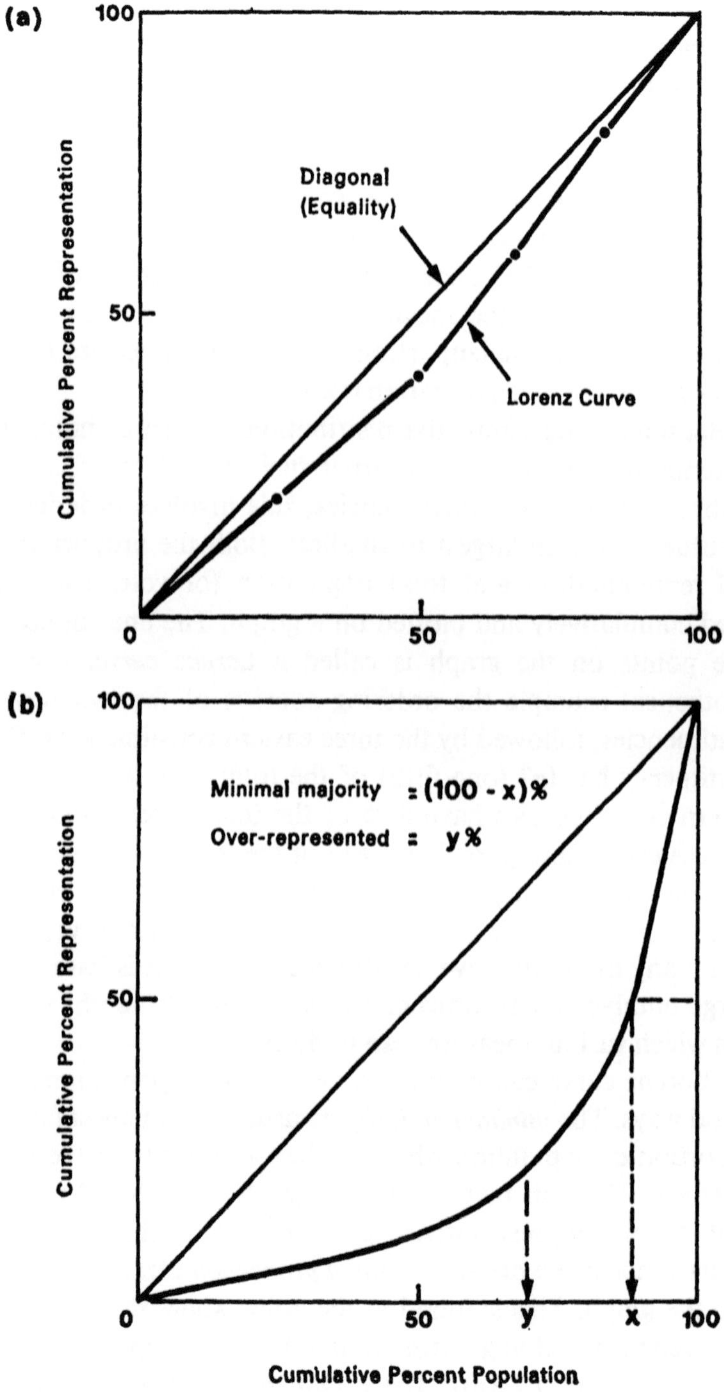

Figure 7.2 The Lorenz curve

measure of malapportionment can be found if we measure the area between the curve and the diagonal. If all constituencies were the same size the Lorenz curve would lie along the diagonal. Hence, the area between the Lorenz curve and the diagonal is a gross measure of malapportionment. If this area is calculated as a proportion of the total area under the diagonal we produce the *Gini index*. This index ranges from zero with perfect apportionment, to one where the Lorenz curve follows the axis of the graph – all the voters, but none of the representatives, are allocated to one constituency! For our simple example in Figure 7.2(a) the Gini index is computed at 0·1.

Our hypothetical example shows that quite low degrees of malapportionment can produce major electoral advantages. This occurs when the pattern of malapportionment corresponds to the pattern of party votes. However, where malapportionment is *not* related to the support of competing parties, it will not have an appreciable effect on party fortunes. There may be quite large differences in constituency sizes, for instance, but if both parties win their fair share of both large and small constituencies neither party will reap any advantage from the malapportionment. We need to distinguish this second situation from the extreme case represented by our hypothetical example. So far we have followed Alker and Russett (1964) and have only discussed measurement of the *degree* of malapportionment; what we now require is a further measure of its partisan *effect*.

There are two ways in which we can calculate a party's overall proportion of the vote. We can sum their total vote from each constituency and divide it by the overall sum of votes. Alternatively we can calculate the *proportion* of the vote a party wins in each constituency, sum these proportions and divide by the number of constituencies. We shall term these two measures the overall proportion of the vote and the average constituency proportion of the vote, respectively. If all constituencies were the same size then these two proportions would be equal. Similarly, if a party's vote is unrelated to sizes of constituencies, the two proportions will be equal. If, however, a party tends to win more of its votes in larger constituencies its average constituency vote proportion will be less than its overall vote proportion. Conversely, a party which tends to win more votes in smaller constituencies will obtain a higher average constituency vote proportion than its overall vote proportion. Hence, we can use the difference between the two vote proportions for a party as a measure of the *malapportionment effect* on that party.

This argument needs clarification by way of a simple example. Let us return to our hypothetical West and East parties. In this example EP's overall vote proportion is 300/600 = 0·5, while its constituency average vote proportion is (0·8+0·8+0·8+0·2+0·2)/5 = 0·56. Hence the malapportionment effect on this party is a positive one of 0·06 or 6 per cent. Since the basic accounting units in the voting system are the constituencies, it follows that the proportion that 'matters' is the last one – the constituency average. Hence, we can interpret this effect of 6 per cent by saying that EP would need to win an extra 6 per cent of the vote for its support to be at the same constituency level with a fair apportionment of equal size constituencies. In this sense the malapportionment is worth an extra 6 per cent of the vote for EP.

Clearly malapportionment is easily measured. One problem is that there are probably too many different measures, so that comparisons are sometimes difficult. We have only presented some of the major methods of measuring malapportionment, with each measuring a different facet of the concept. Some of the simpler measures, such as the largest-smallest ratio, have been useful for propaganda purposes in the American political debate over malapportionment, while the more sophisticated measures such as the Gini index have been particularly useful in comparing across countries. We will use all of these measures in our discussions of actual examples of malapportionment below.

Malapportionment as a British tradition
I. The nineteenth-century reform movement

The most extreme case of malapportionment in any representative assembly was to be found in Britain before 1832 (Seymour, 1915). The unreformed House of Commons remains the classic example of this electoral abuse. The reason for the scale of the malapportionment was legislative inertia. In the early nineteenth century the House of Commons still retained many of its medieval origins. Every county, and selected boroughs, returned two members *each* to Parliament. This meant that small counties such as Rutland had the same number of seats as very populous counties such as Lancashire. However, the main abuses were associated with boroughs. It had been a royal prerogative to bestow parliamentary seats on boroughs, but the right had not been exercised for several hundred years. Hence, the new industrial centres such as Manchester were not directly represented while small towns, even deserted towns, were able to send two members to Parliament. There were 203 boroughs with this right of representation. The most notorious example was a deserted hilltop in Wiltshire known as Old Sarum. The eleven non-residential voters of this constituency had to cast their votes in specially erected tents on the site of the 'town'. In all, there were 36 boroughs with electorates of under 25, and a further 115 with electorates of under 200. The result of this system was that a majority of the House of Commons could be obtained from small boroughs with electorates of under 5000. Many of these boroughs were controlled by powerful lords and commoners so that they became nominated boroughs or 'pocket boroughs'.

The Great Reform Bill of 1832 attempted to curtail these abuses while rationalizing the suffrage rules. The end result was a typical British compromise which eradicated most of the worst cases such as Old Sarum. The bill consisted of five schedules (Seymour, 1915):

Schedule A completely disenfranchised 56 boroughs;
Schedule B reduced representation to one member each for 30 boroughs;
Schedule C allocated two members each to 22 towns;
Schedule D allocated one member to 21 towns;
Schedule F allocated 65 members to new divisions in the counties, with thirteen new members allocated to Scotland and Ireland.

This redistribution produced a massive shift in the geographical pattern of representation. Of the 56 disenfranchised boroughs, 41 were located south of the Thames including 15 in Cornwall alone. Similarly, 21 of the 30 boroughs which had their representation reduced to one were in these southern counties. In contrast, the vast majority of new seats were allocated to the industrial areas of the north and midlands. This changing geography of representation is shown in the first two columns of Table 7.1.

Table 7.1 Nineteenth-century electoral reforms and the changing geography of English representation

Regions	*1832* Losses	*1832* Gains	*1867–8* Losses	*1867–8* Gains	*1885* Losses	*1885* Gains	*Net change of M.P.s*
1. *More agricultural regions*							
South	105	24	25	9	43	13	−127
South Midlands	14	18	11	0	29	7	−29
East	19	9	8	6	15	9	−9
2. *More industrial regions*							
North	14	47	7	18	20	54	+78
North Midlands	0	17	1	6	12	10	+20
London	0	10	0	4	2	44	+56

Source: Adapted from Seymour (1915)

The Great Reform Bill did represent a major change in the pattern of representation, but it by no means eradicated all anomalies. Although the 'importance' of towns was considered in allocating representation, the purpose of the exercise was certainly not to equate representation with population. Malapportionment remained the rule and even some nominated boroughs remained.

Two other major redistributions occurred in the nineteenth century and their regional effects are also shown on Table 7.1. The pattern of change is the same, with representation being progressively transferred largely from south to north, increasingly to match the distribution of population. The 1885 redistribution was in many ways the most fundamental. The traditional two-member constituencies largely gave way to the single-member constituency pattern with which we are familiar today. Although exact population equality was not produced, major anomalies disappeared. All boroughs with populations of less than 15,000, for instance, lost their representation and were incorporated into counties. Table 7.2 shows the differences in population per seat in two

Table 7.2 Population per seat in south-west and north-west England, 1866 and 1886

	1866		*1886*	
	Borough	*County*	*Borough*	*County*
South-west	8,000	68,000	28,000	50,000
North-west	49,000	171,000	58,000	57,000

Source: Seymour (1915)

contrasting regions, the south-west and north-west. After the 1832 reforms large differences remained, as witnessed by the contrast between north-western county constituencies and south-western borough constituencies. After 1885 the differences are far less. A large degree of variation still remained, but after 1885 the geography of representation began to reflect the geography of the population (Seymour, 1915).

Malapportionment as a British tradition II. The Boundary Commissioners

Butler (1955a) has noted that redistributions have been rare events in British electoral history. The redistribution of 1885 was to last until 1918 when constituencies were drawn which were to be more based on population than any previously. The Speaker's Conference of 1917 had recommended equal electoral districts and the Boundary Commissioners appointed to this task tried to make constituencies conform to an overall average electorate per constituency or 'national quota'. This quota principle has been embodied in all subsequent redistributions in 1947, 1954 and 1969. This means that Britain has experienced a total of just seven redistributions of seats in her entire modern parliamentary history. The three redistributions of the nineteenth century moved progressively towards equality of constituencies, as we have seen, while the four redistributions of the twentieth century have explicitly incorporated equal size criteria into the practice of drawing constituency maps.

Unfortunately there has always been a large difference between equality in theory and equality in practice in British redistributions. The rules for Boundary Commissioners in 1918 were soon relaxed when it was realized that strict population equality would entail wholesale boundary changes. The Commissioners were allowed to produce substantially different-sized constituencies in order to maintain county and borough boundaries. Furthermore, population changes soon made these new constituencies even more unequal in size. By 1939 there were 20 constituencies with over 100,000 electors and 13 with under 30,000 (Butler, 1955a). Hence, despite the acceptance of the equality principle in 1918, the 1935 and 1945 elections were fought on grossly unequal constituencies.

In 1944 another Speaker's Conference proposed two ways of overcoming these population discrepancies. First, they proposed that all constituencies should be within 25 per cent of the national quota, and, second, they recommended regular redistributions at frequent intervals. Boundary Commissioners began their new review of constituencies almost immediately and soon requested that the 25 per cent rule be relaxed. This was agreed in 1946 and they were able to produce a new distribution for 1947 with constituency sizes ranging from under 40,000 voters to over 80,000. Equality of constituencies was clearly not even being approximated.

In 1949 a new Redistribution of Seats Act was passed which brought together the rules for drawing boundaries which had previously been operating, and it remains the main basis for redistribution today. The main feature of the act was the setting up of permanent Boundary Commissioners to review constituencies every 4 to 7 years. In 1958 this was changed to 'from 10 to 15' years after both main parties complained about the excessive reorganization entailed by the more frequent reviews (Craig, 1959). Despite this rather elaborate machinery, malapportionment has continued to be a controversial feature of British elections. The reasons for this situation can be found in the nature of the framework within which the Boundary Commissions work. Four main sources for malapportionment can be identified.

(1) Separate Boundary Commissions operate for the four home countries – England, Wales, Scotland and Northern Ireland. These commissions have been required to operate in slightly different ways. First, the Northern Ireland commissioners are given only 12 seats to apportion, on the grounds that Ulster has its own elected assembly and so requires less representation at Westminster. Secondly, the Scottish and Welsh commissioners were allocated minimum numbers of seats, 71 and 36 respectively, so that their representation was 'protected' from declining population. These three countries have had 12, 71 and 36 seats in parliament since 1949. (In 1978, Northern Ireland's number of seats was increased to 18.) In contrast, England's representation has changed as its population has increased. In the 1954 distribution it had a total of 511 seats, while in 1969 this was increased to 516. Nevertheless, England remains under-represented compared with Scotland and Wales, although the main area discriminated against is Northern Ireland. At the 1974 elections the numbers of electors per seat were as follows: England 64,634; Scotland 51,898; Wales 55,798; Northern Ireland 86,376 (Osborne, 1975). This level of malapportionment is very hard to justify, especially since 1972 with the suspension of the Northern Ireland Assembly and the subsequent proposals to set up assemblies in Wales and Scotland with no reduction in seats at Westminster (Taylor, 1974; Osborne, 1975, 1976).

(2) The Boundary Commissioners are required by the 1949 Act to operate a 'boundary rule' whereby constituencies are required

to conform to existing local government boundaries (Taylor and Gudgin, 1976a). This is sometimes justified in terms of maintaining communities of interest, although no attempts are ever made explicitly to measure 'community' in the operation of the rule (Rowley, 1975a, b). This is the rule that leads to the great variety in constituency sizes within each of the home countries. It was the imposition of such boundary constraints that made the equal-size notions of the 1917 Speaker's Conference impossible and the 25-per-cent-range idea of the 1944 Speaker's Conference unworkable. In the 1949 Act the boundary rule is allowed to override the equal electorate criteria. Hence, in the February 1974 election, the first to be held under the 1969 redistribution, there were 54 constituencies with over 80,000 electors and another 54 with under 40,000 (Rowley, 1975a). Clearly, population equality is not even being approximately created.

(3) In the 1949 Act the Boundary Commissioners had another rule which could override the equality criteria – the 'geography' or accessibility rule (Taylor and Gudgin, 1976a). This concerned the problems of representatives serving more remote areas, for instance in the Scottish islands (Butler, 1955). The Boundary Commissioners in 1947 and 1954 interpreted this rule more widely, however, and gave more constituencies to rural areas as opposed to urban areas. Hence malapportionment was consciously created – in the original 1947 distribution urban constituencies had on average 6,000 more voters than rural constituencies and in 1954 the difference was 4,000. This rule has added a systematic basis to the variety of constituency sizes initially created by the boundary rule.

(4) Finally, we need to consider the effect of the period between distributions. As we have seen this was extended to 'from 10 to 15 years' in 1958. This meant that the 1954 distribution did not have to be revised until 1969. In fact the new proposals were not implemented until 1974, so that the 1970 election was contested in constituencies which were 16 years old. At this election malapportionment had become particularly gross – there were 168 constituencies out of 630 which were outside the range 40,000 to 80,000 electors. Ironically, it was the urban constituencies which

lost most population between 1954 and 1970 so that the intentional rural bias of the commissioners was converted into the opposite pattern; in 1970 urban (borough) constituencies had an average of 17,000 less electors than rural (county) constituencies.

Let us now consider the effects of these various forms of malapportionment. Two particular effects have been politically controversial – the national differences and the induced rural bias. In 1947 the Labour government identified the latter bias as being against their party's interest and instructed the English Commissioners to produce another 17 borough constituencies (Butler, 1955a; Williams, 1968). In 1954, however, a Conservative government was in power so that the Boundary Commissioners' preference for smaller rural constituencies came into operation for the 1955 election. The malapportionment effect, as defined above, for Labour in this election was −1 per cent (Taylor and Gudgin, 1976a). By 1970 this rural bias had disappeared, as we have seen, and in fact there was basically no malapportionment effect on parties at that election (see also Johnston, 1976b). This source of malapportionment has now disappeared since the 1969 Commissioners reinterpreted the geography rule so that it no longer involves creating smaller electorates in rural areas.

The national biases source of malapportionment is still with us, however, and is becoming increasingly topical as Scottish and Welsh devolution proposals compete with the Ulster situation as constitutional problems. In the past the national bias has counteracted the rural bias by favouring Labour, who are stronger in Scotland and Wales. This situation is now further complicated, however, by the rise of Nationalist parties in both of these countries and the separation of the Ulster Unionists from the British Conservative Party. At the present time the effect of the national level malapportionment on the balance between the two main parties is problematical.

All our discussion of distributions in Britain has come under the heading of malapportionment as a British electoral tradition. The continuing truth of this assertion is emphasized by comparing current British standards with American practice. We can follow McKay and Patterson (1971) and Rowley (1975a, 1975c) and use the Gini index for this purpose. Before redistribution in 1969 the index had reached 0·17; the redistribution reduced it to 0·14 but by the time of the 1974 election it had already risen to 0·16. In the U.S.A. there has been a major political controversy over population equality which led to the so-called reapportionment revolution of the mid-1960s. However, before this redistricting, the congressional districts for the House of Representatives had a Gini index of 0·15 which is comparable with the situation *after* a British redistribution. After the reapportionment revolution the index had been reduced to only 0.04. Hence the U.S.A. is currently operating on an entirely different plane from Britain when it comes to considering malapportionment. Let us consider how America reached its current situation of almost equal constituencies.

The reapportionment revolution in the U.S.A.

For most of the twentieth century, Chicago voters have suffered discrimination in both state and federal elections. In 1910, for instance, Cook County (which includes Chicago) was allocated 37·3 per cent of the seats in the Illinois state senate on the basis of its 38·1 per cent of the state population. It continued to obtain 37·3 per cent of these seats through the next half a century while its population grew enormously to include over half the state's population. Several attempts were made to change the situation: County taxes were withheld in 1925, and in 1926 consideration was given to Chicago's secession from Illinois. The most dramatic action was taken in 1936 by John Keogh when a judge refused to hear his plea that the legislature was illegally constituted. Keogh pulled a gun, killed the opposing lawyer and only just missed the judge, declaring that 'something drastic has to be done to awaken the people' (Tyler, 1955). Unfortunately the people were not awakened by this manslaughter. Ten years later another Chicago resident, Kenneth Colgrove, argued that since his federal congressional district had a population of 914,653 compared with 112,116 in a downstate district, his vote was worth only an eighth the value of some other Illinois voters. The case went to the

Supreme Court who handed down the verdict in *Colgrove v. Green* that apportionment was a 'political question' and hence beyond the jurisdiction of the courts. This position of judicial inactivity in the face of gross malapportionments was to persist in the U.S.A. until the 1960s.

Numerical discrimination against Chicago was typical of malapportionment in other states. The first half of the twentieth century was a time of rural over-representation and urban under-representation. This has not always been the case however; Hanson (1966) points out that population equality has traditionally been the main criterion for electoral districts. After 1776 the first state constitutions typically allocated representatives to counties by population and, even where counties were allocated equal numbers of representatives, discrimination was small because in any case counties all had similar populations. Of the 20 states which joined the union up until the Civil War, 18 used population as their major criterion and during the reconstruction and after, new constitutions tended to be even more democratic. Hence, America has not experienced any malapportionment equivalent to the unreformed House of Commons in her electoral history.

In many ways 1920 is a key year in American history. The census of that year showed that for the first time the urban population outnumbered the rural population. After 1920 Hanson (1966) argues that there have been fewer 'popular' reforms, because rural politicians were afraid of city politics which they saw as involving political extremists, ethnic politicians and city bosses associated with corrupt practices. In contrast, the rural population were seen as virtuous (Perrin, 1962). This argument is summed up in the statement from a delegate to New York's constitution convention of 1864: 'I say without fear of contradiction . . . that the average citizen in the rural district is superior in intelligence, superior in morality, superior in self government, to the average citizen in the great cities' (Hanson, 1966, p. 19). For people holding this type of view, 1920 was a year of impending disaster for America. However, the cities could be contained from 'ruining' American democracy by the simple expedient of numerical discrimination. America might have a majority of urban population in 1920 but that did not necessarily mean that it would have an overall majority of urban representatives in the various legislatures.

Malapportionment could be produced in one of three ways (Hanson, 1966). Constitutional provisions to redistrict after each census could be ignored. This deliberate failure to implement the state constitution occurred in 26 states (Walter, 1938). Alternatively, state constitutions themselves sometimes produced malapportionment. This occurred where, for instance, all counties were entitled to one representative irrespective of their population. Where urban growth had led to major population changes since implementation of the constitution, its effect was to favour rural voters in small counties. It was estimated by Walter (1938) that this was the cause of the malapportionment in 15 states. Finally, some states actually changed their constitution in order to produce malapportionment. In effect they were attempting to amend their constitutions to maintain the *status quo* in the distribution of power against the demographic trends. Michigan, California and Illinois all introduced 'non-population' factors into their constitutions. Michigan's conservatism is most apparent; this state actually froze the 1920-based districts into the constitution, hopefully ensuring that all subsequent population trends would be of no political account.

The effect of these practices was inevitable gross malapportionment as the urbanization trend was not reflected in any equivalent change in the geography of representation. This has been documented in many studies (see, for instance, the essays in Jewell, 1962). The minimal majority measure was devised in the 1930s to demonstrate the enormous malapportionment in American state legislatures (Tyler, 1955). Figures for this period show that 35·4 per cent of Illinois population could elect a majority to that body. This was the malapportionment that so upset John Keogh. However Illinois senate, at this time, was one of the more representative U.S. state legislatures. In the Connecticut House of Representatives only 8·67 per cent of the population was needed to elect a majority of the legislature. Similarly, Rhode Island's minimal majority was only 8·86 per cent. Clearly Illinois was in no sense a unique or even an extreme case, but neatly fitted into the American way of things, ranking 25th in terms of malapportionment (Tyler, 1955).

Although this malapportionment is normally seen in terms of urban/rural conflicts, the actual negotiations and politicking behind the scenes was much more complicated than this simple dichotomy indicates. Within some states there were city rivalries which prevented a coherent urban lobby developing. This was true in Ohio (Cleveland v. Cincinnati), Texas (Houston v. Dallas), Pennsylvania (Pittsburgh v. Philadelphia) and California (San Francisco v. Los Angeles). There were also regional differences involved, such as northern v. southern California. However, perhaps the most important addition to the simple urban/rural cleavage was to be found in alliances of the right, that is rural conservative areas working with urban business interests. For this latter section of the urban population, conservative rural domination of legislatures was to be preferred to more liberal urban control. This meant that even where urban voters managed to get a referendum on reapportionment in a state, it was not inevitable that a state's urban majority would automatically lead to a victory for a reapportionment question. In California, for example, the senate was based on one representative per county, hence discriminating against both Los Angeles and San Francisco. Attempts to change this were made by referenda in 1948, 1960 and 1962, and in each case the measure was defeated. The *status quo* found its support naturally in the small rural counties but also in the state Chamber of Commerce and most of the urban press. The list of major financial contributors to the campaign against the proposal in 1962 was Pacific Gas and Electric, Standard Oil, Southern Pacific Railroad, Richfield Oil, Bank of America, plus several other oil companies, banks and railroads (Baker, 1966). Clearly, the reapportionment battle in California was no simple reflection of an old rural-urban cleavage. By the 1960s it had taken on a truly modern character with big business showing its political strength.

In party terms the effects of the malapportionment were confused over the nation as a whole. This was because Democrat and

Republican strength is not consistently related to the urban/rural cleavage. In the north the Democrats tended to suffer from malapportionment since their main areas of strength were urban whereas, elsewhere, in Arizona for instance, Republican urban strength was minimized. The main effect was probably to be found in intra-party balances. This was certainly true in the south where urban liberal Democrats were under-represented. In general the overall effect would seem to have been a non-party conservative effect on state legislatures and on the House of Representatives in Washington.

1960 was another important census year in demographic terms. The census of that year showed that the urban population was no longer the largest group in America: suburbanites had overtaken urban dwellers in numbers. In demographic terms, therefore, urban areas were no longer the threat that they had been, thus allowing a complete reappraisal of the apportionment situation. In 1962 the Supreme Court reversed *Colgrove v. Green* in a case concerning malapportionment in Tennessee and ruled that such cases were the concern of the courts. This verdict of *Baker v. Carr* is seen as a milestone in American electoral history. Two years later a series of verdicts confirmed population equality as the sole criterion for apportionment in state legislatures and for the House of Representatives in Washington. In all, fifteen decisions held that the Fourteenth Amendment's equal protection clause must include representation. As Chief Justice Warren baldly stated: 'Legislators represent people, not trees or acres'. The days of malapportionment in America were well and truly over.

The effect of these court decisions was reapportionment on a large scale in every state. This massive amount of activity is usually referred to as the *reapportionment revolution*. Ironically, the main benefactors turned out to be suburban counties since most central cities were in decline by the 1960s and hence were becoming less under-represented. Nonetheless, there was a massive shift of representation away from rural areas.

At first the courts did not specify how equal districts had to be, but as the decade wore on the population requirements became more and more stringent. The courts tended to use the simple measure of the ratio between the most and least populous districts. Table 7.3 shows the immediate transformation in those states which redrew their Congressional District maps as a result of these court guidelines. This is the transformation reflected in

Table 7.3 Judicially prompted Congressional redistricting, 1963–5

State	*Ratio of largest to smallest*	
	1962	*1965*
Texas	4·4	1·2
Michigan	4·5	1·0
Georgia	3·0	1·4
Maryland	3·2	1·3
Ohio	3·1	1·3
Alabama	2·7	1·4
Indiana	2·4	1·2
Connecticut	2·2	1·2
Florida	2·8	1·2
Tennessee	2·8	1·3
South Dakota	2·7	1·1
Colorado	3·3	1·2
Wisconsin	2·2	1·1
Oregon	2·0	1·2
Arkansas	1·7	1·0
Utah	1·8	1·0
Kansas	1·4	1·2
Idaho	1·6	1·2

Source: Baker (1966)

the fall in the Gini index from 0·15 to 0·04 for the House of Representatives reported previously.

At the state level, the compositions of the local legislatures were similarly transformed. This is shown in Table 7.4 where minimum majorities are shown for every state before and after the reapportionment revolution. We can see that the term 'revolution' is not an understatement: the composition of legislatures across America was radically transformed. The change was very

Table 7.4 Changes in representation of state legislatures, 1962–8

	Minimum percentage of population that could elect a majority			
	Senate		*House*	
	1962	1968	1962	1968
Alabama	25	48	26	48
Alaska	35	51	49	48
Arizona	13	52	—	51
Arkansas	44	49	33	48
California	11	49	45	49
Colorado	30	50	32	54
Connecticut	33	48	12	44
Delaware	22	53	19	49
Florida	12	51	12	50
Georgia	23	48	22	43
Hawaii	23	50	48	43
Idaho	17	47	33	47
Illinois	29	50	40	49
Indiana	40	49	35	49
Iowa	35	45	27	45
Kansas	27	49	19	49
Kentucky	42	47	34	45
Louisiana	33	48	34	47
Maine	47	51	40	43
Maryland	14	47	25	48
Massachusetts	45	50	45	46
Michigan	29	53	44	51
Minnesota	40	48	35	47
Mississippi	35	49	29	48
Missouri	48	52	20	49
Montana	16	47	37	48
Nebraska	37	49	—	—
Nevada	8	50	35	48
New Hampshire	45	52	44	46
New Jersey	19	50	47	50
New Mexico	14	46	27	46
New York	41	49	33	49
North Carolina	37	49	27	48

Table 7.4 – cont.

	Minimum percentage of population that could elect a majority			
	Senate		*House*	
	1962	1968	1962	1968
North Dakota	32	47	40	47
Ohio	41	50	30	47
Oklahoma	25	49	30	49
Oregon	48	47	48	48
Pennsylvania	33	50	38	47
Rhode Island	18	50	47	49
South Carolina	23	48	46	46
South Dakota	38	47	39	47
Tennessee	27	49	29	47
Texas	30	49	39	47
Utah	21	48	33	48
Vermont	47	49	12	49
Virginia	38	48	37	47
Washington	34	48	35	47
West Virginia	47	47	40	46
Wisconsin	45	48	40	45
Wyoming	27	47	36	46

Source: Dye (1971)

much geographical in nature with different places within the states now asserting their numerical superiority. This changing geography of representation is illustrated in Figure 7.3 for the nine south-eastern states, from a study by Bushman and Stanley (1971). The percentage deviations from state averages for senate seats are shown in terms of under-representation before reapportionment. There is a very clear relationship with the pattern of metropolitan areas. After the reapportionment this relationship has totally disappeared and the level of malapportionment is much less in any case. The reapportionment revolution has involved a total transformation in the geography of representation in the south-east and elsewhere in the U.S.A.

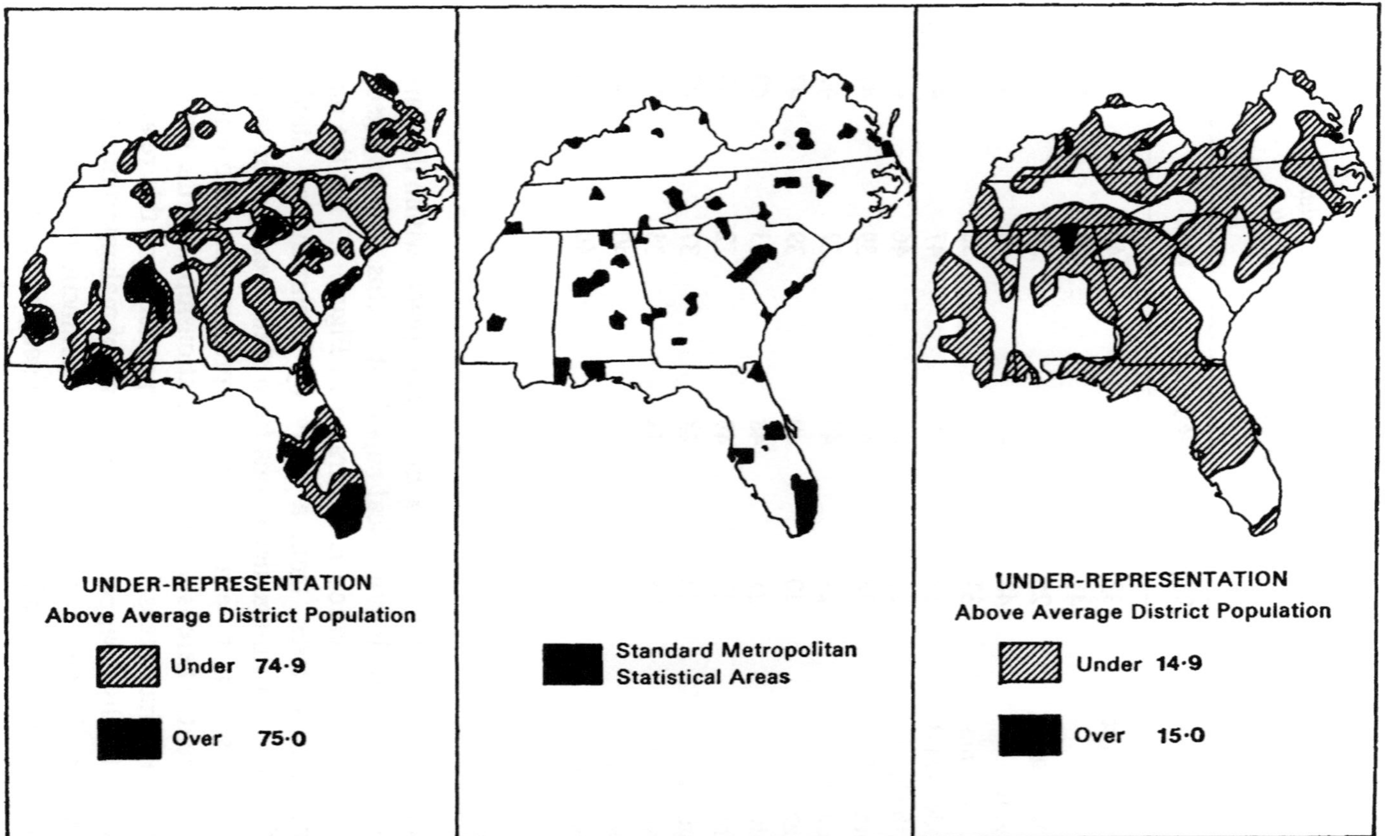

Figure 7.3 Under-representation and metropolitan areas in south-eastern U.S.A., before and after the reapportionment revolution

Despite the massive improvements shown in Tables 7.3 and 7.4 and illustrated in Figure 7.3, not all of the revised plans satisfied the courts. Some of the new plans were challenged and in some cases complaints were upheld. In the 1964 cases, *Wesberry v. Sanders* required that districts must be as equal as 'practical' and in *Reynolds v. Sims* it was argued that they should be 'substantially' equal. By 1969 this had been transformed into a requirement for 'precise mathematical equality' in *Kirkpatrick v. Preisler*. In this latter case a Missouri plan was rejected even though the maximum deviation from the average was only 3·1 per cent. This was despite the fact that the census figures were, by this time, nine years out of date and were thought to be inaccurate by up to 20 per cent in some parts of the state. It is not surprising that some observers have concluded that the American electoral system had become obsessive over malapportionment. In fact all the districts so carefully drawn in the 1960s had to be redrawn again after the publication of the 1970 census. We will consider some of the negative effects of all this districting activity in the next chapter where the reapportionment revolution is assessed in terms of electoral reform in general.

Malapportionment as rural defence

At first sight the stories of malapportionment in Britain and the U.S.A. are very different from one another. One important feature that they do share in common, however, is the linking of the malapportionment issue to rural over-representation. This is explicit in the U.S.A. case but it also underlies the British situation. In the nineteenth century the rural basis of the conflict in Britain is obscured to some degree by the fact that the worst anomalies were 'boroughs'. These were, of course, controlled by rural landed interests which were often aristocratic in nature. On the other side of the coin the under-represented areas were the new urban industrial regions. Even in the twentieth century the Boundary Commissioners have used the 'geography' and boundary rules to override the population equality criterion so as to consciously produce rural over-representation. Hence in both

Britain and the U.S.A. the fight against malapportionment has also been about eroding the over-representation of rural interests.

We can, in fact, generalize beyond these two countries and view malapportionment as a rural defence mechanism which has been used in countries all over the world. It is a convenient way by which formerly dominant groups and areas can maintain their political power long after their numerical majority has been lost to new areas of population growth. It is convenient in the sense that it requires no direct action on the part of the formerly dominant groups; they just have to make changing the *status quo* difficult. As such malapportionment has had a major impact on representation in Japan, South Africa, Australia, New Zealand, France, Chile and Canada. Examples of parties particularly favoured by this mechanism are the Country Party in Australia, the Gaullists in France, the National Party in New Zealand, the Liberals in Japan, and the Nationalist Party in South Africa. This latter party came to power and initially maintained power solely on the basis of the rural bias in representation (Heard, 1974; Lakeman, 1974), with very profound effects upon the future of that country. Other specific examples of malapportionment favouring rural areas can be found in McDonald's (1969) discussion of the Chilean case and Long's (1969) description of the situation in Alberta, Canada. In this section we will describe the Australian example in some detail, first because it incorporates the most explicit procedures for favouring rural areas and secondly because it illustrates clearly the normal party effect of this electoral abuse – discrimination against the left.

Malapportionment in Australia occurs at the level of both Federal and state elections. At the Federal level, the Labor government attempted to overturn rural over-representation by constitutional referenda in 1974 but failed. It is at the state level, however, that this over-representation has long been a crucial factor in the translation of votes into seats (Rydon, 1958). The justification for such malapportionment mirrors the sentiments of rural defenders in the U.S.A. In the Queensland state parliament, for instance, the following arguments have been used to justify rural over-representation (McDonald, 1976):

(1) The greater 'worthiness' of rural populations.
(2) Sparsely settled areas are difficult for a representative to service (see also Chapter 9).
(3) Rural dwellers have developed the state and therefore should have more say in its government.
(4) Rural areas have higher proportions of adult males, who are the major taxpayers.
Remember that these arguments are not required to initiate any change, they are merely statements to justify the *status quo*. Let us consider the actual procedures they are defending.

All Australian states, except Tasmania, are divided into two or more zones to which seats are allocated. Different zones are given different quotas of seats in a sort of 'vote weighting' exercise (Aitkin and Kahan, 1974). It is at this stage that the urban areas are discriminated against. Table 7.5 shows the ratios of seats to votes in the various zones of the five mainland states. In each case

Table 7.5 Rural over-representation in Australian state legislatures

Zone	*New South Wales (1970)*	*Victoria (1971)*	*Queensland (1971)*	*South Aust. (1969)*	*Western Aust. (1966)*
1.					
Seats	63	44	47	47	23
Pop./seat	28,377	25,000	12,657	15,055	11,523
2.					
Seats	33	8	13	19	24
Pop./seat	19,823	22,250	12,603	9,647	5,822
3.					
Seats		21	7		4
Pop./seat		18,200	7,641		2,500
4.					
Seats			15		
Pop./seat			9,976		
Largest-Smallest ratio	2·1	2·9	2·3	2·5	13·2
Metropolitan areas:					
Percentage of votes	73·3	67·4	39·6	71·0	64·7
Percentage of seats	65·6	60·3	36·6	59·6	45·1

Source: Blewett (1972)

Zone 1 includes the more urban parts of the states and is subsequently allocated fewer seats per population than the other zones in each state. The largest/smallest ratios are all over 2 with Western Australia displaying an outstandingly large ratio. Finally the seat and vote proportions for metropolitan areas in each state directly illustrate the anti-city bias of the apportionment.

The Australian Labor Party's main electoral strength lies in the metropolitan areas and so it is the party that suffers severe electoral disadvantage from the apportionment procedure. A very clear example of this occurred in South Australia during the period 1944–70, when the Liberal–Country League won a majority of the votes in only two of ten elections to the House of Assembly but won a majority of seats in eight elections. (During all of this period there was minimal support for any third party to distort the pattern of votes.) Even when Labor managed to win the 1965 election, however, it was unable to redraw the electoral boundaries to remove the effect of the malapportionment because the Upper House – the Legislative Council – was even more biased towards the rural areas and constitutional amendments such as a redistribution required the support of a majority of the members of both houses (Blewett and Jaensch, 1971). It was only after a period of virtual electoral stalemate, and a recognition of the inequity of the 'Playmander' – as the malapportionment was known after its originator Sir Thomas Playford – that the Liberal–Country League leadership accepted the need for a much fairer distribution of seats. In 1969 some of the worst anomalies were removed, thereby curtailing, though not removing entirely, the use of malapportionment as a means of defending rural interests.

Rural over-representation remains a live issue at federal and state level in Australia today. The same can be said of South Africa, Japan and France. Malapportionment has been, and remains, a major electoral abuse in many countries.

Creating malapportionment: the European Assembly

So far we have been concerned with malapportionment as a tool for preserving past power structures in modern legislatures. In this sense it is a reactionary device which has to do with looking backwards. It can, however, be created by those who are looking forward. The new European elected assembly has no rural tradition to uphold but it has not been able to avoid gross malapportionment of its seats.

1979 is planned to be a unique year in European political history. For the first time, a truly international parliament, popularly elected, will be created. This new assembly will be based on the second largest electorate in the world, outstripping the U.S. Congress by about a fifth and being smaller only than the electorate of the faltering Indian democracy. Since a completely new institution is being created it may be thought that electoral abuses can be eradicated right from the start. Here, at least, there are no historical precedents which require reform. Unfortunately, the political world is not as simple as that and the European Assembly is starting out as anything but an 'ideal' parliament. In this section we will be concerned with the failure to deal with malapportionment and in the next chapter we consider other aspects of the electoral laws underlying the election.

Although Birke (1961) has traced proposals for a directly elected European Assembly back to 1923, the modern impetus came with the setting up of the E.E.C. in 1957. Article 38 of the Treaty of Rome set up an assembly based on delegates from national parliaments but instructed the assembly 'to draw up proposals for elections by direct universal suffrage'. No action on this article was taken until after a Heads of Government meeting in 1974 which set 1978 as a target date. This intention left several problems to be resolved, none more difficult than the share-out of assembly seats among the member countries.

Let us begin by considering the distribution of delegates among the countries in the original unelected assembly. The second column of Table 7.6 shows this initial apportionment. Notice that the minimum number of delegates is six, for Luxembourg, and the maximum number is thirty-six for the big four – Germany, Britain, Italy and France. These countries are of course far more than six times larger than Luxembourg, as the column one population figures show. The result of this original apportionment is, inevitably, massive numerical discrimination with

Table 7.6 Alternative apportionments for a European Assembly

Country	Population (millions)	Non-elected	Apportionments Draft	Adopted	Equitable	Populations (thousands) per seat Non-elected	Draft	Adopted	Equitable
Belgium	9·65	14	23	24	13	680	420	400	740
Denmark	4·94	10	17	16	7	490	290	310	710
France	49·78	36	65	81	66	1,380	770	610	750
Germany	60·65	36	71	81	81	1,680	850	750	750
Ireland	2·78	10	13	15	4	280	210	190	700
Italy	54·03	36	66	81	72	1,500	820	670	750
Luxembourg	0·34	6	6	6	1	60	60	60	340
Netherlands	13·33	14	27	25	18	950	490	530	740
United Kingdom	55·36	36	67	81	74	1,540	830	680	750

Luxembourg having one delegate per 60,000 population and the big four all having well over a million people per delegate.

In 1975 a working group of the Assembly produced a draft Convention for the elected Assembly (Green Paper, 1976). It was proposed to increase the seats from 198 to 355. The distribution of seats was based on two principles. First, small states such as Luxembourg were guaranteed adequate representation, and second, the seats per state were to be approximately proportional to population. Unfortunately the two principles are hardly compatible. If we allocate just one seat to Luxembourg, Germany would require 182 seats on a proportionality basis. The end result of such an exercise produces an assembly of over a thousand members which is clearly too unwieldy to contemplate. Instead, the draft Convention proposed a graduated system of allocating seats so that for a state's first million population, or part thereof, each state receives six seats, while at the other end of the scale one seat is allocated for every million and a half population above 50 million. This system of allocation is very arbitrary but it does ensure Luxembourg six seats while increasing representation for the big four. This proposed distribution is shown in Table 7.6.

Although the draft Convention lessens the differences in population per seat, marked discrimination still exists. Figure 7.4 shows the Lorenz curve for this proposal. Two measures are illustrated. The minimal majority is slightly over 40 per cent, consisting of all voters in Luxembourg, Ireland, Denmark, Belgium, Netherlands and France, plus a small proportion of Italian voters. The second measure is simply one of under-representation. It can be seen that in these proposals, a massive 87 per cent of Europe's electorate would be under-represented. To put these figures in perspective, we can compare them with the same measures for American state senates before the reapportionment revolution, since these were the most notorious examples of malapportionment in modern electoral history. In Alker and Russett's (1964) work, measures are presented for 27 senates giving minimal majorities ranging from 7·2 per cent to 46·5 per cent and percentages under-represented from 42·6 per cent to

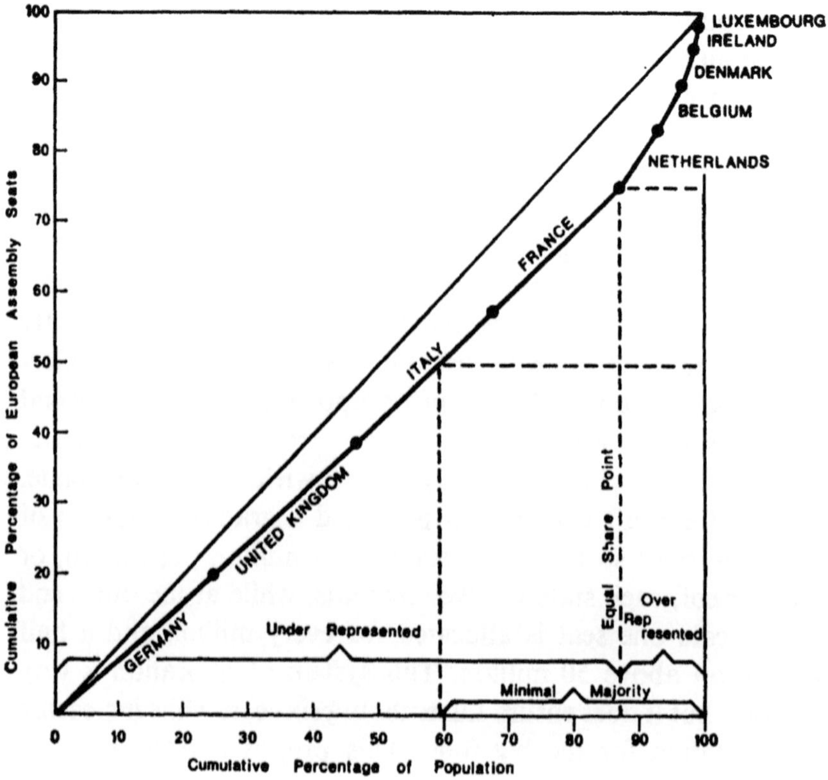

Figure 7.4 The Lorenz curve for the European assembly

80·0 per cent. It seems that, in terms of minimal majority, the proposed assembly fares quite well in this comparison but incredibly, in the case of under-representation, the European assembly is planned to have more under-representation than any of the unreformed American state senates. These proposals define a unique level of under-representation proportions.

The draft Convention of the working party was not implemented. Final agreement from Heads of Governments was not reached until July 1976 when the proposed under-representation of the big four was a major issue. The United Kingdom was particularly sensitive to this issue since adequate representation was required for Scotland, Ulster and Wales. In the final scheme the big four were given 81 seats each, Luxembourg retained her six seats and for some reason Ireland gained some extra representation. The details are given in Table 7.6. With the exception of Ireland discrepancies of populations per seat remain the same, or are reduced, compared with the draft proposals. This is reflected in the minimal majority which increases to 43 per cent, but the percentage under-represented remains at the massive level of 87 per cent. Hence the elections of 1979 will have a basis where the value of a vote quite clearly depends on where the voter lives. Even allowing for the improvements negotiated for the big four, a vote in Luxembourg will be worth fourteen times a vote in Germany. In the context of a totally new democratic institution, this electoral abuse must be considered very disappointing.

Is a high level of malapportionment for the European Assembly inevitable? The answer revolves around what is done with Luxembourg. If Luxembourg retains six seats then malapportionment is inevitable. However if apportionment rules were adopted which are based upon the allocation of seats in the U.S. House of Representatives, then a much more equitable solution is possible. This would involve two rules: (1) All member states must be apportioned a minimum of one seat. (2) Otherwise, seats are apportioned strictly on a population basis. Such rules would ensure Luxembourg's representation while also enabling a fair treatment of the larger countries. If seats were allocated per 750,000 population, then a 336 member assembly would result as shown in Table 7.6. Such an equitable solution reduces malapportionment to a practical minimum.

Why should this creation of malapportionment be a concern beyond theoretical niceties of equality of voters? There are three reasons why this electoral abuse is disturbing. First, it casts doubts on the legitimacy of the new institution. The institution has no tradition of legitimacy to fall back upon; it must create it afresh and electoral abuses must hamper this task. Secondly, it proves a precedent for future apportionment to new members of the community. Without considering the implications of six members each for Monaco, Vatican City, San Marino, Andorra and the Isle of Man, future members of the community are likely to be small population countries (Norway, Portugal, Greece?), so that the big four will continue to be discriminated against.

Finally, there are the possible political effects. Clearly parties that do well in small countries will be favoured over parties whose main strength lies in the larger countries. One simple example will illustrate this point. Communist strength in the new assembly is sure to be highly concentrated in just two countries, Italy and France. Since both are members of the big four, they are discriminated against, hence the Communists are discriminated against. Communist votes in the election to the European assembly will be worth less than votes for other party groups, simply because of where the votes come from. Europe has created a system within which its geography of representation will be a very distorted reflection of the underlying geography of its voting.

Boundary Discrimination: Gerrymandering

The term gerrymandering is sometimes used as a blanket noun to cover all types of electoral abuse. In 1969, for instance, the failure of the Labour Government to implement the Boundary Commission's proposals led to widespread accusations of gerrymandering (Steed, 1969). Similarly the failure to reapportion U.S. districts up to 1962 in the wake of massive changes in the distribution of population has sometimes been referred to as 'the silent gerrymander' (Hacker, 1964). However the term gerrymander is more properly restricted to the particular practice of drawing constituency boundaries to favour one party over another. As such, it can be entirely independent of malapportionment and in no way relies on numerical discrimination to produce its electoral effect.

Let us return to our small hypothetical country with which we illustrated numerical discrimination (Figure 7·1 p. 337). If we return to the initial vote situation on Figure 7·1(a) we can eliminate the malapportionment by producing the simple four constituency solution in Figure 7.5 (a). This reduction to four constituencies enables us to produce a 'fair' result, with both parties equally sharing votes and seats. Such a solution is not the inevitable result of eliminating the malapportionment, however.

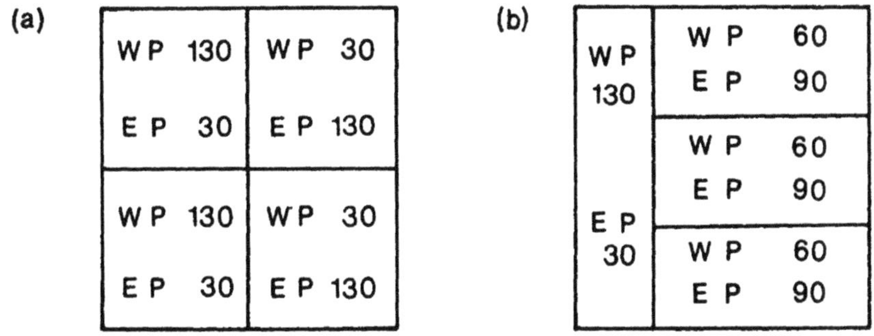

Figure 7.5 Gerrymandering

Consider Figure 7.5(b). This set of four constituencies maintains equal size districts but now EP easily wins three of the four seats. There has been no change in vote or vote pattern from Figure 7.5 (a), all we have done has been to design the boundaries so as to maximize the effect of the EP vote and minimize WP's vote effect. Hence WP are given one safe seat but the rest of the support is spread among three EP-dominated constituencies. All of these WP votes are literally wasted. The boundaries are placed in such a way that WP need a swing of over 10 per cent to win a majority of seats. This means that EP would still win three-quarters of the seats even if they won only 41 per cent of the overall vote. Such is the power of the practice of gerrymandering.

The practice of gerrymandering is usually associated with the U.S.A. However, the opportunity for gerrymandering occurs with every redrawing of boundaries where partisan considerations may influence decisions. At the time of the Great Reform Bill's redistribution, certain borough boundaries were redrawn to ensure government victories. This seems to have been the case with Arundel borough, for instance, which was considered marginal but was made safe for the Liberal government by the addition of the 'Whig' village of Littlehampton (Seymour, 1915). Since 1885, however, such abuses have disappeared from the parliamentary scene in Britain as neutral Boundary Commissioners have been used to delimit constituencies.

In British local government elections, on the other hand, political influences on drawing electoral district boundaries sometimes come to light. Shepherd, Westaway and Lee (1974) give examples in drawing ward boundaries in London. The most clear cut examples of political influences in this matter, however, can be found in Northern Ireland where the political cleavage is most acutely drawn. The classic case is that of Londonderry (Robinson, 1970). In 1840 Londonderry's Municipal Act created three wards – North, East and South – which were given eight representatives each. This resulted in two 'Protestant' wards and one 'Catholic' ward. By this simple division of the town the minority Protestant group were able to maintain control of the city right up until 1969. Other local government gerrymandering is reported by Darby (1976). In County Fermanagh, for example, the Catholic majority was not able to transform its numerical superiority into political control of councils throughout the area. Table 7.7 shows this effect for local government districts; in every

Table 7.7 Local government representation in County Fermanagh

District	*Percentage Catholic*	*Seats* *Unionist*	*Non-unionist*
Dunganon Urban	50	14	7
Dunganon Rural	52	16	6
Omagh Urban	61	12	9
Omagh Rural	60	24	18
Castledorg Rural	50	13	6
Clogher Rural	51	14	5
Cookstown Rural	55	12	7
Strabane Rural	49	22	9

Source: Darby (1976)

case the Unionist Party representing the Protestant groups has complete control of the local council despite general Catholic demographic dominance.

Although these Ulster examples provide a basic example of discrimination in the province, and hence have wider significance beyond electoral politics, for further illustration and understanding of gerrymandering as an electoral abuse one must turn to two countries where it has almost become an accepted part of the electoral game – U.S.A. and France.

Gerrymandering as an American tradition

The American Constitution prescribes that 'each house shall be the judge of the elections . . . of its own members' (Hacker, 1964). One effect of this doctrine has been that the various state legislatures have had the power to draw the boundaries of their electoral districts. They have further inherited the task of drawing the boundaries of their congressional districts for sending representatives to Washington. This direct political involvement in the districting procedure has inevitably led to much gerrymandering as majority parties in state legislatures have attempted to draw boundaries that favour their own party.

The 'original' gerrymander clearly illustrates this procedure. In April 1810 Elbridge Gerry was elected Governor of Massachusetts on a strong anti-Federalist ticket. As governor he signed into law the infamous Massachusetts Senate redistricting bill of 1812. The districts were designed to favour the Republican-Democrats over the Federalists and the results showed how the bill achieved this aim. In fact it was extraordinarily successful. While the Federalists won most votes – 51,766 to 50,164 – the Republican-Democrats achieved a landslide victory in terms of Senate seats – 29 to 11 (Lossing, 1872). The total distortion of the voting intentions was produced by careful manipulation of the district boundaries. It remains the classic example of boundary discrimination.

One district in particular received the attention of Gerry's opponents. In Essex County the Federalist vote was concentrated into a two-member district which was surrounded by a long strung-out three-member district where Republican-Democrats could expect a marginal win. Hence this 'Federalist' county returned only two Federalists out of five senators. The long strung-out district caught the eye of Federalist journalists on the *Columbian Centinel*, one of whom added a few touches to the map to produce head, wings, claws and a tail. The resulting salamander was christened a 'gerrymander' in honour of the governor who had signed the districting bill. This cartoon was distributed as part of a political broadsheet and the term has remained with us, ensuring Elbridge Gerry's political immortality (Dean, 1892).

Figure 7.6 (a) shows a diagram from one of the political broadsheets with Essex County's outer district as the political monster. However in the following year this outer district was won by the Federalists which produced obituaries for the gerrymander in the local press (Figure 7.6 (b)). While the tables may have been turned in this particular example, all the evidence is that the gerrymander has lived and flourished on the American political scene. Let us briefly consider some of this evidence.

The American political literature is full of examples of gerrymandering. A typical example is that concerning the Republican congressman McKinley from Stark County, Ohio. In 1876 his congressional district returned him to Washington with a majority of 3300. What happened subsequently is summarized in Figure 7.7. The Democrat-controlled Ohio legislature repeatedly altered his district's boundaries in attempts to defeat him. However, his support remained surprisingly resilient despite the boundary changes, although he was finally defeated in 1890. The end of this story has two ironies. McKinley's career blossomed after his defeat and he went on to become state governor and U.S. president. However, he finally suffered the ultimate electoral abuse – he was assassinated in office.

The McKinley gerrymanders are examples of personal discrimination which has, no doubt, been quite common in this form of electoral abuse. However, such discrimination will normally be merely part of a larger overall strategy for legislative control as in the original gerrymander. Particular districts may be emphasized, but the overall effects must never be lost sight of. In the more modern New York City gerrymanders which we used in Chapter 1 to introduce the geography of representation, the effect has traditionally been quite traumatic (Tyler and Wells, 1962). While the Democrats quite commonly win over half the vote in New York state elections, they have very rarely won control of the legislature in the twentieth century. Tyler and

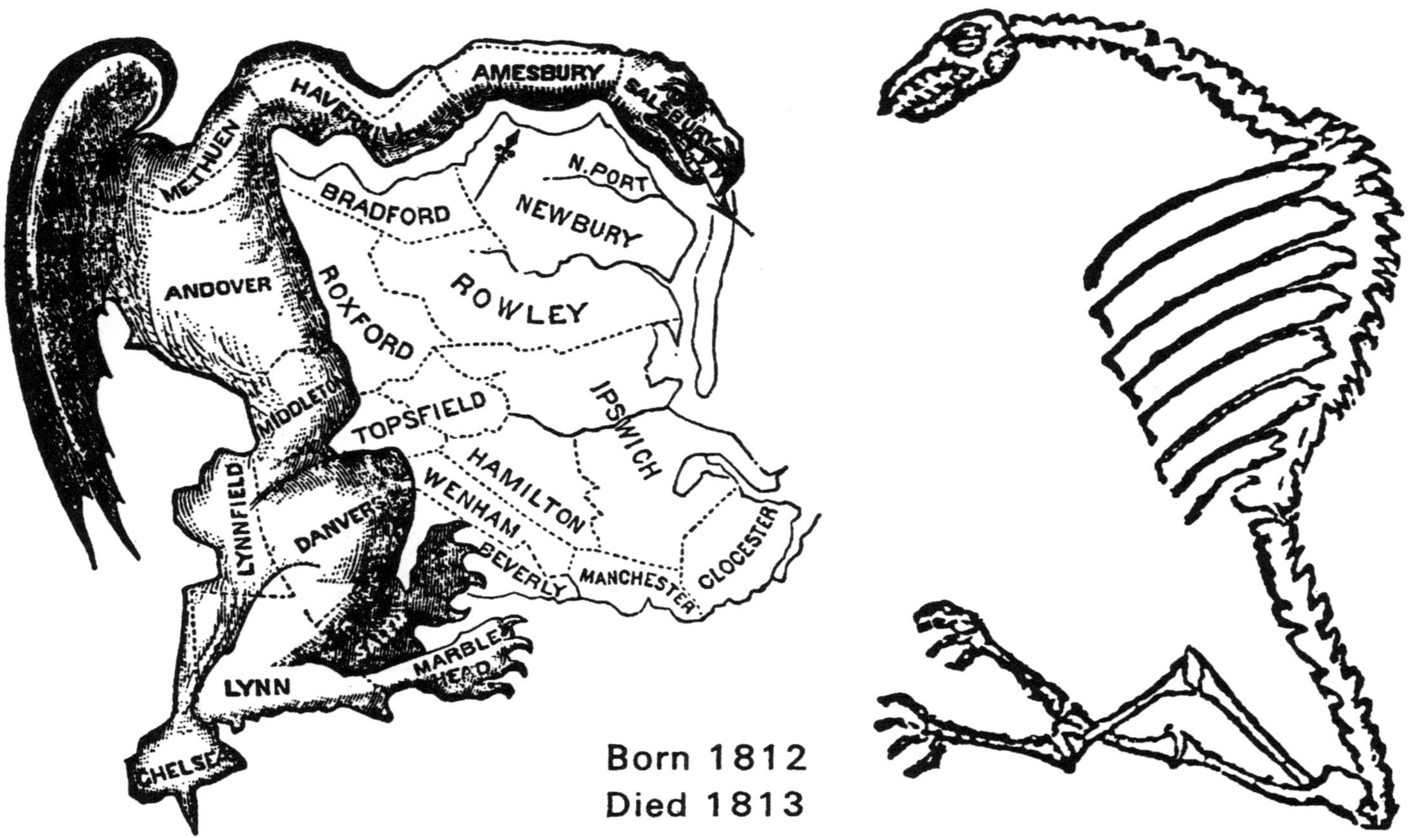

Figure 7.6 The original gerrymander

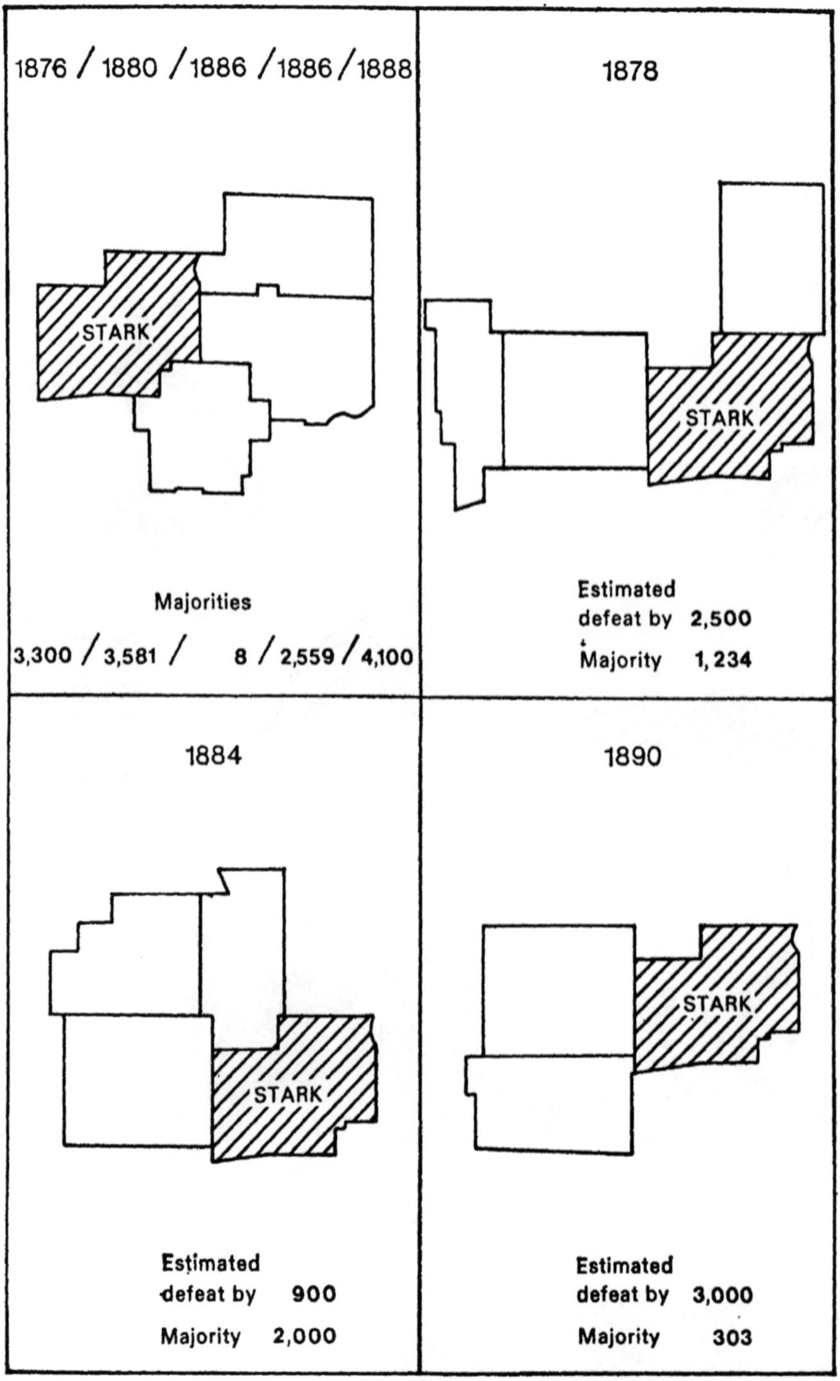

Figure 7.7 The McKinley gerrymanders

Wells's phrase 'two party state with a one party legislature' neatly summarizes the position. New York Republicans have used boundary discrimination to lessen the uncertainties associated with elections as they devalued their opponents' votes.

We could go on almost endlessly quoting examples of gerrymandering in the U.S.A. (e.g. Orr, 1970). That it has existed is proven beyond doubt; what is now required is some estimate of its overall importance in the American political scene. Do legislatures inevitably discriminate in their districting bills? If the answer is yes, how successful are they? We will briefly describe one comprehensive attempt to answer these questions.

Robert Sickels (1966) studied all congressional elections in states with more than ten seats between 1946 and 1964. For all 62 election contests he determined which party had controlled the drawing of the district boundaries upon which the contests were being fought. His results are quite startling. Table 7.8 shows

Table 7.8 Electoral biases and the power to gerrymander, 1946–64

Winning Party:	*Electoral bias*			
	Negative		*Positive*	
	Over 5%	*Up to 5%*	*Up to 5%*	*Over 5%*
(1) Had power to gerrymander	0	0	6	33
(2) Without power to gerrymander	7	7	6	3

Source: Derived from Sickels (1966)

only those parties that won a majority of the state vote. They are divided between 39 parties that had the power to gerrymander and 23 parties without the power to gerrymander. Notice that no party with the power to gerrymander suffered a negative electoral bias, that is, obtained a lower percentage of seats than votes. On the other hand, parties without the gerrymander power commonly suffered negative bias so that although they 'won' their elections in terms of votes, in the majority of cases they still failed to win a majority of their state's congressional seats. If boundary discrimination is so clearly apparent for congressional elections, we can infer that it will be at least as important in state elections where the legislators draw their own district's boundaries (Jewell, 1962). Gerrymandering obviously has a vital role to play in distorting American geographies of voting into geographies of representation.

Ages of gerrymandering in France

So far we have been concerned with electoral abuses in Britain and America. Such abuses are repeated in other Anglo-American democracies to varying degrees (Gudgin and Taylor, 1978). However, in the Scandinavian and other European countries such abuses are far less common because of the widespread adoption of proportional representation forms of electoral law. One major exception among the European democracies is France. This country has frequently changed its electoral law so that while forms of proportional representation have been used, they have not survived as elsewhere in Europe. In France we can find electoral abuses to rival those of the U.S.A.

In terms of spatial organization, France has experienced two basic types of electoral system since 1789. First, there has been the use of multi-member constituencies (often involving P.R.list systems) and second, the use of single-member constituencies. In the former case, administrative units, the departments, have been used as constituencies so that no intentional boundary discrimination could be attempted. In the second case, however, the departments have required division into single-member constituencies, thus giving scope for gerrymandering. Campbell (1958) has designated periods of use of single-member constituencies in the nineteenth century as 'ages of open gerrymandering'. These periods have occurred from 1820 to 1830, 1831 to 1848, 1852 to 1870, 1889 to 1919, 1927 to 1945 and from 1958 to the present. Boundary discrimination has been a part of French political life, sporadically at least, right up until the present day.

According to Campbell (1958) boundaries have been 'designed to favour their makers' since 1820. The need for such abuse, however, was not particularly felt until after the introduction of manhood suffrage in 1848. From this date France experienced the first 'mass' elections in Europe, involving electorates of up to ten million voters. In urban areas many of these voters were 'radical' and the emperor, Louis Napoleon, set out to neutralize their effect after 1852. The main way in which he did this was to draw boundaries around constituencies so that areas of radical support were divided up and hence deprived of representation. In most departments this involved dividing the main town into three or more sections and combining each section with larger rural areas in the remainder of the department (du Vistre, 1869). Figure 7.8(a) shows the division of Nîmes in this way so that the radical elements in the town were separated and electorally swamped by conservative rural votes. Where such simple cartography was unable to ensure radical defeats, more distorted, and sometimes non-contiguous constituencies had to be devised as Figure 7.8 (b) shows. This boundary discrimination helped Louis Napoleon's regime so that it was never seriously challenged electorally throughout the life of the second Empire.

The spatial organization of constituencies in 1927 illustrates a contrasting approach. In this case separate representation of town and country was recognized so that urban areas were used to form constituencies in their own right (Criddle, 1973). A typical example would be Sarthe department where the main town, Le Mans, made up one constituency, while the surrounding rural area was divided in sectors to produce four further constituencies. This 'hub and spokes' pattern of boundaries was quite common and enabled the left to win some seats even in rural regions where they were not generally very popular.

In 1958 the return to power of de Gaulle involved a return to single-member constituencies and the discriminatory districting pattern of Louis Napoleon. Criddle (1973) states simply that 'the decision was taken to neutralize as far as possible the impact of votes for the Communist party'. Separate representation of urban areas was largely abandoned to produce an urban–rural mix in each constituency. Hence, in 1958 Sarthe department kept its five seats but Le Mans was now split up and allocated as small parts

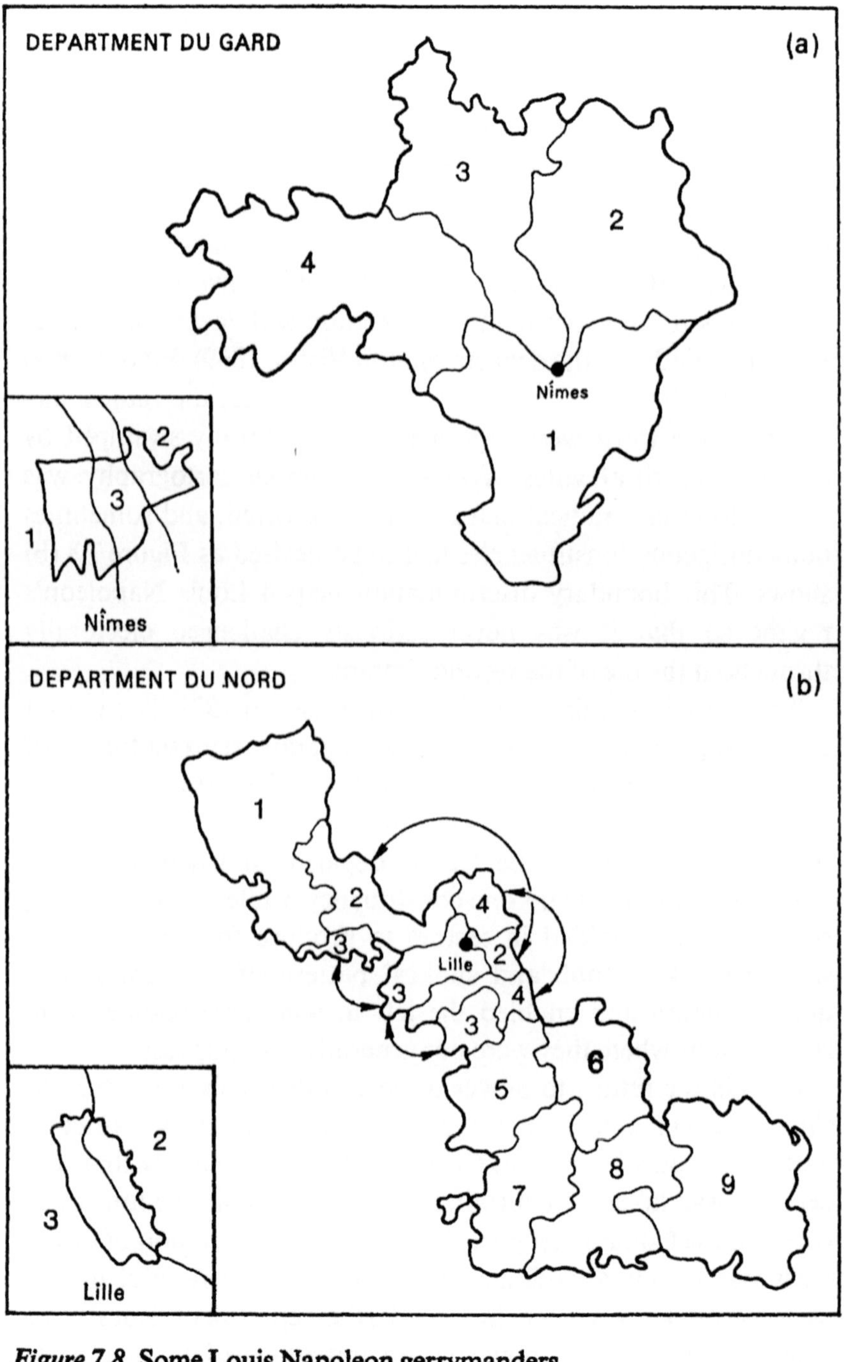

Figure 7.8 **Some Louis Napoleon gerrymanders**

of three separate rural-dominated constituencies. The results have been very predictable – 'whilst in 1936 the Communist party had clear areas of strength and clear areas of weakness, in 1958 it had neither, merely areas of impotence' (Criddle, 1973, p. 158). Such discrimination against the Communists has continued into the 1970s. In this case, an often clear-cut geography of voting had been distorted into a rather blurred and highly limited geography of representation for the Communists.

The basic problem of proof

Although we have generally treated gerrymandering in a similar manner to malapportionment, beginning with a simple description followed by illustrations of its operation, gerrymandering is in fact a much more complicated form of electoral abuse. Hence, although we were able to describe techniques for measuring malapportionment and its effects, we have not attempted any quantitative assessment of gerrymandering. There have been attempts to assess what is termed 'the distribution effect' in election results (Brookes, 1958, 1959, Taylor and Gudgin, 1975a; Johnston, 1976a) using algebraic manipulation of results, but boundary discrimination is treated merely as a 'residual' after other effects have been accounted for. In any case, no account is taken of the intentions of the boundary drawers, so that the electoral abuse of gerrymandering is not even directly tackled.

Gerrymandering is in a very important sense different from malapportionment. With the latter abuse there is a standard, the population quota, against which any particular constituency or set of constituencies can be compared. This simple fact makes the quantification of malapportionment and its effects quite simple, as we have seen. Hence, a country of a million population with a one-hundred-seat legislature should have one representative per ten thousand population. If one constituency has a population of 5,000 we can easily see it is over-represented while a constituency of 20,000 would be under-represented. The quota of 10,000 represents a standard against which all constituencies can be compared. The ideal case, with 100 constituencies with exactly 10,000 population in each, is easily measured on all the methods we described above as having no malapportionment.

Malapportionment is clearly a relatively simple concept to work with and the courts have been able to consider quantitative assessments of malapportionment in their crucial decisions of the 1960s. It has been a relatively easy task to 'prove' that one voter is being discriminated against because he happens to live in a certain constituency and hence is being deprived of his constitutional rights. Once there was a political will, the reapportionment revolution could unfold with comparative ease. In contrast, there has not been similar eradication of gerrymandering.

How can we set standards to control gerrymandering? One suggestion is to define a standard in terms of the areal shape of the constituencies. Thus, whereas the population quota is the standard against which malapportionment is judged, a circle can be viewed as the ideal 'compact' shape against which gerrymandering can be viewed (Bunge, 1966). This suggestion has been most explicitly developed by the American geographer Schwartzberg (1966). He suggests that the notion of compactness can be measured by the ratio of the perimeter of a constituency to the circumference of a circle of equal area. This index has a minimum value of one for a circle (= maximum compactness), and increases as the shape becomes more irregular as represented by its increased perimeter. Schwartzberg (1966) applied his index to the eleven congressional districts of North Carolina and found values ranging from 1·14 to 2·04. He concluded that indices up to 1·67 'should be considered reasonable'. He goes on to produce an alternative set of districts for North Carolina which meet his criterion. Tyler and Wells (1971) have proposed a very similar rule for districting with the same purpose in mind. The argument can be summarized as follows. Malapportionment is reduced by restricting the range of size of constituencies from a standard population (the average quota) and therefore gerrymandering can be similarly reduced by restricting the range of compactness of constituencies from a standard shape (the circle).

Such proposals miss the essence of boundary discrimination, however. Gerrymandering need not involve strange-shaped districts. The original Massachusetts gerrymander had its peculiar shape because that was the way in which anti-Federalist votes were distributed. Notice that it was associated with an adjacent compact district (Figure 7.6). The shapes resulting from boundary discrimination will vary as the geography of votes varies. What circles, or any other abstract geometric shape, have to do with this relationship is problematic. Odd-shaped districts *may* facilitate gerrymandering, but this can only be assessed by considering effects on representation, not by measuring a district's degree of compactness. This idea, that gerrymandering has a shape standard like malapportionment's population standard, has been termed the *myth of compactness* (Dixon, 1968).

Although the vague notion of compactness has been included in some electoral districting laws in the U.S.A., (Hacker, 1964) there has never been a case where explicit measurement of compactness, as suggested above, has been considered in court. Hence, whereas measures of malapportionment, such as the largest/smallest ratio, have been commonly used in malapportionment court cases, there has been no equivalent use of quantitative assessments of gerrymandering in American courts.

What does constitute proof of gerrymandering, therefore? This is a very difficult question to answer. In our discussion of gerrymandering we have asserted that electoral abuses occurred on the basis of the evidence of electoral outcomes. In the original gerrymander, for instance, the key fact was not Essex County's strange-shaped district, but rather the overall effect of the plan which gave Gerry's party nearly three-quarters of the representation with less than half of the votes. The effect of the plan *can* be quantified – it is measured by the electoral bias we defined at the beginning of the chapter. In this case the bias is a massive +23 per cent to the anti-Federalists. Perhaps here we have a standard against which gerrymandering can be compared so that boundary discrimination is measured by the size of the electoral bias. Although this is getting nearer the heart of the matter, the proposal is unfortunately unsatisfactory. This is because even where there is no gerrymandering, as in British parliamentary elections, there will normally be some electoral bias, partly due to malapportionment but also because of the particular distribution of votes in relation to constituency boundaries. Removal of gerrymanderers from the political scene does not produce proportionality of seats and votes and hence zero electoral bias. Electoral bias cannot therefore be used as a measure of gerrymandering effects. The problems of dealing with gerrymandering in a legal context are thus quite horrendous – there seems to be no way of proving the abuse.

Perhaps we can learn from the one successfully fought gerrymander case. Litigation on boundary discrimination usually refers back to the 1960 decision in *Gomillion v. Lightfoot* concerning the so-called Tuskegee gerrymander (Taper, 1962). Tuskegee is a small Alabama town with a black population majority. The town had been white-controlled because of a failure to register black voters. In the 1950s, however, voting restrictions were swept away and the white council attempted to maintain their control by redrawing their town boundary. The town was transformed from a square to 'a twenty-four sided sea horse' (Figure 7.9). This new boundary was carefully drawn so that all but a handful of black voters found themselves outside the town and therefore voting in the county (with its white majority). This gerrymander was prevented from taking effect because of its explicit racial nature. The Supreme Court ruled that the previous boundaries were to be restored. The key question is how far the *Gomillion v. Lightfoot* decision can be held as a general precedent for gerrymandering. Unfortunately, there are two characteristics of the case which make it a poor precedent. First, the boundary discrimination did not involve voting districts *per se*. Although the conflict was about elective control of the town's council, the means of achieving the discrimination involved the boundary of the whole town. Hence the case is more related to town annexation cases, of which it forms a reverse case, than to litigation over voting districts. Second, the case concerns discrimination against a racial group and does not relate to political parties whatsoever. In fact, the case is usually seen as one of the many court victories in the black civil rights movement of the 1950s and 1960s. When seen in this light

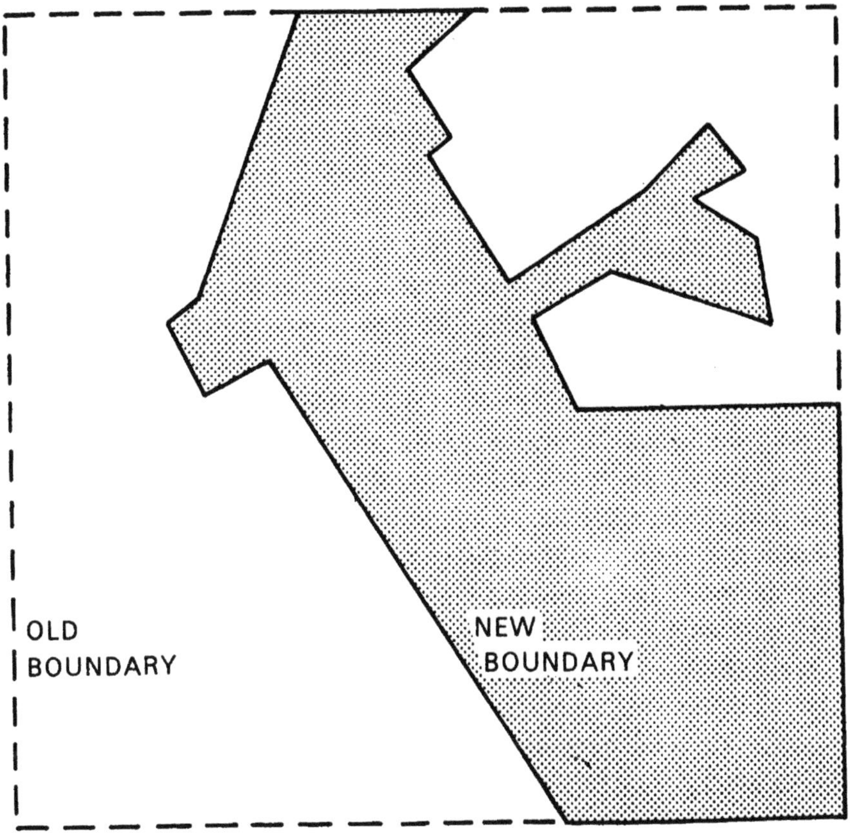

Figure 7.9 The Tuskegee gerrymander

Gomillion v. Lightfoot is even further removed from the vast majority of gerrymandering in American elections, which has normally involved party rather than racial discrimination.

Despite these arguments, *Gomillion v. Lightfoot* is about using boundaries to discriminate against a group of voters for political ends. Hence, it was inevitably invoked in subsequent gerrymandering court cases. The most famous was the 1964 case of *Wright v. Rockefeller* which involved the alleged New York gerrymandering illustrated in Figure 1.3 (p. 31). In Chapter 1 we asserted that this was an example of gerrymandering; this was not the verdict in *Wright v. Rockefeller*. Let us consider the reasons for these differences in interpretation.

In *Wright v. Rockefeller* the plaintiff alleged gerrymandering of the four central New York congressional districts in Manhattan. Although their populations ranged from 382,320 to 445,175 there was no challenge to the districts on malapportionment grounds. The case rested solely on discriminatory districting (Dixon, 1968). Furthermore, like *Gomillion v. Lightfoot*, the allegations were of racial gerrymandering. Three districts had 94·9, 72·5 and 71·5 per cent white populations while the 18th district (Harlem) had 86·3 per cent black-Puerto Rican population. It was argued that this separation of voters on racial lines restricted the influence of black voters unfairly, and hence, in effect, partially disenfranchised the blacks. There were two problems with this argument. First, the motive for drawing the boundaries in New York was most probably party-based so that the Republicans could win one of Manhattan's districts – the famous 'silk stocking' 17th district. Second, it is not clear that the blacks were discriminated against. Is it better to be certain of one black congressman or to have minority influence on all four congressmen who would probably be white? In this case, the black congressman for Harlem appeared for the defendants to support the constitutionality of the existing plan. The result was that black politicians argued on both sides of the case and hence confused the racial issue (Dixon, 1968). In this situation, despite the racial gerrymandering precedent of *Gomillion v. Lightfoot*, the court really had no option but to find in favour of the defendants. The plan was finally overturned on malapportionment grounds, but there remains no example of courts penalizing boundary discrimination of voting districts. Quite simply 'the Supreme Court had refrained from condemning partisan gerrymandering as unconstitutional' (Dixon, 1968, p. 485).

We make no apologies for going into details of these court cases in a geography book, because the issues raised are of basic importance to understanding the geography of representation in the U.S.A. Furthermore, this legal airing of geographical boundary problems has implications for plurality elections beyond the U.S.A. Its major purpose in the context of this chapter, however, has been to illustrate the complexity of what, at first sight, seems to be a quite straightforward topic. Gerrymandering is not the equivalent of the pre-*Baker v. Carr* era of the malapportionment example. Litigation in gerrymandering is different in kind from litigation in malapportionment. There are not going to be any 'breakthrough' cases leading to its eradication. There is no easy solution to the districting problem in America or elsewhere. In the next chapter we will show that boundary discrimination can only be overcome by adopting far more fundamental changes in electoral law than merely tinkering with the cartographic ground rules.

8 Electoral Reform

Electoral abuses spawn electoral reformers. The rate of reform activity and its variable success depends upon many factors, not least of which is the perceived level of abuse. As abuses gradually get worse, as with American malapportionment, or just become more apparent, pressure for reform rises and the electoral *status quo* is forced onto the defensive. This has happened in Britain since the 1974 general elections. A massive increase in Liberal votes from 1970 to 1974 failed to be translated into very many extra seats in parliament; while the Liberal vote approached twenty per cent, Liberal seats stubbornly refused to move beyond the two per cent level. Many commentators outside the Liberal Party proclaimed this situation to be unfair: electoral reform became a live issue again for the first time since 1931 (Finer, 1975; Rogaly, 1976; Hansard Society, 1976).

In the U.S.A. there has been no major third party which has suffered from the plurality voting system in the way that the Liberals have in Britain. Hence, there has been no equivalent attack there on the system of voting for representatives. American reformers are concerned with their most obvious remaining abuse, the gerrymandering described in the last chapter (Dixon, 1968; 1971; Baker, 1971; Mayhew, 1971). Thus reform movements in the two countries operate at two separate levels. In America the cause of concern is districting; in Britain the issue is the system of voting. The British movement is the more fundamental in that it deals directly with the seat-vote relationship, and hence with electoral bias as defined in the last chapter. As we shall see, geographical solutions to districting problems are unlikely to affect electoral bias greatly, since it is an inherent property of single-member constituency systems that up to half the voters *must* lose in every constituency.

This chapter treats both levels of electoral reform. In the first section, we consider reform of districting procedures and substantiate our assertions that such reform is unsatisfactory. The second section deals with the more basic questions that arise when we come to consider changing the voting system. As we might expect, it is easier to criticize the existing system than it is to find its replacement.

The Problem of Alternative Geographies

For any state or country there are literally thousands or even millions of ways in which it can be divided up to form constituencies. Whoever has the task of creating these constituencies usually begins with some smaller administrative units – wards and districts in Britain, precincts and counties in the U.S.A. – which are then added together to make constituencies. Constraints on population size or compactness merely serve to restrict the many different ways in which this can be done. However, even where such rules are strictly adhered to, there will still be many feasible solutions remaining. The districting agency has to pick one of these many feasible solutions as the set of constituencies to be used. This is the environment in which gerrymandering thrives. However, it is also the context within which other districting agencies, the British Boundary Commissioners for instance, have to operate. Unfortunately, the districting problem of plurality voting defined in the last chapter operates whether gerrymanderers are at work or not. This is what makes reform of the districting procedure seem to be so simple in theory yet so difficult in practice.

Non-partisan solutions in theory: the three monkeys policy

Given the partisan gerrymandering described in the last chapter, the most obvious path to reform is to take the task of drawing constituency boundaries out of political hands. This non-partisan solution to the districting problem was developed as part of the British reform of distribution, in the form of neutral Boundary Commissioners. In the last chapter we described the role of Boundary Commissioners in terms of their treatment of malapportionment. Another vital characteristic of their work is that they are formally non-political. Their rules preclude them from considering party-political factors and they operate as if political parties did not exist. Similar institutions have operated in New Zealand (Jackson, 1962) and Australia (McPhail and Walmsley, 1975) for many years and in 1964 Canada adopted this solution to the districting problem (Ward, 1967). This leaves the U.S.A., the home of gerrymandering, as the final country using a plurality voting system which does not normally have neutral districting agencies. However, there has been pressure to make districting into a non-partisan activity in the U.S.A. and this has been associated mainly with attempts to use computers to devise electoral districts. This reform campaign started in the early 1960s and ran parallel to the reapportionment revolution but without any of the latter's success.

The case for non-partisan districting was forcefully put by Vickrey (1961) in a paper ambitiously entitled 'On the prevention of gerrymandering'. His position was quite straightforward: the elimination of gerrymandering would seem to require the establishment of an automatic and impersonal procedure for carrying out a redistricting. This statement summarizes the non-partisan, computer-districting school of thought. In the words of one proponent: 'Since the computer doesn't know how to gerrymander ... the electronically generated map can't be anything but unbiased' (Forrest, 1965). The best-known work in this field is that of Weaver and Hess (1963) who form part of 'a group of civic-minded engineers' known as CROND Inc. (Computer Research on Non-partisan Districting). Their approach is now widely available to other 'civic-minded' groups as a do-it-yourself manual (Weaver, 1970). The most widely used computer districting algorithm, on the other hand, is that of Littschwager (1973) although even his results have only partially been used, in one state – Iowa. In general, computer districting has made little practical headway in the U.S.A. (Nagel, 1972).

Why should this be? The most obvious answer is that political vested interests are operating against neutral solutions. While this is certainly part of the answer, it is by no means the whole story. Many ardent reformers in the U.S.A. have argued against the employment of such computer procedures (Appel, 1965; Nagel, 1965, 1972; Dixon, 1968, 1971, 1973). This is because such procedures do *not* ensure fairness to the parties involved. They may be non-political in procedure, but they cannot fail to be political in their effects. Not to recognize this point is to fail to understand the essence of the districting problem. It involves, in Dixon's terms, the *myth of a non-partisan cartography* (Dixon, 1968; Taylor, 1973; Taylor and Gudgin, 1976a).

A simple example will clarify this argument. Consider Figure 8.1 where figures refer to votes for the two parties, A and B. Four wards have to be combined into two constituencies. If we maintain contiguous pairs of wards for solutions, then there are only two possible sets of constituencies. If a north/south division is made (Figure 8.1) then the majority party (A) wins both con-

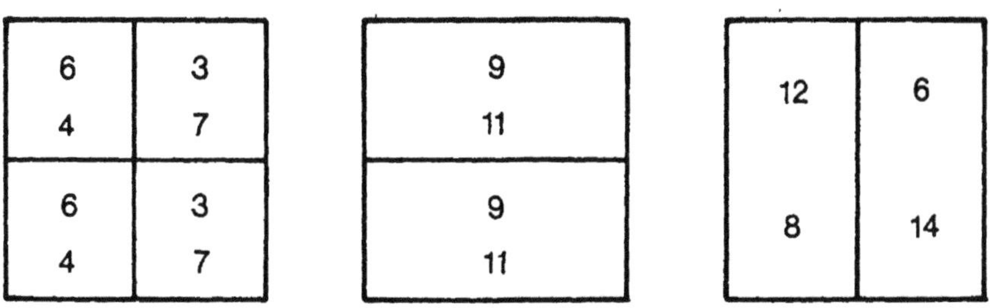

Figure 8.1 The districting problem (vote for A is the lower figure)

stituencies, that is 100 per cent of the seats with only 55 per cent of the vote. This massive electoral bias of 45 per cent for party A is the sort of result we might expect if Party A had gerrymandered the districting. If an east/west division is made (Figure 8.1), on the other hand, both parties win one seat each. In this case, party B wins 50 per cent of the representation with only 45 per cent of the vote, and so receives an electoral-bias bonus of +5%. The point is that *both* solutions lead to bias. If a computer arbitrarily chooses between them it *must* produce a bias. In fact there is a fifty-fifty chance that it will generate the *same* solution as the gerrymanderers and hence produce a massive electoral bias of 45 per cent. Using a computer to select a solution does not overcome the political effects of the plurality voting system. If the computer did choose the north/south solution then it would seem to be of little comfort for the party B candidates that the computer had no political bias against them. Neutral *intentions* are all well and good, but it is the political *effects* – the electoral outcomes – which ultimately matter. Hence, the failure of the non-partisan, computer-districting lobby in the U.S.A. is due in no small measure to a recognition of the paucity of their theory.

There is one very well-known example of a non-partisan solution being employed in the U.S.A. After the 1970 census the state of Washington's legislature could not agree on a districting plan so the Federal District Court there intervened to break the deadlock. The court appointed a geographer, Richard Morrill, as 'master' to carry out the task. He had just one month to do the work and so had no time to develop a computer solution. Hence the districting was 'by hand' in the manner of the British Boundary Commissioners. Some of the rules imposed upon him were also reminiscent of the British situation – he was instructed not to consider any electoral data on voting or to have contacts with party officials. He was simply required to divide up Washington into a set of approximately equal-population districts having no regard to the political effects of his actions.

Morrill (1973) has described this interesting task in some detail. After he presented his plans to the court and had them accepted, he was able to employ voting data to show that his solution was a fair one in the sense that it represents a compromise between the rival Republican and Democrat proposed plans. This equitable political effect is, of course, a pure chance result since the districting was carried out without any consideration of electoral outcomes. Given the rules under which Morrill operated, there is no reason why such a 'fair' solution should be any more likely than a pro-Republican or pro-Democrat plan.

Morrill (1976) has subsequently replicated his work for the court with the use of a computer. He claims to be able to produce 'better solutions' with this electronic aid. Unfortunately, his criteria remain non-partisan so that 'better' largely refers to compactness in the shape of districts, not to the relationship between seats and votes. He maintains an implicit theory that says that a satisfactory electoral districting solution can be obtained without any consideration of electoral outcomes. This theory is widely held outside the U.S.A., as we have seen, but has come in for very strong criticism among American political scientists. They argue that ignoring political effects does not overcome the districting problem. Nagel (1965) suggests that such districting is 'only non-partisan in the sense that it is unpredictable as to which party it will favour'. Dixon (1968) prefers the term 'innocently partisan' and has been particularly scathing in his attack, calling it 'the three monkeys policy – speak no politics, see no politics, hear no politics' (Dixon, 1971). There may be no electoral abuse in the sense of intention to discriminate, but there are electoral biases which do discriminate.

Non-partisan districting in practice: geographical bases of electoral bias

The arguments for non-partisan, computer districting in the U.S.A. and for neutral boundary commissioners elsewhere are all based upon the same theory which we have discredited above. They are different in one important respect, however. In terms of practical applications non-partisan solutions are extremely rare in the U.S.A.; outside the U.S.A. they are overwhelmingly the norm. Hence, in order to illustrate the myth of a non-partisan cartography we must study elections where this reform operates. In the discussion below, we consider electoral biases in British elections.

If non-partisan cartography is a myth, what are the biases which occur? Three main types of electoral bias have been documented and are well known. First there is the 'winner's bias'. Usually, the party that wins most votes wins more than its proportional share of the seats. This is often thought to be a good thing, since it generally leads to stable one-party government. In Britain since 1945, for instance, no party has ever received an overall majority of the votes but only one election has failed to produce a party with a parliamentary majority of seats. Second, there is the bias against small parties. Very often parties such as the Liberals in Britain and Social Credit in New Zealand win very few seats in relation to the votes they receive. Finally, there is an anti-concentration bias that often results from non-partisan districting. Labour parties in Britain, New Zealand and Australia (and Communists in France) have often tended to do less well than their right-wing opponents for similar levels of the overall vote because their votes are more concentrated in constituencies. We will consider each type of bias in turn.

1. *Winner's bias*

In our discussion of non-partisan districting above, we considered just one simple example involving drawing only two constituencies. If we expand our consideration into many constituencies in the manner of real elections we find that certain features of the results become quite predictable. This can be shown by returning to the constituency vote-proportion distributions described in Chapter 3. These are arrays of constituency frequencies for different levels of party vote (Figure 3.9 p. 149). We will begin by considering only the case of two main parties whose support is fairly well mixed across the country as shown in Figure 3.9(c). Kendall and Stuart (1950) have shown that in this voting situation, arbitrarily placed constituency boundaries will result in what is technically called a 'normal' distribution of the percentage vote for any one party. Such a distribution has more central frequencies near the mean than away from that point, and is often described as 'bell-shaped'. An example is shown in Figure 8.2(a). With just the votes and seats of the two main parties being considered, the constituencies that are won lie to the right of the 50 per cent vote line.

In Figure 8.2(a) the party wins half of the two-party vote and,

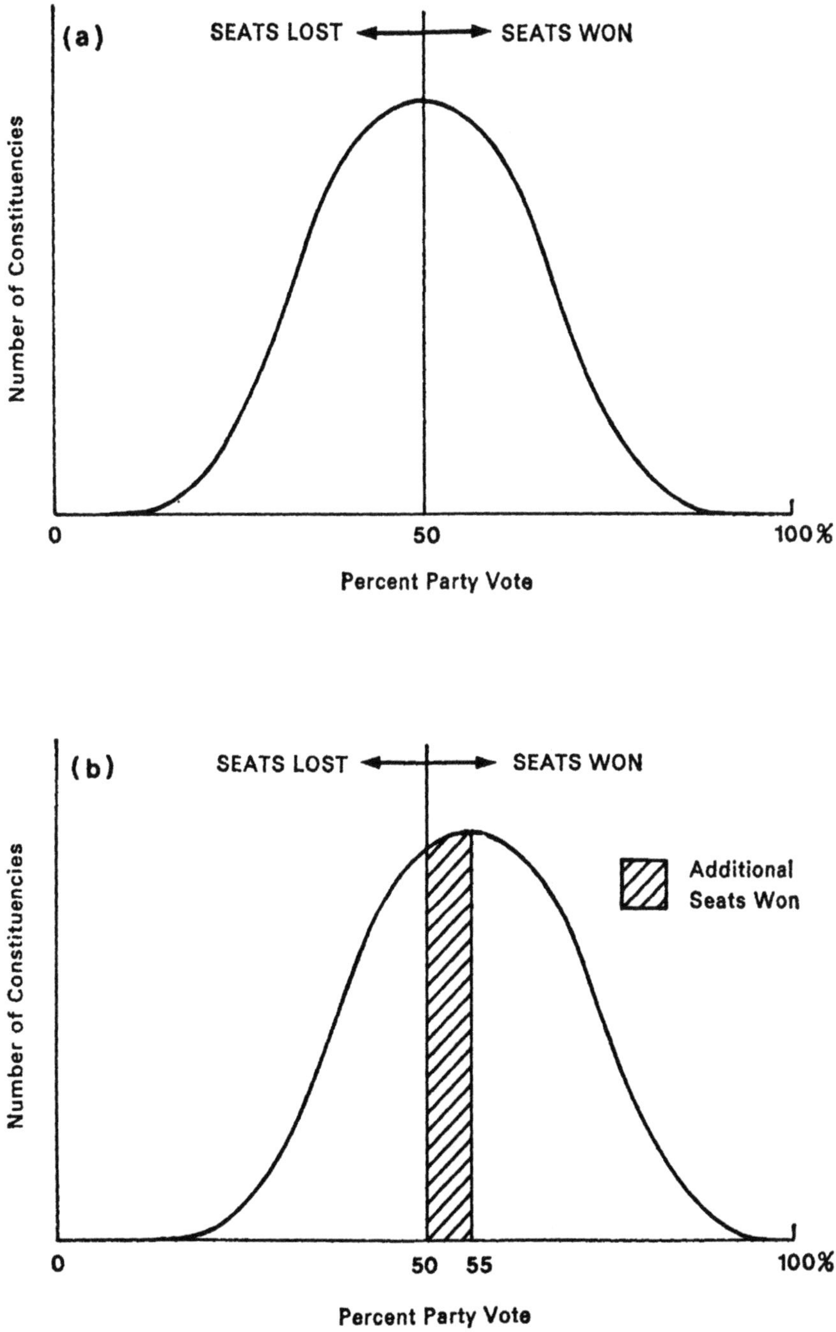

Figure 8.2 Producing a winner's bias: non-partisan solutions

because the normal distribution is symmetrical, it also wins exactly half the seats. Let us consider what happens if there is an even swing of 5 per cent to the party across all constituencies – that is to say, that party's vote proportion increases by 5 per cent of the two-party vote in every constituency. This results in the normal distribution being moved along the vote axis by 5 percentage points – Figure 8.2(b). Notice that because the normal distribution is bell-shaped, more than 5 per cent of the constituencies cross the 50 per cent vote line. Therefore the 5 per cent swing in votes leads to a gain of more than 5 per cent of the seats. The additional seats above 5 per cent are the bonus for this winning party.

The size of this bonus, or winner's bias, depends on the shape of the normal distribution, in particular its 'spread' around the mean. This is measured by the distribution's standard deviation. If the normal distribution is squeezed together, the standard deviation is small and the winner's bias is large. This is because there are very many marginal constituencies to change hands with a small swing of the vote. Alternatively a 'wide' distribution with a large standard deviation produces a relatively small winner's bias because of fewer marginal constituencies (Gudgin and Taylor, 1974).

In modern elections in Britain and New Zealand, and in earlier elections in the U.S.A., this winner's bias has been described by the, so-called, cubic law of proportions. This simply says that the seat odds will be the cube of the vote odds:

$$\frac{S_A}{S_B} = \left(\frac{V_A}{V_B}\right)^3$$

where S_A and V_A are the proportions of seats and votes for party A and S_B and V_B are the proportions for party B. Hence, a party that receives two-thirds of the two-party vote will win $\left(\frac{2}{1}\right)^3$ of the seats giving an 8:1 proportion. This means that the cube law predicts 89 per cent of the seats for a party that obtains 67 per cent of the vote; a winner's bias of 22 per cent! Of course most elections are much closer than 2:1 odds and the winner's bias is correspondingly less extreme.

This cube law has worked fairly well for translating votes into seats in Britain and New Zealand. It is based on the fact that the parties in these two countries have proportion distributions that are approximately normal and with a standard deviation of about 14 per cent. In fact the cube law is an easy way of working out the winner's bias that accrues from the operation of a normal distribution as described previously. However, it relies upon the spread of the distribution being a certain size. With a standard deviation much larger or smaller than 14 per cent the cube law will not operate. This is one of the reasons why the cube law does not apply to most American elections, where, as we shall see, standard deviations are much higher than 14 per cent.

The spread of the normal distribution depends on the interaction between the pattern of constituencies and the underlying mosaic of a voting pattern, as we showed in Chapter 3. Since this voting pattern reflects the socio-economic bases of the voting, it follows that the winner's bias is itself a product of the underlying cleavage structure. The cube law operates best in two countries where simple class-based parties compete for power. This suggests that the spatial pattern of social classes, underlying the voting, produces just the right spread of a normal distribution of constituency vote proportions to generate cube-law type biases (Gudgin and Taylor, 1978).

Alternative bases for voting will produce different spatial patterns of voting and hence different levels of bias. This can be illustrated by contrasting the British elections of 1906 and 1970 (Figure 8.3.). The latter reflects the modern class cleavage and produces a standard deviation of 14·6 per cent. In 1906 the Conservative–Liberal clash was not so much based upon a class cleavage and the distribution is accordingly very different. This much narrower distribution has a standard deviation of only 8·9 per cent. The result of this latter election was a landslide Liberal victory, which was not so much due to a massive lead in terms of votes, but rather reflected the nature of the distribution. In fact, the elections between 1885 and 1910 were typified by landslides.

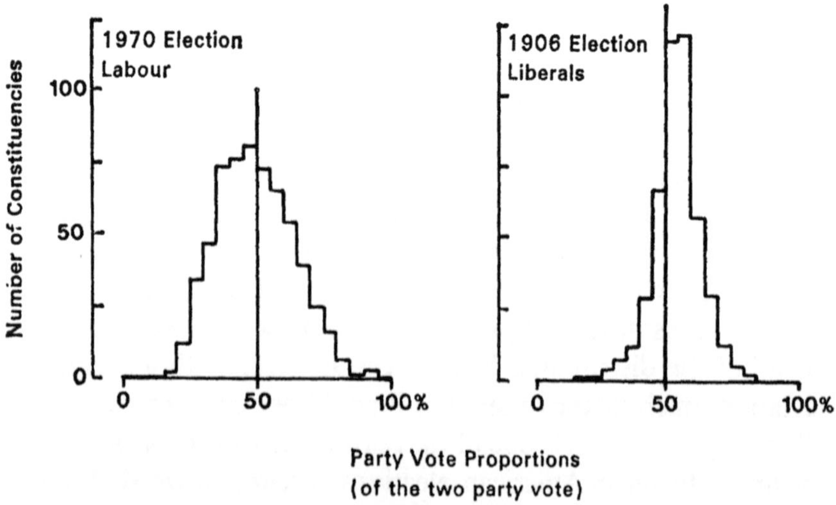

Figure 8.3 Constituency frequency distributions for two major parties

A small swing in votes inevitably led to many seats changing hands and so large winners' biases. Modern British elections based on the class cleavage are much more stable affairs, as illustrated by the 1970 distribution. In fact, we can treat the standard deviation as a simple measure of the stability of an electoral system which itself will reflect the underlying voting cleavage.

2. *Minor party bias*

So far, we have only considered the two main parties in a plurality election. When we come to consider other parties, further electoral biases come to light. The Liberals in Britain may have benefitted from a massive winner's bias in 1906 but they have suffered continuous biases since they became Britain's third party in the 1920s. Such suffering occurs simply because they are a small party with a fairly evenly spread pattern of support. Their constituency proportion distribution usually remains below the winning threshold, so that the vast majority of their votes are wasted. Nobody has ever suggested that the Boundary Commissioners are anti-Liberal in their intentions, but it is this party which typically suffers most from the effects of their work. The

Liberal vote is divided up and split among many constituencies so that it becomes a winning majority in very few.

The Boundary Commissions have little option in their treatment of the Liberals, whose votes are, quite literally, in the wrong places. For a minor party to win seats it must not have a nation-wide pattern of support but, rather, must have regional concentrations of strength. In this way it cuts down on wasted votes and wins more seats. Hence, 'regional' minor parties do much better than nation-wide minor parties. This is true with the current success of the Nationalists in Scotland and Wales, who win far fewer votes than the Liberals but currently have more seats in parliament. Similarly, minor parties have fared far better in the plurality voting system of Canada, almost solely because of the regional nature of electoral politics in that country (Blake, 1967). However, the best contrast lies between the Irish Nationalists

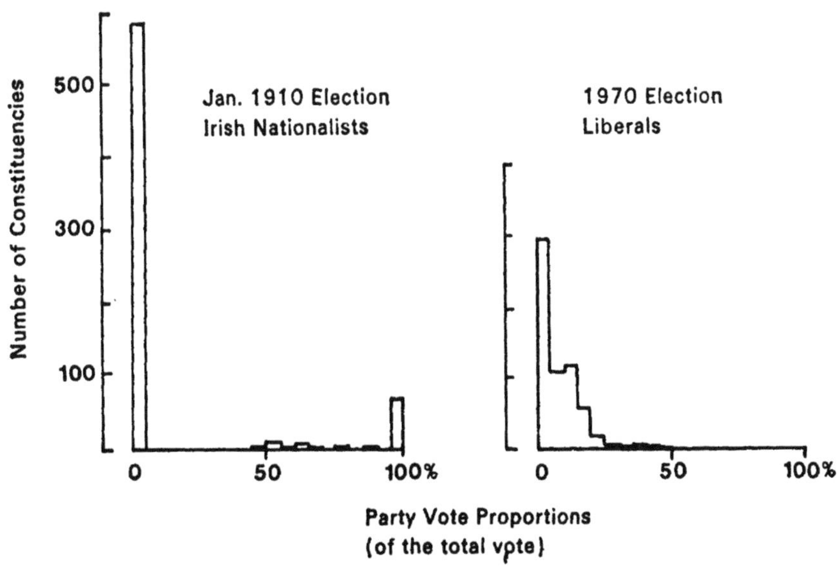

Figure 8.4 Constituency frequency distributions for two minor parties

before 1920 and the modern Liberals. Their distributions are shown in Figure 8.4. Notice that the Liberals in 1970 won a higher proportion of votes, but the Irish Nationalists in 1910 won far more seats. Irish Nationalist strength lay in the geography of its support; conversely Liberal weakness today lies in its contrasting geography of votes.

If single-member constituency systems favour regionally-based parties at the expense of nation-wide parties then we are left with something of a paradox. In order to get a reasonable foothold in parliament, a new minor party needs a regional base. By appealing to regional interests, however, it is not certain that such a party may ever attain national support and hence become a major party. Even in Canada, where minor parties have had numerous state successes, the Liberals and Progressive Conservatives have maintained control of the Federal government with no serious threats from other parties. Clearly the transition from minor to major party would seem to be a very difficult one. One party that has achieved this changeover has been the British Labour Party and we will consider its electoral history in some detail.

3. *Anti-concentration bias*

The British Labour Party was formed in 1900 and relied upon Liberal party support in its early contests (Pelling, 1961). It soon won seats in coalfield areas and this gave it a 'regional base' of about 40 seats in parliament, from which core of support it tried to break out in 1918. Its number of seats rose only slightly to 60 but by the 1922 election it was the second largest party and in 1923 it was able to form its first government. This spectacular success was based on transforming its geography of votes from a concentrated coalfield pattern to a nation-wide mosaic of industrial working-class zones. As its vote rose, however, the Labour party's original cores on the coalfields became veritable strongholds and remain with the party today as the safest seats in Britain.

Strangely, the original advantage of the coalfield support in winning a foothold in parliament is now a disadvantage in terms of wasted votes. As a major party, Labour does not require these extra votes where it wins so easily. All of these additional votes produce no extra seats, and hence are as wasted as Liberal votes in lost seats. Quite simply, many Labour votes are in the wrong place; if they were more evenly spread they would produce more Labour seats. It is this relative concentration of support which leads to the post-1945 bias against Labour, whose constituency proportion distribution for 1970 clearly shows this effect (Figure 8.3). The distribution is positive skewed, that is to say it 'leans' to the left and has a larger 'tail' to the right. This tail includes the safe mining seats where Labour support is wasted. The result is that Labour tends to suffer special electoral bias based on its geographical pattern of support. For the 1950 and 1951 elections Butler (1952) estimated the bias to be about two per cent, or worth half a million votes to the Conservatives, and it was the cause of Labour losing the 1951 election, even though they obtained more votes than the Conservatives. Taylor and Gudgin (1976a) have found the same effect for 1955 and 1970. In the 1974 election the situation became somewhat confused, as some Labour voters seem to have 'tactically' voted Liberal (Steed, 1974) so that the effect is counter-acted to some degree. However, it should be seen as a general problem for all left-wing parties in single-member constituency systems. Rydon (1957) notes its occurrence in New Zealand and Australia and this has more recently been documented by Taylor and Gudgin (1977, but see Johnston, 1976g); Criddle (1973) describes the same bias for French elections.

It would seem that concentration of support is a prerequisite for initial success for a party, but thereafter becomes a handicap. At first, its supporters are in the right place; subsequently, they are less well placed. This is a relatively subtle distortion of the geography of representation by the geography of voting. The argument can be summarized as a schematic diagram. Figure 8.5(a) shows a developmental model in four stages as the party moves from minor to major party status. Figure 8.5(b) shows how the British Labour Party fits this model. From 1945 to 1970 the party obtained less seats than the cube law predicts. This is because its distribution is not perfectly normal. Instead it is skewed, as we have seen, and the difference between these predictions and the actual results is the resulting bias it suffers (Gudgin and Taylor, 1974). Hence, even as a winning party it

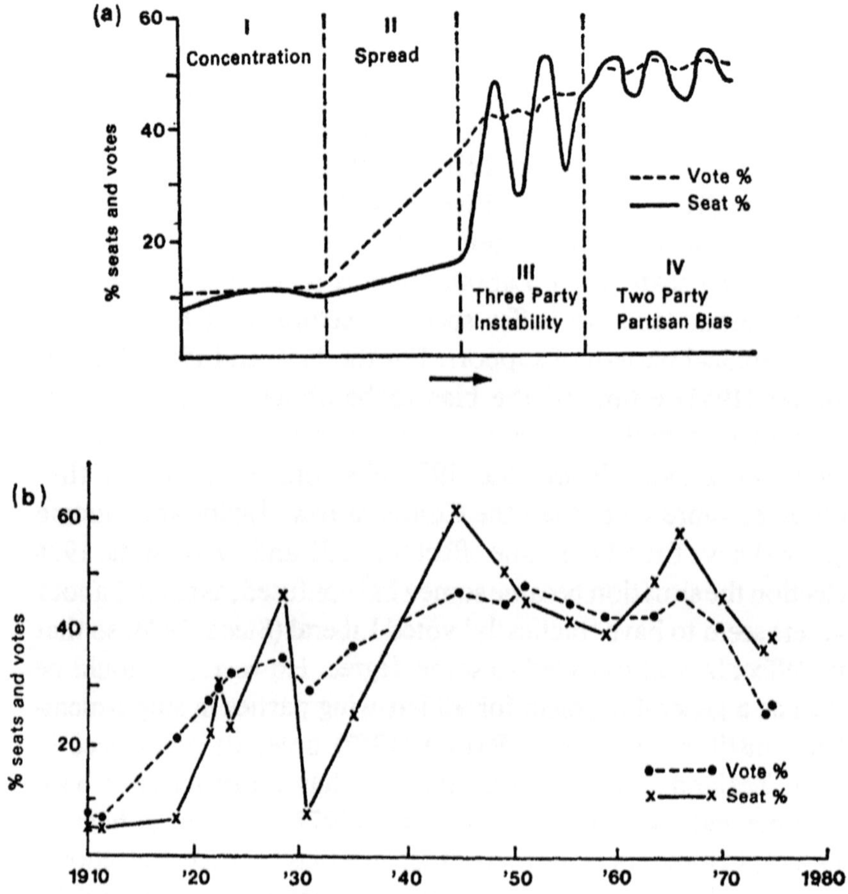

Figure 8.5 A developmental model of party support and biases

tends to obtain less of a bonus than the Conservatives would win. The one exception is 1970, when Labour gained a counter-balancing bias due to the level of malapportionment which favoured it, as we described in the last chapter.

Britain clearly has a long experience of electoral bias to set alongside its tradition of neutral boundary drawing. Hence, although the non-partisan approach may preclude intentional abuses, it certainly does not eradicate electoral bias *per se*. This situation has been recognized by American opponents of the non-partisan school who have continued the search for a satisfactory procedural reform of the constituency boundary problem.

Bi-partisan solutions in theory: recognizing politics

Partisan and non-partisan approaches to districting problems seem to imply a simple, exclusive dichotomy. In fact this is not the case, and there is a third approach. In Morrill's work on Washington he argues that his solution is fair to both parties and assumes that this is highly desirable. If this argument is accepted, then it leads us to suggest that just such a desirable solution should be the *aim* of the districting procedure. Such an aim transcends the non-partisan approach, since it requires consideration of electoral outcomes. Hence, voting data have to be used, not for partisan advantage, but to ensure fairness to both parties. This can only be achieved by explicitly considering the political effects of any districting proposal so that the 'fairest' may be finally chosen. In the American context such an approach has come to be known as bi-partisan districting.

The idea of requiring that a set of constituencies should be fair to all parties concerned is not a new one. It has sporadically occurred in the discussion of the tasks of boundary commissions. Their neutral stance does not necessarily imply a naive non-partisan approach. In Britain, for instance, the commissioners of 1885 had rules allowing them to divide up cities along class lines with known political effects (Pelling, 1967). More recently, it has been suggested that the New Zealand boundary commissioners should consider voting data so that they can ensure fairness to both main parties (Scott, 1955). This 'gerrymandering for democracy', as Scott terms it, was most fully developed in some of the attempts to transfer the Westminster model of parliamentary democracy to parts of the British Empire in the 1950s prior to decolonization (Mackenzie, 1957, 1958). In order to guarantee representation of ethnic-minority groups in plural societies, the colonial boundary commissioners were sometimes required to 'gerrymander in reverse'. For instance, one districting criterion in Mauritius was that 'each main section of the population of Mauritius shall have adequate opportunity to secure representation in the Legislative Council corresponding to its own number in the community as a whole' (Smith, 1960, p. 14). Other such 'gerrymandering' has occurred in Ceylon (Tinkler, 1956) and Malaya (Laponce, 1957) to ensure adequate Tamil and Chinese representation respectively. Clearly, these are cases where the nature of the ethnically plural societies has meant that a bi-partisan approach has been necessary in order to make the plurality voting system acceptable. Obviously electoral biases in terms of ethnic groups involve more serious problems of an integrative nature than mere bias against established political parties and they have thus been explicitly eliminated by British colonial boundary commissions. These examples have now passed into history. Today it is in America that the bi-partisan approach is most consistently argued for in theory and, it seems, adopted in practice.

Bi-partisan districting, like its non-partisan competitor, has come to the fore in the American districting debate by way of a computer-based proposal. In 1965 Stuart Nagel outlined a bi-partisan computer districting approach which explicitly involves feeding in voting data so that the political effects of any plan can be assessed. The criteria for choosing the desired plan can be specified in political terms and the computer should produce the solution which will have the required result. Hence, the solution which comes closest to giving parties seats in proportion to their votes can be found using Nagel's computer program (Nagel, 1965; Taylor, 1973).

One particular feature of Nagel's computer approach is that it disturbs existing constituencies very little. This is because all new plans that are generated are based upon modification of the existing plan of constituencies. This is important in the American context because it results in minimum disruption of local party organization and incumbents (Nagel, 1972). This is all part of Nagel's explicit recognition of the political sensitivity of the districting problem. As he points out in his criticism of the non-partisan approach, it is wholly unreasonable to expect politicians to accept having their political careers cut short at the arbitrary whim of a computer. Nagel's solution is for the computer districting to work with the politicians in a bi-partisan manner.

Dixon (1968, 1971, 1973) has followed Nagel's lead in favouring a bi-partisan approach although he is not particularly concerned with the use of computers. He argues that the job can quite easily be done by a bi-partisan commission on which both parties are represented. These can negotiate a final solution acceptable to both parties and hence avoid narrow partisan districting and 'blind' non-partisan districting. Dixon considers that such a districting agency would be forced to consider the political realities of their task and we would be able to presume that their solutions would incorporate 'representative fairness'. This overcomes the problem of proof in gerrymander cases discussed at the end of the last chapter. Gerrymandering is difficult to prove in court and so the problem is avoided by making partisan districting virtually impossible in the first place. Hence there will be no need for court intervention. Dixon (1971) notes, with approval, that since 1966 several states have set up bi-partisan commissions to redistrict.

The bi-partisan approach has recently gained the approval of the U.S. courts. Knight (1976) notes that since 1973 the equal population criterion of the courts has been relaxed when population deviations can be justified. In *Gaffney v. Cummings* and *White v. Regester*, concerning state legislature districts in Connecticut and Texas, population variations of 7·9 and 9·9 per cent were held to be 'insignificant'. In fact the court developed the concept of 'political fairness' as a key consideration, so that these population deviations were accepted 'as necessary to achieve political fairness' (Knight, 1976, p. 157). Hence, the court is taking political outcomes into account in its evaluation of a districting plan. This retreat from the simple numerical basis of court decisions described in the last chapter represents a victory for the bi-partisan school of thought with its explicit political concern.

It should be emphasized at this stage of the argument that a bi-partisan approach to districting is not new to the American political scene. In fact this approach has commonly occurred where there has been a legislative stalemate in a state (Mayhew, 1971). For instance, one party may control the legislature while the state governor is of the other party, or else the two houses of the legislature may be split between the parties. Since neither party can get its plan accepted, a stalemate ensues. One way out of this situation is for the courts to supervise the redistricting, as in Washington in 1971 (Morrill, 1973). However, politicians are usually suspicious of such arbitrary solutions and have generally preferred to come to some compromise amongst themselves. Hence, bi-partisan solutions are produced even where there is no formally instituted bi-partisan commission for the task. We can therefore study the bi-partisan approach in practice in the U.S.A. where it has operated alongside the partisan districting described in the last chapter.

Bi-partisan districting in practice, or devaluing the vote

Mayhew (1971) identifies the bi-partisan approach we have just described as a form of gerrymandering: he uses the term 'bi-partisan gerrymandering'. This may seem strange, since our discussion of this approach has made frequent reference to fairness and we have even mentioned the notion of 'gerrymandering for democracy'. However, Mayhew uses the term bi-partisan gerrymandering to mean an electoral abuse as we have defined it in the last chapter. He identifies an intentional manipulation of the districting by one group for their own ends. In this case the groups abusing the electoral situation are not the parties acting separately but the politicians of both parties acting together. Bi-partisan districting in practice has meant the creation of more safe seats for incumbents of both parties.

Let us consider what this means in terms of the constituency vote proportion distribution. Figure 8.6(a) shows a bi-modal distribution which is the expected outcome of bi-partisan gerrymandering. The 'hump' on the left defines constituencies which the opposing party win easily; the hump on the right is the safe seats for the party being portrayed. With a small swing of 5 per cent as in Figure 8.2, the distribution produces far fewer additional seats for the winning party (Figure 8.6(b)). Hence there may well be no winner's bias at all. In any case the main effect of the swing is to produce only a few defeats for incumbents.

These predicted effects of the bi-partisan approach can be

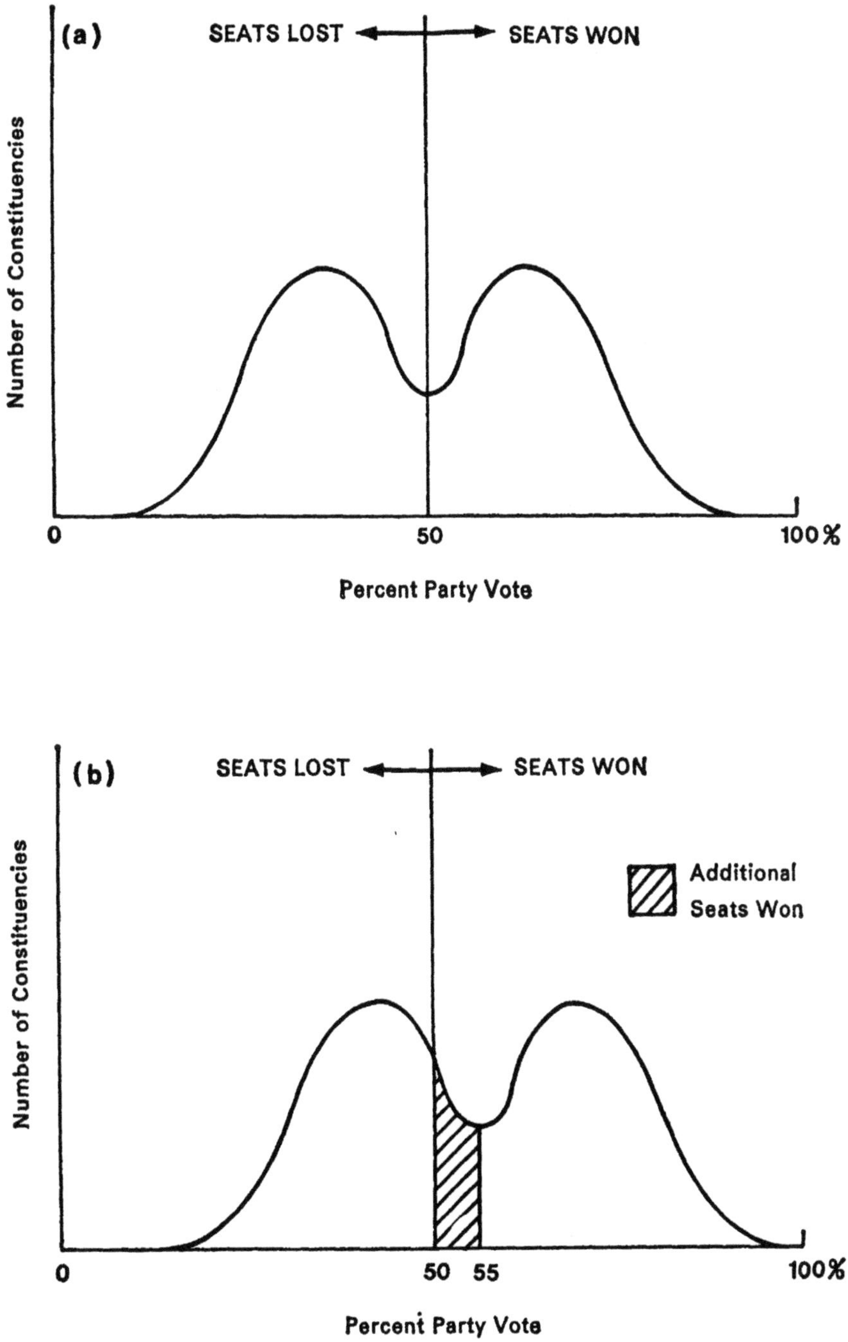

Figure 8.6 Protecting the losers: bi-partisan solutions

clearly seen in the changing frequency distribution of congressional districts. Kendall and Stuart (1950) found that in 1944 the American districts formed a normal distribution with a standard deviation of 13 per cent if the ten southern states are omitted from consideration. In effect they are dividing America into two regions of contrasting political cleavages. Outside the south the U.S.A. seemed to conform to the type of frequency distribution of constituencies reported above for Britain. However, since 1944 the situation has changed markedly. Tufte (1973) has shown that the distribution was still normal in shape in 1948 but by the 'sixties it was being transformed into a bi-modal pattern. In the wake of the increasing redistricting precipitated by the reapportionment revolution, Tufte found two basic types of district – safe Republican and safe Democrat, with very few marginal seats (Noragon, 1973). This distinct divergence from normality directly implies manipulation of constituency boundaries – in this case for bi-partisan ends (Gudgin and Taylor, 1978; for an alternative interpretation see, for example, Ferejohn, 1977). Politicians are saving themselves from the capricious whims of the voters!

A simple example will clarify the situation. In 1974 the fortunes of the Republican party were at a very low ebb. The Watergate scandal had led to expectations of massive losses in the congressional elections in November. From the Democratic point of view it was important for them to win two-thirds of the seats to enable them to override the presidential veto. Such a massive win seemed to be a possibility. However, the optimism did not take into account the bi-partisan districting that had been going on around the country. The expected swing in votes to the Democrats occurred but they failed to win two-thirds of the seats. The reason can be seen in Figure 8.7. The bi-modal distribution of largely safe seats meant that many seats stayed in Republican hands and a massive landslide was avoided. Hence the geography or spatial organization of the election ameliorated the electoral effects of Watergate and saved the Republicans from an even more humiliating defeat.

The effect of a bi-partisan approach is now clear – it lessens the influence of the voters on the outcome of the election. In Britain,

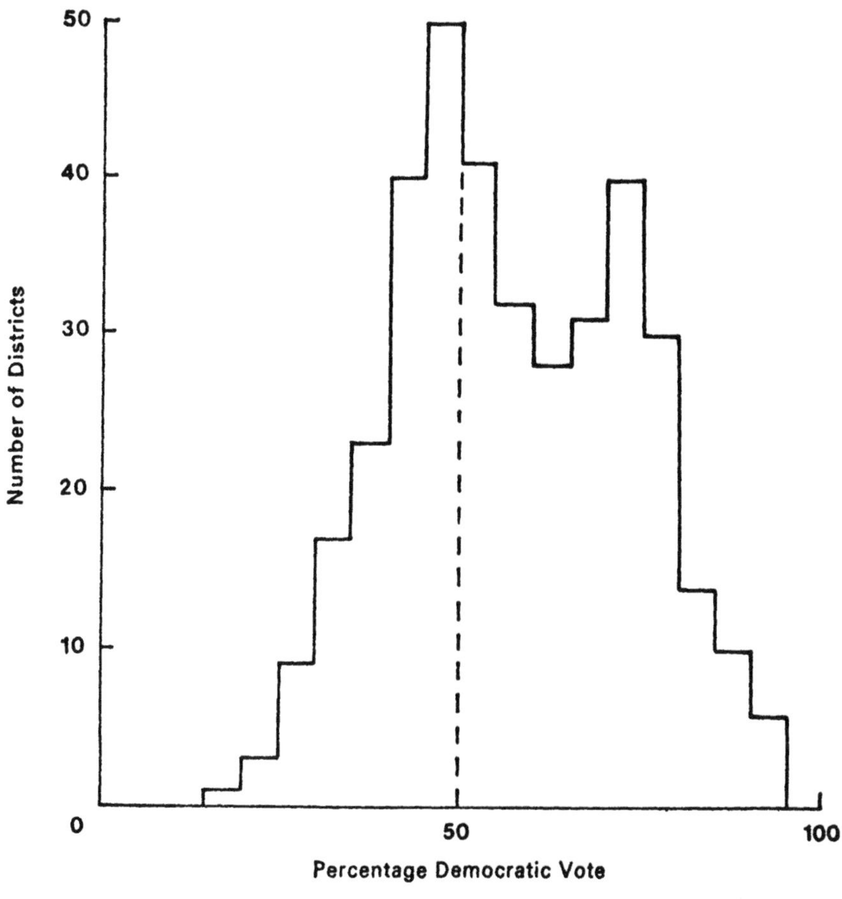

Figure 8.7 Congressional district frequency distribution, U.S.A., 1974

with its non-partisan approach, we identified a winner's bias. In this case a party receiving a one per cent increase in votes wins approximately three per cent more seats. In America the situation is now reversed so that there is no bonus for winners at all – a one per cent increase in the vote is reflected in only about 0·8 per cent increase in seats (Tufte, 1973). More safe seats and hence long political careers may be a satisfactory solution for politicians, but it clearly raises new problems. The ordinary voter's power is diminished, since the number of marginal seats where his vote may count is decreased. In the bi-partisan approach one interested group is omitted from the negotiations – the voters themselves. It seems that all approaches to the districting problem are unsatisfactory in one way or another!

A simple theory of the geography of representation

In the final part of this section we will attempt to combine the three approaches – partisan, non-partisan and bi-partisan – into a single overall framework. This will enable us to see them together as they interrelate.

The districting problem has been defined as one involving many alternative solutions. Such problems are usually best tackled through a statistical perspective. Such a statistical basis merely involves investigating all possible solutions, or a large sample thereof, so that actual solutions can be viewed in the context of all possible outcomes. The particular influences on the actual solutions, such as we have enumerated above, should be reflected in the relationship between a specific, chosen solution and all other solutions (Pulsipher, 1973).

A simple example will clarify this argument. Suppose we have a city with eight wards which are to be grouped into two sets of four to form two constituencies. Even with such a comparatively small problem there are, none the less, 35 different ways in which the wards can be combined. All possible solutions to such a problem are listed in Table 8.1. We have assumed typical ward votes for party A ranging from 31 to 89 per cent, as indicated, and Table 8.1 shows the percentage of the votes gained by each party in each combination of wards (each ward has the same number of voters). These ward results reflect a city-wide dominance for party A of 60 per cent of the vote to party B's 40 per cent. However, in terms of winning seats, party A's dominance seems to be much greater. Table 8.1 shows that in 31 of the 35 solutions, party A wins both seats, that is 100 per cent of the representation. Let us look at the nature of these alternative solutions; in particular, what are the characteristics of the four solutions which would lead to the more equitable result of equal representation?

In the final column of Table 8.1 we have included the standard deviation of each solution. This is a simple measure of spread of

Table 8.1 All possible combinations of eight wards into two constituencies of four wards each

Solution no.	*First constituency* *Wards*	*A's vote %*	*Second constituency* *Wards*	*A's vote %*	*Seats* *A*	*B*	*Standard deviation*
1	1234	48·0	5678	72·0	1	1	12·0
2	1235	48·5	4678	71·5	1	1	11·5
3	1236	49·5	4578	70·5	1	1	10·5
4	1237	51·5	4568	68·5	2	0	8·5
5	1238	55·5	4567	64·5	2	0	4·5
6	1245	49·5	3678	70·5	1	1	10·5
7	1246	50·5	3578	69·5	2	0	9·5
8	1247	52·5	3568	67·5	2	0	7·5
9	1248	56·5	3567	63·5	2	0	3·5
10	1256	51·0	3478	69·0	2	0	9·0
11	1257	53·0	3468	67·0	2	0	7·0
12	1258	57·0	3467	63·0	2	0	3·0
13	1267	54·0	3458	66·0	2	0	6·0
14	1268	58·0	3457	62·0	2	0	2·0
15	1278	60·0	3456	60·0	2	0	0·0
16	1345	51·5	2678	68·5	2	0	8·5
17	1346	52·5	2578	67·5	2	0	7·5
18	1347	54·5	2568	65·5	2	0	5·5
19	1348	58·5	2567	61·5	2	0	1·5
20	1356	53·0	2478	67·0	2	0	7·0
21	1357	55·0	2468	65·0	2	0	5·0
22	1358	59·0	2467	61·0	2	0	1·0
23	1367	56·0	2458	64·0	2	0	4·0
24	1368	60·0	2457	60·0	2	0	0·0
25	1378	62·0	2456	58·0	2	0	2·0
26	1456	54·0	2378	66·0	2	0	6·0
27	1457	56·0	2368	64·0	2	0	4·0
28	1458	60·0	2367	60·0	2	0	0·0
29	1467	57·0	2358	63·0	2	0	3·0
30	1468	61·0	2357	59·0	2	0	1·0
31	1478	63·0	2356	57·0	2	0	3·0
32	1567	57·5	2348	62·5	2	0	2·5
33	1568	61·5	2347	58·5	2	0	1·5
34	1578	63·5	2346	56·5	2	0	3·5
35	1678	64·5	2345	55·5	2	0	4·5

Party A's percentage of the vote by wards:
1–31%, 2–47%, 3–55%, 4–59%, 5–61%, 6–65%, 7–73%, 8–89%.

the results, as we have seen used previously with distributions of more than two results (p. 150). In this case the standard deviation is merely measuring the level of polarization of a solution – the larger the difference between the results for the two constituencies, the larger the standard deviation. From Table 8.1. we can see that the four 1–1 results are associated with the four largest standard deviations. Quite simply the minority party is favoured by the more polarized solutions, since such maps allow them to win one seat while losing very badly in the other. In contrast, the best solutions for the majority party occur when the polarization is minimized (equal results and so zero standard deviations in solutions 15, 24, and 28) so that both seats are relatively safe. Since party A has a city-wide majority it requires both districts to be as similar as possible, so that they both reflect this overall majority and hence produce 2–0 results.

The findings from this artificial example can be replicated in a real situation. The old county borough of Sunderland can be divided into two constituencies in 87 different ways, made up of 9 wards each, so that each group of 9 produces a contiguous constituency. Figure 8.8 shows all 87 possible districting solutions arrayed against their varying levels of polarization (standard deviation). In this case local government election results for wards have been used to predict the electoral outcome for each solution. The majority party in this case is Labour, which wins 58 per cent of the overall vote. As majority party we expect it to do well in most solutions and this is the case. Labour would normally win both seats, 100 per cent of Sunderland's representation, in 73 out of the 87 solutions (Taylor and Gudgin, 1976b). On only 14 occasions is there a 1–1 split and all of these are associated with the largest standard deviations.

We seem to have found a pattern relating types of solutions to electoral outcomes. We can now link it to our previous discussion of different types of districting agency. Let us begin by considering partisan districting. If we were gerrymandering for the majority party then we would presumably choose a less polarized solution. On the other hand gerrymanderers from the minority party (e.g. Republicans gerrymandering New York City) would

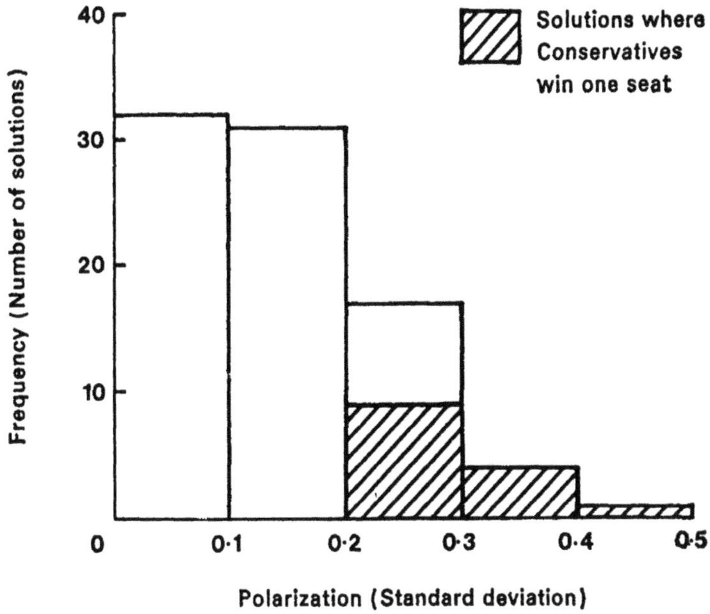

Figure 8.8 Distribution of polarization for all solutions for two Sunderland constituencies

want a highly polarized solution. Clearly these two agencies with opposite intentions would produce opposite types of solution.

What of non-partisan agencies? They will not consider the polarization since they do not take political effects into account. Their solution will display some degree of polarization, however, even if they do not choose the level. In fact we can predict that non-partisan agencies will usually choose *low* polarized results. This is simply because there are more of such solutions and since a non-partisan choice is politically arbitrary, they will tend to select the most common type of solution. Hence, we have the intriguing finding that non-partisan agencies will tend to select similar solutions to gerrymanderers for the majority party (Taylor and Gudgin, 1976b). In Sunderland, for instance, the Boundary Commission's choice is one of the 73 solutions which provide Labour with both parliamentary seats.

We are led to an interpretation of the neutral commissioners' work as being no different *in effect* from what would happen if local councils were allowed to gerrymander for the majority party throughout the country. In Sunderland the Labour-controlled council would have undoubtedly chosen a low polarized solution as the Boundary Commission did. What this means is that the Boundary Commission goes around the country devising constituencies that favour the majority party – Labour in most northern towns like Sunderland, Conservatives in southern rural counties (Taylor and Gudgin, 1975). The neutrality in intention has a very predictable political effect at the local city and county level.

Where does the bi-partisan approach fit into this scheme of things? A bi-partisan solution implies safe seats which in turn suggests high levels of polarization. These agencies will therefore tend to choose one of the rarer solutions with high standard deviations. Hence a bi-partisan agency chooses a solution similar in type to that chosen by gerrymanderers for the minority party.

Our final conclusion is summarized in Figure 8.9 – non-partisan agencies pick solutions similar to those of gerrymanderers for the majority party while, in contrast, bi-partisan agencies pick solutions like gerrymanderers for the minority party. Clearly,

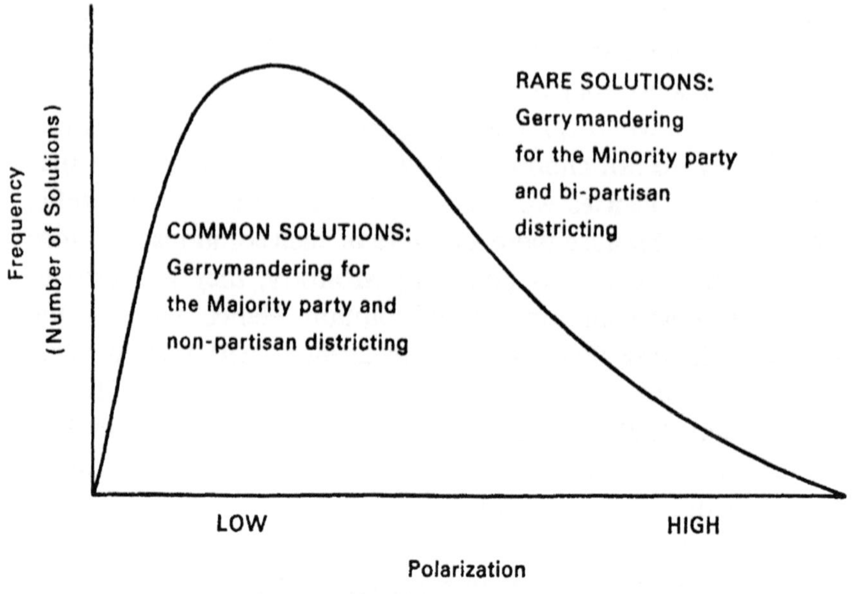

Figure 8.9 Choice of districting solution and polarization

neither type of reform of the districting procedure can be distinguished from these two modes of partisan gerrymandering in its political effects.

When we extend this theory to a situation with more than two constituencies, the relationship between polarization and party fortunes is complicated somewhat. The changes in interpretation are quite minor (Taylor and Gudgin, 1976a; Gudgin and Taylor, 1978) and one feature that remains is that one particular result is overwhelmingly the most common. For instance, Newcastle upon Tyne's 20 wards can be combined into four constituencies, comprising sets of five contiguous wards each, in 334 different ways. In this city, Labour again wins about 58 per cent of the vote; 256 of the solutions predict 3–1 wins for Labour – three-quarters of the representation. This bias towards Labour is the most common result and so we are not surprised that this is the type of solution chosen by the neutral Boundary Commissioners. It is the sort of solution we might expect Labour to gerrymander if they were able to draw the districts themselves, since they do not quite have enough votes to spread around to win all four seats with safety.

By contrast, let us consider the case of Iowa's congressional districts. After the 1970 census, Iowa was apportioned six congressmen and these had to be derived from combinations of their 99 counties (Taylor, 1973). There is a very large number of possible arrangements and we consider a sample of 700 of these alternatives. Of these 700, 556 produce 4–2 wins for the Republicans in terms of seats based upon a 'typical' 54 per cent of the vote for them. The legislature and governor were both Republican at the time of the redistricting so that they had the power to gerrymander. Although tempted to go for a 6–0 or 5–1 win (Taylor, 1973), they decided a 4–2 win was about as far as their percentage of the vote would spread to win seats. Hence, they chose a districting solution on the basis of a predicted 4–2 result, the same as the most common type of solution which we would expect to be chosen by a non-partisan districting agency. Thus, just as in the Newcastle example, the districting agency chose the most common type of solution. This is in line with our theory that asserts that non-partisan and partisan gerrymanders will tend to have the same political effect.

There is an ironic capstone to this in the Iowan example. In the post-Watergate 1974 election the swing to the Democrats *did* have a major effect in Iowa. In this case there was no bi-partisan districting so that safe seats were not produced. Hence, here, unlike many other states, there was a major transfer of seats. In the 1974 election the Democrats won five of the six congressional seats. By attempting a partisan advantage, the Iowa Republicans allowed the voters of Iowa to have a major say in the election of 1974, so that they were voted out in all but one seat. We can predict that if the legislature had been split between both parties in 1970, the resulting compromise solution with safe seats would have protected the Republicans in 1974. There seems to be a raw sort of justice in the demise of the Iowa Republicans, which illustrates nicely the unsatisfactory nature of mere districting reform.

The Problem of Alternative Electoral Systems

The fact that alternative districting solutions are an unsatisfactory answer to problems of electoral bias is very obvious in the case of British elections. It is clear that whatever rules we give to the Boundary Commissioners, there is little they can do for the Liberal Party, and yet it is this party which suffers most consistently from electoral bias. The conclusion that may be drawn from this situation is that far more fundamental electoral reform is required: instead of tinkering with boundaries we need to change the whole system of voting. This seems to be the conclusion reached by reformers in Britain (Hansard Society, 1976) and was generally accepted throughout most of the rest of Europe over half a century ago. The plurality system of voting gave way to a more proportional system in Denmark in 1856 and by 1920 Britain was the odd-man-out in Europe for its maintenance of the plurality principle (Rokkan, 1970). Even in Britain the traditional form of voting only survived because reformers could not agree on its replacement in 1918 (Butler, 1963).

Rokkan views the spread of proportional representation as part of his model of the general evolution of a state's political system. It is the final stage in a process of increasing participation of the population in the political structure of the state and is thus a 'natural' successor to suffrage reform. As noted in Chapter 3, Rokkan has traced the adoption of the P.R. List System to replace plurality voting in Norwegian local government elections as it has spread out from the core to the periphery. Interestingly, he terms parishes that retain the plurality system 'pre-political'. On this definition most of the Anglo-American political realm becomes pre-political!

The decision to replace the plurality system of voting is not necessarily as straightforward as Rokkan implies. There are several competing types of voting system as we have shown in Chapter 2 and there are further variations within each of these general types. Just as with alternative constituencies in a plurality system, alternative voting systems in general will give different election results, in terms of seats for parties, for the *same* pattern of party votes. No two countries have exactly the same system of voting so there is certainly no generally-accepted preferred system, although the list system is the general type which is most common.

Rae (1971) has shown how the relationship of the voting system to the type of party system in a country is a complex one. Many early writers associated P.R. list systems with multi-party situations and associated unstable government: Hermans (1957) has gone so far as to blame the rise of Hitler on the P.R. system used in the Weimar Republic. However Rae's very comprehensive study shows that such simple relationships are not the norm. We have only to think of the stable governments of Scandinavia under P.R. systems and the multi-party situation in Canada with a plurality electoral law to realize this. In fact, as we argued in Part II, party systems reflect the society they develop in; they certainly interact with the voting system but there is no simple pattern as suggested by many earlier writers.

Since different systems of voting give different election results it is perhaps inevitable that this property has sometimes been used for partisan ends. Hence, Rokkan's evolutionary progression which culminates in P.R. does not always occur. This is most clearly illustrated in France where the system of voting has been a perpetual electoral issue for nearly two centuries. In the last chapter we described France's 'ages of gerrymandering' which alternated with multi-member constituencies, based upon administrative units, the departments. The electoral laws of 1919, 1945, 1946 and 1951 all used list systems (Campbell, 1958). We should not assume, however, that this 'reform' was merely to improve the representative quality of the electoral system. In 1951, for instance, the motives were quite different. In this particular law France had two systems of voting, a P.R. list system for the Paris region and a complicated majority system elsewhere. This was to ensure that the parties of the centre would be fairly treated where they were weak (Paris) but would gain a winner's bias where they were strong. Campbell (1958) estimates that this law gave the centre parties an extra 97 seats, 71 of them at the expense of the Communists.

Mackenzie (1958) terms such manipulation of the system of voting *electoral engineering*. It has certainly not been confined to France. Dixon (1968) points out that New York City adopted a P.R. voting system earlier this century but abandoned it in 1945 after it had allowed Communist Party candidates to win representation for the first, and last, time in the city's history. More recently, several cities have altered their voting system in an effort to prevent large-scale black representation on their councils (Sloan, 1969). This is usually achieved by employing at-large elections whereby all representatives are elected on a city-wide vote. This means that the white majority can control all representatives. Cities which have their representatives elected by wards, on the other hand, are shown to produce fairer black representation as black voters can ensure black representatives in those areas where they are locally the majority. Thus, it would seem that alternative systems of voting, just like the alternative constituency patterns previously discussed, can form another basis for electoral abuses.

Despite these new examples of electoral abuses, it remains true that most electoral reform involving the system of voting has not been partisan in nature. Reform of voting is intimately related to the proportional representation movement both in Britain and, at an earlier date, in the U.S.A. The 1970s have seen a massive increase in the momentum of this movement in Britain, as we have previously noted. In the remainder of this section we will consider alternative voting systems for British elections. Since P.R. list systems have never seriously been advocated for Britain we will not consider their adoption here. We describe the possible effects of three systems – the alternative vote, which nearly became law in both 1918 and 1931; the single transferable vote, which has the support of the Electoral Reform Society (Lakeman, 1974) and the Liberal Party; and finally the additional member system which has recently been advocated by the Hansard Society (1976).

Maintaining the spatial organization: the alternative vote

The simplest reform of the plurality voting system is to adopt the alternative vote method, which is used to elect the Australian House of Representatives and has been described in Chapter 2. Its ease of adoption is based upon the fact that the spatial organization of elections need not be modified: the single-member constituencies and use of boundary commissions to revise them periodically can both be maintained. All that is required is to change the actual ballot paper for the voters. Instead of selecting their preferred candidate they have to extend their choice of preferences through all candidates by ranking them from first to last.

The argument for adopting the alternative vote system is based on the fact that in the usual plurality system many representatives are returned to parliament without the support of even half of the voters. Consider these two results from the October 1974 British election:

Ashfield	
D. I. Marquand (Lab.)	35,367 (63·4%)
R. N. Kemm (Con.)	12,452 (22·3%)
H. C. Flint (Lib.)	7,959 (14·3%)

Bodmin	
R. A. Hicks (Con.)	20,756 (45·5%)
R. A. Tyler (Lib.)	20,091 (44·0%)
P. C. Knight (Lab.)	4,814 (10·5%)

In the Ashfield constituency the Labour candidate had a clear majority over all other candidates and was easily elected. In the Bodmin constituency the Conservative candidate won only marginally and failed to obtain an overall majority. It is not unlikely that in Bodmin more voters would have preferred the Liberal candidate *given a straight choice* between him and the Conservative. The intervention of the Labour candidate prevented this straight fight under plurality voting and produced a minority Conservative representative for Bodmin. The advocates of the alternative vote would argue that the Conservative candidate can hardly claim to 'represent' the electors of Bodmin, since fully 54·5 per cent cast their votes against him. The alternative vote procedure attempts to overcome such minority representatives by requiring that a majority of counted preferences be required before a winner is declared.

This argument for majority representatives seems to be a very reasonable one. It does not, however, overcome any of the biases we have described previously. This is because it deals with the problem of *local* representation, whereas we have been concerned with proportionality at the overall parliamentary level. Ensuring local majorities will not necessarily reduce electoral biases. In the case of small parties, for instance, if their support is relatively evenly spread they will normally come bottom in the three-party vote and so in most cases their candidate will be eliminated. Hence, we have no reason to believe that this system should appreciably help minor parties such as the Liberals in Britain. Furthermore, there is evidence that the alternative vote can generate extra biases and so further distort the relationship between seats and votes.

Both Britain and Australia have Labour Parties as major competitors for government power. Since 1945 Labour in Britain have formed six governments from ten contested elections, whereas the Australian Labor Party (A.L.P.) have only formed three governments from contesting thirteen elections. In contrast the A.L.P. have consistently tended to receive a higher proportion of the vote than their British comrades (Taylor and Gudgin, 1977). It has been shown that A.L.P. suffer from the usual problem of Labour parties with their concentrated pattern of support; they had more very large majorities in the 1969, 1972 and 1974 elections than their competitors (McPhail and Walmsley, 1975). Gudgin and Taylor (1978) show that for 1975, A.L.P. had a skewed distribution of constituency votes typical of Labour parties. Hence, A.L.P. suffer the usual concentration bias against Labour. Their results since the war, however, suggest a further bias. This is associated with the use of the alternative vote. A.L.P. is the major sufferer in transfers of votes in the system since most minor party supporters give their second preferences to A.L.P.'s rivals. Butler (1973) notes that in eight elections up to 1972, A.L.P. only once came from behind to win a constituency when lower preferences had to be counted. By contrast, in the 1969 election alone, there were twelve cases where either Liberal or Country Party candidates were behind A.L.P. candidates on the first count, but overhauled them after the lower preferences of eliminated candidates were counted. In 1972 this occurred in fourteen cases. In an assembly of only 122 seats these failures to translate A.L.P. first-preference pluralities into seats explain why this party fares much worse than its British counterpart despite its generally greater popularity.

In Australia the alternative vote system prevents A.L.P. benefitting from a division among its opponents, but allows these opponents to make an anti-Labour alliance with their lower preferences. In the French double-ballot system, similar effects have been observed whereby an anti-Communist alliance can sometimes be found in the second-ballot votes (Criddle, 1973). These examples suggest that if this type of voting system were employed in Britain we might expect the Labour party to suffer. The situation is not that simple, however. We can never know whether this effect would occur, without a real alternative vote election in Britain. Nonetheless, we can attempt to simulate such an election by employing actual results for first preferences and using various assumptions about what the lower preferences would be. When this has been carried out no anti-Labour bias occurs. Let us briefly consider one such simulation.

Berrington (1975) used the October 1974 election results as indicating the pattern of first preferences in a hypothetical, alternative vote election. For all constituencies where there was no majority candidate, he assumed that lower preferences would be determined as follows:

(1) 80 per cent of Liberals give their second preferences to Nationalists and vice versa, in Scotland and Wales.

(2) 80 per cent of both Labour and Conservative voters give their second preferences to Liberal candidates, or 40 per cent each to Liberal and Nationalist in Scotland and Wales.

(3) Both Liberals and Nationalists split their lower choices evenly between Labour and Conservatives.

If these preferences are distributed among candidates in constituencies without a majority candidate, then we can predict results for an alternative-vote election. Table 8.2 shows this procedure in

Table 8.2 An alternative vote simulation for Bodmin constituency

First count:	
Conservative	20,756
Liberal	20,091
Labour	4,814
The Labour candidate is eliminated and second preferences are distributed: 3851 (80%) Liberal, 963 (20%) Conservative.	
Second count:	
Conservative	21,719
Liberal	23,942
The Liberal candidate is elected.	

operation for Bodmin. On this basis Berrington predicts that, overall, Labour would lose 28 seats and Conservatives 53, whereas Liberals would gain 41 and Nationalists 38. This would obviously involve a major change in the balance of power in parliament.

One interesting feature of Berrington's results is that the Conservatives lose more seats than Labour. Berrington carried out three other analyses with slightly changed assumptions and produced a similar anti-Conservative effect. Steed's (1975a) simulations, using the February 1974 election results, again predict that the Conservatives fare worse than Labour under an alternative vote system. This, of course, is the opposite of the Australian situation. It occurs because minor parties come second in constituencies currently held by the Conservatives far more often than in Labour-held constituencies. These are largely Conservative constituencies in the south of England such as Bodmin. Using the above assumptions on lower preferences, it is in these constituencies where the Liberals are able to overhaul the Conservative candidates on the basis of Labour second preferences, as illustrated in Table 8.2. Hence we have the peculiar situation that Labour fare better than the Conservatives because they come *third* in more constituencies. In these constituencies their candidate is eliminated and their second choices counted to the advantage of the Liberals. Because the Conservatives come third in far fewer constituencies, their candidates are not eliminated so that their second choices are counted on far fewer occasions. Hence, the alternative vote system penalizes the Conservatives for not doing as badly as Labour in constituencies they lose.

Berrington (1975) fears that the alternative vote system in Britain would lead to an electoral situation where Labour would always be the largest party, in the Scandinavian manner of things. We must remember, however, that these simulations can never fully replicate what would happen in an alternative vote election. It is not inconceivable, for instance, that an anti-Labour alliance from lower preferences might develop to prevent a Scandinavian-type situation occurring. Speculating on such possibilities is not all that profitable. What we can conclude, is that the alternative vote does *not* eliminate electoral biases but may in fact produce new ones. If the basis of the electoral reform movement is concern over unequal treatment of parties, then the alternative vote system is clearly no solution. Although it had some support among reformers in Britain in 1918 and 1931, it is no longer a major candidate for a change in the British voting system.

Varying the size of constituencies: the single transferable vote

For many years the most popular voting system among British reformers has been the single transferable vote method. It was devised in the mid-nineteenth century by the reformer Thomas Hare and was popularized by the social philosopher John Stuart Mill. It was the product of liberal thinking to give individual voters more choice among candidates. This method for increasing voter power in theory has become, in practice, a means of producing proportional representation for parties (Rae, 1971). Its main application has been in Irish elections since 1922 and we will briefly describe its use there before considering its implementation in Britain.

Although the British House of Commons turned down S.T.V. for electing its own members in 1918, it did stipulate this system of voting for the new Irish state in 1921. The reason for this decision was to ensure some representation for the Unionist minority in the new state (O'Leary, 1975). Minority representation is achieved using this system of voting because multi-member constituencies allow a variety of local political opinions to be represented. In the seventeen elections using this system in Ireland, the levels of electoral bias have been very much lower than in Britain. Each of the two main parties, Fianna Fail and Fine Gael, usually obtain a winner's bonus of about 2 per cent while the third party, Labour, suffers a negative bias of about 2 per cent and other minor parties and independents suffer the remaining negative bias (Gudgin and Taylor, 1978). Rae (1971) points out that no voting system produces pure proportional representation and Ireland's low levels of bias are not very dissimilar to results using list systems on the continent.

In practice, S.T.V. seems to be much fairer to all parties than plurality voting with single member constituencies. Nonetheless, there are opportunities for electoral abuses and these have been reported for Irish elections. In particular, the spatial organization of elections is carried out by the Ministry of Local Government. This government control has inevitably led to accusations of gerrymandering (Gallagher, 1974). In this case, it is not so much the exact location of constituency boundaries that is important, but rather the size of constituencies in terms of seats. Clearly, the more seats in a constituency the easier it is for proportionality to be achieved between seats and votes for each party. With a three-seat constituency, proportionality can only be achieved at a crude level; with a nine-seat constituency, it can be achieved more finely. For instance, a party that wins 46 per cent of the first preferences will likely win just one seat (33 per cent) or two seats (67 per cent) in a three-member constituency, but may win four seats (44 per cent) in a nine-member constituency. This problem is treated theoretically by Lakeman (1974, p. 128) and empirically for Irish elections by Paddison (1976).

In drawing up constituencies the only constraints on the government are that there should be one seat per 20,000 to 30,000 population and a minimum of three seats. Initially, large constituencies were quite common – there were nine constituencies with seven or more members in the initial Electoral Act of 1923. Since 1947, however, there have been no constituencies with more than five members and recent acts (1969 and 1973) have produced about two-thirds of constituencies having the minimum of three seats (Mair and Laver, 1974). Gallagher (1974) has shown how these smaller constituencies have consistently produced larger electoral biases – on average 10 per cent for all three-member constituencies since 1927 – but that such local biases cancel each other out in the national result to produce the high levels of overall proportionality referred to previously. The bias against the smaller party, Labour, may be partly due to the use of small constituencies. Overall, however, this size factor does not lead to major biases.

Size of constituency is important in a second, more subtle way. In constituencies with an odd number of seats there may be a winning party in terms of seats (e.g. 2–1 in a three-member seat), whereas with an even number of seats the seats may be equally shared. Hence, one strategy of electoral abuse is to produce three-member constituencies where your party is strongest and four-member constituencies where your party is the second most popular. The idea is to win where you are strong and draw where you are weaker; that is, to lose nowhere! This form of spatial organization has been identified in Ireland (Mair and Laver, 1974; Paddison, 1976). In practice, the choice has been between having three- or four-member constituencies. Gallagher (1974) suggests that the vital vote threshold should be 46 per cent. With less than 46 per cent of the vote a party should define four-member constituencies and draw 2–2: with more than 46 per cent of the vote the party should define three-member constituencies and win 2–1. Table 8.3 shows the 1969 distribution by the Fianna

Table 8.3 Fianna Fail's share of the vote and the 1969 Irish distribution of seats

Fianna Fail's share of vote	Total seats:	3		4	
	Fianna Fail seats:	1	2	1	2
Less than 46%		8	2	0	12
More than 46%		1	15	0	2

Source: Derived from Paddison (1976)

Fail government as it relates to the party's vote in the election of that year. (The two five-member constituencies are not considered in the table.) Notice that where the party obtains less than 46 per cent of the vote, the majority of constituencies are four-member and the party wins two seats in every case. This is drawing where you are weak. Where Fianna Fail are strong, on the other hand, and win over 46 per cent of the vote, three-member constituencies are the rule and in all but one case two-thirds of the representation is obtained.

The geography of Fianna Fail's strategy is a relatively simple one. The party is strong in the west and weaker in the east: the west tends to have the three-member constituencies; the east the four-member constituencies (Paddison, 1976). The latter are best illustrated in Dublin. The 1969 act divided the city's 27 seats among six four-member constituencies and one three-member constituency. This enabled Fianna Fail to win two seats per constituency with vote proportions ranging from 34 to 43 per cent, while its opponents merely won two seats with from 52 to 61 per cent of the vote (Mair and Laver, 1974). In 1974, however, the new Fine Gael–Labour government revised the constituencies. In Dublin they predictably went for three-member constituencies so that Dublin's 27 seats are now apportioned to nine three-member constituencies. Mair and Laver (1974) suggest that this revised organization in Dublin will lead to an extra four seats for the coalition government. This is a clear example of electoral engineering again, with seats won and lost before the voters have cast their ballots. In the event, only a large and unexpected swing against the government (7 per cent) prevented this manipulation from distorting the 1977 election result.

The issue of constituency size in multi-member systems is an electoral abuse with a simple solution. Mair and Laver (1974) suggest taking the decision of constituency size out of government hands and giving it to a neutral body. This non-partisan solution has all the disadvantages of equivalent solutions described earlier. Ignoring the political effects of constituency size does not make it go away. Where the impartial commission chose three-member constituencies they would favour the local majority party; where they chose four-member constituencies their decision would be detrimental to the local majority party. Whatever their intention, it is their effects that would matter. A much fairer solution would simply be to outlaw small constituencies. Instead of having a minimum size of three seats, Paddison (1976) suggests that this should be changed to five seats, and then provides examples of large-scale spatial organization for Irish elections. With larger constituencies there is much more local proportionality and manipulation of size becomes very much more difficult, if not impossible.

If S.T.V. were used for British elections, it would involve a completely new spatial organization of multi-member constituencies. This makes predictions via simulations much more difficult. Furthermore, multi-member constituencies mean many more candidates, so simulation is made doubly difficult. Detailed presentations of such simulations are not as widely available as for the much simpler alternative vote situation. Table 8.4 shows

Table 8.4 An S.T.V. simulation for Nottingham

Candidates	*1st*	*2nd*	*3rd*	*Counts* *4th*	*5th*	*6th*	*7th*
Lab. 1	22,866	22,866	22,866	22,866	34,299*	—	—
Lab. 2	22,866	22,866	22,866	22,866	34,299*	—	—
Lab. 3	22,865	22,865	22,866	22,866	Elim.	—	—
Con. 1	15,512	15,512	15,512	23,268	23,268	28,687	57,573*
Con. 2	15,512	15,512	15,512	23,267	23,267	28,686	Elim.
Con. 3	15,511	15,511	15,511	Elim.	—	—	—
Lib. 1	7,170	10,755	21,510	21,510	21,510	Elim.	—
Lib. 2	7,170	10,755	Elim.	—	—	—	—
Lib. 3	7,170	Elim.	—	—	—	—	—

Threshold 34,161
* Elected candidates.

a hypothetical S.T.V. constituency of Nottingham which would elect three members as now. Votes for the three individual constituencies for the three main parties in October 1974 have been combined to produce possible first preferences among party candidates under S.T.V. voting. Lower preferences are assumed to go to candidates of the same party and where this is not possible, due to elimination, preferences are split as follows:

(1) Labour and Conservatives split 70–30 in favour of Liberals.

(2) Liberals split evenly for Labour and Conservative.

With three seats the quota for winning is (total vote÷4)+1 (see p. 57) which comes to 34,161. The process of elimination and the declaration of winners is shown in Table 8.4. With single-member constituencies the city produces three Labour M.Ps., and leaves both Conservatives and Liberals unrepresented. S.T.V. does not produce Liberal representation with only three seats, but it does produce a Conservative representative in a more equitable result.

This type of exercise has been carried out for all of Britain (Gudgin and Taylor, 1978) using three sizes of constituency – small (largely three-member), medium (largely five-member), and large (seven to ten-members with a mode at 9). The purpose of having three simulations is to show the relationship between size of constituency and treatment of the four main parties. The results are displayed in Figure 8.10. As expected, seat proportions generally converge on vote proportions as seat size increases. There are important differences between the parties, however. For the Nationalists the adoption of S.T.V. makes only a marginal difference. In contrast, for the Liberals the effect is massive although even with large constituencies they suffer a small bias of about —3 per cent. For Labour and Conservatives, their fortunes decline under S.T.V. but once again the Conservatives tend to do worse than Labour since it is in their areas of strength in the south of England that the Liberals pick up most of their extra seats, especially with the small and medium-sized constituencies.

Figure 8.11 shows the changing geography of Liberal representation. Under plurality voting they win just 13 seats, scattered over the country where they happen to be locally strong. This distorts their geography of voting in many ways. For instance, in the rural south-east they receive 24 per cent of the vote and win no seats; in rural Scotland they receive 11 per cent of the vote and win 3 seats. Such distortions are overcome in the S.T.V. simulations as Figure 8.11 illustrates. With small constituencies, Liberal strength in the south begins to tell and with larger constituencies they are able to win more in the north of England, while Scotland remains little changed from the plurality situation. The S.T.V. simulations, especially with the larger constituencies, do produce a geography of Liberal representation which fairly reflects the geography of their support.

Our brief discussion of voting patterns for the Liberals suggests that S.T.V. not only tends to produce proportionality between parties but that it also affects the intra-party pattern of representation. Let us consider how far this is true for the two main parties.

Table 8.5 shows two contrasting English regions, the south-east and north, and further divides the constituencies between mainly urban and mainly rural types. The geography of voting is fairly simple; Conservatives do better in the south and in rural

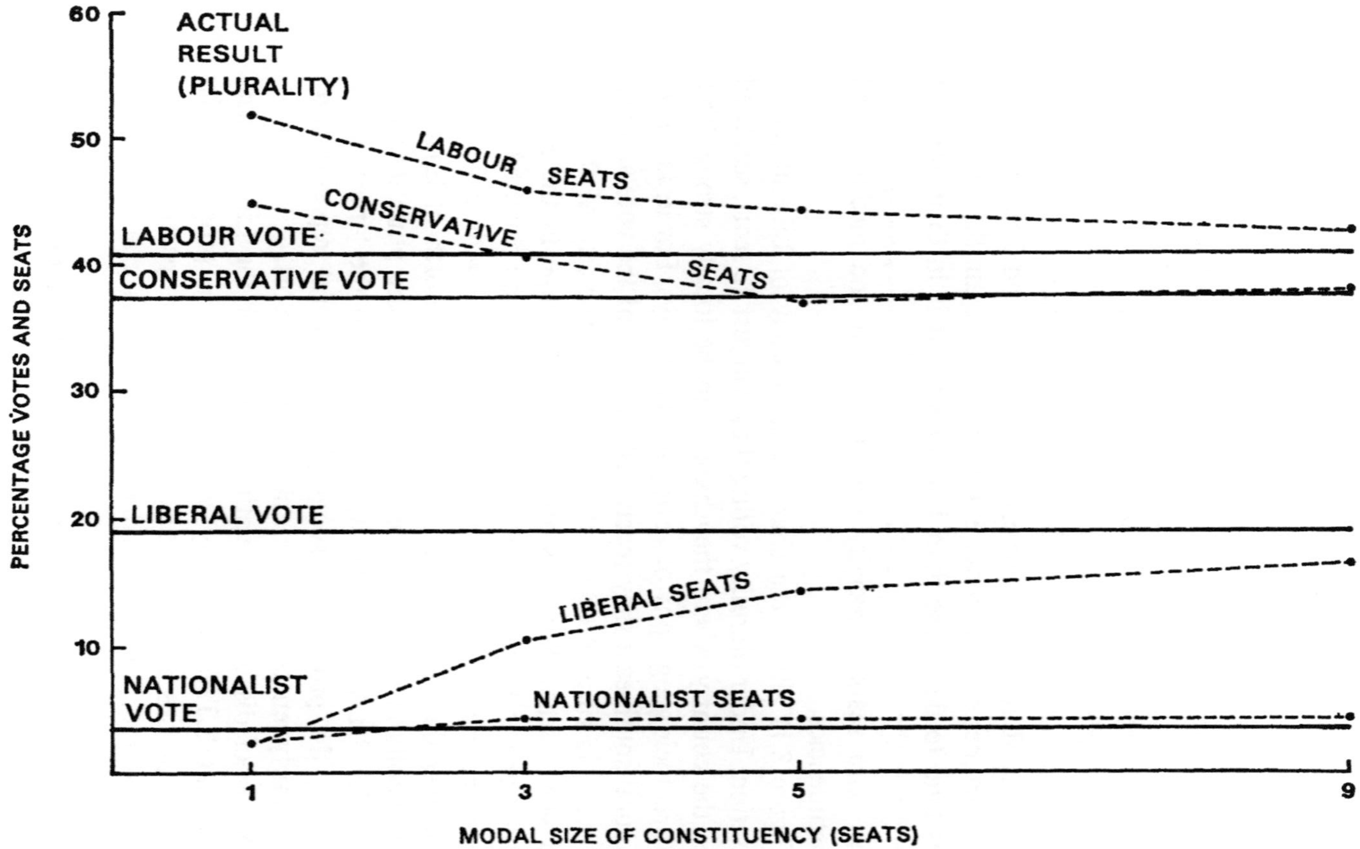

Figure 8.10 Predicted seats for parties in S.T.V. experiments

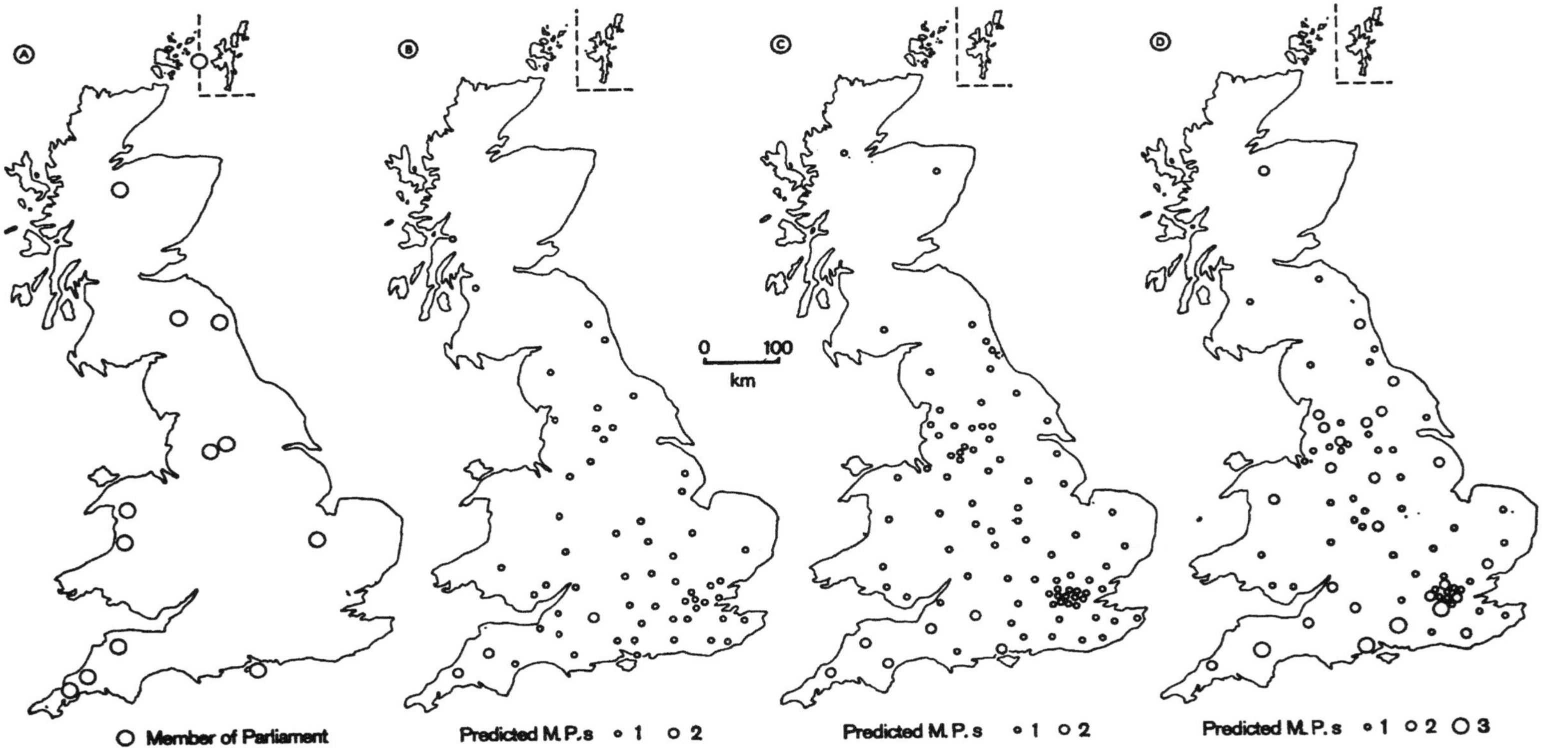

Figure 8.11 The changing geography of Liberal representation (a) M.P.s from October 1974 (b) S.T.V. with small (c) medium and (d) large constituencies

Table 8.5 Changing the geography of representation in Britain

Region		*South-east*		*North*	
Type	*Party*	*Rural*	*Urban*	*Rural*	*Urban*
Percentage vote	Con.	47	39	42	30
	Lab.	29	43	38	52
Percentage actual seats	Con.	95	48	58	12
	Lab.	5	52	42	85
Percentage predicted seats	Con.	46	39	46	29
	Lab.	33	48	35	57

constituencies, hence the most extreme differences between the parties are found in the rural south-east and urban north. This difference is accentuated in the geography of representation from the October 1974 election. In the rural south-east, Conservatives win a massive 95 per cent of seats from their 47 per cent of the total vote and in the urban north, Labour win 85 per cent of the seats with their 52 per cent of the total vote. This is the plurality system converting small regional differences into almost 'one-party states' in terms of representation. The predicted seats in the final part of Table 8.5 are from the S.T.V. simulation using medium-sized constituencies. In this case the geography of representation more accurately reflects the voting. This means that the Conservatives *lose* seats in their strongholds where they are overrepresented but *win* them where they are relatively weak. Hence, in the rural south-east their seats fall from 95 per cent to 46 per cent, while in the urban north they rise from 12 per cent to 29 per cent. The converse of this change can be found in Labour seats. These examples show that S.T.V. not only produces a more proportionate result at the national level, it also achieves the same at a regional level so that it fundamentally changes the geography of representation These simulations and their results are more fully discussed in Gudgin and Taylor (1978).

Before we leave consideration of S.T.V. we must ask why it is that a voting system designed to promote individual voter power should happen to produce approximate party proportionality. In the Irish case, Mair and Laver (1974) suggest that proportionality results largely from the fact that the electorate tend to vote strictly along party lines. In this situation, individual preferences coincide with party preferences so that the original liberal intentions do not conflict with modern party politics. We have no reason to think that such party voting would not also occur in British S.T.V. elections and produce the levels of proportionality reported above.

The new frontrunner in the P.R. stakes

We have previously mentioned that proportional representation in the Weimar Republic has been blamed for the rise of Hitler in 1933. With the defeat of Germany in 1945 it was clear that the old electoral law would not be revived. Instead, a compromise was adopted whereby a normal plurality election using single-member constituencies would be held, but the resulting biases would be cancelled out by giving parties additional members on the basis of their overall votes by Länder (provinces). This method was first used in the British zone of occupation and was then adopted for the 1949 Federal election. It has been used, with only minor changes, since that date. It is ironic that this post-war British compromise for West Germany has become the envy of the British electoral reformers of the 1970s (Hansard Society, 1976).

The German use of the 'mixed system' or 'additional member system' (A.M.S.) has been highly successful in terms of proportionality. Small biases have been produced by using a 5 per cent threshold for parties to qualify for representation at the second stage (see Chapter 2) but certainly in both 1972 and 1976 this was irrelevant since the three main parties won over 99 per cent of the vote. The electoral biases recorded in these two elections have been negligible and allow supporters of A.M.S. to claim, with some justice, that this voting system is the fairest that can be devised (Gudgin and Taylor, 1978).

In Germany, half the seats are elected directly using constituencies and half are allocated on the basis of Land vote totals.

For Britain the Hansard Society has suggested 75 per cent directly elected members in a 640-member house. This means a spatial reorganization to produce 480 constituencies which would be somewhat larger than the existing set. Nevertheless, the spatial reorganization would be much less than with the adoption of S.T.V. The attraction of A.M.S. is that it would involve less change than S.T.V. while it seems that it would do the job of producing proportionality much more effectively. The main contentious point revolves around the scale at which additional members are to be allocated. If the 'topping up' occurs at the U.K. scale it may be that the two small nationalist parties in Scotland and Wales might fail to achieve the vote threshold for additional members and hence suffer electoral biases. However, if the 'home countries' are used for the topping up process then no such biases will occur.

The Hansard Society's proposals are difficult to simulate since it is not possible to combine the existing 623 constituencies (excluding Ulster) into an equitable pattern of 480 new constituencies. Instead, we have assumed that half of the representatives will be additional members, as in Germany. This means that constituency M.P.s will be elected from combined pairs of existing

Table 8.6 Additional members for the British parliament

Party	*Percentage of vote*	*Constituency M.P.s*	*National list M.P.s*	*Total*	*Percentage of seats*
Conservatives	36·7	122	108	230	37·0
Labour	40·8	181	71	252	40·5
Liberal	18·8	1	117	118	19·0
S.N.P.	2·9	7	11	18	2·9
Plaid Cymru	0·6	0	4	4	0·6

constituencies. Using such a system would produce results such as in Table 8.6 if the voting of October 1974 were to be repeated. Notice how the two major parties dominate the constituency M.P.s whereas the Liberals win most additional members. (This type of result also occurs in Germany, where the third party, the Free Democrats, have won only Land representatives since 1961.) This result would be considered highly satisfactory from the point of view of the modern electoral reformers: parliament would proportionately reflect the wishes of the voters.

The effects of proportional representation on the British electoral system are hard to assess. We are literally working in the realms of speculation. Rae (1971) has shown how simple arguments concerning the break-up of the British party system are unfounded. However, one aspect that is not often considered is the effect of the changing geography of representation. With plurality voting the geographical differences between the parties' bases of support are highly accentuated when translated into parliamentary representation. Hence, outside London, inner-city Conservatives are rarely represented, whereas outside the coalfields rural Labour supporters have little or no representation. All this would change with electoral reform. We showed this explicitly with S.T.V. and a similar feature could occur with A.M.S. especially if English regions were to be used, with Wales and Scotland, for allocating additional members. Parties could then choose some degree of interest representation within regions. In this way the distortion of parties would be eradicated along with the distortion of votes.

Why geographies of proportional representation?

The conclusion of this section is that there are no technical problems which would prevent proportional representation being created in the British House of Commons. What is lacking is an effective political will to achieve this goal. Although much of the reformers' literature has an altruistic air, the questions being posed are acutely political and involve specific value judgements. Representation is not an end in itself, it is the means for achieving legislative power. Several writers have emphasized how the current lack of representative proportionality influences many areas of government policy, such as economic strategies and incomes policy (Finer, 1975). Such arguments are beyond the scope of our discussion here but are mentioned to illustrate the perceived importance of electoral reform. Our analyses have extended the P.R. discussion into the realm of party proportional representation by regions and type of constituency. Such changes in the nature of party representation in parliament itself suggest direct influence on policy, especially those policies with direct spatial implications. In the final part of this book we attempt to draw together several themes from this and previous chapters, as we move into the relatively under-developed field of the geographical bases to policy and policy-making.

Part Five

Towards a Geography of Power

9 Geography, Elections, Representation and Power

Our focus in this book has been on the geography of elections, and we have highlighted three particular aspects of that geography; (1) the spatial variations in voting for different candidates, parties and issues which reflect the spatial division of labour and the process of politicization; (2) the locational variables which are related to information flows and influence how voters react to various political issues; and (3) the effect of the division of a territory into constituencies on the translation of votes into seats, and hence on the pattern of representation. Within such a framework, we have considered the election as an event in its own right, worthy of study for its own sake. But the purpose of an election is to allocate political power (as compared with a referendum or plebiscite, which is conducted to obtain a decision on a particular issue). If there are important geographical influences on voting and representation, then these should be followed by similar influences on the allocation of power, and so it is to this topic that we address our final chapter. In doing so, our interest moves away from the interaction between voters and political actors and focuses instead on the roles and performances of the successful actors in the election process. As Cox (1976) has pointed out in a recent review, such a concern with the outputs of the electoral process is unusual among geographers, but it is crucial if the value of geographical study of the whole political system is to be demonstrated.

The concept of power is a crucial one to much analysis in social science, and its definition has been the focus of much debate. Our concern here is with a relatively narrow view of power, which is that level of control over political decision-making which is allocated to different elected representatives. This is in line with the general positivist tone of the whole book; we accept the current electoral systems as given and analyse their inputs and outputs rather than focus on their position in the wider socio-economic system (Miliband, 1969). Our aim is simply to illustrate the political implications of electoral systems.

The political implications of electoral systems form a topic of continuing interest, especially among those who favour some form of electoral reform. We have already looked at some of the implications of reform for the geography of representation in the preceding chapter; here we unravel that geography somewhat and investigate the political, as against the electoral, implications of 'reform'. Interpretation of these implications must rest on models of how political systems should work; on whether, for example, the political arena should be one of conflict between adversaries or of consensus between people of differing shades of opinion (Finer, 1975). More than a concluding chapter in a book on the geography of elections would be necessary to examine all of these implications and interpretations. The most we can do here is to outline their nature, and to set the study of electoral and political geography firmly in the mainstream of social science.

Much of the debate on electoral reform has been *ad hoc* in nature, being based on reactions – especially among losers – to particular election results. But the topic has also been of continuing interest to political theorists and to philosophers, especially those concerned with such issues as equality and justice. Both the pragmatic and the theoretical points of view are being widely aired during the 1970s. In the United States, for example, the 1960s was a decade of great activity in reapportionment, with attempts, largely generated from outside the established political parties, to obtain democratic equality through redistricting (see Chapter 7), and there is still much discussion about the fairness of the electoral college system for electing presidents. In the United Kingdom, the two general elections of 1974 were judged by many as unfair to the Liberal Party and its supporters, and several groups – most of them self-appointed –

have been researching and writing about electoral reform (Finer, 1975; Mayhew, 1976; Rogaly, 1976). Interest increased during 1976 when the related issues of direct elections to the European Parliament, with the need for a common, community-wide electoral system for the second election in the early 1980s, and the nationalist revivals in Scotland and Wales came to the forefront of British political debate. Meanwhile, the Electoral Reform Society continues to argue for a certain electoral system to allow individuals the maximum freedom of choice, and in Australia the ever-interesting topic of rural over-representation was fiercely debated in both Houses in Canberra before the fall of Whitlam's A.L.P. government.

Within this general topic of electoral reform is the question, 'Can some, if not all, of the geographical influences on elections be removed, to what end, and why?'. For some of the topics we have discussed in this book the answer is a clear 'no', at least as an independent action. The voting patterns which are consequent upon the spatial division of labour (Chapters 3 and 4) cannot be altered without one or both of: (1) a spatial reorganization of society which removes most of the current socio-economic segregation; and (2) a removal of the class bias to so much political behaviour, which undoubtedly would involve the removal of class itself. Discussion of the feasibility of such policies lies beyond the compass of this brief volume; in our context, the argument is that voting is a process deeply embedded in the existing social structure, and that changing this structure of society is the only way of changing the salient elements of the geography of voting.

The topics we dealt with in Chapters 5 and 6, under the general heading of geographical influences in voting, concern small-scale features which lead to various warpings of the general geographies of voting produced by the processes outlined in Chapters 3 and 4. In them, we take a micro-spatial view, based on the assumption that much of politics involves individuals trying to persuade others to pursue certain courses of action – whether to vote, who to vote for, etc. Whilst we continue to live most of our lives within the confines of relatively small areas, frequently called neighbourhoods, then most of our social contacts are likely to remain local and some political discussion will be with our neighbours. And whilst housing markets are largely in the hands of capitalist institutions, spatial segregation of socio-economic classes will continue and so will class-based politics; the neighbourhood effect is not independent of the society which creates the neighbourhoods. Similarly, for as long as elections have a strong component of being between individual candidates, home-based friends-and-neighbours effects are always likely.

Local issues, local campaigns, and the geography of representation are the remaining topics. As with local candidates, local issues are always likely to arise in a particular electoral contest. Their impact could perhaps be reduced – the larger the average constituency the less likely that a local issue in one part will affect the whole result – but whether local issues should be important depends on one's theory of representation, a topic we take up later. And with limited resources, including time as well as money, available to political contestants, campaigning is likely to be localized. We pointed out in Chapter 6 that the major effect of most campaigns is on turnout levels, and so their efficacy, indeed necessity, could be removed by the introduction of compulsory voting. While constituencies remain as integral parts of an electoral system (and not just for convenience, as in the Netherlands – p. 63), however, and particularly if they are single-member constituencies, then some places will be seen by candidates and parties as more important to them than others. If campaigning simply involves door-knocking and exhortations to 'please vote', there seems to be little to worry about, but if further research confirms the hypotheses concerning vote-buying in marginal constituencies (p. 314), then it could well be argued that the spatial allocation of public funds for the maintenance of a particular government is an abuse of political power. Even here, however, the amount spent on place-particular campaigns, relative to that on general programmes not aimed at particular areas, may well prove to be fairly small.

If local issues and local campaigns are undesirable aspects of the geography of elections, this will arise because of the geography of representation. This brings us firmly into the debate about the relative desirability of different electoral systems. In order to discuss this topic we need to be clear about the purposes of elections, most of which are conducted with more than one end in view. As one British prime minister, Ramsay MacDonald, argued in a House of Commons debate on electoral reform (the quote is from Butler, 1963, p. 59): 'One view . . . is the static view where we are an exact replica, on a very small scale, of the millions of electors . . . the other view is that the real, final purpose of an election is to elect a government – and I use the word rather apart from merely electing a House of Commons'. The British parliament, therefore, comprises members who combine two major roles, representing the electorate and forming a government/opposition system in which one group or coalition of groups has the major political power without fear that it may lose it on any particular issue; most parliaments (including various local government bodies) are similarly composed of members who perform these two roles.

In constructing an electoral system, the following four criteria are generally considered important:

(1) Elections should be organized so as to ensure democratic equality for the participants – 'one man, one vote; one vote, one value'.

(2) Elections should be organized so that the different views held by the electorate are proportionally represented in the parliament.*

(3) Elections should produce governments which do not have a narrow, sectional base in the geography of representation.

(4) Elections should give voters the maximum possible choice.

Before examining various electoral systems, and in particular their geographical aspects, within the context of these four criteria, however, it is necessary to look in more detail at the question of representation.

* The terms parliament and members are used throughout this chapter as synonyms for all elected bodies and elected candidates respectively.

The Geography of Representative Behaviour

The nature of representatives

Elections produce members to sit in parliaments and, except in certain non-partisan bodies such as the state legislatures of Minnesota and Nebraska, to form permanent coalitions which are either government or opposition. But what is the relationship between those members and the people who have elected them? As was shown in Chapter 2, there is a number of theories of the nature of representation and the role of members relative to their constituents (Birch, 1971, reviews these). Rather then review those theories here, we confine our discussion to a typology of role orientations of representatives developed by Newton (1976) from his interviews with 66 councillors and aldermen in the now-defunct City of Birmingham. He identified six such roles, all of which are expressed as polar opposites although several involve intermediate categories.

(1) *Delegate or trusteee.* Members who are delegates are sent to a parliament to represent the views of those who elected them and to act in a predetermined way, according to policies debated prior to the election, perhaps with periodic reference back. Trustees, on the other hand, are elected as members not only because of specific things which they agree to do but also because the voters have confidence in their general ability to legislate and to make decisions on issues of the moment, irrespective of whether possible reactions to such issues were discussed during the election campaign. As we have shown throughout this book, opinions differ widely on the relative importance of these two roles. Members of the Japanese Diet, for example, are very much elected on what they can get for those who voted for them, and many American members act similarly, for example in the committee assignments they undertake. In Birmingham, Newton found that 27 per cent of those he interviewed considered themselves delegates, whereas 47 per cent acted as trustees; the remaining 26 per cent – dubbed politicos – operated both roles depending on the particular circumstances.

(2) *Party member or individual.* In most elections, members are

successful because of their association with a political party, whose label is extremely influential in securing their return to the parliament. Once elected, however, is the member expected to be loyal to that party – unless it breaks its pledges to the electorate – or is he or she an individual who is trusted to use personal judgement and where necessary to speak and vote against the party? (An alternative which may be less injurious to party, and to member, is to abstain.) Of the Birmingham sample, 23 per cent had abstained from certain votes when their party did not, and 26 per cent had voted against their party.

(3) *Local representative or territorial governor.* If members are sent to a parliament as representing the constituents of a particular area, is their responsibility solely to those people or do they have a wider responsibility to the entire electorate whom the parliament represents? Newton found that 42 per cent of his interviewees interpreted their main role as providing city-wide government, whereas 21 per cent perceived themselves as local (ward) representatives; 27 per cent claimed that both roles were important.

(4) *Policy-makers or errand-boys.* This difference is largely a continuation of the previous one, except that it need have no overt localism in the errand-boy function. Those members who see their main role as policy-makers for the electorate as a whole, almost certainly consider the local representation function as relatively unimportant; those who see themselves as some form of ombudsman, acting as intermediaries between electors and government/bureaucracy, and as solvers of problems for individuals, probably also see the representation of the views of their local constituents as important. As Newton (1976, p. 130) found, the latter are also more likely to be in frequent contact with their electorate through constituency 'surgeries' and like meetings, although some played 'errand-boy' for all.

(5) *Legislative specialist or generalist.* Parliaments and like bodies are responsible for a very wide range of administrative functions in modern states and few individual members have the time or resources to command a detailed knowledge of all of these, or even to debate effectively on matters of detail as against

general principles. Thus they tend to specialize, either in areas of administration for which they have been trained or have developed some expertise or, as is often so with American congressional committeees (Bullock, 1971), in those which are of particular relevance to their constituency. Even in the relatively simpler British local government, 88 per cent of the Birmingham respondents considered themselves specialists, which means that their roles as local representatives could often be confined merely to transmitting queries etc., rather than fighting local issues if they were irrelevant to their specialism. (In such cases, members may well pass cases to relevant specialists elected by different constituencies.)

(6) *Independent or subject to pressure groups.* Another consequence of the increased complexity of parliaments is the growth of pressure groups to ensure that certain sectional interests are kept before the legislators; such pressure groups are often legalized and institutionalized, as with the official lobbies which operate in Washington and the 'consultancies' and 'sponsorships' which British M.P.s accept from, for example, trade unions and professional associations. These pressure groups are important channels in the flow of information to legislators, most of whom in Newton's survey (82 per cent) welcomed their participation in government.

These six different representation role-orientations illustrate the twin functions of a parliament identified in the quotation from Ramsay MacDonald; representing electors and forming governments. From his Birmingham data, Newton was able to recognize five types of member: (1) *the parochial* – 'a special sort of unpaid social worker or ombudsman' (Newton, 1976, p. 137) – who was neither ideological nor partisan with regard to the governmental function, tending to act as a loyal party member when not representing his own constituents; (2) *the people's agent*, similar to the parochial except that he was an errand-boy for everybody and not just his ward constituents; (3) *the policy advocate*, an ideological partisan elected to run the city on his party's manifesto; (4) *the policy broker*, also oriented to city-wide government but less ideological in his reactions to particular problems; and

(5) *the policy spokesman*, a party delegate except when representing constituents in general, as against on individual problems. The proportion of borough councillors and aldermen in the different categories is of no interest to us; the importance of the various types will vary by time, place, and type of government. What is of interest is the relationship between representational roles and the geography of representation in Birmingham. Birmingham City Councillors, but not the aldermen, were elected by the plurality system in single-member constituencies. Some of their seats were safe for one party or another, whereas others were marginal and continued membership was less certain. There were clear differences between the members from these safe and marginal wards in their perceived representational roles (Table 9.1); incumbents of marginal wards were much more inclined to become closely involved with local issues and the problems of individual constituents.

Newton (1976, p. 138) also found that parochials were 'not committed political activists from a young age, but "amateurs" who take up council work in their late middle-age'; that 'the most junior and short-service members are more likely to lean towards the ward focus' (p. 125); and that recently elected councillors 'contain a clear majority who prefer dealing with the problems of individuals' (p. 127). These statements suggest that the differences illustrated in Table 9.1 may reflect the nature of the members from safe and marginal wards, since inexperienced candidates usually serve a political apprenticeship in a marginal seat before being rewarded with a safe constituency when their value to the party as a whole becomes clear. (This was so, for example, with New Zealand's prime minister from 1972 to 1974, Norman Kirk, who was member for the marginal seat of Lyttleton from 1957 to 1969 before being transferred to his party's safe seat of Sydenham.) Whether it is the youth and the inexperience of the members, the sorts of seat they represent, or a combination of the two which determine their representative behaviour is difficulty to ascertain.

American data strongly support an argument that there is a strong relationship between constituency type and member's

Table 9.1 Role orientations and constituency type: Birmingham city councillors

	Percentage of councillors from	
	Safe wards	*Marginal wards*
Type of representative		
Delegate	19	42
Trustee	57	31
Politico	24	27
Voting record		
Had abstained against party	23	23
Had voted against party	24	27
Faithful to party	52	50
Areal role		
Ward representative	19	38
City governor	43	42
Both	38	19
Function		
General policy-maker	29	23
Local 'errand boy'	33	54
Both	38	33
Area of interest		
Specialist	100	77
Generalist	0	23
Attitude to pressure groups		
Anti	14	15
Pro	86	77
Other	0	8

Source: from Newton (1976, pp. 120 and 128)

activities. Because of the relatively weak party discipline in parliaments there, many members see themselves as individuals rather than as party members (role 4 above) in their decisions on how to vote, and so analysis of voting records is often informative. MacRae's (1952) pioneer study of the Massachusetts House of Representatives showed that members' voting was strongly predicated on their perceptions of their constituents' attitudes, a finding later validated in a more sophisticated analysis by Cnudde and McCrone (1966). Analyses of the federal Congress have been less conclusive, but Brady (1973) has argued that when competition for House of Representatives seats is strong, members from marginal states are more likely to defect from the 'party line'. Shannon (1968) has shown that both Republican and Democrat representatives from the northern states, and especially the former, were more likely to vote against their party if they came from marginal constituencies (Table 9.2). This was because

Table 9.2 Constituency type and voting behaviour: representatives from the northern states, 1960

	Percentage with a party opposition score of[a]				
Type of district[b]	*0–10*	*11–20*	*21–30*	*31–40*	*41+*
	Republican representatives				
Predominantly Democrat	0	50	0	50	0
Marginal	5	26	16	11	42
Predominantly Republican	16	42	21	8	13
Safe Republican	32	55	9	5	0
	Democrat representatives				
Safe Democrat	20	61	16	4	0
Predominantly Democrat	20	48	29	4	0
Marginal	17	70	13	0	0
Predominantly Republican	16	37	27	5	5

[a] The higher the party opposition score, the greater the frequency of a representative voting against his party in an inter-party division.

[b] Districts were classified according to their voting averages over the period 1952–60.

Source: Shannon (1968, pp. 160 and 162)

their party views were more likely to be at odds with those of a large number of their constituents, so that during 1960 Democrats who represented districts which usually returned a Republican member 'apparently were more conservative . . . or else they were convinced that they must deviate towards the opposition to gain re-election' (Shannon, 1968, pp. 160–61), whereas Republican members whose electoral base was less secure than that of their colleagues were either more liberal than were the members from safe seats, or they felt compelled to moderate their voting in order to win favour with their electorate. Similar constituency influences have been noted for other elected officials in the United States; judges are elected by partisan contests in twenty states, for example (Vines, 1965), and several researchers have sought relationships between constituency characteristics and judicial behaviour (Adamany, 1969; Jarus and Canon, 1971). An interesting examination of the spatial pattern of voting in the geographical literature is Smith and Hart's (1955) analysis of roll-calls in the House of Representatives on the issue of tariff between 1929 and 1953. They show that basically the Republican party was protectionist and the Democrat party liberal and that the general pattern of voting followed party lines. Of the Democrats who either voted against their party or abstained, many represented congressional districts west of the Mississippi whose economic interests were strongly in favour of protectionism; of the dissident Republicans, half of those voting against protection were from large-city districts, notably in the north-east. The nature of local opinion on the issue clearly was important in producing defections from the party ideology.

Government by representatives, it would seem, is influenced by how the representatives feel they should behave, what they believe their constituents demand of them, and the importance of courting electors' favours in order to retain power. In addition, many are also influenced by their beliefs about the general needs, short and long term, of the whole electorate. Each representative will balance out the importance of the constituency influence (and may mis-judge it as some, such as Senator J. W. Fulbright and Miss Jennie Lee, have found to their cost) and behave accordingly. Is the importance of the constituency influence, at least in part, a function of the type of electoral system, so that members of different systems emphasize different representational roles?

The nature of constituencies

Most electoral systems are geographically based, in that the members are elected as representatives for particular constituencies. But is the type of representation which results a necessary feature of constituency-based politics, and are constituencies themselves necessary? In other words, are constituencies *real* and therefore areas which require representation, or are they merely administrative conveniences with their influence on representational roles an unexpected side-effect?

These questions are crucial, since the nature of the constituencies strongly influences election results, as shown in a study of the Democrat primary elections of 1972 in the United States (Lengle and Shafer, 1976). Three types of system were then used in the various states:

(1) Winner-takes-all, in which the candidate with a state-wide plurality got all of the state's delegates.

(2) Proportional representation, in which delegates were allocated to candidates according to what percentage each got of the state-wide poll.

(3) District pluralities, in which each district (usually a congressional district) was allocated a number of delegates and the candidate with a district-wide plurality won them all.

The results of the first fifteen primaries (excluding Illinois and the District of Columbia) if all states had adopted the same system vary widely with the system used (Table 9.3; the actual result was Humphrey 284, Wallace 291, McGovern 401·5, Muskie 56·5, Others 59). Compared to the winner-take-all system, McGovern and Muskie would have done much better with district pluralities, and Humphrey much worse. But what defence can be offered for a district system? If Humphrey was the most popular candidate in state X as a whole, should he have received all of state X's delegates, or only those delegates for the districts he was most popular in, or only a percentage of the delegates proportional to his percentage of the poll? If the last alternative is chosen, the state is only an administrative convenience for counting the national vote; if the second is chosen, then the dis-

Table 9.3 The results of fifteen Democrat primaries, 1972, under different rules

Candidates	*Winner-takes-all*	*Proportional representation*	*Districting*
Humphrey	446	314	324
Wallace	379	350	367
McGovern	249	319	343
Muskie	18	82	52
Others	0	27	6

Source: Lengle and Shafer (1976, p. 29)

tricts are seen as 'real' areas deserving representation at the nominating convention. The importance of this choice is indicated by two quotations from Lengle and Shafer (1976, pp. 34 and 38):

a winner-take-all victory in Pennsylvania would have been equivalent to victories in all *six* of the smallest states, [but] any *two* of these states could have offered about the same delegate margin as the Keystone state [Pennsylvania] under districted regulations . . .

Of the three basic primary plans, districting promises the most sharply divided conventions and the most severe problems in postconvention electioneering . . . the more radical candidates on both ends of the party's ideological spectrum will have a maximum number of delegates.

The defence of districting occurs in the theory of representation which focuses on the parochial aspect of members' roles. It suggests that the districts are 'real' areas, whose constituents have common interests posing common problems for the member to solve. This is reflected in the requirements in several countries that district boundaries be drawn so as to enclose areas with 'community of interest' (Taylor and Gudgin 1975, 1976b; Morrill, 1973); in the United Kingdom boroughs and 'county areas' must not be combined into parliamentary constituencies, for example, and wards must not be subdivided. The 'sense of place' is an important element in human make-up (Tuan, 1976) and many now believe, with Ardrey (1966), that the 'territorial imperative' and its associated defensive functions are major aspects of human behaviour. But the major territories with which most people identify are their homes, their neighbourhoods, perhaps their counties/states, and their countries. Research on 'home areas' has led Lee (1976, p. 179) to conclude that with regard to neighbourhoods, 'in the majority of cases the area is found to be considerably smaller than the smallest local government unit in which the elector resides, and this reinforces the dubiety of using these units as the scale of reference', which is in line with the research commissioned by the Royal Commission on Local Government in England (1969).

Many districts used for electoral constituencies are merely administrative conveniences, therefore, which bear little relationship to the ways in which residents structure their mental maps. Only in federal systems is this not usually so. In these, the states retain some sovereignty which is constitutionally protected (Dahl, 1956) and states' rights are usually jealously guarded, particularly where the federation has come about through some cession of freedoms (Dikshit, 1975). Both the American and the Australian senates were founded as states' houses, with each state having an equal voice so that any legislation passed would be approved by a majority of the federation's members as well as by a majority of the federal population (districting for the lower Houses of Representatives being based on population). The takeover of the senates, especially in Australia, by the party system suggests that states' houses are now irrelevant, but the arguments over the size of the E.E.C. Parliament in 1976 suggest otherwise; in any case, the areas referred to are more 'meaningful' in everyday life than, say, the counties on which several American state senates were based (Jewell, 1962).

The Value of Votes: in Search of Power

The various roles of parliamentary members are many and complex. Several of them refer to their relationships with their constituencies, and as constituencies are basic elements in the design of most electoral systems the nature of these relationships and the roles which the members adopt may be associated with, if not influenced by, the type of electoral system used. In the debate about electoral reform, the constituency link is often produced in defence of certain types of system and yet, as we have suggested, most constituencies are simply administratively-convenient territorial divisions and nothing more.

In turning to the topic of electoral reform, our discussion is set in the context of the four criteria outlined earlier (p. 441). Our aim is not another polemic on the issue, and we will not conclude with a 'best buy'. The type of electoral system adopted should be related to the type of representation a society wants, via its theories on the roles of parliament and of its members. This is not to argue a form of socio-spatial determinism, that certain systems *will* produce certain representation and government; all the statements are probabilities, not certainties. We can only suggest what types of representation are likely to emerge from various electoral systems, so that the approach can then be inverted and readers can decide (1) what they want from members and parliaments and (2) what electoral systems are most likely to produce these ends.

Elections and democratic equality: 'one man, one vote; one vote, one value'

Adult suffrage is virtually universal in the countries we have been considering, although putting it into operation is not always conducive to full adult enjoyment of the suffrage, as illustrated by the voter registration rules in some American states. Thus 'one man, one vote' has largely been achieved, although there are some anomalies. (As recently as 1971, one of us had three votes in a New Zealand County Council election because he was legally considered as the property-owner; his wife had only one vote in the same election.) Although 'one man, one vote' exists, however, it is far from the case that we also have 'one vote, one value'. In plurality systems, as we showed in Chapters 7 and 8, many votes are 'wasted', being cast either for a losing candidate or for a candidate who would have won without them. Spatial variations in vote wastage result from gerrymanders, intentional or otherwise, amd also from differences in constituency size. Thus in the United Kingdom, each vote cast in a small, marginal seat such as Halesowen and Stourbridge (October 1974: Conservative, 34,387; Labour 23,537; Liberal, 14,672) was potentially of much more importance to the candidates, since at least two had an excellent chance of winning, than was one in Rother Valley (October 1974: Labour, 44,670; Conservative, 11,983; Liberal, 9828), whereas one in Ross and Cromarty (October 1974: Conservative, 7924; S.N.P., 7291; Labour, 3440; Liberal, 1747) was even more crucial because the number of electors entitled to vote in the Scottish constituency was only 30 per cent of that for Halesowen and Stourbridge. Similarly, in the American State Senates and congressional districts there was considerable variation in the ratios of voters in the smallest and largest districts in the southern states, even after the reapportionment of the 1960s in the case of State Senates (Table 9.4).

We indicated in Chapter 8 how difficult it is to produce a districting system for plurality elections without, either or both, a

Table 9.4 Ratios of votes in largest and smallest districts: southern states

	State senate districts		*U.S. congressional districts*	
State	*Before reapportionment*	*After*	*1963*	*1969*
Alabama	19·6	1·5	a	1·2
Florida	98·3	1·1	2·8	1·1
Georgia	1·5	1·4	3·0	1·4
Kentucky	2·9	2·0	1·7	1·1
Mississippi	9·1	1·3	2·1	1·1
North Carolina	2·3	1·3	1·8	1·0
South Carolina	25·0	1·3	2·0	1·1
Tennessee	6·0	1·4	2·8	1·0
Virginia	5·5	1·4	1·7	1·0

[a] Alabama's representatives were elected 'at large' at this time.
Source: Bushman and Stanley (1971, p. 656)

size and an unintentional gerrymander effect on the representation. Boundary Commissioners are likely to produce biased results in a neutral way (Taylor and Gudgin, 1976b), and although electorates of unequal size are now being deemed illegal in many countries (for example, in Japan; *The Times*, 15 April 1976), it is almost impossible to avoid them, as one geographer found when a court gave him the task of creating a constituency system (Morrill, 1973); even if the latter end is almost reached, without constant revision population movements will soon destroy it again (Hughes and Savage, 1967). But were equal-size districts possible, and other criteria such as shape and compactness satisfied (Taylor, 1976), unintentional gerrymanders are much harder to prevent. Arguments have been made that deliberate 'gerrymandering for democracy' is possible (Scott, 1955; Hermens, 1976), but the safest conclusion would seem to be Dixon's (1968, p. 462) that 'all districting is gerrymandering'.

Only a national constituency, as in Israel and the Netherlands, could ensure an absence of gerrymandering, therefore. Large constituencies, as in Belgium and Italy where up to 32 and 36 members respectively are returned from one district, may reduce the problem considerably although some vote wastage is bound to occur (as it would with a national constituency). The systems used in Germany of list members to correct the problems created by plurality gerrymanders and in Scandinavia to correct biases in multi-member constituency lists, are also ways of circumventing the issue.

Most elections for multi-member constituencies use the list system for voting (p. 62). This involves the elector selecting between parties, and perhaps candidates within the selected party. A major objection against it is that the party is thereby institutionalized, since it is based on an, implicit at least, concept of a member as a loyal party delegate rather than as a trustee, probably as a specialist rather than as a generalist, and probably also little concerned with the problems of individual constituents. This was recognized by Headlam-Morley (1929) in her critique of the constitutions of the new European states created by the 1919 Treaty of Versailles (Germany, Czechoslovakia, Poland,

Finland, Yugoslavia and the Baltic States). All had adopted list systems in which, she pointed out:

> The object . . . is not only to prevent the waste of votes, but to enable the parties to obtain the election of candidates of intellectual ability or practical experience who may not have any local connexion or do not wish to enter an electoral campaign . . . (p. 106).

> This system . . . is the only one that makes possible the combination of a comparatively simple procedure with one that secures the minimum of wasted votes. It has the disadvantage that the freedom of choice of the elector is severely curtailed and the influence of the party managers increased (p. 113).

Individuals can stand as independents, perhaps under the cloak of their own party, but will need large personal followings, particularly in large constituencies, to have any hope of success. Members elected on party lists can decide to adopt the trustee role, and vote with their consciences, but, to quote Headlam-Morley (1929, p. 115) again: 'A deputy who voted against his party would be ejected from the party organization and, unless he were influential enough to form a new party of his own, he would have no opportunity of re-election.' This is not peculiar to list systems, however. It occurs under Britain's plurality system, where party rebels standing as independents rarely do well for long, but not – it is to be noted – under the United States plurality system.

Preferential voting is also unlikely to produce the equality of 'one man, one vote; one vote, one value', although, as Knight and Baxter-Moore (1973) show in their analyses of Irish elections, under the Single Transferable Vote (S.T.V., p. 57) system the percentage of votes wasted per constituency is invariably less than thirty. In single-member constituencies, preferential voting using the Alternative Vote (A.V., p. 51) system allows choices other than the electors' first ones to be considered, but only where no candidate obtains a majority of the first preferences and, as we illustrated from the Australian use of this method, the unintentional gerrymander can mean that the counting of preferences occurs infrequently. Thus, many can claim that they are partly disenfranchised in that only their first preferences are counted, and this occurs both between constituencies and between parties. For example, if the A.V. system had been used in England at the October 1974 general election the percentage of each party's supporters whose second preferences would have been counted – assuming that the votes cast at the election would have formed the first preferences – are given in Table 9.5. In three-party contests,

Table 9.5 The alternative vote in England, October 1974

Party given first preference	*Percentage of voters whose second preferences would have been allocated* Conservative	Labour	Liberal
Type of constituency			
Borough	2·5	3·8	46·8
Rural	1·1	16·8	51·0
Regional breakdown			
North	2·4	4·3	16·0
Northwest	2·5	2·8	42·6
Yorkshire and Humberside	2·0	6·6	32·8
West Midlands	2·2	3·9	46·4
East Midlands	0	8·1	69·9
Southwest	2·3	32·6	45·2
East Anglia	0	27·3	85·0
Southeast	1·7	8·9	56·0
London	1·7	5·7	51·1

Source: Johnston (1976d, Table 1)

only the last-placed candidate's second preferences will be distributed, and as the table shows, this was usually the Liberal aspirant, but Liberal party supporters were more than five times more likely to have their second preferences counted in East Anglia than were those in the north (Johnston, 1976d).

The purpose of the A.V. is to produce a member for whom there is a consensus of general support; the person elected should be the least disliked. On one view, seats won with an initial majority of the votes cast already have such a consensus but, as we showed in the earlier discussion of the voting paradox known as Arrow's theorem (p. 56), when all preferences are counted the consensus may look rather odd. Thus, A.V. provides only a limited definition of a consensus candidate, albeit one which will always produce a favourable result for one, and only one, candidate.

Is such a consensus desirable in terms of various theories of representation? It could be argued that the A.V. is likely to produce conservatism, with radical parties of the right and the left which do not obtain absolute majorities being outflanked by those of the middle-of-the-road as voters from one flank deny success to those of the other. This can happen in Australia, for example, where an Australian Labor Party (A.L.P.) candidate may obtain most first preference votes, only to be defeated because the Liberal–Country Coalition (L.C.P.) aspirant receives most of the second preferences from the third-place right-wing Democratic Labor Party (D.L.P.) contestant. This occurred in the Riverina division of New South Wales in May 1974 where the count was:

First preferences		*After Mackay's and Thomson's second preferences*	
Sullivan	16,128	Sullivan	24,689
Grassby	23,233	Grassby	23,897
Mackay	8,868		
Thomson	357		

Alternatively, it can be argued that the A.V. gives minorities a chance to express their opinions on a particular issue, and thereby influence the government, without entirely wasting their vote on that issue. Lakeman (1974, p. 64) gives an example of this for the English constituency of Gravesend at the 1955 election. The former Labour member (Acland) dissented from his party's policy on nuclear disarmament and stood as an independent on this issue. As a result, the seat was lost, but if A.V. had been used and most of Acland's second preferences had gone to the official Labour candidate, instead of the vote – Conservative, 22,058; official Labour, 19,149; Acland, 6514 – producing a Conservative victory, Labour would have retained the seat and been made aware of the substantial body of feeling against the official policy on nuclear weapons. Such a procedure was in fact the reason why the A.V. system was introduced in Australia, to stop the splitting of a coalition (p. 52), and it allows individuals greater flexibility in expressing opinions, both on particular issues and on general policy directions when 'independent' candidates stand, without feeling that at the same time they are harming the party which they most want to see form a government. In terms of representation, therefore, the A.V. allows voters greater influence on the actions of the loyal party delegates they eventually return. It also allows new parties to float themselves and voters to respond to them without again feeling that they are casting wasted votes with respect to the election of a government.

Votes and voting power

What is the value of votes in terms of the power that they bring to the members? As a simple example of the argument, assume a parliament comprising four parties in each of which discipline is very tight and no member ever votes against his or her party. The membership of the parties is: A, 10; B, 10; C, 7; and D, 4. No one party has a majority in the parliament of 31, therefore, and a coalition is necessary for continuous government. All of the possible coalitions are listed in Table 9.6. The number of votes each coalition commands is given, and those with asterisks are the coalitions whose vote total exceeds the necessary majority of 16; they are the groupings which could form a government. Also listed are the 'destructors', which are those parties that could destroy a coalition's majority if they withdrew. Thus if either A or B withdrew from a coalition involving just those two parties, it would no longer command a majority, but if party D withdrew from coalition BCD the majority would remain. The political power of each party is thus the number of coalitions it could destroy by unilateral withdrawal (Coleman, 1972); this indicates its bargaining power, since the more important a party's votes are in determining a coalition's success, the greater its influence is

Table 9.6 Votes and power in a hypothetical parliament

Votes	A 10	B 10	C 7	D 4	
Possible coalition	*Votes*	*Destructors*	*Possible coalition*	*Votes*	*Destructors*
A B	20*	A B	A B C	27*	
A C	17*	A C	A C D	21*	A C
A D	14		A B D	24*	A B
B C	17*	B C	B C D	21*	B C
B D	14		A B C D	31*	
C D	11				

Coalitions each party could destroy A 4 B 4 C 4 D 0

Party	A	B	C	D
Percentage of votes	32	32	23	13
Percentage of power	33	33	33	0

likely to be over the coalition's policies which are put together when governments are being formed.

In our hypothetical example of Table 9.6, we see that parties A, B, and C have equal percentages of the power, in that each could destroy four potential coalitions, despite C having three fewer votes than the other two; D, on the other hand, has four votes but no apparent power to influence government decisions. A more realistic example of this variation between vote distributions and power distributions concerns the European parliament, constituted with 410 members in July 1976. If we assume that each country's members vote as a bloc on certain issues, what is their power? Table 9.7 shows that although membership of the parliament was designed to give each country approximately equal representation per voter, with the exception of Luxembourg, the smallest country, this 'one man, one vote' provision is not matched by 'one vote, one value' (Taylor and Johnston, 1978); the smaller countries, particularly Luxembourg, have much more power than their votes would apparently entitle them to, and the larger countries slightly less. Similar maldistribution of power occurs in another of the E.E.C.'s institutions, the Coun-

Table 9.7 Votes and power in the European parliament

Country	*Members*	*Ratio of population to members*	*Percentage of members*	*Percentage of power*
Belgium	24	400,000	5·9	8·7
Denmark	16	310,000	3·9	4·3
France	81	610,000	19·8	17·4
Germany	81	750,000	19·8	17·4
Ireland	15	190,000	3·7	4·3
Italy	81	670,000	19·8	17·4
Luxembourg	6	60,000	1·5	4·3
Netherlands	25	530,000	6·1	8·7
United Kingdom	81	680,000	19·8	17·4

cil of Ministers (Johnston and Hunt, 1977), and has important implications with regard to national sovereignty (Johnston, 1977d).

With governments based on coalitions of members, therefore, it is almost certain that the number of members in a party will not equate with that party's power to influence government policies. (It should not be assumed that the larger parties are always disadvantaged, since the distribution of power depends on the combinatorial structure; Johnston, 1977d.) The bargaining procedures out of which a ruling coalition emerges will undoubtedly involve various ideological issues not discussed in the simple examples here – such as the refusal in 1976 of other political parties in Italy to join a coalition which included the Communists – but the general principles remain the same (de Swaan, 1973). As we showed in Chapter 6 with the discussion of the American electoral college, power is not distributed in line with the number of delegates a state has (Mann and Shapley, 1964) – which has a variety of policy implications (see p. 312). Our conclusion must therefore be, that even if electoral systems can be designed which prevent vote-wasting and so ensure 'one man, one vote', the concurrent achievement of 'one vote, one value' is unlikely to occur also. Particularly with regard to party, but also country or state in the European and American examples, certain groups, often representing only relatively few voters, may well be much more powerful in government and opposition than others, irrespective of their size.

Elections and proportional representation: representation and power

Advocates of proportional representation (P.R.) argue that the distribution of votes over a whole territory – usually their distribution across political parties – should be reflected as accurately as possible in the distribution of parliamentary membership. Thus the Liberal Party in Britain claims that because it received 18·3 per cent of all the votes cast in October 1974 it should have received a similar percentage of seats in the House of Commons; it actually got only 2·1 per cent. Such arguments see members very largely as delegates, as loyal party supporters because their election is based on voter acceptance of that party's manifesto. Parliament is seen as a microcosm of the electorate in terms of its political attitudes.

No constituency-based electoral system can ensure P.R. The plurality system with single-member constituencies is the least likely to approach it, but both list and preferential systems can also result in considerable mis-matches between the percentage distributions of votes and of seats (Rae, 1971; Johnston, 1977a; Gudgin and Taylor, 1978). List systems and S.T.V. often come close to P.R., especially with relatively large constituencies, but the absence of complete matches with list systems has led several Scandinavian countries to adopt 'topping-up' allocations to overcome the possible distortions (Elder, 1975; see p. 70). With S.T.V., Lakeman (1974, p. 129) points out that the advantages of increasing constituency size beyond 5–10 members are few – although this depends on the relative size of minor parties (Gudgin and Taylor, 1978) – and any discrimination is almost always against small parties, as with Labour in Ireland (O'Leary, 1961; Mair and Laver, 1975).

With regard to P.R. there are two main strands to the debate over the relative desirability of list/preference systems over pluralities. (A third – the greater difficulty of S.T.V. – is really a smokescreen despite frequent arguments to the contrary, e.g. *Second Report* . . . 1976. Interestingly, experiment suggests that list systems are as likely to produce P.R. as is S.T.V.; Johnston, 1977a.) One of these concerns *fairness*, especially with respect to minority victories, and the other relates to the *uncertainties of coalitions*, which many believe are an inevitable consequence of P.R.

Plurality systems occasionally give governmental power to a party which has not won most votes (as with Conservative in 1951 and Labour in February 1974, in recent British elections). More frequently – in fact almost always (Rae, 1971) – they give a parliamentary mandate to a party supported by only a minority of all those who voted, although that party has obtained more votes than any other; no party in Britain has won half of the votes cast in any election since 1945, although Conservative came very close in 1955 and 1959 with 49·6 and 49·4 per cent respectively. (Given that many voters abstain, no party has won the support of even 40 per cent of the electorate since 1945 – Rogaly 1976, p. 19 – and the Labour governments elected in 1974 had the support of only 29·3 per cent in February and 28·6 per cent in October of all qualified voters.) Leaving aside for the moment the 'mistakes' – the victories of parties without the support of most votes – the main argument in favour of giving a parliamentary majority to a party with only minority (i.e. less than 50 per cent) support is that it encourages strong government 'capable of taking bold initiatives in a coherent and at the same time flexible manner' (Hansard Society, 1976, p. 21). This case was put by a former British prime minister (Harold Wilson) in an interview (*The Times*, 2 August 1976) as follows:

> what is good for Britain – if you can't have a Labour government with a decent majority – is, though I don't like the thought, a Conservative government with a decent majority. So that you get decisions taken which are all of a pattern with some particular political philosophy and strategy, whereas a coalition, I mean an inter-party coalition, would, in my view, lead to weak and fudged decisions and compromises . . .

Because the two main parties are very evenly balanced in Britain, so that a slight swing in votes away from the one in government is likely to bring the other to power, the result is what Finer (1975, p. 3) has defined as 'adversary politics' involving

> two rival teams of politicians in open contention which goes on before an election, during an election and – above all – continues after the election, in the form of a continuous polemic across the floor of the Commons where a powerless opposition confronts an all-powerful government

and (p. 6)

> Governments enjoying this plenitude of power, patronage and information do, however, alternate with one another. Our system is one of alternating single-party government.

He goes on to argue (p. 12 ff.) that such an alternating system is 'inimical to the good conduct of the nation's affairs', for the following five reasons:

(1) Although governments may be elected by voters whose ideologies are mainly middle-of-the-road (Downs, 1957), such governments are usually the more extreme in their policies because of the power of small radical groups (such as the Tribune group in the October 1974 Labour government and the 'deposing' in 1975 of 'a moderate' minister, Reg Prentice, who had much voter support, by the executive of his local party).

(2) Neither party has the support of a majority of the voters, let alone of the electorate.

(3) The alternation of parties and the strength of extremist groups within them – especially when the parliamentary majorities are small – ensures that a change of government brings radical shifts in policy direction.

(4) Powerless oppositions cannot amend government legislation – 'the House as such has been reduced to the role of a pianola playing out jaded tunes that have been recorded elsewhere' (Finer, 1975, p. 14) – and the major determinants of legislation are secret intra-party bargains (see Mitchell, 1968).

(5) Uncertainty is generated, since decision-makers outside

politics (investors etc.) realize that changes of government could well influence them greatly (on regional policy, for example; see Wilson, 1975; Donaldson, 1973). And because governments are frequently – at least once every five years – having to court the electorate, they are unable effectively to control the countervailing forces of unemployment and inflation, perhaps thereby exaggerating if not generating the well-known economic cycles of boom and slump (Wilson, 1975; Stout, 1975).

The alternative to plurality systems usually propounded is one that is more likely to produce P.R., which in most countries would probably mean that governments could only be formed by coalitions of parties. (Minority governments are possible, though these are 'quasi-coalitions' in most cases, relying on the support of other parties providing that they do not introduce certain legislation or, as occurred in Italy after the 1976 election, the agreement of one major party to abstain on votes of confidence in the government.) Harold Wilson's attitude to coalitions has already been quoted – they 'lead to weak and fudged decisions and compromises'. (The next sentence of that interview says, 'of course, I ran a coalition for years . . . every prime minister is head of a kind of coalition', but presumably intra-party coalitions do not fudge or compromise!) Anti-coalition attitudes are often based on a belief that inter-party bargaining prior to the formation of a government involves policy decisions – usually moderating ones – in which the electorate does not participate. If voters consider their members as delegates, then unless they clearly direct them before the election on the acceptable terms for entering a coalition, elector control of the member is reduced and the trustee role becomes more important, even if often as a loyal party member. Party A may differ from party B on seven issues and from party C on three; should it renounce its differences on two of the three in order to form a government with C? And should it allow a member of C to lead the government? (This last question has raised some interest in the Netherlands, where it has been argued that separate elections for prime minister should be held.) Often the conditions are known before the election. In Australia, for example, it is accepted that the Country Party will form a federal government with the Liberal Party, and that the former will take the minority role, at least in the number of cabinet offices allocated to it; the British Liberal Party leader, David Steel, has indicated that an electoral system ensuring P.R. would be a condition of his party entering a coalition (*The Times*, 31 August 1976; this is somewhat paradoxical since it says that 'in the unlikely event of a coalition being necessary after a plurality election we would insist on a system being adopted which virtually ensures coalitions'); and several parties indicated before the Italian 1976 election that they would not enter a coalition with the Communists. In such cases, the electorate has a clearer indication of what their representatives will and will not do.

The partial delegation of powers which may follow from the use of systems which are likely to produce coalitions encourages, in some people's minds, the development of parties which pursue sectional, individual interests only; in terms of representational roles they are specialists rather than generalists, and this applies to parties as a whole rather than to individual members. From this, it can be argued, parliament becomes a number of groups seeking to promote one or a few particular policies rather than a chamber dominated by a party elected because of its perceived ability to legislate over the whole range of government activity. Minorities pursuing their particularistic aims can then come to dominate the policy directions.

The proper representation of minorities is a topic of considerable interest for many. Should they receive P.R.? In Australia this has been a source of much debate. In the determination of electoral divisions for the House of Representatives, a deviation of 20 per cent above or below the average number of electors per division is allowed, and has been used to provide much smaller rural than urban constituencies (Blewett, 1972), because the Electoral Commissioners are required to 'heed disabilities arising out of remoteness or distance, the density or sparsity of population in the division, and the area of the division' (May, 1975, p. 132). Such 'rural over-representation' is particularly irksome to the urban-focused A.L.P., which attempted to remove it in 1973 but failed because it lacked a majority in the Senate. May's (1974, 1975) critique of that debate suggests that representation involves more than equality of voting power on election day. The rationale for rural over-representation rests, at least in part, on the difficulty of rural residents influencing policy through contacts with their members and the administration, often many miles away. But do such peculiar disadvantages require weighted votes? Should poorer people be given weighted votes because they have less accessibility to legislators than do wealthier residents who are easier to organize (Harvey, 1973)? If they are not given such protection do they, as an Irish supporter of P.R. suggested, become 'muzzled, silent, discontented minorities predisposed to doctrines of violence' (O'Leary, 1961, p. 34).

The coalition models developed earlier (Table 9.6) are relevant here with regard to the rights of minorities, for by giving them weighted representation they may be given even greater power. Assume a five-party parliament with members as shown in Table 9.8, in which party A will not serve with E, and E will not govern with B. As a result of these constraints, imposed by the parties themselves or, less likely, by their supporters, we see that parties B and, particularly, E have little power relative to their vote totals, whereas C and D have a lot of bargaining potential. Parliamentary representation of minority parties might be encouraged by P.R., therefore, but it may in addition give them substantial power as well as proportional representation.

Arguments for and against P.R. have been frequent in both the United Kingdom and Ireland. In the latter, de Valera attempted to replace S.T.V. by pluralities in 1958, arguing that coalition government involved 'too much "post-election" bargaining, in which the people obviously could not have a say' (O'Leary, 1961, p. 64). Among the arguments against this were that pluralities produce 'unrepresentative parliaments and arrogant governments', with weak political opposition and a lack of protection for 'small men' against 'jackboot policies'. The move was eventually defeated by referendum in 1959, as was another in 1968, the electorate presumably believing that 'Irish politics ... had been remarkably stable and permanent ... Fianna Fail supremacy

Table 9.8 Votes and power in a hypothetical parliament with constrained coalitions

Votes	A 20	B 8	C 10	D 4	E 15

Possible coalition	*Votes*	*Destructors*
A B	28	
A C	30*	A C
A D	24	
A B C	38*	A C
A B D	32*	A B D
A B C D	42*	A
B C	18	
B D	12	
C D	14	
C E	25	
D E	19	
B C D	22	
C D E	29*	C D E

Party	A	B	C	D	E
Percentage of votes	35	14	18	7	26
Percentage of power	36	9	27	18	9

would be too high a price to pay for the alleged blessings of single-party government' (O'Leary, 1975, p. 170). In the United Kingdom, a Speaker's Conference and both the Commons and the Lords voted in favour of some form of P.R. in 1918, but lack of agreement on which method to adopt led to the proposed reform being lost (Butler, 1963; Steed, 1975). Further bills were introduced during the confused political situation of the 1920s, when Labour's gradual replacement of Liberal as the second major party required several coalitions. One such bill seemed likely to succeed in 1931, as the price of Liberal support for Labour, but the latter's government fell before the reform was effected.

The debate continues. It has been claimed (Butler, 1963, pp. 191–2) that if P.R. had applied in Britain at previous elections –

> Strong majority governments would have been rare. Elections would not have decided which party should form the Cabinet or what general policy it should have. Responsible government and the power of the ordinary elector would thereby have been weakened ... On the other hand ... The necessity of coalition might have made parliament a more genuinely deliberative body ... [with the government lacking] a majority so much greater than was necessary for the control of legislation and policy that it ran the danger of riding roughshod over an opposition too weak adequately to do its job.

Such deterministic arguments, often based on somewhat irrelevant analogies, continue (Butler, 1963, p. 192):

> In Great Britain ... the statistician can say with little fear of contradiction that it [P.R.] would have made minority government the rule and not the exception. The student of politics can assert with almost equal confidence that it would have had a drastic, if largely uncalculable, influence upon the structure and programmes of the parties and upon the conduct and thought of politicians.

Anti-coalitionists point to the instability of governments in Italy and in the French Fourth Republic – both under list electoral systems – and claim that this is what would happen in Britain; pro-P.R. supporters point out, as does Lakeman (1974, p. 173), that the type of system is in no way associated with the number of parties in parliament, that stable, effective minority government, and even majority government, can result under P.R., as in Scandinavian countries, in Ireland, and in Australia. Sectional minorities, especially spatially clustered ones such as Welsh and Scottish nationalists, can obtain parliamentary representation in plurality systems, and may get great power in the parliament; P.R. is apparently acceptable for some parts of Great Britain – i.e. Ulster – proving its feasibility for the electorate; protection of minorities can be ensured by other institutions, such as the judiciary in America, where congressional members can act as parochial delegates because a separately determined executive – appointed by a popularly-elected president – is responsible for general policy direction, constrained by Congress, and individual rights are protected by the judiciary: and so the pros and cons go on. P.R. can be achieved, though only by electoral engineering of the types used in Germany, Denmark and Sweden, but election of a parliament is only one part of the total political-institutional structure of society. What is required of the parliament depends on its role in that structure, and though the nature of parliament and government may be influenced by the electoral system, it is more likely to be influenced by the wider social structure. Might not the deep structural cleavages in Italian society produce unstable government whatever the electoral system, whereas the lack of such cleavages in Ireland will similarly ensure governmental stability?

The unfairness of two systems?

Even if the claim that the strong government a plurality system can provide is worth buying, through the diminution of minority voices, that pluralities occasionally reward the losing major party with governmental power should be much harder to defend. Taylor (1976) has shown that when this has occurred in the United Kingdom during the last three decades:

(1) the government party received only a small parliamentary majority; and

(2) the smaller the party's majority the shorter its term of office, because of difficulties in ensuring parliamentary victories and the usual attrition of majorities which results from by-elections. Thus, although two 'mistakes' were made between 1945 and 1976, during that period the percentage of time each of the two main parties held office has been very much proportional to their percentage of votes cast in all ten elections, so that (Taylor, 1976, p. 8), 'Although we have not had proportional representation in our legislature for *individual* elections, we have had *proportionality of government office* between the parties'. Long-term roundabouts versus short-term swings!

Taylor's argument is based on the assumption that the prime purpose of an election is to produce a government with a workable parliamentary majority. This is backed up by many responses to opinion polls that indicate a concern with the executive role of government. (Governments are elected to govern. On the other hand, of course, there are those who argue that no party which was supported by less than 29 per cent of the eligible voters – the British Labour government elected in October 1974 – has a mandate to introduce all of the policy proposals of its manifesto.) The smaller a party's majority, the shorter its term of office. Thus between 1945 and October 1974, the British population elected nine different governments. The relationship between the size of their parliamentary majority (X) and the number of months before the next election (Y) is extremely close ($r = 0{\cdot}95$; $Y = 14{\cdot}8 \log X - 14{\cdot}9$) indicating that ninety per cent of the variation in the length of parliaments is accounted for by the size of the government's parliamentary majority. From this relationship, Taylor predicts that the government elected in October 1974 would last until the winter of 1977–8. (It lasted another year, because of the Lib-Lab pact, a 'partial coalition' between the Labour and Liberal parties.) By then, Labour would have occupied the government benches at Westminster for 188 months in the years from 1945, compared to 197 months for Conservative; this equates almost exactly with the distribution of votes between the two parties in all post-war elections – 122 million to Conservative and 124 million to Labour. If one accepts the two-party dominance of the plurality system, therefore, one can agree with Taylor that 'the even balance of the electorate is reflected by the even allocation of Conservative and Labour months in office'. Even the lack of power for the minority Liberal Party can be accounted for. After the February 1974 election, that party was offered a place in a coalition with the Conservatives, which was refused; if accepted, the Liberals might have enjoyed about 20 months' occupation of the government benches, proportional to their total showing over all elections since 1945.

Another example of a possibly unfair plurality system concerns the U.S. electoral college, in which a candidate could win a minority of the votes cast, but a majority of the delegates (see p. 45 and p. 312). In 1960, the election turned on Kennedy defeating Nixon by 9000 votes in Illinois, and so winning all 27 of the state's delegates; in 1948 and 1968 if the third-party candidates

(Thurmond and Wallace respectively) had prevented Truman and Nixon getting a majority of electoral college votes, the decision would have gone to 'backstairs intrigue' in the House of Representatives rather than remain with the electorate. One consequence of the immense power of the larger states, it is claimed, is that they are over-represented both in the selection of presidential candidates (of the 70 between 1836 and 1972, 32 of the Democrat and Republican aspirants came from either New York or Ohio; 28 states have never produced a presidential candidate), and in the presidential cabinet appointments (between 1900 and 1968, of the 168 appointed 33 were from New York alone and 12 each from Pennsylvania and Illinois: see Brunn, 1974). Furthermore, three 'runner-up' presidents have been elected (including vice-presidents but excluding Ford) – as well as another 15 who received less than 50 per cent of the popular vote. Of the three 'mistakes', that in 1824 (Adams 30·5 per cent of the vote beat Jackson with 43·1 per cent) occurred largely because of support for Adams in six states where the electoral college delegates were selected by the legislatures, whereas in 1876 Hayes (48 per cent) defeated Tilden (51 per cent) because, it is alleged, of corruption and intimidation in three states (Best, 1975, p. 52). And so, there has been only one *real* 'runner-up' president, Benjamin Harrison, who in 1888 won 47·86 per cent of the votes and yet defeated Grover Cleveland, who received 48·66 per cent.

Victories such as Harrison's over Cleveland are defended by Best as an advantage of the electoral college system, which ensures success for the candidate with the widest appeal. Amassing extra votes in 'safe' states brings no further electoral advantage; a candidate must appeal to widely-different groups across the whole country, so that (Best, 1975, pp. 58 and 70) 'a runner-up presidency is as much the fault of the losing party as of the electoral count system ... The Republic's only undisputed runner-up president, Benjamin Harrison, won because his opponent, Grover Cleveland, ran a sectional campaign'. Thus as a single representative, the sole elected member of the executive (except the vice-president), the president should according to this theory of representation be a generalist in his appeal rather than a specialist; the trustee for many states' residents rather than the delegate of a few. Again, the debate continues, however. The House of Representatives decided by 339 to 70 in September 1969 to replace the college by a single plurality election, but this was never voted on in the Senate.

And so, are these two plurality electoral systems unfair? The answer depends entirely on the criteria which are used to judge fairness. Taylor's case is that any one British government elected since the war may have been over-represented in parliament, and so possessing an unfair allocation of power, but that over the whole post-war period, power has been allocated equitably. The validity of such an argument rests on the assumption that when a party holds its portion of the power is irrelevant. Best's case rests upon the argument that the electoral college ensures that presidential aspirants appeal to a wide range of interest-groups rather than build up massive support among a few major sections of the population. The consequence is, in Harold Wilson's words (p. 462), coalition of interests represented in the White House; does this produce executives that make 'weak and fudged decisions, and compromises'? If so, what do the people want?

The Geography of Power

If it is accepted that a major function of elections is to produce governments strong enough to legislate widely, then a case can be made that such a party should be broadly based in terms of the parts of the country which its members represent. The class basis of many political parties, and the spatial segregation of these classes, makes equal representation of the various parts very difficult even if, as Seliger pointed out for Britain (*The Times Higher Education Supplement*, 27 August 1976, p. 19), rarely less than 40 per cent of the working-class vote is cast for parties other than Labour and at most elections about half of the Conservative vote comes from one-third of the working class. Under the plurality system, Labour representation is over-emphasized in the areas with pro-Labour majorities and under-emphasized where it is in a minority relative to Conservative.

This representational spatial bias can be illustrated from Wales (Johnston, 1977a). In West Glamorgan, comprising five constituencies, the Conservative party polled 20 per cent of the votes to Labour's 58 per cent at the October 1974 general election, but the latter party won all five seats (Table 9.9). And so, if the Conservative party had formed a government after that election, its benches, front and back, would have included no West Glamorgan member. In its formulation of policy, the government would have been denied a West Glamorgan voice, and West Glamorgan residents would have had no access to a representative of theirs who was of the government party. This situation is typical of all plurality systems; in Britain it leads to a pattern whereby 'Labour becomes a more urban party and the Conservatives more "county" in character' (Taylor and Gudgin, 1975, p. 415), so that the geography of government membership is very much more spatially polarized than is the geography of party voting. One of the consequences of this is that some governments find it hard to staff certain ministries – urban-based Labour governments in plurality systems such as those in Britain and New Zealand, for example, often have few members with farming backgrounds and farming constituencies, who are potential candidates for minister of agriculture.

Table 9.9 Voting in West Glamorgan, October 1974 general election

	Votes (with percentages) for				
Constituency	*Conservative*	*Labour*	*Liberal*	*Plaid Cymru*	*Total*
Aberavon[a]	7931 (17)	29,683 (63)	5178 (11)	4032 (9)	47,251
Gower	8863 (20)	25,067 (57)	5453 (12)	4369 (10)	43,752
Neath	4641 (11)	25,028 (61)	3759 (9)	7305 (18)	40,733
Swansea East	6014 (14)	26,735 (64)	5173 (12)	3978 (9)	41,900
Swansea West	17,729 (36)	22,565 (46)	6842 (14)	1778 (4)	48,914
Total	45,168 (20)	129,078 (58)	26,405 (12)	21,462 (10)	222,550

[a]an Independent obtained 427 votes in Aberavon.

Whether members are representative of the constituencies who elect them and are always able to identify local problems depends on what societies demand of their politicians (see below). Nevertheless, alternative systems to the plurality at least ensure that voters for certain parties in larger areas than single constituencies are not entirely unrepresented. If West Glamorgan had been a single constituency using either a list or the S.T.V. system, Conservative would certainly have won one seat to Labour's three, with the other going to either Liberal or Plaid Cymru depending on the system (Johnston, 1977a). (Representation of smaller parties is largely a function of constituency size: Fig. 8.11, p. 429.) In this way, not only would the spatial polarization of government and opposition be reduced, but some of the basis for place-specific campaigning and vote-buying (p. 319) would be replaced by a greater need for nation-wide campaigning (which is somewhat contradictory to Best's defence of the modified plurality system of the American electoral college!).

In parliamentary elections, people vote for members who will undertake a wide range of representative roles – local 'errand boy', government legislator, specialist investigator of certain issues, etc. Under the plurality system they must focus all these issues into a single vote, which usually reflects their choice of party with regard to the governmental role. Under list systems, too, they must choose one party, although in many cases they can express opinions about its various candidates, so that again the governmental role is salient. Under S.T.V. in multi-member constituencies, however, advocates – notably the members of Britain's Electoral Reform Society – claim that the voter can exercise choice for several roles, which thereby 'overrides that of any party organization' (Lakeman, 1974, p. 150). According to Rogaly (1976, p. 140), such a system 'is fairer to voters than to political parties'. In a five-member constituency, for example, a voter could decide that party A would form the best government, that candidate x of party B would be valuable in opposition, and that Mrs y of party C would be an excellent local representative following-up particular problems and issues of constituents in the corridors of power. How he allocated his first five preferences – three for party A, one for x and one for y – would then depend on his perception of the relative importance of the three roles and his beliefs on how others will vote. (S.T.V. is not necessary for this; the at-large plurality elections in Christchurch allow it too: p. 43 and p. 283.)

Arguments ranged against this choice argument include those already discussed, that it will ensure parliamentary coalitions and dominance of parliamentary business by sectionally oriented minorities. Associated with this is the often-expressed fear that with multi-member constituencies the important link between voter and member would never be forged.

Rogaly (1976, pp. 142–3) argues strongly against this from the Irish experience:

> Members of Parliament from *all* constituencies, and not just marginals, would feel obliged to be seen in their constituencies, and to respond to calls from individual voters . . . The Southern Irish M.P., working in a culture that expects good service from politicians . . . probably does more constituency work than his British counterpart . . . Members of the Irish Parliament are far more likely to be local men, originating from or living in their constituencies, than are Westminster M.P.s. Many are prominent in local government. They probably do more social work . . . than the average British M.P. would think was reasonable. They have to – the voters demand it.

(Similar data regarding the primacy of the errand-boy role are available for Austrian representatives, elected by a list system: Crane, 1962.) Again, the important issue is the total socio-political milieu and not just the electoral system acting as an independent influence. As Chubb (1963) has pointed out for the Irish case, most members prefer the errand-boy role, leaving general policy to the party leaders; this, he feels, may reflect on the still rural and parochial nature of much extra-Dublin Irish society. Whether the arguments are transferable to Britain, where in any case constituencies contain many more voters, is dubious (but see Crewe, 1975). Party politics may dominate voting under S.T.V. there, as it does in Australian Senate elections because of the minor errand-boy role of the senators. Once again, we are in the land of probabilities, and clear-cut effects of changing the electoral system cannot be deduced.

Direct Democracy: Avoiding the Geography of Representation

Classical democracy involved government *by* the people; it has been replaced in modern, large-scale societies with government *for* the people. As we have shown in this book, creation of that form of government involves elections. The major influences on how people vote are social and economic, and so we get the geographies of voting described in Chapters 3 and 4, spatial patterns which are often warped by the effects of local influences on self-interested voting (Chapters 5 and 6). The results of such voting are indirect democracy, with decisions made for the electorate by their chosen representatives. In Chapters 7 and 8, however, we showed how there are also strong geographical influences on and patterns in representation, so that the degree of congruence between the democratic desires expressed in the ballot box and the nature of the representation is not always too close. This has consequences for the geography of power, as discussed in the present chapter. So far we have focused on the nature of the geography of power, and the possible effects upon it of various proposed electoral reforms. In this final section we look at aspects of direct democracy through voting which avoids the problems of the geography of representation.

Most of the representatives elected to national parliaments and to the executives of major local governments are trustees in whom the voters have expressed their general confidence. Their range of action may be constrained in some ways; a British Labour M.P., for example, could face a hostile reaction when he appears for re-election if he has voted against some major item in the party's manifesto, and an American Representative who failed to get a cherished irrigation scheme financed for his constituents might receive a cool reception. But on many issues, the trustee representative is given wide scope and his behaviour – voting or otherwise – is unlikely to produce substantial electorate sanctions.

With indirect democracy, therefore, representatives are given considerable legislative latitude. They may use this to 'lead' the electorate, enacting or repealing laws against the views of a majority of voters. In Britain, for example, it is often claimed that a majority of voters probably favour the death penalty and do not approve of 'liberal' attitudes to such issues as divorce and abortion. Such views have not prevented parliamentary votes to the contrary.

National election campaigns almost invariably focus on issues such as economic management, and the behaviour of representatives on a variety of other topics is rarely called into question. (Although when it is, as we showed in Chapter 6 with respect to the immigration issue in Britain, the local impact may be quite intense.) If, as is generally the case, representatives are not typical of those who elect them – in socio-economic characteristics and life styles, in attitudes, values and beliefs – then it is quite easy for this élite group to impose its views on the society as a whole. Further, since the geography of representation if anything accentuates the biases just described, and small interest groups are usually much easier to mobilize and articulate than is the mass of the voting population, then minority pressure groups can quite readily 'lead the leaders'!

To avoid this enforced abdication of much power by the electorate, some form of direct democracy, of government *by* the people, is required. It can be achieved by some proportional representation electoral systems which allow for the election of minority parties representing certain sectional interests. Not all interests can be represented in this way, however, and, as we have shown in this chapter, the power of such minority groups depends very much on the configuration of voting strengths.

Referenda form one possible avenue for direct democracy. In terms of their usage, four types of referenda can be identified:

(1) *Traditional direct democracy.* The major example of this is the Swiss system, in which the referendum is an obligatory mechanism for determining the will of the people on many issues, at all levels of government (see Chapter 6). The number of referenda held there is large. Many attract very small turnout of voters, but it is the existence of the mechanism, as a compulsory part of the system, which ensures the democratic will.

(2) *Anti-government referenda.* These are characteristically American, and reflect the fears of powerful government in the minds of the legislators who wrote many of the state constitutions around the turn of the last century. The purpose of the referenda was to ensure that governments didn't get into large-scale debt without first obtaining public approval to raise a loan.

In 21 states, governments (state and local) cannot borrow without a constitutional amendment; in another 21, legislative approval and a majority of votes in a referendum (⅔rds in some cases) are needed (Sharkansky, 1969, p. 88). The initiative is a public-sponsored referendum, introduced by the reform movement in local government which aimed at removing the big-city political machines and creating non-partisan businesses to replace sectional conflicts. Both see the perils of representative government, and attempt to dilute the indirect democracy that it involves.

(3) *Executive versus legislature.* Many governments comprise more than one elected component, and these parts may be in conflict with each other. To over-rule a hostile legislature, therefore, an executive may make use of the referendum. This was a common ploy of de Gaulle's in France after 1958 to obtain popular approval for his policies; it was used by the Whitlam government in Australia in its attempts to bypass a hostile Senate; and in Britain it was used by a dominant group in the Labour Party in 1975 to isolate a majority of members who opposed it over a major issue.

(4) *National sovereignty referenda.* There is a tradition in several parts of the world that territorial reorganization requires public approval. Thus plebiscites were held after the Treaty of Versailles in 1919 to establish popular support for the new pattern of boundaries, and, at another scale, in a number of countries approval by referendum of the affected parties is required for the redrawing of local government boundaries. On these issues, therefore, the role of territory is crucial, illustrating the strong ties which exist between peoples and places (p. 449).

Re-emergence of core–periphery cleavages

The referenda on national-sovereignty issues produce some interesting examples of the spatial patterns of voting under direct democracy, which on occasions are very different from those under indirect democracy. Thus in 1948, Newfoundlanders voted by 52 to 48 in favour of joining the Canadian Confederation rather than independence. Over the 24 electoral districts in the island there were no correlations between the percentage voting 'yes' to confederation and socio-economic variables such as income which indexed the main basis of party cleavages (Warntz, 1955). Instead, the strongest correlation was with accessibility. The more isolated the community, the greater the support for confederation, suggesting a core–periphery cleavage to voting on this issue of national sovereignty rather than a class-based cleavage.

Core–periphery cleavages have been strong in Scandinavian countries in the recent past, as we demonstrated in Chapters 3 and 4. More recently, they have been replaced by a class-based cleavage, but in the voting at referenda held in 1972 on E.E.C. membership, the core–periphery (urban–rural) voting pattern re-emerged in both Denmark and Norway. In both countries, it was the rural areas which were crucial in these acts of direct democracy, a result which would have been very unlikely if indirect democracy had been used to settle the issue in the Folketing and Storting (the respective parliaments).

Table 9.10 illustrates the urban–rural dimension to the voting pattern in Denmark, as well as a class-based cleavage within Copenhagen where the working-class districts (like the areas of 'left' support in several other countries) were against entry (Petersen and Elklit, 1973). Within the general pattern of these two cleavages, neighbourhood effects can be identified, in both urban and rural areas. In the former, for example, middle-class central city areas follow the dominant working-class ethos of anti-E.E.C., whereas in the suburbs, working-class residents seem drawn towards the middle-class view. The agricultural industry was expected to profit from E.E.C. membership, and so, according to survey data, whereas 'workers' in urban areas were only 49 per cent in favour of joining compared to 79 per cent for professional people, in rural areas members of these two groups were 64 and 100 per cent in favour respectively (Valen, Alklit and Tonsgaard, 1975, p. 277).

Re-emergence of the core–periphery cleavage was even stronger in Norway's voting on a similar referendum. Overall, 53·5 per cent of those voting were against E.E.C. membership, compared

Table 9.10 Percentage 'Yes' votes in the Danish E.E.C. referendum by region and type of constituency

Region	*Type of constituency*	*Per cent 'yes' vote*
Greater Copenhagen	Working-class city	36·0
	Working-class suburb	50·0
	Middle-class city	47·3
	Middle-class suburb	61·8
Three largest provincial cities		52·8
The Islands	More urbanized	59·5
	Less urbanized	62·4
Jutland	More urbanized	59·1
	Less urbanized (east)	64·7
	Less urbanized (west)	67·7
	Less urbanized (south)	67·8

Source: Petersen and Elklit (1973)

to only 30 per cent of those who had been elected to the Storting in 1969. Regional patterns of support for the proposal ranged from 64·5 per cent in Oslo to 37·5 per cent in Nordland; by type of community, the range was from 57·4 per cent in the mixed service-and-manufacturing municipalities to only 19·7 per cent in the fishing communities. Table 9.11 illustrates the clear spatial pattern which these variations produced, highlighting the polarization between the accessible and inaccessible areas, both within and between regions.

Whereas in Denmark the core–periphery cleavage joined the class-based cleavage in producing the referendum result, in Norway the former almost entirely replaced the latter. Unlike the Danes, the Norwegians believed that membership of the E.E.C. would be against the interests of their (heavily subsidized) agricultural and fishing industries. Thus, the Centre (Agrarian) Party was against joining, whereas the Conservative Party, representing urban-business interests, was in favour; the majority of its supporters followed each party's lead (Table 9.12). But the Labour

Table 9.11 Percentage 'Yes' votes in the Norwegian E.E.C. referendum by region and accessibility

Region	*Accessibility*	*Per cent 'yes' vote*
	Low	32·6
East	Intermediate	37·5
	High	57·0
	Low	21·3
South	Intermediate	37·0
	High	47·0
	Low	28·2
West	Intermediate	31·3
	High	52·9
	Low	26·6
Middle	Intermediate	32·2
	High	43·8
	Low	23·1
North	Intermediate	34·3

Source: Central Bureau of Statistics of Norway (1972)

Party (then the governing party) and the Liberal Party were both split; within the former, whereas 45 per cent of Labour supporters in the 'core' were against membership, in the periphery 61 per cent voted 'no'.

There are two possible interpretations of the core–periphery vote in Norway (Hellevik and Gleditsch, 1973): the first is that the implications of the benefits of membership had not sufficiently permeated the periphery by 1972; the other is that membership was in the interests of the majority in the Storting, where urban-business-professional interests are over-represented and the views of the rural voters are under-represented. A single referendum cannot discriminate between these two plausible hypotheses. Hellevik and Gleditsch (1973, p. 233) note, however, that 'many voters simply will not change either position or party even when they disagree with their party on the most central issue in the

Table 9.12 Party voting and referendum voting in Norway

Party support in 1969 election	*Per cent 'yes' vote*
Labour	58
Liberal	47
Christian	22
Centre (Agrarian)	7
Conservative	82

Source: Central Bureau of Statistics of Norway (1972)

campaign. Well aware of this, representatives can deviate considerably from their voters without worrying unduly about the next election'. In 1972, if the second hypothesis is correct, this party loyalty disappeared and direct democracy contradicted the establishment of indirect democracy. And so, whereas the Labour minister of fisheries won 49 per cent of his constituency's votes in 1969, in 1972 the same people voted 92 per cent against E.E.C. membership.

These two Scandinavian referenda, and the earlier one in Newfoundland, suggest that on issues of national sovereignty spatial cleavages may be more important in referenda voting than in the more general election of representatives. Is the same true in Britain? In the prolonged debate over devolution to Scotland and Wales in the mid-1970s, residents of peripheral areas in Scotland (the Shetland Islands and the Western Isles) made it clear that they feared rule from Edinburgh (and the undoubted political power of the Strathclyde region – including Glasgow) more than they disliked the current base in Westminster (*The Times*, 12 January 1977). But in the 1975 referendum on continued membership of the E.E.C., no core–periphery cleavage emerged, perhaps because of the lack of a powerful agricultural lobby. This was demonstrated by Kirby and Taylor (1976) who used the scores for the two factors identified in Table 2.7 (p. 92) as their independent variables (Figure 9.1). The resulting regression equation –

$$\% \text{ Yes} = 0{\cdot}85\ F_{11} + 0{\cdot}04\ F_{1}$$

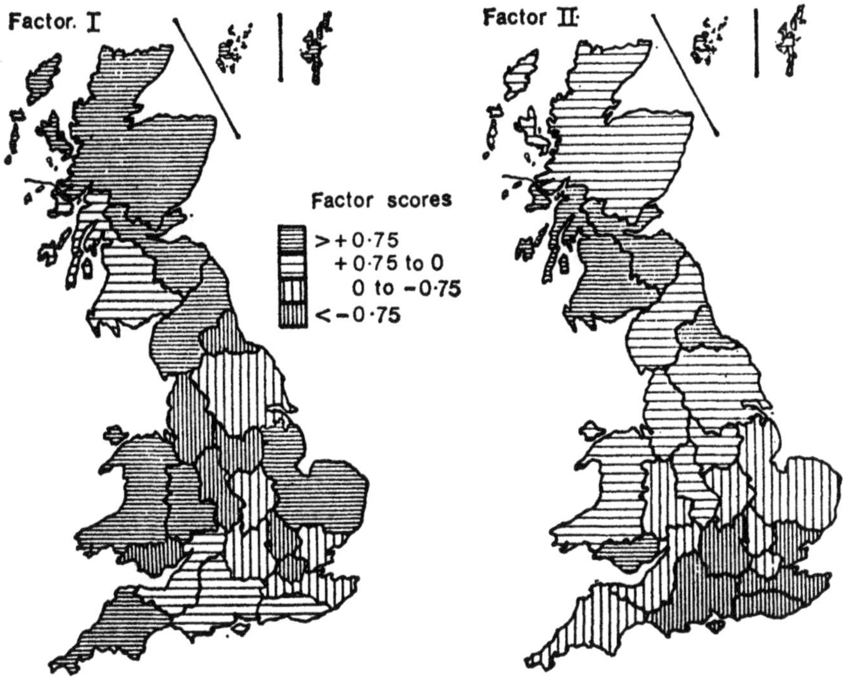

Figure 9.1 Scores, for the 23 'regions' of the United Kingdom for which data were available, on the core-periphery (*left*) and affluence (*right*) factors identified in Table 2.7.

– accounted for about 64 per cent of the spatial variation in the voting pattern. Both regression coefficients have positive signs, indicating that support for continued membership was greatest in the Conservative-dominated areas (Factor II) and in the core (Factor I), but of the two only the former made a substantial contribution to the regression equation, thereby indicating a triumph for class-based voting (centre and right versus a diluted left, as in Denmark and Norway) over spatial cleavages.

Although the 1975 British referendum was held on an issue of national sovereignty, and indeed some of the strongest campaigners for a 'no' vote (including Enoch Powell and Tony Benn) stressed the sovereignty issue, nevertheless, in many ways the vote was used as an executive versus legislature contest. One group within the Labour Cabinet, led by the Prime Minister, was pro-E.E.C. membership, and it used the novel procedure (for

Britain) of direct democracy in order to sidestep the major difference of opinion within the ruling party. Because it was the first use of such a tactic, there was a clear question of its legitimacy, since British governments have always argued that their election provides them with a mandate to govern as they see fit. From an analysis of abstentions and spoiled ballots, Bristow (1976) indicates that the procedure was deemed legitimate, with Labour supporters apparently more inclined towards this use of direct democracy than their Conservative counterparts.

Opinion polls as direct democracy

Direct and indirect democracy are far from independent of each other, of course, for voters and representatives are continually learning from one another. Where direct democratic procedures are obligatory, elected representatives will often attempt to lead the electorate, as did the Swiss government over the immigrant issue (Johnston and White, 1977), and as American city governments do with regard to bond issue referenda (Archer and Reynolds, 1976).

Representatives used to learn from their constituents through personal contacts. Increasingly they now use the frequent public opinion polls for this purpose. Members of Norway's Storting, for example, were well aware that, while in September 1971 67 per cent of their countrymen favoured E.E.C. membership, in December 1972 this figure had fallen to 47 per cent (Hellevik and Gleditsch, 1973, p. 227). Some of them reacted to this by changing their own positions and so removing the 75 per cent majority in the Storting in favour of membership that could have overruled the referendum decision (which was not binding): in Britain, on the other hand, in 1972 'a simple majority in parliament voted Britain into the Common Market against a majority of the voters' (Hellevik and Gleditsch, 1973, p. 229).

Political opinion polls are, therefore, increasingly used as instruments of direct democracy, albeit imprecise ones. In Norway, they, and then the referendum, were used to educate the representatives, as the former have been in many countries to aid governments in deciding when to call elections. Over the E.E.C. issue, in the United Kingdom, the polls were used to monitor the degree to which the electorate was learning from the representatives before the decision was made to use the referendum to legitimize the representatives' view. Of course, there are problems in using opinion polls to monitor public opinion, as we suggested in Chapter 2. Although pollsters were confident that Britain's membership of the E.E.C. would be confirmed by the referendum, the polls had indicated that the size of the pro-E.E.C. majority varied from 2 per cent to 18 per cent depending upon *how* the question was phrased (Butler and Kitzinger, 1976). More generally Wheeler (1976) has illustrated many disturbing examples of American pollsters influencing government policy over such issues as Vietnam by taking on the role of 'scientific surrogates' for direct democracy. Clearly if public opinion may be easily manipulated by pollsters the dangers of governments manipulating direct democracy are immense. Direct democracy via referenda may remove some power from representatives, therefore, but where use of the method is non-obligatory it should only seriously upset them when they have misread public opinion.

Although direct democracy might seem more preferable than the various forms of indirect democracy as a means of matching public policy to public attitudes, it does have the further disadvantage of removing any power from minority groups. This is demonstrated by the anti-government referenda in the United States. Many local governments are in serious financial straits, and are unable to undertake large-scale programmes of investment because those who must pay are not prepared to vote for public rather than private interests in the relevant referenda. Further, since the 'reformed' governments, where referenda and initiatives are widely used, are most typical of small suburban municipalities, especially in the west, it is the upper-middle-class business community's private interest which prevails and redistribution of real income from rich to poor is kept to a low level.

Just as all forms of electoral system have their disadvantages, with complete 'one man, one vote; one vote, one value' apparently unattainable, so direct democracy does not offer only benefits. It may avoid some of the problems of the geography of representation, but if the issues are based on conflicts of interest between classes and other groups, then permanent minority exclusion from decision-making may be ensured, perhaps enhancing class polarization. Our analyses here have shown that this need not always be so, and that new 'coalitions' may form on particular issues, as in the Danish and Norwegian examples. Opinion polling could lead to new spatial biases. Instead of the hundred most marginal constituencies receiving disproportionate attention, for example, it may be more beneficial to parties to concentrate on the constituencies in which the sampling takes place (Chapter 2, p. 94). Furthermore, the value of the vote (opinion) of the 2000 or so chosen respondents would seem to be potentially far greater than anything so far discussed here. Direct democracy can have its own geography of power too.

Conclusion

And so the debate can, and certainly will, continue. Because of the multi-functional role of elections, there can be no single, simple answer as to what is the best electoral system. It depends very much on the dominant roles expected of representatives and of parties, and of the social milieu within which the electoral system operates. If you want P.R. and only P.R., with party-machine-dominated politics, then the German system is probably the best bet; if you want to avoid coalitions, but again to be dominated by parties, then select the plurality system; and if you want maximum choice for voters, then go for S.T.V.: if you want all three, and more besides, then . . . All we have been able to do here is illustrate the complex inter-relationships between society, geography and electoral systems, and to indicate that if you believe that social engineering is possible through spatial engineering of the electoral system, then before you build the machine you must specify the sort of environment you want it to work in and with.

References

ABLER, R. F., ADAMS, J. S., and GOULD, P. R. (1971) *Spatial Organization*. Prentice-Hall, New Jersey.

ADAMANY, D. (1969) 'The party variable in judges' voting: conceptual notes and a case study', *American Political Science Review*, 63, 57–73.

AITKIN, D., and KAHAN, M. (1974) 'Australia: class politics in the New World', in Rose, R. (editor), *Electoral Behavior: A Comparative Handbook*. The Free Press, New York, 437–80.

ALFORD, R. R. (1963) *Party and Society*. Rand McNally, Chicago.

ALKER, H. R. (1969) 'A typology of ecological fallacies', in Dogan, M., and Rokkan, S. (editors), *Quantitative Ecological Analysis in the Social Sciences*. The M.I.T. Press, Cambridge, Mass., 69–86.

ALKER, H. R., and RUSSETT, B. M. (1964) 'On measuring inequality', *Behavioral Science*, 9, 207–19.

ALLARDT, E., and PESONEN, P. (1967) 'Cleavages in Finnish politics', in Lipset, S. M., and Rokkan, S. (editors), *Party Systems and Voter Alignments*. The Free Press, New York, 325–66.

ALLARDT, E., and ROKKAN, S., editors (1970) *Mass Politics*. The Free Press, New York.

ALMY, T. A. (1973) 'Residential location and electoral cohesion: the pattern of urban political conflict', *American Political Science Review*, 67, 914–23.

ALT, J. (1971) 'Some social and political correlates of county borough expenditure', *British Journal of Political Science*, 1, 49–62.

ANDREWS, J. H. (1966) 'Illinois' at-large vote', *National Civic Review*, 55, 253–7.

APPEL, J. S. (1965) 'A note concerning apportionment by computer', *American Behavioral Scientist*, 7, 36.

ARCHER, J. C., and REYNOLDS, D. R. (1976) 'Locational logrolling and citizen support of municipal bond proposals: the example of St Louis', *Public Choice*, 27, 21–40.

References

ARDREY, R. (1966) *The Territorial Imperative*. Atheneum Press, New York.

ARROW, K. J. (1951) *Social Choice and Individual Values*. John Wiley, New York.

BAKER, G. E. (1966) *The Reapportionment Revolution*. Random House, New York.

BAKER, G. E. (1971) 'Gerrymandering: privileged sanctuary or next judicial target?', in Polsby, N. W. (editor), *Reapportionment in the 1970s*. University of California Press, Berkeley, 121–142.

BANFIELD, E. C., and WILSON, J. Q. (1963) *City Politics*. Harvard University Press, Cambridge, Mass.

BANZHAF, J. F. III (1968) 'One man, 3·312 votes: a mathematical analysis of the Electoral College', *Villanova Law Review*, 13, 304–32.

BARNES, S. H. (1974) 'Italy: religion and class in electoral behavior', in Rose, R. (editor), *Electoral Behavior: A Comparative Handbook*. The Free Press, New York, 171–226.

BARNETT, J. R. (1973) 'Scale components in the diffusion of the Danish Communist Party, 1920–63', *Geographical Analysis*, 5, 35–44.

BARNETT, M. J. (1973) 'Aggregate models of British voting behavior', *Political Studies*, 21, 121–34.

BARONE, M., UJIFUSA, G., and MATTHEWS, D. (1972) *The Almanac of American Politics: The Senators, the Representatives – their Records, States and Districts*. Macmillan, London.

BARRY, B. (1974) 'Review article: exit, voice and loyalty', *British Journal of Political Science*, 4, 79–107.

BENNEY, M., and GEISS, P. (1950) 'Social class and politics in Greenwich', *British Journal of Sociology*, 1, 310–27.

BERELSON, B. R., LAZARSFELD, P. F., and MCPHEE, W. N. (1954) *Voting*. University of Chicago Press, Chicago.

BERGER, B. (1960) *Working Class Suburb*. University of California Press, Los Angeles.

BERRINGTON, H. (1964) 'The General Election of 1964', *Journal of the Royal Statistical Society*, Series A, 128, 17–66.

BERRINGTON, H. (1975) 'Electoral reform and national government', in Finer, S. E. (editor), *Adversary Politics and Electoral Reform*. Anthony Wigram, London, 269–92.

BEST, J. (1975) *The Case against Direct Election of the President: A Defense of the Electoral College*. Cornell University Press, Ithaca.

BIEL, H. S. (1972) 'Suburbia and voting behavior in the London metropolitan area: an alternative perspective', *Tijdschrift voor Economische en Sociale Geografie*, 63, 39–43.

BIRCH, A. H. (1971) *Representation.* Pall Mall, London.

BIRCH, A. H. (1975) 'Economic models in political science: the case of "exit, voice and loyalty"', *British Journal of Political Science*, 5, 69–82.

BIRDSALL, S. S. (1969) 'Preliminary analysis of the 1968 Wallace vote in the Southeast', *Southeastern Geographer*, 9, 55–66.

BIRKE, W. (1961) *European Elections by Direct Suffrage.* Sythoff, Leyden.

BLACK, E., and BLACK, M. (1973) 'The Wallace vote in Alabama: a multiple regression analysis', *Journal of Politics*, 35, 730–36.

BLAKE, D. E. (1967) 'The measurement of regionalism in Canadian voting patterns', *Canadian Journal of Political Science*, 5, 55–81.

BLAU, P. M. (1960) 'Structural effects', *American Sociological Review*, 25, 178–93.

BLEWETT, N. (1972) 'Redistribution procedures', in H. Mayer, and H. Nelson (editors), *Australian Politics: A Third Reader.* Cheshire, Melbourne, 295–300.

BLEWETT, N. (1976) 'Dunstan, the Council, and electoral innovation', *The Australian Quarterly*, 48, 83–97.

BLEWETT, N., and JAENSCH, D. (1971) *Playford to Dunstan: Politics of Transition.* Cheshire, Melbourne.

BLONDEL, J. (1963) *Voters, Parties and Leaders: The Social Fabric of British Politics.* Penguin Books, Harmondsworth.

BLYDENBURGH, J. C. (1971) 'A controlled experiment to measure the effects of personal contact campaigning', *Midwest Journal of Political Science*, 15, 365–81.

BLYDENBURGH, J. C. (1974) 'The effect of ballot form on city council elections', *Political Science*, 26, 47–55.

BLYDENBURGH, J. C. (1976) 'An application of game theory to political campaign decision-making', *American Journal of Political Science*, 20, 51–66.

BOCHEL, J. M., and DENVER, D. T. (1971) 'Canvassing, turnout and party support: an experiment', *British Journal of Political Science*, 1, 257–69.

BOCHEL, J. M., and DENVER, D. T. (1972) 'The impact of the campaign on the results of local government elections' *British Journal of Political Science*, 2, 239–44.

BRADY, D. W. (1973) 'A research note on the impact of interparty competition in Congressional voting in a competitive era', *American Political Science Review*, 67, 153–6.

BRAMS, S. J. (1975) *Game Theory and Politics.* Free Press, New York.

BRAMS, S. J., and DAVIS, M. D. (1973) 'Resource-allocation models in presidential campaigning: implications for democratic representation', *Annals of the New York Academy of Sciences*, 291, 105–23.

BRAMS, S. J., and DAVIS, M. D. (1974) 'The 3/2s rule in presidential campaigning', *American Political Science Review*, 68, 113–34 and 155–6.

BRISTOW, S. L. (1976) 'Partisanship, participation and legitimacy in Britain's E.E.C. referendum', *Journal of Common Market Studies*, 14, 297–310.

BROOKS, R. C. (1933) *Political Parties and Electoral Problems.* Harper, New York.

BROWN, J. (1958) 'Local party efficiency as a factor in the outcome of British elections', *Political Studies*, 6, 174–8.

BRUNN, S. D. (1974) *Geography and Politics in America.* Harper and Row, New York.

BRUNN, S. D., and HOFFMAN, W. L. (1970) 'The spatial response of negroes and whites toward open housing: the Flint referendum', *Annals, Association of American Geographers*, 60, 18–36.

BUCHANAN, J. M. (1974) *The Limits of Liberty.* University of Chicago Press, Chicago.

BUDGE, I., CREWE, I., and FAIRLIE, D., editors (1976) *Party Identification and Beyond.* John Wiley, London.

BULLOCK, C. S. III (1971) 'The influence of state party delegations on House committee assignments', *Midwest Journal of Political Science*, 15, 525–46.

BUNGE, W. (1966) 'Gerrymandering, geography and grouping', *Geographical Review*, 56, 256–63.

BURGHARDT, A. F. (1963) 'Regions and political party support in Burgenland (Austria)', *Canadian Geographer*, 7, 91–8.

BURGHARDT, A. F. (1964) 'The bases of support for political parties in Burgenland', *Annals, Association of American Geographers*, 54, 372–90.

BURNHAM, W. D. (1967) 'Party systems and the political process', in Chambers, W. N., and Burnham, W. D. (editors), *The American Party System.* Oxford University Press, New York, 277–307.

BURNHAM, W. D. (1974) 'The United States: the politics of heterogeneity', in Rose, R. (editor), *Electoral Behavior: A Comparative Handbook.* The Free Press, New York, 653–726.

BURNHAM, W. D. (1975) 'American politics in the 1970s: beyond party?', in Burnham, W. D., and Chambers, W. N. (editors), *The American Party Systems: Stages of Political Development.* Oxford University Press, New York, 308–58.

BURSTEIN, P. (1976) 'Social networks and voting: some Israeli data', *Social Forces*, 54, 833–47.

BUSH, G. W. A. (1975) 'Local body elections', *Political Science*, 27, 140.

BUSHMAN, D. O., and STANLEY, W. R. (1961) 'State Senate reapportionment in the Southeast'. *Annals, Association of American Geographers*, 61, 654–70.

BUSTEED, M. A. (1975) *Geography and Voting Behaviour*. Oxford University Press, London.

BUSTEED, M. A., and MASON, H. L. (1970) 'Irish Labour in the 1969 election'. *Political Studies*, 18, 373–9.

BUSTEED, M. A., and MASON, H. L. (1974) 'The 1973 General Election in the Irish Republic', *Irish Geography*, 7, 97–106.

BUTLER, D. E. (1947) 'The relation of seats to votes', in McCallum, R. B., and Readman, A., *The British General Election of 1945*. Oxford University Press, London, 277–92.

BUTLER, D. E. (1955a) 'The redistribution of seats'. *Public Administration*, 55, 125–47.

BUTLER, D. E. (1955b) *The British General Election of 1955*. Macmillan, London.

BUTLER, D. E. (1963) *The Electoral System in Britain since 1918*. The Clarendon Press, Oxford.

BUTLER, D. E., and KING, A. (1966) *The British General Election of 1966*. Macmillan, London.

BUTLER, D. E., and KITZINGER, U. (1976) *The 1975 Referendum*. Macmillan, London.

BUTLER, D. E., and PINTO-DUSCHINSKY, M. (1971) *The British General Election of 1970*. Macmillan, London.

BUTLER, D. E., and STOKES, D. E. (1969) *Political Change in Britain: Forces shaping Electoral Choice*. Macmillan, London. (References are to page numbers in the Penguin edition, published in 1971, except those to the 1974 second edition published by Macmillan.)

BUTLER, J. R., BEVAN, J. M., and TAYLOR, R. C. (1973) *Family Doctors and Public Policy: A Study of Manpower Distributions*. Routledge and Kegan Paul, London.

CAIRNS, A. C. (1968) 'The electoral systems and the party system in Canada, 1921–1965', *Canadian Journal of Political Science*, 1, 55–80.

CAMPBELL, A., and MILLER, W. E. (1957) 'The motivational basis of straight and split ticket voting', *American Political Science Review*, 51, 293–312.

CAMPBELL, P. (1958) *French Electoral Systems and Elections since 1789.* Faber and Faber, London.

CAMPBELL, R. V., and KNIGHT, D. B. (1976) 'Political territoriality in Canada – a choropleth and isopleth analysis', *Canadian Cartographer,* 13, 1–10.

CAPECCHI, V., and GALLI, G. (1969) 'Determinants of voting behavior in Italy: a linear causal model of analysis', in Dogan, M. and Rokkan, S. (editors), *Quantitative Ecological Analysis in the Social Sciences.* The M.I.T. Press, Cambridge, Mass. 235–84.

CARTER, H., and THOMAS, J. G. (1969) 'The referendum on the Sunday opening of licensed premises in Wales as a criterion of a culture region', *Regional Studies,* 3. 61–71.

CARVALHO, C. M. D. (1962) 'Geography of languages', in Wagner, P. L., and Mikesell, M. W. (editors), *Readings in Cultural Geography.* University of Chicago Press, Chicago.

CHAMBERS, W. N. (1967) 'Party development and the American mainstream', in Chambers, W. N., and Burnham, W. D. (editors), *The American Party System.* Oxford University Press, New York, 3–32.

CHAMBERS, W. N., and BURNHAM, W. D., editors (1967) *The American Party Systems.* Oxford University Press, New York.

CHI, N. H. (1976) 'Class cleavage' in Winn, C., and McMeneny, J. (editors), *Political Parties in Canada.* McGraw-Hill, Toronto.

CHUBB, B. (1963) 'Going about persecuting civil servants: the role of the Irish parliamentary representative', *Political Studies,* 11, 273–86.

CLUBB, J. M., and ALLEN, H. W., editors (1971) *Electoral Change and Stability in American Political History.* The Free Press, New York.

CNUDDE, C. F., and MCCRONE, D. J. (1966) 'The linkage between constituency attitudes and Congressional voting behavior: a causal model', *American Political Science Review,* 60, 1966, 66–72.

COATES, B. E., and RAWSTRON, E. M. (1971) *Regional Variations in Britain.* Batsford, London.

COLEMAN, J. S. (1964) *Introduction to Mathematical Sociology.* The Free Press, Glencoe, Illinois.

COLEMAN, J. S. (1972) 'Control of collectivities and the power of a collectivity to act', in Liebermann, B. (editor), *Social Choice.* Gordon and Breach, New York, 269–300.

COLMAN, A., and POUNTNEY, I. (1975a) 'Voting paradoxes: A Socratic dialogue I', *Political Quarterly,* 46, 186–90.

COLMAN, A., and POUNTNEY, I. (1975b) 'Voting paradoxes: a Socratic dialogue II', *Political Quarterly,* 46, 304–309.

Congressional Quarterly Service (1966) *Representation and Reapportionment.* Washington, D.C.

CONVERSE, P. E. (1966) 'The concept of a normal vote', in Campbell, A., Converse, P. E., Miller, W. E., and Stokes, D. E., *Elections and the Political Order.* John Wiley, New York, 9–39.

COPE, C. R. (1971) 'Regionalization and the electoral districting problem', *Area*, 3, 190–95.

CORNFORD, J. (1964) 'The adoption of mass organization by the British Conservative Party', in Allardt, E., and Littunen, Y. (editors), *Cleavages, Ideologies, and Party Systems.* Contributions to Comparative Political Sociology. Transactions of the Westermarck Society, 10, Helsinki, 401–11.

CORNFORD, J. (1970) 'Aggregate election data and British party alignments, 1885–1910', in Allardt, E., and Rokkan, S. (editors), *Mass Politics.* The Free Press, New York, 107–16.

COX, K. R. (1968) 'Suburbia and voting behavior in the London metropolitan area', *Annals, Association of American Geographers*, 58, 111–27.

COX, K. R. (1969a) 'The voting decision in a spatial context', *Progress in Geography*, 1, 81–117.

COX, K. R. (1969b) 'The spatial structuring of information flow and partisan attitudes', in Dogan, M., and Rokkan, S. (editors), *Quantitative Ecological Analysis in the Social Sciences.* The M.I.T. Press, Cambridge, Mass., 157–85.

COX, K R. (1969c) 'Voting in the London suburbs: a factor analysis and a causal model', in Dogan, M., and Rokkan, S. (editors), *Quantitative Ecological Analysis in the Social Sciences.* The M.I.T. Press, Cambridge, Mass., 343–70.

COX, K. R. (1970a) 'Geography, social contexts, and voting behavior in Wales, 1861–1951', in Allardt, E., and Rokkan, S. (editors), *Mass Politics.* The Free Press, New York, 117–59.

COX, K. R. (1970b) 'Residential relocation and political behavior: conceptual model and empirical tests', *Acta Sociologica*, 13, 40–53.

COX, K. R. (1971) 'The spatial components of urban voting response surfaces', *Economic Geography*, 47, 27–35.

COX, K. R. (1972) 'The neighborhood effect in urban voting response surfaces', in Sweet, D. C. (editor), *Models of Urban Structure.* D.C. Heath, Lexington, Mass., 159–76.

COX, K. R. (1973) *Conflict, Power and Politics in the City: A Geographical View.* McGraw-Hill, New York.

COX, K. R. (undated) 'The spatial evolution of national voting response surfaces: theory and measurement', Department of Geography, Ohio State University, *Discussion Paper* No. 9, Columbus.

CRAIG, J. T. (1959) 'Parliament and boundary commissions', *Public Law*, 24, 23–45.

CRANE, W. JR (1962) 'The errand-running function of Austrian legislators', *Parliamentary Affairs*, 15, 160–69.

CREWE, I. (1973) 'The politics of "affluent" and "traditional" workers in Britain: an aggregate data analysis', *British Journal of Political Science*, 3, 29–52.

CREWE, I. (1975) 'Electoral reform and the local M.P.', in Finer, S. E. (editor), *Adversary Politics and Electoral Reform*. Anthony Wigram, London, 317–42.

CREWE, I., FOX, T., and ALT, J. (1977) 'Non-voting in British general elections', *British Political Sociology Yearbook*, 3 Croom Helm, London.

CREWE, I., and PAYNE, C. (1971) 'Analysing the census data', in Butler, D., and Pinto-Duschinsky, M., *The British Genera Election of 1970*. Macmillan, London, 416–36.

CREWE, I., and PAYNE C. (1976) 'Another game with nature: an ecological regression model of the British two-party vote ratio in 1970', *British Journal of Political Science*, 6, 43–81.

CRIDDLE, B. (1975) 'Distorted representation in France', *Parliamentary Affairs*, 26, 154–79.

CROSSMAN, R. H. S. (1975) *The Diaries of a Cabinet Minister: Volume One, Minister of Housing 1964–66*. Hamish Hamilton and Jonathan Cape, London.

CROTTY, W. J. (1971) 'Party effort and its impact on the vote', *American Political Science Review*, 65, 439–50.

CUMMINGS, M. C. JR (1966) *Congressmen and the Electorate: Elections for the U.S. House and the President, 1920–1964*. The Free Press, New York.

CURTIS, G. L. (1971) *Election Campaigning Japanese Style*. Columbia University Press, New York.

CUTRIGHT, P. (1963) 'Measuring the impact of local party activity on the General Election vote', *Public Opinion Quarterly*, 27, 372–86.

CUTRIGHT, P., and ROSSI, P. H. (1958a) 'Grass roots politicians and the vote', *American Sociological Review*, 23, 171–9.

CUTRIGHT, P., and ROSSI, P. H. (1958b) 'Party organization in primary elections', *American Journal of Sociology*, 64, 262–9.

DAHL, R. A. (1956) *A Preface to Democratic Theory*. University of Chicago Press, Chicago.

DARBY, J. (1976) *Conflict in Northern Ireland: The Development of a Polarised Community*. Gill and Macmillan, Dublin.

DAVIDSON, N. (1976) *Causal Inferences from Dichotomous Variables*. CATMOG 9, Geoabstracts Ltd., Norwich.

DAWIDOWICZ, L. S., and GOLDSTEIN, L. J. (1963) *Politics in a Pluralist Democracy*. Institute of Human Relations Press, New York.

DAWSON, R. E. (1975) 'Social development, party competition and policy', in Chambers, W. D., and Burnham, W. D. (editors), *The American Party Systems: Stages of Political Development*. Oxford University Press, New York, 203–37.

DEAKIN, N. (1965) *Colour and the British Electorate 1964: Six Case Studies*. Pall Mall, London.

DEAN, J. W. (1892) 'The gerrymander', *New England Historical and Genealogical Register*, 44, 374–83.

DE KLERK, W. A. (1976) *Puritans in Africa: A Story of Afrikanerdom*. Penguin Books, Harmondsworth.

DENVER, D. T., and HANDS, G. (1972) 'Turnout and marginality in local elections: a comment', *British Journal of Political Science*, 2, 513–15.

DE SWAAN, A. (1973) *Coalition Theories and Cabinet Formation*. Elsevier, Amsterdam.

DEUTSCH, K. W. (1953) *Nationalism and Social Communication*. The M.I.T. Press, Cambridge, Mass.

DEUTSCH, K. W. (1969) *Nationalism and its Alternatives*. A. A. Knopf, New York.

DIKSHIT, R. D. (1975) *The Political Geography of Federalism: An Inquiry into Origins and Stability*. Macmillan, New Delhi.

DIXON, R. G. JR (1968) *Democratic Representation: Reapportionment in Law and Politics*. Oxford University Press, New York.

DIXON, R. G. JR (1971) 'The court, the people and "one man, one vote"', in Polsby, N. W. (editor) *Reapportionment in the 1970s*. University of California Press, Berkeley, 7–46.

DOGAN, M. (1967) 'Political cleavage and social stratification in France and Italy', in Lipset, S. M., and Rokkan, S. (editors), *Party Systems and Voter Alignments*. The Free Press, New York, 129–95.

DOGAN, M. (1969) 'A covariance analysis of French electoral data', in Dogan, M., and Rokkan, S. (editor), *Quantitative Ecological Analysis in the Social Sciences*. The M.I.T. Press, Cambridge, Mass., 285–98.

DOGAN, M., and ROKKAN, S., editors (1969) *Quantitative Ecological Analysis in the Social Sciences*. The M.I.T. Press, Cambridge, Mass.

DONALDSON, P. (1973) *Economics of the Real World*. Penguin Books, Harmondsworth.

DOWNS, A. (1957) *An Economic Theory of Democracy*. Harper and Row, New York.

DUNBABIN, J. P. D. (1966) 'Parliamentary elections in Great Britain, 1868–1900: a psephological note'. *English History Review*, 81, 82–99.

DYE, T. R. (1965) 'State legislative politics', in Jacobs, H., and Vines, K. N. (editors), *Politics in the American States: A Comparative Analysis*. Little, Brown and Company, Boston, 151–206.

ELDER, N. C. M. (1975) 'The Scandinavian states', in Finer, S. E. (editor), *Adversary Politics and Electoral Reform*. Anthony Wigram, London, 185–202.

ELDERSVELD, S. J. (1956) 'Experimental propaganda techniques and voting behavior', *American Political Science Review*, 50, 154–65.

Election Expenses. Return to an Address of the Honourable the House of Commons dated 7 November, 1974 (1975) H.M.S.O., London.

ENNIS, P. H. (1962) 'The contextual dimension in voting', in McPhee, W. N., and Glaser, W. A. (editors), *Public Opinion and Congressional Elections*. The Free Press, Glencoe, Ill., 180–211.

EULAU, H., ZISK, B. H., and PREWITT, K. (1966) 'Latent partisanship in nonpartisan elections: effects of political milieu and mobilization', in Jennings, M. K., and Zeigler, L. H. (editors), *The Electoral Process*. Prentice-Hall, Englewood Cliffs, New Jersey, 208–37.

FENTON, J. H. (1966) *People and Parties in Politics*. Scott, Foresman and Co., Glenview, Ill.

FENTON, J. H., and CHAMBERLAYNE, D. W. (1969) 'The literature dealing with the relationships between political processes, socio-economic conditions and public policies in the American states: a bibliographical essay', *Polity*, 1, 388–404.

FEREJOHN, J. A. (1974) *Pork-Barrel Politics: Rivers and Harbors Legislation, 1947–1968*. Stanford University Press, Stanford.

FEREJOHN, J. A. (1977) 'On the decline of competition in congressional elections', *American Political Science Review*, 71, 166–75.

FIFER, J. V. (1976) 'Unity by inclusion: core area and Federal state at American independence', *Geographical Journal*, 142, 402–10.

FINER, S. E., editor (1975) *Adversary Politics and Electoral Reform*. Anthony Wigram, London.

FINER, S. E. (1975) 'Adversary politics and electoral reform', in Finer, S. E. (editor), *Adversary Politics and Electoral Reform*. Anthony Wigram, London, 3–32.

FISHER, S. L. (1973) 'The wasted vote thesis', *Comparative Politics*, 5, 293–300.

FITTON, M. (1973) 'Neighbourhood and voting: a sociometric explanation', *British Journal of Political Science*, 3, 445–72.

FLETCHER, P. (1969) 'An explanation of variations in turnout in local elections', *Political Studies*, 17, 495–502.

FOLADARE, I. S. (1968) 'The effect of neighborhood on voting behavior', *Political Science Quarterly*, 83, 526–9.

FOOT, P. (1965) *Immigration and Race in British Politics*. Penguin Books, Harmondsworth.

FOOT, P. (1969) *The Rise of Enoch Powell*. Penguin Books, Harmondsworth.

FORREST, E. (1965) 'Apportionment by computer', *American Behavioral Scientist*, 7, 23, and 35.

FORREST, J., and JOHNSTON, R. J. (1973) 'Spatial aspects of voting in the Dunedin City Council elections of 1971', *New Zealand Geographer*, 29, 166–81.

FORREST, J., MARJORIBANKS, E., and JOHNSTON, R. J. (1977) 'Local effects at New Zealand local elections', in Johnston, R. J. (editor), *People Places and Votes: Essays on the Electoral Geography of Australia and New Zealand*. University of New England, Department of Geography, Armidale, 35–50.

FREEMAN, H. E., and SHOWEL, M. (1962) 'The political influence of voluntary organizations', in McPhee, W. N., and Glaser, W. A. (editors), *Public Opinion and Congressional Elections*. The Free Press, Glencoe, Ill., 212–21.

GALLACHER, M. (1974) 'Disproportionality in a proportional representation system: the Irish experience', *Political Studies*, 23, 501–13.

GARRAHAN, P. (1977) 'Housing, the class milieu and middle-class conservatism', *British Journal of Political Science*, 7, 125–6.

GINGRAS, F. P., and WINN, C. (1976) 'Bicultural cleavage', in Winn, C., and McMeneny, J. (editors), *Political Parties in Canada*. McGraw-Hill, Toronto.

GIROD, R. (1964) 'Geography of the Swiss party system' in Allardt, E., and Littunen, Y. L. (editors), *Cleavages, Ideologies and Party Systems*. Transactions of the Westermarck Society, 10, Helsinki, 132–61.

GOGUEL, F. (1970) *Géographie des Élections Françaises sous la Troisième et la Quatrième République*. A Colin, Paris.

GOLDTHORPE, J. H. *et al.* (1968) *The Affluent Worker: Political Attitudes and Behaviour*. Cambridge University Press, Cambridge.

GOODEY, B. R. (1968) *The Geography of Elections: An Introductory Bibliography*. University of North Dakota, Center for the Study of Cultural and Social Change, Monograph 3, Grand Forks, North Dakota.

GOULD, P. R. (1969) *Spatial Diffusion*. Association for American Geographers, Commission on College Geographers, Research Paper No. 4, Washington, D.C.

GRAHAM, B. D. (1962) 'The choice of voting method in Federal politics, 1902–1918', *Australian Journal of Politics and History*, 8, 164–82.

GREEN, G. (1972) 'National, city and ward components of local voting', *Policy and Politics*, 1, 45–54.

GREEN PAPER (1976) *Direct Elections to the European Assembly*. H.M.S.O., London.

GUDGIN, G., and TAYLOR, P. J. (1974) 'Electoral bias and the distribution of party voters', *Transactions, Institute of British Geographers*, 63, 53–73.

GUDGIN, G., and TAYLOR, P. J. (1978) *Seats, Votes and the Spatial Organization of Elections*, Pion, London.

GUMP, W. R. (1971) 'The functions of patronage in American party politics: an empirical reappraisal', *Midwest Journal of Political Science*, 15, 87–107.

HACKER, A. (1964) *Congressional Districting*. The Brookings Institute, Washington, D.C.

HANSARD SOCIETY (1976) *The Report of the Hansard Society Commission on Electoral Reform*. The Hansard Society for Parliamentary Government, London.

HANSON, R. (1966) *The Political Thicket*. Prentice-Hall, Englewood Cliffs, New Jersey.

HARMATUCK, D. J. (1976) 'Referendum voting as a guide to public support for mass transit', *Traffic Quarterly*, 30, 347–70.

HARTLEY-BREWER, M. (1965) 'Smethwick', in Deakin, N. (editor), *Colour and the British Electorate 1964: Six Case Studies*. Pall Mall, London, 77–105.

HARTZ, L. (1964) *The Founding of New Societies*. Harcourt, Brace and World, New York.

HARVEY, D. W. (1973) *Social Justice and the City*. Edward Arnold, London.

HEADLAM-MORLEY, A. (1929) *The New Democratic Constitutions of Europe*. Oxford University Press, London.

HEARD, K. A. (1974) *General Elections in South Africa, 1943–1970*. Oxford University Press, London.

HEER, D. M. (1958) 'The sentiment of white supremacy: an ecological study', *American Journal of Sociology*, 64, 592–8.

HELLEVIK, O., and GLEDITSCH, N. P. (1973) 'The Common Market decision in Norway: a clash between direct and indirect democracy', *Scandinavian Political Studies*, 8, 227–35.

HENIG, S., and PINDER, J., editors (1969) *European Political Parties*. George Allen and Unwin, London.

HERBERT, D. T. (1976) 'Urban education: problems and policies', in Herbert, D. T., and Johnston, R. J. (editors), *Social Areas in Cities: Volume II Spatial Perspectives on Problems and Policies*. John Wiley, London, 123–58.

HERBERT, G. (1975) 'Party voting contagion in city regions', *Politics*, 10, 58–68.

HERMANS, F. A. (1958) *The Representative Republic*. University of Notre Dame Press, Notre Dame, Indiana.

HERMANS, F. A. (1976) 'Electoral systems and political systems: recent developments in Britain', *Parliamentary Affairs*, 29, 47–59.

HESS, S. W., WEAVER, J. B., SIEGFELDT, H. J., WHELAN, J. N., and ZITLAU, P. A. (1965) 'Non-partisan political districting by computer', *Operational Research* 13, 998–1006.

HICKS, J. D. (1971) *The Populist Revolt*. University of Minnesota Press, Minneapolis.

HINDESS, B. (1967) 'Local elections and the Labour vote in Liverpool', *Sociology*, 1, 187–95.

HIRSCHMANN, A. O. (1970) *Exit, Voice and Loyalty: Responses to Decline in Firms, Organizations and States*. Harvard University Press, Cambridge, Mass.

HOLT, A. T., and TURNER, J. E. (1968) *Political Parties in Action*. The Free Press, New York.

HOROWITZ, G. (1966) 'Conservatism, Liberalism and Socialism in Canada: an interpretation', *Canadian Journal of Economics and Political Science*, 32, 179–201.

HUGHES, C. A., and GRAHAM, B. D. (1968) *A Handbook of Australian Government and Politics 1850–1964*. Australian National University Press, Canberra.

HUGHES, C. A., and SAVAGE, E. E. (1967) 'The 1955 Federal redistribution', *Australian Journal of Politics and History*, 13, 8–27.

HYMAN, H. H. (1959) *Political Socialization.* The Free Press, Glencoe, Ill.

JACKSON, W. K. (1962) 'The electoral framework', in Chapman, R. M., Jackson, W. K., and Mitchell, A. V. *New Zealand Politics in Action: The 1960 General Election.* Oxford University Press, London, 3–12.

JAENSCH, D. (1970) 'A functional gerrymander - South Australia 1944–1970', *Australian Quarterly*, 42, 96–101.

JAROS, D., and CANON, B. C. (1971) 'Dissent on State Supreme Courts: the differential significance of characteristics of judges', *Midwest Journal of Political Science*, 15, 322–46.

JENKINS, M. A., and SHEPHERD, J. W. (1972) 'Decentralizing high school administration in Detroit: an evaluation of alternative strategies of political control', *Economic Geography*, 48, 95–106.

JEWELL, M. E. (1962) 'Political patterns in apportionment', in Jewell, M. E. (editor), *The Politics of Reapportionment.* Atherton Press, New York, 1–48.

JOHNSON, R. W., and SCHOEN, D. (1976) 'The "Powell effect": or how one man can win', *New Society*, 37, 22 July 1976, 168–72.

JOHNSTON, R. J. (1971) *Urban Residential Patterns: An Introductory Review.* G. Bell and Sons Ltd, London.

JOHNSTON, R. J. (1972) 'Spatial elements in voting patterns at the 1968 Christchurch City Council election', *Political Science*, 24(1), 49–61.

JOHNSTON, R. J. (1973) 'Spatial patterns and influences on voting in multi-candidate elections: the Christchurch City Council election, 1968', *Urban Studies*, 10, 69–82.

JOHNSTON, R. J. (1974a) 'Local effects in voting at a local election', *Annals, Association oƒ American Geographers*, 64, 418–29.

JOHNSTON, R. J. (1974b) 'Social distance, proximity and social contact', *Geografiska Annaler*, 56B, 57–67.

JOHNSTON, R. J. (1976a) 'On contagion and voting', *Politics*, 11, 102–103.

JOHNSTON, R. J. (1976b) 'Contagion in neighbourhoods: a note on problems of modelling and analysis', *Environment and Planning*, A, 8, 581–6.

JOHNSTON, R. J. (1976c) 'Parliamentary seat redistribution: more opinions on the theme', *Area*, 8, 30–34.

JOHNSTON, R. J. (1976d) 'Geography and an alternative electoral system', *The Globe* (Manchester University Geographical Society), 49, 3–13.

JOHNSTON, R. J. (1976e) 'Resource allocation and political campaigns: notes towards a methodology', *Policy and Politics*, 5, 181–99.

JOHNSTON, R. J. (1976f) 'Political behaviour and the residential mosaic', in Herbert, D. T., and Johnston, R. J. (editors) *Social Areas in Cities: Volume II, Spatial Perspectives on Problems and Policies.* John Wiley, London, 65–88.

JOHNSTON, R. J. (1976g) 'Spatial structure, plurality systems and electoral bias', *Canadian Geographer*, 20, 310–28.

JOHNSTON, R. J. (1977a) 'The compatibility of spatial structure and electoral reform: observations on the electoral geography of Wales', *Cambria*, 4, 125–51.

JOHNSTON, R. J. (1977b) 'Political geography and welfare: observations on interstate variations in AFDC programs', *Professional Geographer*, 29, 347–52.

JOHNSTON R. J. (1977c) 'Contagious processes and voting patterns: Christchurch, 1965–1972', in R. J. Johnston (editor), *People, Places, and Votes: Essays in the Electoral Geography of Australia and New Zealand.* University of New England, Department of Geography, Armidale, 11–34.

JOHNSTON, R. J. (1977d) 'National sovereignty and national power in European institutions', *Environment and Planning, A*, 9, 569–77.

JOHNSTON, R. J. (1977e) 'The electoral geography of an election campaign', *Scottish Geographical Magazine*, 93, 98–108.

JOHNSTON, R. J. (1978a) *Multivariate Statistical Methods in Geography: A Primer on the General Linear Model.* Longman, London.

JOHNSTON, R. J. (1978b) 'Politics and social well-being: an essay on the political geography of the welfare state', in Busteed, M. A. (editor), *Developments in Political Geography.* Academic Press, London.

JOHNSTON, R. J., and HUNT, A. J. (1977) 'Voting power in the E.E.C.'s Council of Ministers: an essay on method in political geography', *Geoforum* 8, 1–9.

JOHNSTON, R. J., and WHITE, P. E. (1977) 'Reactions to foreign workers in Switzerland: an essay in electoral geography', *Tijdschrift voor Economische en Sociale Geografie*, 67, 341–54.

KAREIL, E. (1916) 'Geographical influences in British elections', *Geographical Review*, 6, 419–32.

KASPERSON, R. (1969) 'On suburbia and voting behavior', *Annals, Association of American Geographers*, 59, 405–11.

KATZ, E., and LAZARSFELD, P. F. (1955) *Personal Influence.* The Free Press, Glencoe, Ill.

KATZ, R. S. (1973) 'The attribution of variance in electoral returns: an alternative measurement technique', *American Political Science Review*, 67, 817–28.

KAVANAGH, D. (1970) *Constituency Electioneering in Britain.* Longmans, London.

KENDALL, M. G., and STUART, A. (1950) 'The law of cubic proportions in election results', *British Journal of Sociology*, 1, 183–97.

KERR, H. H. (1974) *Switzerland: Social Cleavages and Partisan Conflict.* Sage Professional Paper in Contemporary Political Sociology 1, 06–002. Sage Publication, Beverly Hills.

KEY, V. O. JR (1949) *Southern Politics in State and Nation.* Alfred A. Knopf Inc., New York.

KEY, V. O. JR (1955) 'A theory of critical elections', *Journal of Politics* 17, 3–18.

KEY, V. O., and MUNGER, F. (1959) 'Social determinism and electoral decision: the case of Indiana', in Burdick, E., and Brodbeck, A. J. (editors), *American Voting Behavior*, The Free Press, Glencoe, Ill., 281–99.

KINNEAR, M. (1968) *The British Voter: An Atlas and Survey since 1885.* Batsford, London.

KIRBY, A. M., and TAYLOR, P. J. (1976) 'A geographical analysis of the voting pattern in the E.E.C. referendum, 5 June 1975', *Regional Studies*, 10, 183–92.

KLAPPER, J. T. (1960) *The Effects of Mass Communication.* The Free Press, Glencoe, Illinois.

KNIGHT, B. B. (1976) 'The states and reapportionment: one man, one vote reevaluated', *State Government*, 49, 155–60.

KNIGHT, J., and BAXTER-MOORE, N. (1973) *Republic of Ireland: The General Elections of 1969 and 1973.* The Arthur MacDougall Fund, London.

KRAMER, G. H. (1966) 'A decision-theoretic analysis of a problem in political campaigning', in Bernd, J. (editor), *Mathematical Applications in Political Science*, 2, Dallas, SMU Press, 137–60.

KRAMER, G. H. (1970) 'The effects of precinct-level canvassing on voter behavior', *Public Opinion Quarterly*, 34, 560–72.

LAKEMAN, E. (1974) *How Democracies Vote.* Faber and Faber, London, Fourth Edition.

LANCELOT, M-T, and A (1970) *Atlas des Circonscriptions Électorales en France depuis 1875.* A. Colin, Paris.

LAPONCE, J. A. (1957) 'The protection of minorities by the electoral system', *Western Political Quarterly*, 10, 318–39.

LASERWITZ, B. (1960) 'Suburban voting trends: 1948–1956', *Social Forces*, 39, 29–36.

LAUX, H. D., and SIMMS, A. (1973) 'Parliamentary elections in West Germany: the geography of electoral choice', *Area*, 5, 161–71.

LAVER, M. (1976) 'On introducing S.T.V. and interpreting the results: the case of Northern Ireland 1973–1975', *Parliamentary Affairs*, 29, 211–29.

LAZARSFELD, P. F., BERELSON, B. R., and GAUDET, H. (1944) *The People's Choice*. Columbia University Press, New York.

LAZARSFELD, P. F., and THIELENS, J. R. W. (1958) *The Academic Mind: Social Scientists in a Time of Crisis*. The Free Press, Glencoe, Ill.

LEE, T. R. (1976) 'Cities in the mind', in Herbert, D. T., and Johnston, R.J. (editors), *Social Areas in Cities: Volume II, Spatial Perspectives on Problems and Policies*. John Wiley, London, 159–88.

LELEU, C. (1971) *Géographie des Élections Françaises depuis 1936*. Presses Universitaires de France, Paris.

LENGLE, J. I., and SHAFER, B. (1976) 'Primary rules, political power, and social change', *American Political Science Review*, 70, 25–40.

LEVIN, M. L. (1961) 'Social climates and political socialization', *Public Opinion Quarterly*, 25, 596–606.

LEWIS, P. F. (1965) 'Impact of negro migration on the electoral geography of Flint, Michigan, 1932–62: a cartographic analysis', *Annals, Association of American Geographers*, 55, 1–25.

LEWIS, P. W., and SKIPWORTH, G. E. (1966) *Some Geographical and Statistical Aspects of the Distribution of Votes in Recent General Elections*. University of Hull, Department of Geography, Miscellaneous Series No. 32, Hull.

LEY, D. (1974) *The Black Inner City as Frontier Outpost*. Association of American Geographers, Washington.

LIITTSCHWAGER, J. M. (1973) 'The Iowa redistricting system', *Annals, New York Academy of Science*, 219, 221–35.

LIJPHART, A. (1971) 'Class voting and religious voting in European democracies', *Acta Politica*, 6, 158–71.

LIJPHART, A. (1974) 'The Netherlands: continuity and change in voting behavior', in Rose, R. (editor), *Electoral Behavior*. The Free Press, New York, 227–68.

LIPSET, S. M., and ROKKAN, S. (1967) 'Cleavage structures, party systems, and voter alignments: an introduction', in Lipset, S. M., and Rokkan, S. (editors), *Party Systems and Voter Alignments*. The Free Press, New York, 3–64.

LIPSET, S. M., TROW, M. A., and COLEMAN, J. S. (1956) *Union Democracy*. The Free Press, Glencoe, Ill.

LIPSON, L. (1959) 'Party systems in the United Kingdom and the older Commonwealth: causes, resemblances and variations', *Political Studies*, 7, 12–31.

LOCKARD, D. (1959) *New England State Politics*. Princeton University Press, Princeton.

LONG, J. A. (1969) 'Maldistribution in western provincial legislatures: the case of Alberta', *Canadian Journal of Political Science*, 2, 345–55.

LOSSING, B. J. (1872) 'The natural and political history of the gerrymander', *American Historical Record*, 1, 504–7.

MCCARTY, H. H. (1952) 'McCarty on McCarthy: the spatial distribution of the McCarthy vote, 1952', unpublished manuscript, State University of Iowa, Iowa City; discussed in Thomas, E. N. (1968) 'Maps of residuals from regression', in Berry, B. J. L., and Marble, D. F. (editors), *Spatial Analysis*. Prentice-Hall, Englewood Cliffs, New Jersey, 326–52.

MCCLOSKY, H., and DAHLGREN, H. E. (1959) 'Primary group influence on party loyalty', *American Political Science Review*, 53, 757–76.

MCCORMICK, R. P. (1967) 'Political development and the second party system', in Chambers, W. N., and Burnham, W. D. (editors) *The American Party Systems*. Oxford University Press, New York, 90–116.

MCCREADY, D., and WINN, C. (1976) 'Geographic cleavage: core vs periphery', in Winn, C., and McMeneny, J. (editors), *Political Parties in Canada*. McGraw Hill, Toronto.

MCDONALD, G. T. (1976) 'Rural representation in Queensland state parliament', *Australian Geographical Studies*, 14, 33–42.

MCDONALD, R. H. (1969) 'Apportionment and party politics in Santiago, Chile', *Midwest Journal of Political Science*, 13, 455–70.

MCKAY, D. H., and PATTERSON, S. C. (1971) 'Population equality and the distribution of seats in the British House of Commons', *Comparative Politics*, 4, 59–76.

MACKENZIE, W. J. M. (1957) 'The export of electoral systems', *Political Studies*, 5, 240–57.

MACKENZIE, W. J. M. (1958) *Free Elections*. Allen and Unwin, London.

MCKENZIE, R. T., and SILVER, A. (1968) *Angels in Marble: Working Class Conservatives in Urban England*. Heinemann, London.

MACKERRAS, M. (1970) 'Preferences and donkeys', *Politics*, 5, 69–76.

MCLEAN, I. (1973) 'The problem of proportionate swing', *Political Studies*, 21, 57–63.

MCLEAN, I. (1975) *Elections*. Longman, London.

MACOBY, E. E., MATTHEWS, R. E., and MORTON, A. S. (1954) 'Youth and political change', *Public Opinion Quarterly*, 18, 25–39.

MCPHAIL, I. R. (1971a) 'Recent trends in electoral geography', *Proceedings of the Sixth New Zealand Geography Conference*, Christchurch, 1, 7–12.

MCPHAIL, I. R. (1971b) 'The vote for Mayor of Los Angeles in 1969', *Annals, Association of American Geographers*, 61, 744–58.

MCPHAIL, I. R., and WALMSLEY, D. (1975) 'Government', *Atlas of Australian Resources*, Second Series (Booklet), Department of Minerals and Energy, Canberra.

MACRAE, D. (1952) 'The relationship between roll-call votes and constituencies in the Massachusetts House of Representatives', *American Political Science Review*, 46, 1046–55.

MAIR, P., and LAVER, M. (1975) 'Proportionality, P. R. and S.T.V. in Ireland', *Political Studies*, 23, 491–500.

MANN, I., and SHAPLEY, L. S. (1964) 'The *a priori* voting strength of the Electoral College', in Shubik, M. (editor), *Game Theory and Related Approaches to Social Behavior*. John Wiley, New York, 151–64.

MARTIN, F. M. (1952) 'Social status and electoral choice in two constituencies', *British Journal of Sociology*, 3, 231–41.

MASTERMAN, C. J. (1964) 'The effect of the "Donkey Vote" on the House of Representatives', *Australian Journal of Politics and History*, 10, 221–5.

MAY, J. D. (1974) 'Democracy and rural over-representation', *Australian Quarterly*, 46, 52–6.

MAY, J. D. (1975) 'Rural over-representation: pros and cons in recent Australian debate', *Journal of Commonwealth and Comparative Politics*, 13, 132–45.

MAY, R. J. (1972) 'Federal finance: politics and gamesmanship', in Mayer, H., and Nelson, H. (editors), *Australian Politics: A Third Reader*. Cheshire, Melbourne, 237–58.

MAYHEW, C. (1976) *The Disillusioned Voter's Guide to Electoral Reform*. Arrow Books, London.

MAYHEW, D. R. (1971) 'Congressional representation: theory and practice in drawing the districts', in Polsby, N. W. (editor), *Reapportionment in the 1970s*. University of California Press, Berkeley, 249–85.

MERCER, C. (1976) *Living in Cities*. Penguin Books, Harmondsworth.

MEYER, J. W. (1962) 'A reformulation of the "coattails" problem', in McPhee, W. N., and Glaser, W. A. (editors), *Public Opinion and Congressional Elections*. The Free Press, Glencoe, Ill., 52–64.

MICHELSON, W. (1970) *Man in his Urban Environment: A Sociological Approach*. Addison-Wesley, Reading, Mass.

MIKESELL, M. W. (1960) 'Comparative studies of frontier history', *Annals, Association of American Geographers*, 50, 62–74.

MILIBAND, R. (1969) *The State in Capitalist Society*. Quartet Books, London.

MILLER, W. E. (1956) 'One-party politics and the voter', *American Political Science Review*, 50, 707–25.

MILLER, W. E. (1964) 'Majority rule and the representative system of government', in Allardt, E., and Littunen, Y. (editors), *Cleavages, Ideologies, and Party Systems*. Transactions of the Westermarck Society, 10, Helsinki, 343–76.

MILLER, W. E., and STOKES, D. E. (1963) 'Constituency influence in Congress', *American Political Science Review*, 57, 45–56.

MILLER, W. L., RAAB, G., and BRITTO, K. (1974) 'Voting research and the population census 1918–71: surrogate data for constituency analyses', *Journal, Royal Statistical Society*, A, 137, 384–411.

MILLS, G. (1967) 'The determination of local government boundaries', *Operational Research Quarterly*, 18, 243–55.

MITCHELL, A. V. (1968) 'Caucus: The New Zealand Parliamentary Parties', *Journal of Commonwealth Political Studies*, 6, 3–33.

MORRILL, R. L. (1970) *Spatial Organization of Society*. Wadsworth Publishing Company, Belmont, California.

MORRILL, R. L. (1973) 'Ideal and reality in reapportionment', *Annals, Association of American Geographers*, 63, 463–77.

MORRILL, R. L. (1976) 'Redistricting revisited', *Annals, Association of American Geographers*, 66, 548–56.

MOSER, C., and SCOTT, W. (1961) *British Towns*. Oliver and Boyd, London.

MUELLER, J. E. (1970) 'Choosing among 133 candidates', *Public Opinion Quarterly*, 34, 395–402.

MYRDAL, G. (1969) *Objectivity in Social Research*. Random House, New York.

NAGEL, S. S. (1965) 'Simplified bi-partisan computer redistricting', *Stanford Law Review*, 17, 863–99.

NAGEL, S. S. (1972) 'Computers and the law and politics of redistricting', *Polity*, 5, 77–93.

NEWTON, K. (1972) 'Turnout and marginality in local elections', *British Journal of Political Science*, 2, 251–5.

NEWTON, K. (1976) *Second City Politics: Democratic Processes and Decision-Making in Birmingham*. Oxford University Press, London.

NORAGON, J. L. (1973) 'Redistricting, political outcomes, and the gerrymandering of the 1960s', *Annals, New York Academy of Science*, 219, 314–33.

O'LEARY, C. (1961) *The Irish Republic and its Experiment with Proportional Representation.* University of Notre Dame Press, Notre Dame, Indiana.

O'LEARY, C. (1975) 'Ireland: the north and south', in Finer, S. E. (editor), *Adversary Politics and Electoral Reform.* Anthony Wigram, London, 153–84.

O'LOUGHLIN, J., and BERG, D. A. (1977) 'The election of Black mayors, 1969 and 1973', *Annals, Association of American Geographers*, 67, 223–38.

ORBELL, J. M. (1970) 'An information-flow theory of community influence', *Journal of Politics*, 32, 322–38.

ORR, D. M. JR (1970) *Congressional Redistricting: The North Carolina Experience.* University of North Carolina, Department of Geography, Studies in Geography, No. 2, Chapel Hill.

OSBORNE, R. D. (1975) 'Parliamentary seat distributions', *Area*, 7, 199–201.

OSBORNE, R. D. (1976) 'Northern Ireland: representation at Westminster and the Boundary Commission', *Irish Geography*, 9, 115–20.

PADDISON, R. (1976) 'Spatial bias and redistricting in proportional representation systems: a case study of the Republic of Ireland', *Tijdschrift voor Economische en Sociale Geografie*, 67, 230–40.

PEDERSEN, M. H. (1966) 'Preferential voting in Denmark: the voters' influence on the election of Folketing candidates', *Scandinavian Political Studies*, 1, 167–87.

PEELE, S., and MORSE, S. J. (1974) 'Ethnic voting and political change in South Africa', *American Political Science Review*, 68, 1520–41.

PELLING, H. (1967) *The Social Geography of British Elections 1885–1910.* Macmillan, London.

PELLING, H. (1971) *A Short History of the Labour Party.* Macmillan, London.

PERRIN, N. (1962) 'In defence of country votes', *Yale Review*, 52, 16–24.

PESONEN, P. (1974) 'Finland: party support in a fragmented system', in Rose, R. (editor), *Electoral Behavior: A Comparative Handbook.* The Free Press, New York, 271–314.

PETERSEN, S. (1968) *A Statistical History of the American Presidential Elections.* Ungar, New York.

PETERSEN, N., and ALKLIT, J. (1973) 'Denmark enters the European communities', *Scandinavian Political Studies*, 8, 198–213.

PETRAS, J., and ZEITLIN, M. (1967) 'Miners and agrarian radicalism', *American Sociological Review*, 32, 578–86.

PETRAS, J., and ZEITLIN, M. (1968) 'Agrarian radicalism in Chile', *British Journal of Sociology*, 19, 254–70.

PIEPE, A., PRIOR, R., and BOX, A. (1969) 'The location of the proletarian and deferential worker', *Sociology*, 3, 239–44.

POLLOCK, J. K. (1952) 'The electoral system of the Federal Republic of Germany – a study in representative government', *American Political Science Review*, 46, 1056–66.

POLSBY, N. W. (1968) 'The institutionization of the U.S. House of Representatives', *American Political Science Review*, 62, 144–68.

POLSBY, N. W. (1969) 'The growth of the seniority system in the House of Representatives', *American Political Science Review* 63, 787–807.

POLSBY, N., and WILDAVSKY, A. (1964) *Presidential Elections: Strategies of American Electoral Politics.* Scribner's, New York.

POUNDS, N. J. G., and BALL, S. S. (1964) 'Core areas and the development of the European states system', *Annals, Association of American Geographers*, 54, 24–40.

PRESCOTT, J. R. V. (1959) 'The functions and methods of electoral geography', *Annals, Association of American Geographers*, 49, 296–304.

PRESCOTT, J. R. V. (1969) 'Electoral studies in political geography', in Kasperson, R. E., and Minghi, J. V. (editors), *The Structure of Political Geography.* Aldine Press, Chicago, 376–83.

PRESCOTT, J. R. V. (1972) *Political Geography.* Methuen, London.

PRICE, D. E., and LUPFER, M. (1973) 'Volunteers for Gore: the impact of a precinct-level canvass in three Tennessee cities', *Journal of Politics*, 35, 410–38.

PULSIPHER, A. G. (1973) 'Empirical and normative theories of apportionment', *Annals, New York Academy of Science*, 219, 234–41.

PULSIPHER, A. G., and WEATHERBY, J. L. JR (1962) 'Malapportionment, party competition, and the functional distribution of government expenditures', *American Political Science Review*, 62, 1207–19.

PUTNAM, R. D. (1966) 'Political attitudes and the local community', *American Political Science Review*, 60, 640–54.

QUAIFE, G. R. (1969) 'Make Us Roads, No Matter How', *Australian Journal of Politics and History*, 15, 47–54.

RAE, D. W. (1971) *The Political Consequences of Electoral Laws.* Yale University Press, New Haven.

RANNEY, A. (1965) 'Parties in state politics', in Jacob, H., and Vines, K. N. (editors), *Politics in the American States: A Comparative Analysis*. Little, Brown and Company, Boston, 61–100.

RANNEY, A. (1976) 'Review article: thirty years of psephology', *British Journal of Political Science*, 6, 217–30.

RANTALA, O. (1967) 'The political regions of Finland', *Scandinavian Political Studies*, 2, 117–42.

RASMUSSEN, J. (1973) 'The impact of constituency structural characteristics upon political preferences in Britain' *Comparative Politics*, 5, 123–45.

REAGAN, M. (1972) *The New Federalism*. Oxford University Press, New York.

REYNOLDS, D. R. (1969a) 'A "friends-and-neighbors" voting model as a spatial interactional model for electoral geography', in Cox, K. R. and Golledge, R. G. (editors), *Behavioral Problems in Geography*. Northwestern Studies in Geography 17, Northwestern University, Evanston, 81–100.

REYNOLDS, D. R. (1969b) 'A spatial model for analyzing voting behavior'. *Acta Sociologica*, 12, 122–30.

REYNOLDS, D. R. (1974) 'Spatial contagion in political influence processes', in Cox, K. R., Reynolds, D. R., and Rokkan, S. (editors), *Locational Approaches to Power and Conflict*. Halsted Press, New York, 233–73.

ROBERTS, G. K. (1975) 'The Federal Republic of Germany', in Finer, S. E. (editor), *Adversary Politics and Electoral Reform*. Anthony Wigram, London, 203–22.

ROBERTS, M. C., and RUMAGE, K. W. (1965) 'The spatial variations in urban left-wing voting in England and Wales in 1951', *Annals, Association of American Geographers*, 55, 161–78.

ROBINSON, A. (1970) 'Londonderry, Northern Ireland: a border study', *Scottish Geographical Magazine*, 86, 208–21.

ROBINSON, J. P. (1976) 'Interpersonal influence in election campaigns: *two* step-flow hypotheses', *Public Opinion Quarterly*, 40, 304–19.

ROBINSON, W. S. (1950) 'Ecological correlation and the behavior of individuals', *American Sociological Review*, 15, 351–7.

ROGALY, J. (1976) *Parliament for the People*. Maurice Temple-Smith, London.

ROGIN, M. P., and SHOVER, J. L. (1969) *Political Change in California*. Westport, Connecticut.

ROKKAN, S. (1970) *Citizens, Elections, Parties*. McKay, New York.

ROKKAN, S., and MEYRIAT, J. (1969) *International Guide to Electoral Statistics*. Mouton, Paris.

ROKKAN, S., and VALEN, H. (1970) 'Regional contrasts in Norwegian politics', in Allardt, E., and Rokkan, S. (editors), *Mass Politics*. The Free Press, New York, 190–250.

ROSE R. (1967) *Influencing Voters*. Faber and Faber London.

ROSE, R., editor (1974) *Electoral Behavior: A Comparative Handbook*. The Free Press, New York.

ROSE, R. (1974) 'Comparability in electoral studies', in Rose, R. (editor), *Electoral Behavior*. The Free Press, New York, 3–25.

ROSE, R. (1976) *The Problem of Party Government*. Penguin Books, Harmondsworth.

ROSE, R., and URWIN, D. W. (1970) 'Resistance and change in Western party systems since 1945', *Political Studies*, 18, 287–319.

ROSE, R., and URWIN, D. (1975) *Regional Differentiation and Political Unity in Western Nations*. Sage Professional Papers, Contemporary Political Sociology Series, 06–007, Sage Publications, Beverly Hills.

ROSSI, P. H., and CUTRIGHT, P. (1961) 'The impact of party organization in an industrial setting', in Janowitz, M. (editor), *Community Political Systems*. The Free Press, Glencoe, Ill., 81–116.

ROWLEY, G. (1965) 'The Greater London elections of 1964: some geographical considerations' *Tijdschrift voor Economische en Sociale Geografie*, 56, 113–14.

ROWLEY, G. (1970) 'Elections and population change', *Area*, 3, 13–18.

ROWLEY, G. (1971) 'The Greater London Council elections of 1964 and 1967: a study in electoral geography', *Transactions, Institute of British Geographers*, 53, 117–32.

ROWLEY, G. (1975a) 'The redistribution of parliamentary seats in the U.K.: themes and opinions', *Area*, 7, 16–21.

ROWLEY, G. (1975b) 'Parliamentary seat redistribution elaborated', *Area*, 7, 279–81.

ROWLEY, G. (1975c) 'Electoral change and reapportionment: prescriptive ideals and reality', *Tijdschrift voor Economische en Sociale Geografie*, 66, 108–20.

ROYAL COMMISSION ON LOCAL GOVERNMENT IN ENGLAND 1966–1969 (Chairman: The Rt Hon. Lord Redcliffe-Maud, 1969) *Volume III: Research Appendices*. H.M.S.O., London.

RUSSETT, B. M. (1967) *International Regions and the International System*. Rand McNally, Chicago.

RYDON, J. (1968a) 'Malapportionment Australian style', *Politics*, 3, 133–47.

RYDON, J. (1968b) 'Compulsory and preferential: the distinctive features of Australian voting methods', *Journal of Commonwealth Political Studies*, 6, 183–201.

SACKS, P. (1970) 'Bailiwicks, locality and religion: three elements in an Irish Dail Constituency election', *Economic and Social Review* 1, 531–54.

SALTER, P. S., and MINGS, R. C. (1972) 'The projected impact of Cuban settlement on voting patterns in metropolitan Miami, Florida', *Professional Geographer*, 24, 123–31.

SARLVIK, B. (1974) 'Sweden: the social bases of the parties in a developmental perspective', in Rose, R. (editor), *Electoral Behavior: A Comparative Handbook*. The Free Press, New York, 371–436.

SAUER, C. O. (1918) 'Geography and the gerrymander', *American Political Science Review*, 12, 403–26.

SCAMMON, R. M., and WATTENBERG, B. J. (1970) *The Real Majority: An Extraordinary Examination of the American Electorate*. Coward-McCann, New York.

SCHEUCH, E. K. (1969) 'Social context and individual behavior', in Dogan, M., and Rokkan, S. (editors), *Quantitative Ecological Analysis in the Social Sciences*. M.I.T. Press, Cambridge, Mass., 133–56.

SCHWARTZ, M. A. (1975) 'Canadian voting behavior', in Rose, R. (editor), *Electoral Behavior: A Comparative Handbook*. The Free Press, New York, 437–80.

SCHWARTZBERG, J. J. (1966) 'Reapportionment, gerrymanders, and the notion of compactness', *Minnesota Law Review*, 50, 443–52.

SCOTT, K. J. (1955) 'Gerrymandering for democracy', *Political Science*, 7, 118–27.

SECOND REPORT FROM THE SELECT COMMITTEE ON DIRECT ELECTIONS TO THE EUROPEAN ASSEMBLY (1976). H.M.S.O., London.

SEGAL, D. R., and MEYER, M. W. (1969) 'The social context of political partisanship', in Dogan, M., and Rokkan, S. (editors), *Quantitative Ecological Analysis in the Social Sciences*. M.I.T. Press, Cambridge, 217–32.

SEYMOUR, C. (1915) *Electoral Reform in England and Wales*. Oxford University Press, London.

SHANNON, W. W. (1968) *Party, Constituency and Congressional Voting: A Study of Legislative Behavior in the United States House of Representatives*. Louisiana State University Press, Baton Rouge.

SHAPLEY, L. S., and SHUBIK, M. (1954) 'A method of evaluating the distribution of power in a committee system', *American Political Science Review*, 48, 787–92.

SHARKANSKY, I. (1968) *Regionalism in American Politics.* Bobbs-Merrill, Indianapolis.

SHARKANSKY, I. (1969) *The Politics of Taxing and Spending.* Bobbs-Merrill, Indianapolis.

SHEINGOLD, C. (1973) 'Social networks and voting: the resurrection of a research agenda', *American Sociological Review*, 38, 712–20.

SHEPHERD, J., WESTAWAY, J. and LEE, T. (1974) *A Social Atlas of London.* Oxford University Press, London.

SICKELS, R. J. (1966) 'Dragons, bacon strips and dumbells – who's afraid of reapportionment?', *Yale Law Review*, 75, 1300–1308.

SIEGFRIED, A. (1913) *Tableau Politique de la France de l'Ouest.* A. Colin, Paris.

SIEGFRIED, A. (1949) *Géographie Électorale de l'Ardèche sous la IIIe République.* A. Colin, Paris.

SILVA, R. C. (1965) 'Reapportionment and redistricting', *Scientific American*, 213(5) 20–27.

SILVA, R. C., and BOYD, W. J. D. (1968) *Selected Bibliography on Legislative Apportionment and Districting.* National Municipal League, New York.

SIMEON, R., and ELKINS, D. J. (1974) 'Regional political cultures in Canada', *Canadian Journal of Political Science*, 7, 397–437.

SLOAN, L. (1969) '"Good government" and the politics of race', *Social Problems*, 17, 161–75.

SMITH, H. R., and HART, J. F. (1955) 'The American tariff map', *Geographical Review*, 45, 327–46.

SMITH, T. E. (1960) *Elections in Developing Countries.* Macmillan, London.

SOOT, S., KORTHEISER, J., and WOJKIEWICZ, S. (1976) 'The Chicago Area Regional Transportation Authority Referendum: analysis of the voter demand support implications', *Traffic Quarterly*, 30, 329–46.

SPIERS, M. (1965) 'Bradford', in Deakin, N. (editor), *Colour and the British Electorate 1964: Six Case Studies.* Pall Mall, London, 120–56.

SPILERMAN, S., and DICKENS, D. (1975) 'Who will gain and who will lose under different electoral rules', *Americal Journal of Sociology*, 80, 443–77.

STEED, M. (1966) 'Analysis of the results', in Butler, D. E., and King, A., *The British General Election of 1966.* Macmillan, London, 271–95.

STEED, M. (1969) 'Callaghan's gerrymandering', *New Society*, 13, 996–97.

STEED, M. (1974) 'The results analysed', in Butler, D. E., and Kavanagh, D., *The British General Election of February, 1974*. Macmillan, London, 313–39.

STEED, M. (1975a) 'The results analysed', in Butler, D. E., and Kavanagh, D., *The British General Election of October, 1974*. Macmillan, London, 313–39.

STEED, M. (1975b) 'The evolution of the British electoral system', in Finer, S. E. (editor), *Adversary Politics and Electoral Reform*. Anthony Wigram, London, 35–53.

STEHOUWER, J. (1967) 'Long term ecological analyses of electoral statistics in Denmark', *Scandinavian Political Studies*, 2, 94–116.

STOCKWIN, J. A. A. (1975) *Japan: Divided Politics in a Growth Economy*. Weidenfeld and Nicolson, London.

STOKES, D. E. (1965) 'A variance components model of political effects', in Claunch, J. M. (editor), *Mathematical Applications in Political Science*. Southern Methodist University Press, Dallas.

STOKES, D. E. (1967) 'Parties and the nationalization of electoral forces' in Chambers, W. N., and Burnham, W. D. (editors), *The American Party Systems*. Oxford University Press, New York, 182–202.

STOKES, D. E. (1969) 'Comment: On the measurement of electoral dynamics', *American Political Science Review*, 64, 829–31

STOKES, D. E., and MILLER, W. E. (1962) 'Party government and the saliency of Congress', *Public Opinion Quarterly*, 26, 531–47.

STOUT, D. K. (1975) 'Incomes policy and the costs of the adversary system', in Finer, S. E. (editor), *Adversary Politics and Electoral Reform*. Anthony Wigram, London, 117–40.

TAPER, B. (1962) *Gomillion versus Lightfoot: The Tuskegee Gerrymander Case*. McGraw-Hill, New York.

TARR, J. A. (1971) *A Study in Boss Politics*. University of Illinois Press, Chicago.

TATALOVICH, R. (1975) '"Friends and neighbors" voting: Mississippi, 1943–73', *Journal of Politics*, 37, 807–14.

TATE, C. N. (1974) 'Individual and contextual variables in British voting behavior: an exploratory note', *American Political Science Review*, 68, 1656–62.

TAYLOR, A. H. (1972) 'The effect of party organization: correlation between campaign expenditure and voting in the 1970 election', *Political Studies*, 20, 329–31.

TAYLOR, A. H. (1973a) 'Variations in the relationship between class and voting in England, 1950 to 1970', *Tijdschrift voor Economische en Sociale Geografie*, 64, 164–8.

TAYLOR, A. H. (1973b) 'Journey time, perceived distance, and electoral turnout – Victoria Ward, Swansea', *Area*, 5, 59–63.

TAYLOR, A. H. (1973c) 'The electoral geography of Welsh and Scottish nationalism', *Scottish Geographical Magazine*, 93, 44–52.

TAYLOR, A. H. (1974) 'Kilbrandon: electoral implications', *Area*, 6, 88–91.

TAYLOR, P. J. (1969) 'Causal models in geographic research', *Annals, Association of American Geographers*, 59, 402–4.

TAYLOR, P. J. (1973) 'Some implications of the spatial organization of elections', *Transactions, Institute of British Geographers*, 60, 121–36.

TAYLOR, P. J. (1974) 'Electoral districting algorithms and their applications', Institute of British Geographers, Quantitative Methods Study Group, *Working Paper Set*, No. 2.

TAYLOR, P. J. (1976) 'Time for electoral reform?', unpublished paper, Department of Geography, University of Newcastle upon Tyne.

TAYLOR, P. J. (1977) *Quantitative Methods in Geography: An Introduction to Spatial Analysis*. Houghton Mifflin, New York.

TAYLOR, P. J., and GUDGIN, G. (1975) 'A fresh look at the Parliamentary Boundary Commissions', *Parliamentary Affairs*, 28, 405–15.

TAYLOR, P. J., and GUDGIN, G. (1976a) 'The statistical basis of decision making in electoral districting', *Environment and Planning*, A, 8, 43–58.

TAYLOR, P. J., and GUDGIN, G. (1976b) 'The myth of non-partisan cartography: a study of electoral biases in the English Boundary Commission's Redistribution for 1955–1970', *Urban Studies*, 13, 13–25.

TAYLOR, P. J., and GUDGIN, G. (1977) 'Antipodean demises of Labour', in R. J. Johnston (editor), *People, Places and Votes: Essays in the Electoral Geography of Australia and New Zealand*. University of New England, Department of Geography, Armidale, 111–20.

TAYLOR, P. J., and JOHNSTON, R. J. (1978) 'Population distribution and political power in the European Parliament.' *Regional Studies*, 12, 61–8.

TEER, F., and SPENCE, J. D. (1973) *Political Opinion Polls*. Hutchinson, London.

THORBURN, H. G. (editor) (1972) *Party Politics in Canada*. Prentice Hall, Scarborough, Ontario.

TINKLER, I. (1956) 'Malayan elections: electoral pattern for plural societies?', *Western Political Quarterly*, 9, 258–82.

TUAN, YI-FU (1976) 'Humanistic geography', *Annals, Association of American Geographers*, 66, 266–76.

TUFTE, E. R. (1973) 'The relationship between seats and votes in two-party systems', *American Political Science Review*, 67, 540–54.

TULLOCK, G. (1976) *The Vote Motive*. Institute of Economic Affairs, Hobart Paperback 9, London.

TURNER, F. J. (1920) *The Frontier in American History*. Holt, New York.

TYLER, G. (1954) 'The House of Un-Representatives', *New Republic* (28 June 1954), 14–15.

TYLER, G. (1955) 'The majority don't count', *New Republic* (22 August 1955), 13–15.

TYLER, G., and WELLS, D. I. (1961) 'Camel bites dachshund', *New Republic*, 145 (11 November 1961), 9–10.

TYLER, G., and WELLS, D. I. (1962) 'New York: Constitutionally Republican', in Jewell, M. E. (editor), *The Politics of Reapportionment*, Atherton Press, New York, 221–47.

TYLER, G., and WELLS, D. I. (1971) 'The new gerrymander threat', *The American Federalist*, 78 (2), 1–7.

VALE, V. (1969) 'The computer as Parliamentary Boundary Commissioner?', *Parliamentary Affairs*, 22, 240–49.

VALEN, H., ALKLIT, J., and TONSGAARD, O. (1975) 'E.E.C. – a rural decision', *New Society* (1 May 1975), 277–8.

VALEN, H., and ROKKAN, S. (1967) 'The Norwegian program for electoral research', *Scandinavian Political Studies*, 2, 294–305.

VALEN, H., and ROKKAN, S. (1974) 'Norway: conflict structure and mass politics in European periphery', in Rose, R. (editor), *Electoral Behavior: A Comparative Handbook*. The Free Press, New York, 315–70.

VICKREY, V. (1961) 'On the prevention of gerrymandering', *Political Science Quarterly*, 76, 105–111.

VINES, K. N. (1965) 'Courts as political and governmental agencies', in Jacob, H., and Vines, K. N. (editors), *Politics in the American States: A Comparative Analysis*. Little, Brown and Company, Boston, 239–89.

DE VISTRE, J. (1869) 'Les circonscriptions électorales', *L'Illustration, Journal Universel*, 53, 265–6.

WALTER, D. O. (1938) 'Reapportionment and urban representation', *Annals, American Academy of Political and Social Science*, 195, 9–21.

WARD, N. (1967) 'A century of constituencies', *Canadian Public Administration*, 10, 105–22.

WARNTZ, W. (1955) 'A methodological consideration of some geographic aspects of the Newfoundland referendum on confederation with Canada, 1948', *Canadian Geographer*, 1, 39–49.

WEAVER, J. B. (1970) *Fair and Equal Districts*. National Municipal League, New York.

WEAVER, J. B., and HESS, S. W. (1963) 'A procedure for nonpartisan redistricting', *Yale Law Journal*, 73, 288–308.

WEBBER, R. (unpublished) 'A typology of parliamentary constituencies', Centre for Environmental Studies, London.

WEINSTEIN, J. (1967) *The Decline of Socialism in America, 1912–1925*. Monthly Review Press, New York.

WESTERGAARD, J. H., and RESSLER, H. (1976) *Class in a Capitalist Society*. Penguin Books, Harmondsworth.

WHEELER, M. (1976) *Lies, Damn Lies, and Statistics: The Manipulation of Public Opinion in America*. Dell, New York.

WHYTE, J. H. (1974) 'Ireland: politics without social bases', in Rose, R. (editor), *Electoral Behavior: A Comparative Handbook*. The Free Press, New York, 619–52.

WILLIAMS, P. M. (1968) 'Politics of redistribution', *Political Quarterly*, 39, 239–54.

WILLIAMS, P. M. (1970) *French Politics and Elections 1931–1969*. Cambridge University Press, Cambridge.

WILSON, J. Q., and BANFIELD, E. C. (1964) 'Public-regardingness as a value premise in voting behavior', *American Political Science Review*, 58, 876–87.

WILSON, T. (1975) 'The economic costs of the adversary system', in Finer, S. E. (editor), *Adversary Politics and Electoral Reform*. Anthony Wigram, London, 99–116.

WINN, C., and MCMENENY, J. editors (1976) *Political Parties in Canada*. McGraw-Hill, Toronto.

WOHLENBERG, E. H. (1976) 'Interstate variations in AFDC programs', *Economic Geography*, 52, 252–66.

WRIGHT, G. C. JR (1975) 'Interparty competition and State social welfare policy: when a difference makes a difference', *Journal of Politics*, 37, 796–803.

WRIGHT, G. C. JR (1977) 'Contextual models of electoral behavior: the Southern Wallace vote', *American Political Science Review*, 71, 497–508.

WRIGHT, J. E. (1974) *The Politics of Populism*. Yale University Press, New Haven, Connecticut.

Acknowledgements

The publishers acknowledge permission to reproduce material in this book from the following sources:

Tables

2.8, 2.9 From R. Rose (editor), *Electoral Behaviour* (1974), copyright © 1974 The Free Press, a Division of Macmillan Publishing Co., Inc. Reprinted by permission.

3.2, 3.3, 3.4, 3.5 From S. Rokkan, *Citizens, Elections Parties* (1976), Universitetsforlaget, Oslo, by permission of the publisher.

3.6, 3.7, 3.8 From R. Rose and D. W. Urwin, 'Regional Differentiation and Political Unity in Western Nations' in *Contemporary Political Sociology* (1975) Sage Publications, by permission of the publisher.

3.10 From William N. Chambers and Walter D. Burnham *The American Party Systems: Stages of Political Development*, copyright © 1967 by Oxford University Press Inc. Reprinted by permission.

3.11 From J. Ross Barnett, 'Scale Components in the Diffusion of the Danish Communist Party, 1920–64' in *Geographical Analysis*, Volume 5, Number 1, January 1973, Ohio State University Press.

4.1 From Arend Lijphart, in *Class Voting and Religous Voting in the European Democracies*. Acta Politica, Vol. 6, No. 2 (April 1971).

4.2 From R. Rose (editor), *Electoral Behaviour* (1974), copyright © 1974 The Free Press, a Division of Macmillan Publishing Co., Inc. Reprinted by permission.

4.3, 4.4, 4.5, 4.6 From E. Allardt and S. Rokkan (editors), *Mass Politics* (1970), copyright © 1970 The Free Press, a Division of Macmillan Publishing Co., Inc. Reprinted by permission.

4.7 From R. Rose (editor) *Electoral Behaviour* (1974), copryight © 1974 The Free Press, a Division of Macmillan Publishing Co., Inc. Reprinted by permission.

4.8, 4.9 From S. Lipset and S. Rokkan, *Party Systems and Voter*

Alignments (1967), copyright© 1967 The Free Press, a Division of Macmillan Publishing Co., Inc. Reprinted by permission.

4.10, 4.11, 4.12 From R. Rose (editor), *Electoral Behaviour* (1974), copyright © 1974 The Free Press, a Division of Macmillan Publishing Co., Inc. Reprinted by permission.

4.13 Reprinted from Dogan and Rokkan (editors) *Quantitative Ecological Analysis in the Social Sciences* by permission of the M.I.T. Press, Cambridge, Massachusetts.

4.15 From E. D. Blake, 'The Measurement of Regionalism in Canadian Voting Patterns' in the *Canadian Journal of Political Science*, Volume 5, (March 1972) by permission of the Canadian Political Science Association.

4.16 Reprinted with permission of The American Jewish Committee from L. S. Dawidowicz and L. J. Goldstein, *Politics in a Pluralist Democracy* (1963), all rights reserved.

4.17 From I. R. McPhail, *The Vote for Mayor of Los Angeles in 1969* in the ANNALS of the Association of American Geographers, Volume 61 1969.

4.18, 4.19 From Stokes and Butler, *Political Change in Britain* (1975) by permission of Macmillan London Ltd.

4.20, 5.1 From Crewe and Payne in the *British Journal of Political Science*, volume 6, by permission of Cambridge University Press.

5.2, 5.3 From Lazarsfeld *et al*: *The People's Choice*, third edition, (1968), Columbia University Press. By permission of the publisher.

5.4 From the *British Journal of Sociology* No. 3 (1952) edited by F. M. Martin by permission of Routledge and Kegan Paul Ltd.

5.5 From M. Dogan and S. Rokkan (editors), *Quantitative Ecological Analysis in the Social Sciences* by permission of the M.I.T. Press, Cambridge, Massachusetts.

5.7 From James Petras and Maurice Zeitlin, 'Miners and Agrarian Radicalism' in the *American Sociological Review*, Vol. 32, 1967, by permission of The American Sociological Association.

5.8 From Stokes and Butler, *Political Change in Britain* (1975) by permission of Macmillan London Ltd.

5.9 From Crewe and Payne in the *British Journal of Political Science*, Vol 6, by permission of Cambridge University Press.

5.10 From Irving Foladare, 'The Effects of Neighbourhood on Voting Behaviour', the *Political Science Quarterly*, Vol. 83, 1968.

6.2 From William N. Chambers and Walter D. Burnham *The American Party Systems: Stages of Political Development*, copyright © 1967 by Oxford University Press Inc. Reprinted by permission.

6.3 From V. O. Key, Jr, *Southern Politics in State and Nation* by permission of Alfred A. Knopf, Inc.

6.4 From R. Tatalovich, '"Friends and Neighbors" Voting: Mississippi, 1943–73' in the *Journal of Politics*, Vol 37 (August 1975). Reprinted by permission.

6.8 From N. Deakin *Colour and the British Electorate* (1965). Reprinted by permission of Pall Mall Press.

6.10 From Brams and Davis, 'The 3/2's Role in Presidential Campaigning' in the *American Political Science Review*, Vol. 68 (1974), by permission.

6.11 From Phillips Cutright and Peter H. Rossi, 'Grass Roots, Politicians and the Vote', in the *American Sociological Review*, Vol. 23, 1958, by permission of the American Sociological Association.

6.12 From Phillips Cutright and Peter H. Rossi, 'Party Organisation in Primary Elections' in the *American Journal of Sociology*, Vol. 64, No. 3 (1958) © University of Chicago Press.

6.13 From J. Brown, 'Local Party Efficiency as a Factor in the Outcome of British Elections' in *Political Studies*, Vol. 6 (1958). By permission of Oxford University Press.

6.14 From John C. Blydenburgh, 'A Controlled Experiment to Measure the Effects of Personal Contact Campaigning' in the *Midwest Journal of Political Science*, Vol. 15, No. 2 (1971). By permission of the Wayne State University Press.

7.1, *7.2* From Charles Seymour, *Electoral Reform in England and Wales* (originally 1915). By permission of Yale University Press.

7.3 From Gordon E. Baker, *The Reapportionment Revolution* (1966). By permission of Alfred A. Knopf, Inc.

7.4 From Thomas R. Dye, 'State Legislative Politics', in Herbert Jacob and Kenneth N. Vines (editors), *Politics in the American States: A Comparative Analysis*, 2nd edition, p. 170. Copyright © 1971 by Little, Brown and Company, Inc. Reprinted by permission.

7.5 From Blewett, 'Redistribution Procedures' in *Australian Politics*, Mayer and Nelson (editors) (1972). Reprinted by permission of Longman Cheshire Pty., Ltd., Melbourne.

7.7 Reprinted from an article by D. Birrell in Volume 20 of *Sociological Review*, by permission.

9.1 From K. Newton, *Second City Politics*, Oxford University Press, by permission of the author.

9.2 From Sharman, *Party Constituency and Congressional Voting* (1968) Louisiana State University Press, by permission.

9.3 From Lengle and Shafer, 'Primary Rules, Political Power and

Social Change', in the *American Political Science Review*, Vol. 70 (1976), by permission.

9.4 Reproduced by permission from the ANNALS of the Association of American Geographers, Vol. 61, 1971 D. O. Bushman and W. K. Stanley.

Figures

1.1 From A. Siegfried, *Geographie Electorale de l'Ardèche* (1949), Librairie Armand Colin, Paris.

1.2 From V. O. Key, Jr, *Southern Politics in State and Nation*, by permission of Alfred A. Knopf, Inc.

2.6 From W. S. Robinson, 'Ecological Correlations and the Behaviour of Individuals' in the *American Sociological Review*, Vol. 15, 1950, by permission of the American Sociological Association.

3.1 From S. M. Lipset and S. Rokkan, *Party Systems and Voter Alignments* (1967). Copyright © 1967 The Free Press, a Division of Macmillan Publishing Co., Inc. Reprinted by permission.

3.5 From A. F. Burghardt, *The Bases of Support for Political Parties in Burgenland* in the ANNALS of the Association of American Geographers, Volume LIV (1964).

3.6 From S. V. Fifer, 'Unity By Inclusion' in *Geographical Journal*, Volume 142, 1976.

4.1 From R. Rose (editor), *Electoral Behaviour* (1974), copyright © 1974 The Free Press, a Division of Macmillan Publishing Co., Inc. Reprinted by permission.

4.2 From S. M. Lipset and S. Rokkan, *Party Systems and Voter Alignments* (1967), copyright © 1967 The Free Press, a Division of Macmillan Publishing Co., Inc. Reprinted by permission.

4.3 From Williams, *French Politicians and Elections 1951–1969*, by permission of Cambridge University Press.

4.4, *4.5* From S. M. Lipset and S. Rokkan, *Party Systems and Voter Alignments* (1967), copyright © 1967 The Free Press, a Division of Macmillan Publishing Co., Inc. Reprinted by permission.

5.1, *5.2* From Stokes and Butler, *Political Change in Britain* (1975) by permission of Macmillan London Ltd.

5.4, *5.5* From K. R. Cox, 'The Spatial Components of Urban Voting Response Surfaces' *Economic Geography*, Vol. 47, 1971. Reproduced by permission.

6.1 From Duane Lockard, *New England State Politics* copyright © 1959 Princeton University Press. Reprinted by permission.

6.2 From J. L. Brian Berry and Duane F. Marble, *Spatial Analysis: A Reader in Statistical Geography*, © 1968. Reprinted by permission of Prentice-Hall, Inc., Englewood Cliffs, New Jersey.

6.3, *6.4* From P. M. Sacks, 'Bailiwicks, Locality and Religion: Three Elements In An Irish Dail Constituency Election' in *Economic and Social Review*, Vol. 1, 1970. Reprinted by permission of Economic and Social Studies, Dublin.

6.11 From S. D. Brunn, *Geography and Politics in America*, Harper and Row, 1974.

7.3 Reproduced by permission from the ANNALS of the Association of American Geographers, Vol. 61, 1971, D. R. Bushman and W. R. Stanley.

7.7 From Charles S. Olcott, *The Life of William McKinley* by permission of Houghton Mifflin Company, Boston, Massachusetts.

Index

For Product Safety Concerns and Information please contact our EU representative GPSR@taylorandfrancis.com
Taylor & Francis Verlag GmbH, Kaufingerstraße 24, 80331 München, Germany

www.ingramcontent.com/pod-product-compliance
Ingram Content Group UK Ltd.
Pitfield, Milton Keynes, MK11 3LW, UK
UKHW022005180926
475701UK00003B/213
* 9 7 8 1 1 3 8 8 1 4 2 7 1 *